1993

In Pursuit of Equality

Women, Public Policy, and the Federal Courts

In Pursuit of Equality

Women,
Public Policy,
and the
Federal Courts

Susan Gluck Mezey

Loyola University

St. Martin's Press / New York

Senior editor: Don Reisman
Managing editor: Patricia Mansfield
Project editor: Elise Bauman
Production supervisor: Alan Fischer
Cover design: Darby Downey

Manufactured in the United States of America.
65432
fedcba

For information, write:
St. Martin's Press, Inc.
175 Fifth Avenue
New York, NY 10010

ISBN: 0-312-03706-6
       0-312-06520-5

Mezey, Susan Gluck, 1944–
    In pursuit of equality : women, public policy, and the federal
courts / Susan Mezey.
        p.   cm.
    Includes bibliographical references and index.
    ISBN 0-312-03706-6
    ISBN 0-312-06520-5
    1. Women—Legal status, laws, etc.—United States.   2. Sex
discrimination against women—Law and legislation—United States.
3. Women's rights—United States.   4. Courts—United States.
I. Title.
KF478.M49   1992
346.7301'34—dc20
[347.306134]   90-63547
                                                                         CIP

FOR MICHAEL

Preface

In writing *In Pursuit of Equality,* I expand the literature on women and public policy by discussing the role of the federal courts, primarily the Supreme Court, in determining the status of women in America. The book combines my scholarly interests in the study of the federal judiciary as a policy-making institution and the study of American women.

Written from a feminist perspective, the chapters focus on women as citizens, workers, students, and mothers — women in all roles, striving to achieve equality and to put an end to discrimination. As the book demonstrates, feminists may agree on the need to empower women as political, economic, social, and legal actors but often disagree over the methods needed to accomplish these goals. Sometimes all viewpoints will be compelling and readers will have a difficult time choosing sides. If that happens, I will consider the book a success because I think it is healthy to debate the *best* way to achieve an agreed-upon goal. By showing where women are now and where we have come from, I also hope my book will indicate how far we still have to go, and perhaps suggest ways of getting there as well.

The completion of this book was facilitated by the generosity of Loyola University in awarding me a research leave and a summer grant. These permitted me to devote myself to research and writing without the additional pressure of teaching duties. The university's willingness to fund the time spent writing this book is a measure of its commitment to the professional development of its faculty. I also would like to acknowledge my colleagues in the Department of Political Science and the Women's Studies Program at Loyola, who helped create the conditions which allowed me to teach courses and do research on the subject of women and law.

More generally, I owe a huge debt to the women and men who researched and wrote in the area of women and politics and made the study of women a respectable scholarly endeavor. I began my research and writing on women and politics in the middle 1970s as political scientists were starting to pay attention to the legal and political status of women. Under the auspices of the National Women's Caucus for Political Science and, later, the Organized Research Section on Women and Politics of the American Political Science Association, I participated in panels at annual meetings and was part of an intellectual network of scholars, many of whom also became good friends.

I would like to thank Liane Kosaki who read and commented on parts of the book in draft. I also wish to thank Don Reisman, senior editor at St. Martin's Press, for letting me write the book I wanted to write and always being supportive about the outcome, and Elise Bauman, who oversaw the transformation of a manuscript into a bound book. Thanks are also due to those who reviewed the prospectus and text and provided many helpful comments: Elizabeth Hull, Rutgers University–Newark; Helen Swartzfager Ridley, Kennesaw State College; Jill Norgren, John Jay College of Criminal Justice and the Graduate Center–City University of New York; Bette Novit-Evans, Creighton University; Judith A. Baer, Texas A&M University; Joyce Baugh, Central Michigan University; and Joan Tronto, Hunter College, City University of New York.

I would also like to acknowledge the students in my class on women and law at Loyola University, especially Kim, Bridget, Kate, Catherine, Julianne, Patsy, and Steve. They helped me to clarify the issues and sharpen the arguments by asking and answering questions arising out of the cases and laws we discussed in class. My graduate research assistants, Steven Doherty and Michael Walsh, provided a good deal of labor in tracking down cases and articles and checking citations in the manuscript. Needless to say, any errors are mine alone.

Finally, and most importantly, I want to acknowledge the role my family has played in this book. My husband Michael, my daughter Jennifer, and my son Jason, all committed feminists, have always given their help and encouragement to any project I have worked on. In this case, they provided assistance by reading and commenting on various chapters in draft. Jennifer and Jason also helped me with some of the menial but necessary chores required to produce a book. To them and to Michael, thanks for being in my life.

Susan Gluck Mezey

Contents

In Pursuit of Equality

Women, Public Policy, and the Federal Courts

Introduction

The first women's movement grew out of the antislavery struggle in the mid-1800s and ended with the passage of the Nineteenth Amendment in 1920. Disagreement over movement goals after its success in securing the franchise led to dissension within the movement and its eventual decline.

The next wave of the fight for women's equality in the United States began to take shape in the 1960s as women began the slow—and as yet unfinished—task of transforming themselves from subordinates to equals. The second women's movement was born out of women's participation in the civil rights and antiwar protests of the 1960s. Committed to the goals of these groups, women discovered that they were often forced to assume subordinate roles within the organizations.[1]

Women rallied under the banner of feminism, an ideology that seeks to empower women by altering their political, social, and economic status in society.[2] The feminist movement, also known as the women's movement or the women's liberation movement, became the driving force for making demands to end the subordination of women in American society.

Feminism and Law

Feminists do not always agree about the sources of women's oppression or the strategies for freeing women from male domination. Liberal feminists and radical feminists, with different perspectives on sexual inequality, each

1

identify a cause of women's subordination and offer solutions to advance their vision of an egalitarian society.

Liberal feminism represents the most commonly held approach to achieving equality between men and women. Liberal feminists believe that "female subordination is rooted in a set of customary and legal constraints that blocks women's entrance and/or success in the so-called public world."[3] Their chief goal is to remove the constraints that impede women's access to the rights and opportunities that men have. Because the battle for sexual equality in the United States has largely been fought within the liberal paradigm, much of the debate among feminists today involves the accuracy and sufficiency of the liberal feminist critique of U.S. society.

Even among liberal feminists, however, there is disagreement over how to eliminate barriers to equality. At one end of the continuum are classical liberal feminists who believe "that after discriminatory laws and politics have been removed from the books, thereby formally enabling women to compete equally with men, not much else can be done." At the other end are the welfare liberal feminists who believe that "society . . . should not only compensate women for past injustices but should also eliminate socioeconomic, as well as legal, impediments to women's progress today."[4] Underlying both approaches of liberal feminism is a heavy reliance on legal remedies.

Other feminists are more pessimistic about the law's ability to limit male dominance. For them, legal change is just the beginning of the struggle for equality. They argue that because law is aimed primarily at women's public lives and tends to ignore their private lives, it has limited utility in effecting social change.

Radical feminism, for example, the most popular competitor to liberal feminism, contends that women's oppression is rooted in male control over female bodies. It directs attention to instruments of control such as laws regulating contraception, sterilization, and abortion, as well as physical and verbal abuse directed against women in the form of pornography, sexual harassment, rape, and battery.[5]

Radical feminists argue that women will not free themselves from oppression in a liberal state. To achieve equality, they insist, women must wrest power over their sexuality and reproduction away from men. Formal rights and legal equality can play only a limited role in accomplishing this end. A prominent critic of the liberal feminist's approach to law, radical feminist Catherine MacKinnon charges that "much of what has passed for feminism in law has been the attempt to get for men what little has been reserved for women or to get for women some of the plunder that some men have previously divided (unequally) among themselves."[6]

While the debate among feminist theorists continues, it is important to recognize the contributions each has made. Liberal feminists have been primarily responsible for the litigation strategy that led to advances of individual rights for women. Radical feminists have been largely responsible for placing such issues as sexual harassment, pregnancy, and reproductive rights on the political agenda. They have insisted that the political system respond to the needs of a variety of women (poor women, women of color, and young women, for example). The chapters in this book demonstrate the influence of both liberal and radical feminism in the struggle to advance women's rights.

Law and Equality

Implicit in the debate over liberal feminism is the controversy over the law as an instrument of entrapment or freedom. Some feminists argue that the law has served to maintain and reinforce women's disadvantaged position in society. Others look upon the law as an instrument to end women's subordination and achieve equality with men.[7] According to feminist scholar Deborah Rhode, the rights-oriented legal approach has played a key role in securing access to educational, employment, and political institutions for women. But, she cautions, it has not proven very helpful in forcing the institutions to alter their values and behavior in order to accommodate women's needs and desires.[8]

Ambivalence over legal reform has led to questions about how effectively law can remedy sexual inequities in society. Recognizing that until very recently courts used sex differences to enforce legal inequality, the question is whether legal reform can generate sexual equality.

The fight for legal rights has always assumed a prominent place on the feminist agenda, yet many feminists claim that law is a male preserve that reinforces male dominance in all sectors of society. Radical feminists contend that liberal feminism will not lead to genuine equality because it merely seeks access to power defined in male terms rather than attempting to change the way power is used in our society. They believe that when male behavior is used as the norm, remedies for inequality are bounded by the extent to which women deviate from the male model. The radical feminists point out that following the liberal model means that women who are similarly situated to men are most benefited by laws, others less so.

Counseling against a reliance on legal reforms, radical feminists such as MacKinnon warn that the law is not an effective force for creating social change. Admitting that it can aid in the process, she adds that "so far, it has helped remarkably little."[9] Others, such as Rhode, also see the shortcomings of law, yet are more optimistic about its usefulness. They acknowledge that law has proven less successful in confronting the informal obstacles that stand in the way of opportunities for women yet insist that it has played a critical role in eradicating formal barriers to equality between the sexes.[10]

Amid these views, there is agreement that legal reform is an important vehicle for effecting societal changes that women need. Although laws can go only so far in eliminating social and economic inequality, they set a standard and create a tone. Most important, the debate over legal rights results in national recognition of the importance of feminist issues and placement of these issues on the public policy-making agenda.

Federal Court Litigation and Sexual Equality

Before making a judgment about the effectiveness of law as an agent of feminist change, it is necessary to establish what law reform and the federal courts have done, and what they have not done, to create a more egalitarian society.

As part of its commitment to civil rights during the 1960s and 1970s, Congress enacted laws banning discrimination on the basis of sex. Despite these gains, women soon discovered that getting laws passed was only the first step toward equality between the sexes. In many cases, the legislative victories had to be solidified in court. The courts played an increasingly important role in defining sexual equality as women demanded that they make good on the promise of equal treatment under the law. Federal court litigation therefore served as a focal point for debate over the expansion of rights as well as a barometer of women's demands for social reform. The decisions rendered by the courts frequently informed the limits of these demands.

Women's groups had used litigation in the past to further sexual equality with only limited success. In 1966, the women's movement undertook a new commitment to litigation strategy to end sex discrimination with the formation of the National Organization for Women. Other groups, such as the Women's Rights Project of the American Civil Liberties Union and the Women's Equity Action League, also used litigation as a political weapon in the fight for greater sexual equality. Whether won or lost, their lawsuits often served as a catalyst to legislative and executive policy-making.[11]

It was not surprising that women turned to the courts. Because most social reform movements in America are infused with legal concepts of equality, the courts have frequently served as the arena for the debate over change.[12] Following the example of other minority groups seeking to empower themselves, women utilized litigation strategy for two purposes: to cement legislative or administrative gains in nondiscrimination policy and to raise constitutional challenges to existing discriminatory laws or policies on the state or federal level.

Outline of the Book

In this book, I examine the role played by the law and the federal courts in contributing to sexual equality in the United States. Emphasizing judicial decision-making through analysis of Supreme Court and lower federal court cases, I also look at policy-making in Congress and the executive branch because most decisions made there ultimately find their way to the federal courts.

Although state law plays a significant role in determining women's rights, theoretical and practical considerations dictate against including state judicial decisions and statutes in this analysis. Because state laws are not controlling outside the state's jurisdiction, and because there are fifty state jurisdictions, analysis of the law of a single state does not accurately depict the status of the law outside that particular state.

Because of powers reserved to the state for regulation of health, safety, and public welfare, matters of divorce, marriage, rape, battery, and surrogacy are controlled by state law. While such issues are important to women, they are for the most part outside the province of federal law and are omitted here except when they conflict with federal statutes or constitutional protections. Leaving them out of this book in no way denigrates their importance as public policy issues; it simply acknowledges the difficulty of presenting the law of fifty states in one book.

The book traces the development of sexual equality in federal law since 1960. Beginning with a brief history of the origins of the feminist movement, Chapter One looks at the formation and application of the Supreme Court's constitutional sex equality doctrine. The cases, brought by women and men as challenges to state and federal laws, cover a wide variety of issues including women's status in the military, widower's pensions and widow's tax benefits, drinking age limits, pregnancy disability, rights of inheritance, and illegitimacy. The chapter explores the reasons behind the Supreme Court's decisions to uphold certain laws and strike down others.

The next three chapters focus on the passage and implementation of Title VII of the Civil Rights Act of 1964, the primary federal law attacking employment discrimination on the basis of sex. By observing the interaction among the three branches of the federal government, these chapters explore the political and legal debates over equal employment opportunity in U.S. society.

Chapter Two discusses the early—and largely successful—lawsuits that challenged the legal barriers to equal opportunity for women. Chapter Three looks at different theories of discrimination and the requirements for proving and defending against discrimination suits. It concludes by showing how the proposed Civil Rights Act of 1990 would have affected employment discrimination litigation. Chapter Four analyzes the controversy over affirmative action as a remedy for employment discrimination and assesses the future of affirmative action policy in light of the attacks on it by the executive branch and the judiciary.

Chapter Five offers another view of employment discrimination by examining the effort to secure pay equity between the sexes through the Equal Pay Act of 1963. It shows how the effectiveness of the statute is limited by the requirement that men and women perform equal work. It concludes by presenting the political and legal debate over comparable worth and discusses actions taken by state and local governments to implement pay equity.

Chapter Six explores the conflict that women face between pregnancy and work. It looks at the evolution of laws affecting pregnancy from the restrictions imposed by forced maternity leaves to the debate over special policies benefiting pregnant working women. It concludes by examining the proposed Family and Medical Leave Act, which attempted to reduce the conflict between pregnancy and work for American women.

Chapter Seven is devoted to the topic of educational equality, including constitutional challenges to sex-separated educational facilities and congressional attempts to forbid discrimination on the basis of sex through enactment of Title IX of the Education Amendments of 1972. The last part of the chapter examines congressional passage of the 1988 Civil Rights Restoration Act to reverse the Supreme Court's restrictive view of Title IX.

Chapter Eight looks at sexual harassment in the workplace. It begins by showing the federal court's initial indifference to the problem and then traces the judiciary's gradual acceptance of Title VII suits in cases of harassment. It also looks at sexual harassment suits brought against faculty and university administrators under Title IX.

Chapter Nine focuses on the distinct legal issues concerning career advancement for business and professional women. It explores the special problems such women face in convincing courts they were discriminated against, largely because of the judiciary's reluctance to override collegial evaluations of the quality of professional work. It concludes by examining the difficulties of balancing career and family that hinder the achievements of women in the business and professional world.

The last two chapters revolve around the legal status of abortion in the United States. Beginning with a history of abortion laws, Chapter Ten traces the origins of the constitutional right to privacy and how the Court legalized abortion by including it within the right to privacy. While proclaiming the right to abortion as fundamental, the Court refused to declare it absolute. The cases show the Court's attempts to balance restrictions on abortion with a woman's right to control her own reproduction.

Chapter Eleven focuses on cases in which the Supreme Court accepted parental consent and notice laws for minors and funding restrictions for poor women as valid exercises of state authority over abortion. It includes discussion of the latest Supreme Court rulings on abortion and presents the current status of the political and legal debate over a woman's right to choose an abortion.

NOTES

1. Jo Freeman, *The Politics of Women's Liberation* (New York: David McKay Company, 1975).

2. Mine is an inclusive definition of feminism, comprising the goals of a range of feminist theorists.

3. Rosemarie Tong, *Feminist Thought: A Comprehensive Introduction* (Boulder: Westview Press, 1989), p. 2. Tong's book provides an overview of the major types of feminist thought, including liberal feminism, radical feminism, Marxist feminism, socialist feminism, and postmodern feminism. See also Vicky Randall, *Women and Politics,* 2d ed. (Chicago: University of Chicago Press, 1987); Joyce Gelb, *Feminism and Politics* (Berkeley: University of California Press, 1989).

4. Tong, *Feminist Thought,* p. 29.

5. Tong, *Feminist Thought,* chapters 3 and 4.

6. Catherine MacKinnon, *Feminism Unmodified* (Cambridge: Harvard University Press, 1987), p. 4.

7. See Ava Baron, "Feminist Legal Strategies: The Powers of Difference," in Beth B. Hess and Myra Marx Ferree, eds., *Analyzing Gender: A Handbook of Social Science Research* (Beverly Hills: Sage, 1987) for discussion of the debate over the law and women's rights.

8. Deborah L. Rhode, *Justice and Gender* (Cambridge: Harvard University Press, 1989), introduction.

9. MacKinnon, *Feminism Unmodified,* p. 26.

10. Deborah L. Rhode, "Equal Protection: Gender and Justice," in Michael W. McCann and Gerald L. Houseman, eds., *Judging the Constitution: Critical Essays on Judicial Lawmaking* (Glenview: Scott, Foresman, 1989).

11. Karen O'Connor, *Women's Organizations' Use of the Courts* (Lexington: Lexington Books, 1980); Ruth Cowan, "Women's Rights through Litigation: An Examination of the American Civil Liberties Union Women's Rights Project, 1971–1976," *Columbia Human Rights Law Review* 8(1976). For analysis of litigation as a political activity, see Susan Olson, *Clients and Lawyers* (Westport: Greenwood Press, 1984); Richard Kluger, *Simple Justice* (New York: Alfred A. Knopf, 1976); Richard C. Cortner, "Strategies and Tactics of Litigants in Constitutional Cases," *Journal of Public Law* 17(1968); Clement Vose, "Litigation as a Form of Pressure Group Activity," *The Annals of the American Academy of Political and Social Sciences* 319(1958).

12. See Ann E. Freedman, "Sex Equality, Sex Differences, and the Supreme Court," *Yale Law Journal* 92(1983).

1

The Constitution
and Equality

The legal status of women has been shaped by an ideology grounded in cultural and physical differences between the sexes. Beginning in the nineteenth century, this "ideology of separate spheres—in which the public sphere of work was considered men's and the private world of family was women's—became the justification for sex-based laws."[1] Although claiming to maintain adherence to equal treatment under the law, the courts of the United States upheld laws that treated women differently on the basis of their physical characteristics and their roles within the family.

The separate spheres doctrine had a profound influence on public policy-making in the United States. Even though women eventually overcame many of the barriers to equality in the public realm, their lives continue to be shaped by their physical and cultural roles as wives and mothers, and their legal status continues to reflect these traditional assumptions about their "proper" roles in the family.

Early Battles for Equality

One of the opening salvos in the fight for women's equality in the United States was fired by Abigail Adams at her famous husband, John. Writing to him on March 31, 1776, about the "new code of laws" he and his compatriots were about to draft, Abigail urged him to "remember the ladies and be more generous and favorable to them than your ancestors. Do not put such unlimited power into the hands of the husbands." She reminded him that "all men would be tyrants if they could. [And that] if particular care and attention is not paid to the ladies, we are determined to foment a rebellion, and will not hold ourselves bound by any laws in which we have no voice or representation."

Husband John responded on April 14, 1776: "As to your extraordinary code of laws, I cannot but laugh. . . . [Y]our letter was the first intimation that another tribe, more numerous and powerful than all the rest, were grown discontented." She chided him in a letter dated May 7, 1776: "I cannot say that I think you are very generous to the ladies; for whilst you are proclaiming peace and good-will to men, emancipating all nations, you insist on retaining an absolute power over wives." She cautioned that "arbitrary power is like most other things which are very hard, very liable to be broken."[2]

Abigail's admonitions to John were largely unheeded. While the framers of the U.S. Constitution debated over the legal status of the slave in the new document, there is no evidence that they gave any thought to the legal position of women.

The Seneca Falls Convention

The Declaration of Sentiments, adopted at the first Women's Rights Convention in Seneca Falls, New York, in July 1848, echoed Abigail Adams's indictment against male-dominated society in the United States. The Seneca Falls Convention was inspired by the experiences of two women attending the World Anti-Slavery Convention in London in 1840. After much debate, and despite the opposition of the American delegation, convention leaders decided that female delegates would not be seated on the convention floor and would have to observe the proceedings from the galleries. Two women forced to sit upstairs, Lucretia Mott and Elizabeth Cady Stanton, spent their time in London pondering their fate as women and agreeing on a need to act.

Eight years later an announcement appeared in the *Seneca County Courier*:

> Women's Rights Convention—A convention to discuss the social, civil and religious rights of woman will be held in the Wesleyan Chapel, Seneca Falls, New York, on Wednesday and Thursday, the 19th and 20th of July current; commencing at 10:00 A.M.

Borrowing from the Declaration of Independence, the convention organizers, including Mott and Stanton, drafted a statement of principles for the meeting:

> When in the course of human events it becomes necessary for one portion of

the family of man to assume among the peoples of the earth a position different from that they have hitherto occupied . . .

We hold these truths to be self evident: that all men and women are created equal; that they are endowed by their Creator with certain inalienable rights; that among these are life, liberty, and the pursuit of happiness . . .

The history of mankind is a history of repeated injuries and usurpations on the part of man toward woman, having in direct object the establishment of an absolute tyranny over her.[3]

The struggle for women's rights, propelled by the Seneca Falls Convention, had grown out of the abolitionist movement. Most early feminists, Elizabeth Cady Stanton, Lucretia Mott, Henry Ward Beecher, Lucy Stone, Frederick Douglass, Susan B. Anthony, and Henry Blackwell, among them, combined the antislavery struggle with the fight for women's rights. With the Civil War looming, however, everyone's attention turned away from women's rights.

Women's Suffrage

After the Civil War, women renewed their efforts to secure the right to vote, but the nation was not ready to accept women voters. The newly ratified Fourteenth Amendment of 1868 was a major setback to women's rights, explicitly inserting the word *male* into the Constitution for the first time.[4] Section two of the amendment warned of the consequences if men over twenty-one were denied the right to vote by stating that

representatives shall be apportioned among the several States according to their respective numbers, counting the whole number of persons in each State, excluding Indians not taxed. But when the right to vote at any election . . . is denied to any of the *male* inhabitants of such State being twenty-one years of age, and citizens of the United States, or in any way abridged . . . the basis of such representation therein shall be reduced in the proportion which the number of such *male* citizens shall bear to the whole number of *male* citizens twenty-one years of age in such State. [emphasis added]

Women lost again when, two years later, they lobbied to have sex included in the Fifteenth Amendment. They were disappointed when the Fifteenth, guaranteeing that the "right of citizens of the United States to vote shall not be denied or abridged . . . on account of race, color, or previous condition of servitude," did not mention sex.

The fight for suffrage dominated the women's rights movement in the latter part of the nineteenth century and the early part of the twentieth.[5] Women sought enfranchisement so they could use their voting power for social reform. Optimistically, "they anticipated that by strategic use of their political power women would break open new occupations, raise the level of their wage scales to that of men, win strikes, and force reforms in marriage and family law in order to protect themselves from sexual abuse, the loss of their children, and the unchecked tyranny of their husbands."[6]

Although the suffragists eventually won the right to vote with the ratification of the Nineteenth Amendment in 1920, their vision of influencing public policy through political power was at best premature; at worst, it was illusory.[7]

The Right to Practice Law

While women sought the right to vote through the political arena, they also pursued women's equality — fruitlessly — in the courts. Reflecting the influence of the separate spheres ideology, the Supreme Court consistently rejected women's appeals for equal rights.

The first Supreme Court test of sexual equality resulted in a disappointing ruling against a woman's right to choose an occupation. Myra Bradwell, who learned law under her husband's guidance, successfully qualified for the Illinois bar but was denied admission because she was a married woman.[8] She took her case to the Supreme Court, basing her claim on the Fourteenth Amendment's privileges and immunities clause, which provides that "no State shall make or enforce any law which shall abridge the privileges and immunities of citizens of the United States." She argued that this section protected her "privilege of earning a livelihood."

Speaking for the Court, in *Bradwell v. Illinois,* 1873, Samuel Miller agreed that the Fourteenth Amendment guaranteed rights of national citizenship but added that "the right to admission to practice in the courts of a State is not one of them. This right," he continued, "in no sense depends on citizenship of the United States."[9]

Bradwell was based on the Court's earlier ruling in the *Slaughterhouse Cases,* where the scope of the privileges and immunities clause was so narrowed that it became virtually useless as a claim for rights.[10] Decided the day before *Bradwell,* the *Slaughterhouse Cases* revolved around definitions of federal and state citizenship and the relationship between the federal and state governments.

The *Slaughterhouse Cases* arose when Louisiana butchers challenged a Reconstructionist law that created a monopoly of the slaughterhouse trade. The Court ruled that the right to earn a living was within the bounds of state citizenship, but it was not within the scope of the privileges and immunities clause — which only guaranteed federal protection of federal constitutional rights or laws. With her case being decided on the heels of the *Slaughterhouse Cases,* Myra Bradwell was an unfortunate victim of the Court's narrow interpretation of the privileges and immunities clause.

By relying on the *Slaughterhouse Cases,* the Court was able to sidestep the issue of Bradwell's rights as a woman. But Joseph Bradley's concurring opinion, joined by Noah Swayne and Stephen Field, squarely addressed — and rejected — Bradwell's equal rights claim. In a strong affirmation of the separate sphere's ideology, Bradley denied that women enjoyed the same rights as men to pursue an occupation. He contended that

> the civil law, as well as nature herself, has always recognized a wide difference in the respective spheres and destinies of man and woman. Man is, or should be, woman's protector and defender. The natural and proper timidity and delicacy which belongs to the female sex evidently unfits it for many of the occupations of civil life. The constitution of the family organization, which is found in the divine ordinance, as well as in the nature of things, indicates the domestic sphere as that which properly belongs to the domain and functions of womanhood. The harmony, not to say identity, of interests and views which belong, or should belong, to the family institutions is repugnant to the idea of a woman adopting a distinct and independent career from that of her husband.

Continuing, he admitted that "many women are unmarried" but explained that they "are exceptions to the general rule. The paramount destiny and mission of woman are to fulfill the noble and benign offices of wife and mother. This is the law of the Creator."[11]

The Right to Vote

Soon after *Bradwell,* women suffered another defeat before the Supreme Court in *Minor v. Happersett* in 1875. Three years earlier, Virginia Minor sued a St. Louis voting registrar for refusing to allow her to register to vote. Losing her case in the Missouri Supreme Court, she appealed to the United States Supreme Court, claiming that the right to vote was a privilege of national citizenship protected from state infringement by the Fourteenth Amendment.

In a decision reminiscent of the *Dred Scott* case of 1857, in which the Court cavalierly denied that blacks were citizens entitled to constitutional protection, Minor's argument was rejected.[12] As in *Bradwell,* the Court diminished the force of the privileges and immunities clause by denying that the Fourteenth Amendment added "to the privileges and immunities of a citizen. It simply furnished an additional guaranty for the protection of such as *he* already had. No new voters were necessarily made by it."[13]

Speaking for the Court, Morrison Waite explained that because the Fourteenth Amendment did not confer suffrage, Minor could only win her case if women had the right to vote at the time the Constitution was adopted. After surveying the laws of several states that limited suffrage to men, he concluded women did not. Why the Court chose to model *Minor* on the thoroughly discredited *Dred Scott* opinion is not known, but according to historian W. William Hodes, it suggests that the Court viewed women as "second-class citizens — citizens with less legal rights than other citizens."[14]

The Right to Work

Around the turn of the century, increasing industrialization of the American economy prompted state regulation of conditions of work, hours, and wages to ameliorate the harsh life of the American worker. The legality of these regulations was soon tested in the courts, with industry arguing that the legislation exceeded state authority. Initially, the Court relied on the *Slaughterhouse Cases* to allow states to regulate industry under their authority to promote the public welfare.

But in 1905, in *Lochner v. New York,* the Court reversed direction by striking down a New York law that prohibited employment in bakeries for more than sixty hours a week or ten hours a day. It ruled that this public welfare measure violated the due process clause of the Fourteenth Amendment guaranteeing that "no State shall . . . deprive any person of life, liberty, or property, without due process of law." The Court explained that "the general right to make a contract in relation to his business is part of the liberty of the individual protected by the Fourteenth Amendment of the Federal Constitution."[15]

The law was struck on a number of grounds: first, baking is not an unhealthy industry; second, bakers could make their own decisions about how many hours to work; and third, the quality of the baked goods is not improved if made by bakers working fewer hours. Convinced that bakers did not require special protection, the Court found no reason to interfere with their liberty to make contracts to work longer hours if they desired.

Lochner marked the beginning of an era of judicial support for laissez-faire economics that lasted until the 1930s.[16] The decision prompted Justice Oliver Wendell Holmes, Jr., to protest that the "Constitution is not intended to embody a particular economic theory."[17]

Three years later, in *Muller v. Oregon,* despite its commitment to a "hands off" approach to industry, the Court upheld an Oregon statute limiting female laundry workers to a maximum ten-hour day.

Curt Muller, owner of the Grand Laundry in Portland, Oregon, was convicted and fined $10.00 for requiring one of his employees, Mrs. E. Gotcher, to work more than ten hours on September 4, 1905. His conviction was upheld by the Oregon Supreme Court, and he appealed to the

United States Supreme Court. The attorney for the state, future Supreme Court Justice Louis D. Brandeis, presented a 113-page brief to the Court arguing that, unlike male bakers, female laundry workers needed the state's protection because they were physically incapable of working long hours. The Brandeis brief, an exegesis to the separate spheres ideology, focused on the physical differences between the sexes and presented evidence on the necessity of restricting women's working hours.

In *Muller*, the Court began its opinion by restating its commitment to allowing workers to contract their labor without government interference. But because women are physically different from men and play different roles in society, the Court believed that the laissez-faire principle articulated in *Lochner* did not apply. Echoing the separate spheres ideology, the Court found that a woman's "physical structure and a proper discharge of her maternal functions . . . justify legislation to protect her from the greed as well as the passion of man."[18] While claiming to endorse equality between the sexes, the Court accepted the state's limitations on women's employment.

Although some labor reformers welcomed *Muller*, the Court's ruling justified restrictive legislation aimed only at female workers. Denying job opportunities under the guise of protection, these laws made women more expensive to employ and limited their availability for work. In her article on the family and the labor market, Frances Olsen points out that "*Muller* was based on the thesis that women differ from men in important ways, and although the case might have seemed to exalt women, it effectively degraded them by treating the asserted differences as evidence of women's inferiority."[19]

Also concerned about its female workers, New York enacted a statute in 1917 prohibiting them from working in restaurants between 10:00 P.M. and 6:00 A.M. Turning aside a challenge to the statute in *Radice v. New York*, 1924, the Supreme Court accepted the state's argument that "night work . . . so injuriously affects the physical condition of women, and so threatens to impair their peculiar and natural functions, and so exposes them to the dangers and menaces incident to night life in large cities."[20]

Once again, as in *Muller*, women were denied opportunities for employment because of their "differences." The Court did not question the state's logic in barring women from nighttime restaurant work while allowing them to work at night as performers, ladies' cloakroom attendants, or hotel kitchen help (all exempted from the law). Nor did it inquire whether the statute was enacted to preserve a male monopoly on the more lucrative nighttime restaurant jobs.

Forty years after *Muller*, in *Goesaert v. Cleary*, 1948, the Supreme Court again allowed a state to "protect" women out of jobs. For their "safety," under Michigan law women could only be licensed as bartenders if they were related to male bar owners. Speaking for the Court, Felix

Frankfurter set the tone of the decision when he said, "beguiling as this subject is, it need not detain us long." His amusement was evident as he reminded the Court that "we are, to be sure, dealing with a historic calling. We meet the alewife, sprightly and ribald, in Shakespeare, but centuries before him she played a role in the social life of England."[21]

In a more serious vein, Frankfurter noted that Michigan could forbid all women from working behind a bar but could not make irrational distinctions among women. Nonetheless, he was persuaded that the state had sufficient reason to believe that only relatives of tavern owners would be protected from the dangers attendant to working behind a bar.

Frankfurter refused to question the logic of allowing women to work as tavern waitresses where they were in closer proximity to sources of danger than they would be behind the width of a two-foot bar. After rejecting the insinuation that the legislation was prompted by the desire to retain bartending jobs for returning World War II veterans, he concluded that the law survived constitutional scrutiny.

The Right to Serve on a Jury

The separate spheres ideology also led to restrictions on women's participation in the responsibilities of citizenship, such as service on juries. The question of access to jury service was presented to the Supreme Court in *Hoyt v. Florida* in 1961. Attempting to relieve women of unwanted obligations that might interfere with their duties at home, Florida only called them to serve on juries if they voluntarily registered.

The case arose when Mrs. Hoyt was tried for killing her husband with a baseball bat in revenge for his infidelity. Following her trial before an all-male jury, she was convicted of second-degree murder. Appealing her conviction, she argued that female jurors would have been more sympathetic to her and that her trial before a jury of men violated her rights.

Speaking for the Court, John Marshall Harlan pointed out that defendants are not entitled to juries of their choice; they are only entitled to juries "indiscriminately drawn from among those eligible in the community for jury service."[22] Florida did not exclude women from juries, Harlan noted, it merely exempted them from jury service at their option.

Reflecting the traditions of the separate spheres ideology, the Court ruled that "despite the enlightened emancipation of women from the restrictions and protections of bygone years, and their entry into many parts of community life formerly considered to be reserved to men, woman is still regarded as the center of home and family life." And because of a woman's familial role, Florida could relieve her "from the civic duty of jury service unless she herself determines that such service is consistent with her own special responsibilities."[23] Acknowledging that the jury exemptions could have been restricted to women with childcare responsibilities, Harlan refused to condemn the law as "irrational."

In accepting suspect motives, illogical thinking, and overbroad generalizations in these cases, the Court demonstrated its reluctance to depart from separate spheres thinking.[24] Finally, in 1971, ten years after *Hoyt,* the Court began to take issue with states' assumptions about differences between the sexes and started to inquire more deeply into the purpose and effect of legislative distinctions based on sex.

The Modern Equal Protection Clause

The equal protection clause of the Fourteenth Amendment provides that "no State shall . . . deny to any person within its jurisdiction the equal protection of the laws." In guaranteeing equality under the law, the Constitution put states on notice that they must justify their legislative decisions to treat persons (that is, to classify them) as legally different. Under equal protection doctrine, differential treatment is constitutionally permissible when it is based on *relevant* differences among individuals.[25] Because laws based on immutable characteristics such as race or national origin bear no relationship to ability and are irrelevant to valid legislative goals, the Court views them as inherently suspicious and carefully scrutinizes them. The prototypical suspicious (or suspect) classification is race, and the government is under a heavy burden to justify such a distinction in law.[26]

The Supreme Court first articulated the concept of a suspect classification based on race in *Korematsu v. United States*, 1944, the World War II Japanese exclusion case. Although it accepted the government's defense of the exclusion order, the Court proclaimed that "all legal restrictions which curtail the civil rights of a single racial group are immediately suspect."[27]

Levels of Scrutiny

When Earl Warren was chief justice of the Supreme Court, from 1953 to 1969, the Court formulated a two-tier level of scrutiny for determining the constitutionality of laws: strict and minimal. Under the strict scrutiny doctrine, invoked in cases involving a suspect classification (such as race), the Court requires the state to show a "compelling" reason for the classification and to demonstrate that the means (the classification) are "necessarily" related to the ends sought to be achieved by the statute and are the least restrictive means to achieve those ends.

The Court applies minimal scrutiny to laws based on classifications involving changeable characteristics (such as wealth) or classifications that are related to ability (such as age). Under minimal scrutiny, the state simply has to produce a "legitimate" reason for the classification and to demonstrate that the means are "rationally" related to the ends desired by the statute.

The level of scrutiny used is crucial to the outcome of the case. Statutes reviewed under minimal scrutiny almost always receive the Court's approval. Conversely, after *Korematsu*, the Supreme Court has never upheld an explicit racial classification.[28] Because of this result, over the years a mystique has surrounded strict scrutiny. The mystique stems not only from the language and mind-set accompanying strict scrutiny review but also, and perhaps more important, from a strong presumption of unconstitutionality against the classification.[29]

Developing a New Level of Scrutiny for Sex-based Laws

In the 1970s, for a number of reasons, including the assertiveness of the women's movement, congressional attacks on sex discrimination in employment and education, and the rising consciousness of women fueled by the struggle for ratification of the Equal Rights Amendment, the federal courts became a forum for the debate over sexual equality. In response to mounting litigation efforts, the Supreme Court under Warren Burger as chief justice (1969–1986) developed a constitutional doctrine to judge legislative assertions of relevant sex differences in light of the equal protection clause.[30]

The modern era of women's struggle for equal rights began in 1971, with most state laws challenged under the Fourteenth Amendment's equal protection clause and federal laws challenged under the due process clause of the Fifth Amendment.[31] In 1971, the Court's opinion in *Reed v. Reed* marked the beginning of a new approach to constitutional sex equality doctrine when, for the first time ever, the Court invalidated a law on the grounds of sex discrimination.

The case arose when Sally Reed and her ex-husband, Cecil Reed, vied for the post of administrator of their deceased son's estate.[32] Because of the Idaho law compelling a preference for the man when there was a choice between an equally qualified man and woman, the probate court selected Cecil to administer the estate. The judge made no attempt to determine who was better suited for the position.

The state district court found the statute unconstitutional, but the Idaho Supreme Court reversed, rejecting Sally Reed's constitutional argument. On appeal before the United States Supreme Court, the state argued that the statute was designed to prevent conflict within the family and to reduce the workload of probate courts in assessing the qualifications of competing estate administrators. Conceding the objectives of the statute were legitimate, the United States Supreme Court reversed the state high court.

Moving away from its usual deference to sex-based classifications, the Court noted that to withstand constitutional scrutiny, the classification must bear a "fair and substantial relation to the object of the legislation." Speaking for a unanimous Court, Burger warned that

> to give a mandatory preference to members of either sex over members of the other, merely to accomplish the elimination of hearings on the merits, is to make the very kind of arbitrary legislative choice forbidden by the Equal Protection Clause of the Fourteenth Amendment; and whatever may be said as to the positive values of avoiding intrafamily controversy, the choice in this context may not lawfully be mandated solely on the basis of sex.[33]

Without openly acknowledging it, the Court edged toward a stricter review of sex-based classifications. The statute under attack in *Reed* was based on the reasonable (and accurate) assumption that men generally had more business experience than women. And although the law was more defensible than others that had survived judicial scrutiny in the past, the Supreme Court invalidated it. Perhaps signaling its desire to enter a new phase of sex discrimination law, the Court cited no sex discrimination case in its opinion.

Frontiero v. Richardson, 1973, built on the *Reed* precedent. In her suit against the secretary of defense, Lieutenant Sharon Frontiero challenged an armed-forces regulation requiring married women to prove they provided over one-half the family support before they could obtain increased quarters allowance and medical and dental benefits. Married men automatically received the additional benefits without having to show they supported their wives.

Women were doubly disadvantaged by the military's rule: first, they had to prove their spouses were dependent on them while men did not; and second, they did not receive benefits unless they contributed at least 50 percent of the family support while men received dependency benefits no matter what their level of support. Although Sharon's husband, Joseph, was a student, his veterans' benefits made him ineligible to be her dependent.

A plurality of four justices consisting of William Brennan, Thurgood Marshall, Byron White, and William Douglas declared sex an inherently suspect classification and held that the regulation violated Frontiero's constitutional right of equality. While agreeing that the military regulation was unconstitutional, four other justices, Potter Stewart, Lewis Powell, Harry Blackmun, and Warren Burger were unwilling to join the plurality and declare sex a suspect category. They concurred, citing *Reed* as precedent. Powell added that the Court should not usurp the democratic process by declaring sex a suspect classification while the states were considering ratification of the Equal Rights Amendment.[34] William Rehnquist dissented without opinion.

Brennan's plurality opinion explained that by rejecting the state's "apparently rational" explanation for its probate scheme in *Reed*, the Court had departed from a "'traditional' rational basis analysis." Justifying the use of strict scrutiny, Brennan characterized the history of sex discrimination in the United States as "'romantic paternalism' which, in practical effect, put women, not on a pedestal, but in a cage."[35]

Like race and national origin, Brennan said, sex was not related to ability and deserved the same searching scrutiny as these other classifications. He observed that Congress demonstrated its belief that sex was an "inherently invidious" classification by passing the Equal Pay Act of 1963 and Title VII of the 1964 Civil Rights Act and by submitting the Equal Rights Amendment to the states for ratification.

Without offering proof, the government contended that the dependency rule was administratively convenient and saved money. The Court was not satisfied with the government's flat assertion that the rule achieved these ends. More important, it held, even if the government could prove its claim, this drawing of lines between the sexes "*solely*" to achieve administrative convenience was constitutionally forbidden.[36]

Frontiero represented a milestone in the development of the Supreme Court's sexual equality doctrine because four justices agreed that strict scrutiny should be applied to laws based on sex. But although the Court continued to move toward stricter judicial review of sex-based classifications, strict scrutiny itself has remained out of reach.

In 1976, in *Craig v. Boren,* the Court abandoned its two-tier analysis and formally adopted a new level of scrutiny for review of laws involving sex-based classifications. The case arose over a seemingly innocuous Oklahoma law that allowed eighteen-year-old women—but not men—to buy 3.2 or "near" beer. A three-judge federal district court upheld the law but the Supreme Court reversed on appeal. Brennan delivered the opinion of the Court for himself, White, Marshall, Powell, and the newly appointed John Paul Stevens. Blackmun and Stewart concurred while Burger and Rehnquist dissented.

Without acknowledging the shift toward stricter scrutiny, Brennan simply asserted that "previous cases establish that classifications by gender must serve important governmental objectives and must be substantially related to achievement of those objectives."[37] Reviewing earlier cases, he noted that the Court refused to approve laws based on "archaic and overbroad generalizations"; or on "'old notions' of role typing"; or on "outdated misconceptions concerning the role of females in the home rather than in the 'marketplace and world of ideas.'"[38]

Within these guidelines, Brennan examined the use of sex as a "classifying device." He accepted Oklahoma's assertion that its goal was to reduce incidents of driving under the influence of alcohol. But despite the factual basis for the sex-based classification (a statistically significant difference between women and men being arrested for driving under the influence of alcohol), the Court held the law did not pass the heightened scrutiny test.

In finding the law unconstitutional, Brennan applied the new heightened scrutiny standard to a law that disadvantaged men. And in his dissent, Rehnquist objected to the adoption of a stricter standard of review without "citation to any source," arguing it was particularly inappropriate in cases of men challenging sex-based classifications. He pointed out that the Court justified its departure from minimal scrutiny in past sex discrimination cases because women had been victims of historical discrimination. But because there was no history of discrimination against men, Rehnquist said he would only apply minimal scrutiny to the Oklahoma law. And, using the lower level of scrutiny, he found the law reasonable and therefore constitutional.[39]

After *Craig*, unable to attract a fifth vote to make sex a suspect category (especially after losing Douglas to retirement), the Court applied the new heightened, or intermediate, scrutiny to sex-based classifications. Table 1.1 summarizes the approach the Supreme Court has taken to equal protection analysis since 1976.

Classifying Cases

Since 1971, there have been twenty-five Supreme Court cases decided on equal protection grounds.[40] The Court struck the sex-based classification in thirteen cases. Seventeen cases were brought by men, two by a married couple, and six by women. Table 1.2 summarizes the cases, dates, issues, and the Court's vote in these twenty-five cases.

Striking the Sex-based Laws

The decisions furthering sex equality, in which the Court struck down the sex-based laws, were mostly "easy" cases because the laws under review were grounded in separate spheres thinking that defined women's and

Table 1.1   Analysis of Equal Protection Cases

Classification	Scrutiny	Ends	Means
Suspect (e.g., race)	Strict	Compelling	Necessarily related
Semisuspect (e.g., sex)	Heightened*	Important	Substantially related
Nonsuspect (e.g., age)	Minimal	Legitimate	Rationally related

*Also known as intermediate scrutiny.

men's lives in old-fashioned, stereotypical roles.[41] *Reed, Frontiero,* and *Craig* were such easy cases. Some of the others were: *Stanley v. Illinois,* 1972, in which the Court held that as a matter of due process, unwed fathers were entitled to individualized custody hearings the same as married fathers or unwed mothers (in denying such hearings, said the Court, the state violated the unwed father's equal protection rights); *Stanton v. Stanton,* 1975, in which the Court invalidated a Utah law specifying a higher age of majority for men and ordered a divorced father to support his daughter until she was twenty-one — the same as his son; *Orr v. Orr,* 1979, in which the Court struck an Alabama law that only entitled women to alimony; *Kirchberg v. Feenstra,* 1981, in which the Court struck a Louisiana statute that gave men the right to dispose of jointly held community property without their wives' consent; and *Mississippi University for Women v. Hogan,* 1982, in which the Court ordered a women-only nursing program at a state university to admit men.[42]

In deciding the easy cases, the Court served notice that classifications based on stereotypical generalizations about sex differences could not serve as the foundation for legislative distinctions. While not revolutionary because the Court was merely recognizing the reality of women's roles as wage earners in modern U.S. society, the decisions were significant because they marked a decline in the Court's adherence to the separate spheres ideology. Ironically, although the cases were brought as part of a rising feminist consciousness, most of the immediate beneficiaries were men.

Other easy cases, revolving around issues of dependency and survivor's rights under the Social Security Act and worker's compensation laws, were: *Weinberger v. Wiesenfeld,* 1975, in which the Court struck a provision of the Social Security law allowing only widows to receive childcare benefits; *Califano v. Goldfarb,* 1977, in which the Court invalidated another provision of the Social Security Act requiring a widower to have received at least one-half his support from his deceased wife before receiving survivors' benefits; *Califano v. Westcott,* 1979, in which the Court ordered the Aid to Families with Dependent Children – Unemployed Father program to pay benefits to eligible families when either parent is unemployed; and *Wengler v. Druggists Mutual Insurance Company,* 1980, in which the Court struck a provision of the Missouri workers' compensation law requiring a widower to prove incapacitation or dependency on his deceased wife before receiving her death benefits.[43]

The laws at issue in these cases presumed that men were heads of households with women dependent on them. By extending government benefits to men and their children, the Court demonstrated it was aware of the discriminatory assumptions behind the laws. Agreeing that the laws were unconstitutional, the justices were often divided on whether the laws discriminated against the men only or also discriminated against women workers by depriving them of the opportunity to provide for their hus-

Table 1.2   Equal Protection Cases, 1971–Present

Case	Date	Issue	Vote	+/−[b]
Reed	1971	Preference for men as estate administrators	9–0	+
Stanley[a]	1972	Unwed fathers automatically denied child custody	5–2[d]	+
Frontiero	1973	Dependent benefits to servicewomen restricted	8–1	+
Kahn[a]	1974	Automatic tax exemption restricted to widows	6–3	−
Geduldig	1974	Pregnancy excluded from disability plan	6–3	−
Ballard[a]	1975	Women naval officers allowed longer time in rank	5–4	−
Wiesenfeld[a]	1975	Childcare benefits restricted to widowed mothers	8–0	+
Stanton	1975	Teenage daughters denied support because reach majority earlier than sons	8–1	+
Craig[a]	1976	Age to purchase beer higher for men	7–2	+
Goldfarb[a]	1977	Nondependent widowers not entitled to dependent benefits	5–4	+
Webster[a]	1977	Advantage to women in calculating pensions	9–0	−
Vorchheimer	1977	Public high school restricted to male students	4–4	−
Fiallo[a]	1977	Immigration preference for mothers of illegitimate children	6–3	−

(*continued on p. 23*)

bands and children the way men ordinarily do—through insurance and pension benefits.

Upholding the Sex-based Laws: The Compensation Cases

The cases in which the Court upheld the sex-based laws were grounded on either of two premises: first, that women could receive preferential treatment (or compensation) for discrimination against them; second, that laws could distinguish between the sexes when women and men were not similarly situated because of differences in physical characteristics.[44]

The four compensation cases, *Kahn v. Shevin,* 1974; *Schlesinger v. Ballard,* 1975; *Califano v. Webster,* 1977; and *Heckler v. Mathews,* 1984, all resulted in decisions upholding the sex-based legislative classification.[45]

Table 1.2   (cont.)

Case	Date	Issue	Vote	+/−[b]
Quilloin[a]	1978	Unmarried father unable to veto adoption of illegitimate child	9–0	−
Orr[a]	1979	Alimony restricted to women	6–3	+
Parham[a]	1979	Unmarried father unable to sue for wrongful death of illegitimate child	5–4	−
Caban[a]	1979	Unmarried father unable to veto adoption of illegitimate child	5–4	+
Westcott[c]	1979	Benefits restricted to families with unemployed fathers	9–0	+
Wengler[a]	1980	Nondependent widowers not entitled to worker compensation benefits	8–1	+
Kirchberg	1981	Husband's right to unilaterally dispose of community property	9–0	+
Michael M.[a]	1981	Statutory rape liability restricted to men	5–4	−
Rostker[a]	1981	Draft registration restricted to men	6–3	−
Hogan[a]	1982	State nursing school restricted to women students	5–4	+
Lehr[a]	1983	No notice to unmarried fathers in adoption of illegitimate child	6–3	−
Mathews[c]	1984	Nondependent men required to offset pension	9–0	−

[a]Case brought by a man.
[b]+ = The Court struck the sex-based classification.
 − = The Court upheld the sex-based classification.
[c]Case brought by a husband and wife.
[d]Decided on due process and equal protection grounds.

Kahn, ironically written within a year of *Frontiero,* when the Court seemed on the verge of adopting strict scrutiny, epitomizes the stereotypical image of needy women. Under Florida law, widows were entitled to a $500.00 property tax exemption. Quoting the lower court opinion in his ruling, Douglas stated that the purpose of the law was to reduce "'the disparity between the economic capabilities of a man and a woman.'"[46]

Accepting the state's claim that the law was a remedy for women's depressed economic status, the Court approved the Florida widows-only property tax exemption. What Douglas neglected to point out was that the state's attempt to redress economic inequality between the sexes amounted to a benefit of only $15.00 a year.

In *Webster,* the Court ruled on a provision of the Social Security Act that allowed women to exclude three more lower earning years than men in computing their average monthly wage on which their pension was based. But since Congress had eliminated this computation method in 1972, it was no longer applicable by the time the Court heard the case except to men who reached sixty-two before 1972.

Similarly, in *Mathews,* the Court allowed women an exemption to a pension offset requirement of the Social Security Act. In 1977, as a result of *Goldfarb,* Congress repealed the dependency requirement for spousal benefits. But to avoid financial problems in the Social Security trust fund, the government deducted the amount of any pension received from the state or federal government from the benefits. Women (and dependent men) were exempted from the pension offset requirement until 1982. The law was thus merely a temporary measure that benefited women for the five-year period between 1977 and 1982.

Ballard arose over a U.S. Navy rule allowing women to accrue thirteen years (compared to nine for men) as commissioned line officers before being discharged for lack of promotion. The government argued that differential treatment was justified because the navy limited women's opportunities for advancement by restricting their participation in combat and sea duty. The Court accepted the argument, expressing no concern about the denial of equal opportunity for women in the navy.

The wisdom of the Court's rulings in the compensation cases has been debated among women's rights advocates. Some have commended the Court for recognizing a need to remedy the discriminatory effects of the economic system.[47] But this view is shortsighted because each of these opinions also demonstrates the Court's refusal to break with traditional thinking about women depending on men (or the government) for support and protection. Although denying that it was motivated by stereotypical generalizations, in upholding these laws the Court reinforced the traditional image of dependent women and caretaker men.

While the Court accepted the government's justification that the laws were intended to remedy past or present discrimination against women, with the exception of *Ballard* the benefit to women was probably not worth the price of continuing the tradition of classifying them as needy dependents. Although the laws may have been well intentioned, the Court could have refused to accept the legislatures' decisions to use sex as a dividing line. It could have required Congress to allow any worker absent from the job market for a number of years to exclude a specified number of lower earning years and to exempt dependents of either sex from the pension offset requirement. It could have insisted that Florida help all poor surviving spouses by drawing a line based on need, not sex. By accepting these sex-based laws, the Court reaffirmed its commitment to the separate spheres ideology. Although *Ballard* may provide needed compensation to female naval officers, it also reflects the Court's acceptance of traditional attitudes towards women and highlights its unwillingness to address the sexual inequality that led to the compensation scheme. Moreover, it illustrates how one sex-based law, such as the exclusion of women from combat, can place men and women in different legal categories for purposes of equal protection analysis. In reaching its decision, the Court ignored the underlying sex discrimination in the navy's regulation and, by focusing on the last layer of discrimination, allowed one sex-based law to justify a second one.

Upholding the Sex-based Laws: The Physical Differences Cases

The cases in which the Court upheld challenged laws based on physical differences between the sexes illustrate the contradictions within the Court's sex equality doctrine most sharply. Feminist scholar Wendy Williams calls these the "hard" cases and contrasts them with the "easy" ones, which "rest on an economic model of the family that no longer predominates." According to Williams, the hard cases are especially difficult for the Court to decide because they revolve around "more basic, sex-role arrangements" derived from society's view of the proper role of women. Additionally, she argues that because the challenged laws are often traceable to physiological sex differences such as childbearing, these cases push the Court's willingness to abandon the separate spheres ideology to the limit.[48]

The first case in which the Court upheld a legislative distinction derived from physical differences between the sexes was *Geduldig v. Aiello.* In this 1974 case, somewhat surprisingly, the Court found that a law affecting pregnancy did not differentiate between men and women. And because it believed the law was not based on sex differences, the Court applied minimal scrutiny and upheld the state's decision to exclude benefits for normal pregnancy from a state-operated disability insurance program.[49]

In two 1981 cases, *Michael M. v. Superior Court* and *Rostker v. Goldberg,* the Court upheld a men-only statutory rape law and a men-only military registration law.[50] In these cases, the Court permitted the legislative distinctions, ruling that because men and women were not similarly situated, the sex-based classifications were valid.

Michael M. involved a California law punishing men for engaging in sexual intercourse with underage women. The case arose when $17\frac{1}{2}$-year-old Michael M. was convicted of statutory rape for having sexual intercourse with $16\frac{1}{2}$-year-old Sharon. Using strict scrutiny, the California Supreme Court upheld the conviction, accepting the state's claim that the law was intended to prevent teenage pregnancy.[51] And since the fear of pregnancy would deter teenage women from sexual relations, men needed the extra deterrent that the law provided.

147,106

In a 5–4 decision, Rehnquist announced the judgment of the Court, joined by Burger, Stewart, and Powell, with Blackmun concurring. The Court upheld the sex-based classification, agreeing that men and women were not similarly situated with respect to the purpose of the law. Since only women faced the risk of pregnancy, "a criminal sanction imposed solely on the males thus serves to roughly 'equalize' the deterrents on the sexes."[52] Although the statutory rape laws of most states punished the adult partner of *either* sex, the Court concluded that the equal protection clause did not require a sex-neutral law.

Contrary to the Court's oft-stated contention that sex-based classifications must be "substantially related" to the goal of the legislation, Rehnquist proclaimed that the California law "was entitled to great deference." Under a heightened scrutiny standard, the state should have been required to show that its goal was the prevention of pregnancy and to demonstrate that the classification served this goal. Its legislative history showed that the law was based on traditional notions of man as agressor and woman as victim and was intended to protect the woman's virtue more than prevent pregnancy.[53] Additionally, there was no evidence that the law contributed to lowering the pregnancy rate among teenage women. Because of the Court's deferential approach, these inconsistencies and omissions did not disturb its decision to uphold the law.

The second 1981 case, *Rostker v. Goldberg,* arose when President Jimmy Carter reactivated a military draft registration following the invasion of Afghanistan in 1979. Although Carter recommended that Congress amend the Military Selective Service Act to allow women to register, Congress authorized funds to register men only. Several young men subject to the new registration policy brought suit against Bernard Rostker, director of the Selective Services.

A three-judge district court held that the law violated the due process clause of the Fifth Amendment and ordered the registration stopped. In a 6–3 vote, the Supreme Court reversed, with Rehnquist again delivering the opinion of the Court for himself, Burger, Stewart, Blackmun, Powell, and Stevens. Deferring to congressional authority over military affairs, the Court applied almost no scrutiny to the male-only registration scheme.

Rehnquist stated that registration was intended to prepare for a draft of combat troops. With women ineligible for combat, he said, the sexes are not similarly situated and the law can distinguish between them.[54] Again, as in *Ballard,* the Court expressed no concern over the different rules applied to men and women military personnel. Even the dissenting justices offered no objection to the restrictions on women's combat status. They simply argued that women could be registered and drafted as needed.

The government successfully argued that administrative convenience, an argument often rejected in earlier cases, justified the sex-based classification. Under the *Craig* standard, the Court should have examined the relationship between the classification and the government's goal of maintaining an effective defense force. Here, it simply accepted the government's assertion that all registrants must be suitable for combat despite evidence that all male registrants were not combat eligible.

These hard cases arose out of circumstances in which men and women were not similarly situated with respect to the asserted purpose of the law. According to Rehnquist and Stewart, the primary proponents of the similarly situated doctrine, the *Craig* heightened scrutiny doctrine should be applied only when the two sexes are similarly situated and one sex is deprived of a benefit the other has. When the sexes are *not* similarly situated, because, for example, there are physical differences between them, Rehnquist and Stewart advocate the use of a two-prong test that requires the government to show that the challenged law does not "make overbroad generalizations based on sex which are entirely unrelated to any differences between men and women or which demean the ability or social status of the affected class."[55]

Because there is rarely a law affecting women that is "entirely unrelated" to a difference between the sexes, the first prong of the test is readily met. The second prong of the test is also easily satisfied because the Court does not usually find that sex-based laws are demeaning to women. Applying the Rehnquist-Stewart test is akin to applying minimal scrutiny and virtually guarantees that the Court will uphold the law.[56]

In part, women have been caught in a trap of their own making because they argued for a sex equality doctrine based on the premise that women and men in the same circumstances—that is, men and women similarly situated—should be treated equally. As Martha Minow points out, "unfortunately . . . embracing the theory of 'sameness' mean[s] that any sign of difference between women and men could be used to justify treating women differently from men."[57]

Fathers and Illegitimate Children

The Court also allowed legislative distinctions between the sexes in four unwed father-illegitimate child cases: *Fiallo v. Bell*, 1977; *Quilloin v. Walcott*, 1978; *Parham v. Hughes*, 1979; and *Lehr v. Robertson*, 1983.[58] The Court appeared to take a contrary position in *Caban v. Mohammed*, 1979, when it struck down a New York law that permitted unwed mothers, but not fathers, to block the adoption of their children simply by withholding their consent. But even though the law was invalidated, the vote was 5–4, and the opinion was narrowly drawn and appeared to be limited to fathers of older children with whom they had long-standing relationships.[59]

In *Fiallo*, an immigrant father challenged a provision of the Immigration and Nationality Act of 1952 allowing mothers, but not fathers, of illegitimate children to claim preferential immigration status for their children. *Quilloin* involved a Georgia law permitting mothers, but not fathers, to veto the adoption of an illegitimate child. *Parham* was also about a Georgia statute that permitted an illegitimate child's mother to sue for the wrongful death of her child; the father could only sue if he had legitimated the child. And finally, *Lehr* concerned a challenge to a New York law denying the father of an illegitimate child the right to receive notice of an adoption proceeding involving his child.

Stewart's plurality opinion in *Parham* for himself, Burger, Rehnquist, and Stevens probably best illustrates the use of the similarly situated doctrine. The Court accepted the state's argument that the law served the important purpose of encouraging unwed fathers to legitimate their children and avoiding lawsuits by men claiming to be fathers of children born out of wedlock.

Stewart reasoned that "mothers and fathers of illegitimate children are not similarly situated [because] under Georgia law, only a father can by voluntary unilateral action make an illegitimate child legitimate."[60] He said this case is unlike cases such as *Reed* and *Frontiero* in which all members of one sex were placed apart in a class even though they were similarly situated with members of the other sex. Here, men and women are not similarly situated and the legislature has simply distinguished among fathers who have legitimated their children and those who have not. Finding that the law did not discriminate *between* the sexes, Stewart applied minimal scrutiny and, as might be expected, upheld the statute because he found it rationally related to the state's purpose.

In accepting the legislative distinctions in these cases involving fathers and their illegitimate children, the Court upheld statutes in which the biological reality of women bearing children was intertwined with the cultural role of women assuming primary care for children. By not probing the cultural biases behind the laws, the Court accepted the government's assertion that the sexes were not similarly situated. In upholding these and other laws involving physical differences between the sexes, as Ann Freedman argues, "The paradoxical—although hardly surprising result . . . has been to uphold those views about sex differences that are most entrenched in cultural beliefs and legislation, which in turn pose the greatest dangers of stereotyping and subordination of women."[61]

A Critique of the Court's Equal Protection Doctrine

Contrasted with the record of its predecessors, the Burger Court's performance in responding to equal protection challenges in sex-based cases was path-breaking.[62] Although recognizing that this Court deserves credit for advancing women's constitutional rights, critics assail it for accepting many current sex role arrangements. The primary criticism has been directed toward the Court's refusal to explore the relationship between physiological distinctions between the sexes and societal norms about appropriate sex role behavior.

Having traveled a long way from the days of *Muller, Goesaert,* and *Hoyt,* the Supreme Court has been reluctant to abandon the separate spheres ideology entirely and adopt a more searching scrutiny of sex-based classifications, especially in areas where physical differences are implicated. Its position in such cases demonstrates that while it has become more receptive to demands for sexual equality and has struck down many laws based on "stereotypical" or "overbroad generalizations" about the sexes, the separate spheres ideology persists. By failing to disentangle biological differences from culturally imposed roles, the Court lost the opportunity to repudiate the separate spheres doctrine and promote greater sexual equality in public policy.

Feminists such as Deborah Rhode, Catherine MacKinnon, Herma Hill Kay, and Sylvia Law view the Court's approach to the physical differences cases as the greatest obstacle to achieving a sex equality doctrine divorced from the separate spheres ideology.[63] While varying in their recommendations for change, they generally agree that the Court must engage in stricter scrutiny of sex-based laws and show more sensitivity to the harm perpetuated by sex-based classifications. They contend that the major problem with the Court's sexual equality doctrine is its approach to physical differences cases in which it abandons the heightened scrutiny standard developed in *Craig* and uses a lower standard of review requiring the legislation only to satisfy a test of reasonableness. And they argue that because such laws are often based, at least in part, on actual (that is, physiological) sex differences, they will virtually always seem reasonable.

Although they offer different remedies for change, these feminist scholars agree that laws based on physical differences between the sexes must be included within the Court's sex equality doctrine and subjected to more searching scrutiny. They argue that such laws often reflect cultural biases, and by upholding them, the Court validates and reinforces sex role stereotypes derived from the separate spheres ideology. What is needed, they assert, is a revised equal protection doctrine that recognizes the reality of biological differences between the sexes but does not allow the differences to overwhelm the principles of legal equality.

From a feminist perspective, it is clear that the Court needs to undertake a more rigorous review of sex-based classifications than the one it is currently using. Whether strict scrutiny will accomplish the ends sought is not known (after all, the California Supreme Court used strict scrutiny in upholding the statutory rape law in *Michael M.*). Certainly, however, a *stricter* scrutiny is called for, one in which the Court subjects sex-based classifications to a more rigorous analysis and requires a state to prove that the classification is very closely related to the goal of the legislation without resorting to stereotypical and paternalistic generalizations about the sexes.

Applying strict scrutiny would underscore the fact that the Court believes that sex-specific laws are presumptively unconstitutional because sex, like race, is an immutable characteristic that is virtually always unrelated to ability. It would serve as a warning to states that except under rigidly controlled circumstances, the Court believes that sex should not serve as a basis for classifying individuals under the law. It would also signal that the Court has renounced the separate spheres doctrine.

NOTES

1. Ava Baron, "Feminist Legal Strategies: The Powers of Difference," in Beth B. Hess and Myra Marx Ferree, eds., *Analyzing Gender* (Beverly Hills: Sage Publications, 1987), p. 477. See also Frances Olsen, "The Family and the Market: A Study of Ideology and Legal Reform," *Harvard Law Review* 96(1983); Nadine Taub and Elizabeth M. Schneider, "Perspectives on Women's Subordination and the Role of Law," in David Kairys, ed., *The Politics of Law: A Progressive Critique* (New York: Pantheon, 1982).

2. *Familiar Letters of John Adams and His Wife, Abigail Adams during the Revolution* (New York, 1876), reprinted in Eve Cary and Kathleen Willert Peratis, eds., *Woman and the Law* (Skokie: National Textbook Company, 1977), pp. 1–2.

3. See Eleanor Flexner, *Century of Struggle* (New York: Atheneum, 1974) for analysis of the Seneca Falls Convention. According to Flexner, the rise of the modern women's rights movement can be dated to 1790 when Mary Wollstonecraft published her *Vindication of the Rights of Women*.

4. W. William Hodes, "Women and the Constitution: Some Legal History and a New Approach to the Nineteenth Amendment," *Rutgers Law Review* 25(1970), pp. 35–37, reprinted in Kermit L. Hall, ed., *Women, the Law, and the Constitution* (New York: Garland Publishing, 1987). Aileen S. Kraditor, *The Ideas of the Woman Suffrage Movement 1890–1920* (Garden City: Anchor, 1971), chapters 1 and 7 discuss how the disagreement over ratification of the Fourteenth Amendment led to a split in the women's rights movement in 1869. Anthony and Stanton argued that the amendment should be defeated while Stone, speaking for a majority of feminists, argued that women should support political freedom for blacks even if women were not included in the amendment.

5. During this time, however, married women in the United States began to be freed from some of the legal disabilities with which they were burdened. The laws relating to women's property rights developed from the English common law doctrine of coverture, in which a married woman's legal identity was subsumed into her husband's. Most states began to move away from coverture beginning in the middle of the nineteenth century until the early part of the twentieth century by enacting Married Women's Property Acts. Under these acts, women were given the benefits of property ownership such as the right to contract, the right to sue and be sued, and the right to sell. The current prevailing view of these reforms is that the women's movement did not play a major role in getting these laws enacted and that the acts did little to alter the economic and social status of women. In any event, they were narrowly construed by most courts and did not have a major impact on women's lives. See Liane Kosaki and Susan Gluck Mezey, "Judicial Intervention in the Family: Interspousal Immunity and Civil Litigation," *Women & Politics* 8(1988); Baron, "Feminist Legal Strategies," pp. 476–77.

6. Ellen Dubois, "The Radicalism of the Woman Suffrage Movement: Notes toward the Reconstruction of Nineteenth-Century Feminism," *Feminist Studies* 3(1975), p. 66, reprinted in Kermit L. Hall, ed., *Women, the Law, and the Constitution* (New York: Garland Publishing, 1987).

7. The Nineteenth Amendment states "the right of the citizens of the United States to vote shall not be denied or abridged by the United States or by any State on account of sex."

8. Under Illinois law, because married women could not make contracts, as lawyers they could not contract with their clients.

9. *Bradwell v. Illinois,* 83 U.S. (16 Wall) 130, 139 (1873).

10. *Slaughterhouse Cases,* 83 U.S. (16 Wall) 36 (1873). The Court limited the privileges and immunities clause of the Fourteenth Amendment to protection of a narrow range of federal rights, such as freedom to use U.S. navigable waters.

11. *Bradwell,* 83 U.S. at 141 (Bradley, J., concurring). Twenty years later in *In re Lockwood,* 154 U.S. 116 (1894), the Supreme Court also rejected Belva Lockwood's request to order her admission to the Virginia bar.

12. In *Dred Scott v. Sanford,* 60 U.S. (19 How.) 393 (1857), the Supreme Court denied citizenship to an alleged slave, Dred Scott, who sued to establish his freedom under the law. The Court also found the Missouri Compromise of 1850 unconstitutional, ruling that Congress could not bar slavery in the territories. The Court's 7–2 decision in *Dred Scott* was its last opinion on slavery and is considered one of the precipitating factors of the Civil War.

13. *Minor v. Happersett,* 88 U.S. (21 Wall) 627, 629 (1875) (emphasis added).

14. Hodes, "Women and the Constitution," pp. 45–46. See also Joan Hoff Wilson, "The Legal Status of Women in the Late Nineteenth and Early Twentieth Centuries," *Human Rights* 6(1977), p. 131, reprinted in Kermit L. Hall, ed., *Women, the Law, and the Constitution* (New York: Garland Publishing, 1987).

15. *Lochner v. New York,* 198 U.S. 45, 53 (1905).

16. Under the "substantive due process doctrine" adopted in *Lochner,* the Court looked at the substance of the law to determine if it was "reasonable" or not. In earlier cases, the Court simply reviewed a state statute to determine if it had been properly passed. The Court's assessment of reasonableness was heavily influenced by the current laissez-faire attitude that looked on regulation of working conditions as undue interference with the prerogatives of industry. The era ended in the 1930s when the Court finally started to uphold New Deal legislation.

17. *Lochner,* 198 U.S. at 75 (Holmes, J., dissenting).

18. *Muller v. Oregon,* 208 U.S. 412, 422 (1908).

19. Olsen, "The Family and the Market," p. 1557. See also Deborah L. Rhode, "Equal Protection: Gender and Justice," in Michael W. McCann and Gerald L. Houseman, eds., *Judging the Constitution: Critical Essays on Judicial Lawmaking* (Glenview: Scott, Foresman, 1989).

20. *Radice v. New York,* 264 U.S. 292, 294 (1924).

21. *Goesaert v. Cleary,* 335 U.S. 464, 465 (1948).

22. *Hoyt v. Florida,* 368 U.S. 57, 59 (1961).

23. *Hoyt,* 368 U.S. at 61–62.

24. During this period, two men brought complaints of sex discrimination to the Supreme Court. In *Quong Wing v. Kirkendall,* 223 U.S. 59 (1912) and in *Breedlove v. Suttles,* 302 U.S. 277 (1937), the Supreme Court refused to invalidate statutes making it easier for women to operate hand laundries and exempting women from paying poll taxes. In each case, the Court echoed the separate spheres ideology by basing its opinion on a woman's special role in the family.

In only one case during this period, *U.S. v. Dege,* 364 U.S. 51 (1960), did the Court veer away from separate spheres thinking by refusing to dismiss an indictment charging a husband and wife with conspiracy. The Court ruled that the defendants were two individuals and hence could conspire with each other.

25. Various approaches to equal protection analysis can be found in Stephanie M. Wildman, "The Legitimation of Sex Discrimination: A Critical Response to Supreme Court Jurisprudence," *Oregon Law Review* 63 (1984); Owen Fiss, "Groups and the Equal Protection Clause," *Philosophy and Public Affairs,* 5(1976); Gerald Gunther, "Foreword: In Search of Evolving Doctrine on a Changing Court: A Model for a Newer Equal Protection," *Harvard Law Review* 86(1972); Joseph Tussman and Jacobus tenBroek, "The Equal Protection of the Laws," *California Law Review* 37(1949).

26. Because the Court treats race as a suspect classification at all times, it is less likely to approve laws intended to benefit minority groups in affirmative action cases.

27. *Korematsu v. United States*, 323 U.S. 214, 216 (1944). Despite this sweeping statement, the Court upheld the racial classification.

28. Laurence Tribe, *American Constitutional Law*, 2d ed. (Mineola: Foundation Press, 1988), pp. 1451–52. The Court has allowed an explicit racial classification to be used as a remedy for racial discrimination, such as the use of busing to integrate racially segregated schools.

29. See Michael W. McCann, "Equal Protection for Social Inequality: Race and Class in Constitutional Ideology," in Michael W. McCann and Gerald L. Houseman, eds., *Judging the Constitution: Critical Essays on Judicial Lawmaking* (Glenview: Scott, Foresman, 1989). Classic studies of the equal protection clause include: Fiss, "Groups and the Equal Protection Clause"; Gunther, "Foreword: In Search of Evolving Doctrine on a Changing Court"; Tussman and tenBroek, "The Equal Protection of the Laws."

30. Warren Burger stepped down as chief justice in 1986 and was replaced by William Rehnquist. Although the Rehnquist Court has decided a few sex discrimination cases since 1986, none of these were based on equal protection claims. Therefore, Burger Court decisions are the only relevant ones for this analysis of constitutional sexual equality.

31. The equal protection clause of the Fourteenth Amendment applies to states and local government units, not the federal government. In *Bolling v. Sharpe*, 347 U.S. 497 (1954), a case involving segregated schools in the District of Columbia, the Supreme Court ruled there was an equal protection component of the due process clause of the Fifth Amendment that applied to the federal government. Some state laws were also challenged under the Fourteenth Amendment's due process clause; these cases are generally not included in the Court's constitutional sex equality doctrine.

32. Their adopted son, Richard, died without a will while still a minor, leaving an estate worth less than $1,000. Under Idaho law, both parents were equally qualified to be appointed administrator of Richard's estate.

33. *Reed v. Reed*, 404 U.S. 71, 76–77 (1971).

34. The Equal Rights Amendment would have transformed sex into a suspect category, although it appears likely that the Court would have allowed exceptions to equality of rights for reasons of privacy or where unique physical differences between the sexes were involved. Barbara Brown, Thomas Emerson, Gail Falk, and Ann E. Freedman, "The Equal Rights Amendment: A Constitutional Basis for Equal Rights for Women," *Yale Law Journal* 80(1971). See Mary Frances Berry, *Why ERA Failed* (Bloomington: Indiana University Press, 1986); Jane Mansbridge, *Why We Lost the ERA* (Chicago: University of Chicago Press, 1986); Janet Boles, *The Politics of the Equal Rights Amendment* (New York: Longman, 1979) for politics of the ERA ratification movement.

35. *Frontiero v. Richardson*, 411 U.S. 677, 684 (1973).

36. Wildman, "The Legitimation of Sex Discrimination," pp. 278–79, claims that despite the plurality's assertion that it was using the strict scrutiny doctrine, the justices were not really following a strict scrutiny approach. She argues that the opinion suggests that the Court would have accepted the dependency rule if the government had shown that it saved money.

37. *Craig v. Boren*, 429 U.S. 190, 197 (1976).

38. *Craig*, 429 U.S. at 198–99.

39. Leo Kanowitz, "'Benign' Sex Discrimination: Its Troubles and Their Cure," *Hastings Law Journal* 31(1980), p. 1394, argues that "sex discrimination against males in statutes and judicial decisions has been widespread and severe."

40. In *Personnel Administrator of Massachusetts v. Feeney*, 442 U.S. 256 (1979), the Court upheld a Massachusetts law granting a permanent employment preference to military veterans despite the adverse impact of this law on women who did not have the same opportunities as men to become veterans. The Court ruled that this was a facially neutral law that was not intended to discriminate against women. The Court based its ruling in *Feeney* on *Washington v. Davis*, 426 U.S. 229 (1976), in which the Court held that the equal protection clause only applies to laws or policies that intentionally discriminate. Under this rule, a law that adversely affects women but does not specifically classify on the basis of sex does not fall within equal protection analysis. Some other constitutional cases affecting women's rights such as *Roberts v. United States Jaycees*, 468 U.S. 609 (1984); *Harris v. McRae*, 448 U.S. 297 (1980); *Turner v. Department of Employment Security*, 423 U.S. 44 (1975); *Cleveland Board of Education v. LaFleur*, 414 U.S. 632 (1974); *Pittsburgh Press v. Pittsburgh Commission on*

Human Relations, 413 U.S. 376 (1973); *Roe v. Wade,* 410 U.S. 113 (1973) concern other legal issues and are discussed in later chapters.

41. See definitions of "easy" cases and "hard" cases in Wendy Williams, "The Equality Crisis: Some Reflections on Culture, Courts, and Feminism," *Women's Rights Law Reporter* 7(1982), pp. 178–80.

42. *Stanley v. Illinois,* 405 U.S. 645 (1972); *Stanton v. Stanton,* 421 U.S. 7 (1975); *Orr v. Orr,* 440 U.S. 268 (1979); *Kirchberg v. Feenstra,* 450 U.S. 455 (1981); *Mississippi University for Women v. Hogan,* 458 U.S. 718 (1982). *Hogan* is discussed in Chapter Seven.

43. *Weinberger v. Wiesenfeld,* 420 U.S. 636 (1975); *Califano v. Goldfarb,* 430 U.S. 199 (1977); *Califano v. Westcott,* 443 U.S. 76 (1979); *Wengler v. Druggists Mutual Insurance Company,* 446 U.S. 142 (1980).

44. These two categories incorporate eleven of the twelve cases in which the Court upheld the laws. In the twelfth case, *Vorchheimer v. School District of Philadelphia,* 430 U.S. 703 (1977), the Court affirmed, without opinion, a lower court decision that a public high school could be restricted to male students. This case is discussed in Chapter Seven.

45. *Kahn v. Shevin,* 416 U.S. 351 (1974); *Schlesinger v. Ballard,* 419 U.S. 498 (1975); *Califano v. Webster,* 430 U.S. 313 (1977); *Heckler v. Mathews,* 465 U.S. 728 (1984).

46. *Kahn,* 416 U.S. at 352 (quoting *Shevin v. Kahn,* 273 So.2d 72, 73 (Fla. 1973)).

47. See Judith Baer, *Equality under the Constitution* (Ithaca: Cornell University Press, 1983); Ruth Bader Ginsburg, "Some Thoughts on Benign Classification in the Context of Sex," *Connecticut Law Review* 10(1978).

48. Williams, "The Equality Crisis," p. 180.

49. *Geduldig v. Aiello,* 417 U.S. 484 (1974). This case is discussed in Chapter Six.

50. *Michael M. v. Superior Court,* 450 U.S. 464 (1981); *Rostker v. Goldberg,* 453 U.S. 57 (1981).

51. In *Sail 'er Inn v. Kirby,* 485 P.2d 529 (Cal. 1971), the California Supreme Court declared sex a suspect category.

52. *Michael M.,* 450 U.S. at 473.

53. Williams, "The Equality Crisis," p. 181 n. 47.

54. See Cynthia Enloe, *Does Khaki Become You?* (Boston: South End Press, 1983) for discussion of women's exposure to combat under various conditions and the military's (often vain) attempts to make distinctions clear between combat and noncombat roles. The controversy over women in combat was stirred up again when, during the American invasion of Panama, Captain Linda Bray led a police military unit into combat against troops of the Panamanian Defense Forces. Women are barred from combat but are permitted to serve in military police units. Bray led a force of thirty soldiers to capture a kennel holding guard dogs. Although intelligence reports indicated the kennel was not defended, it turned out to be "heavily defended [and] three P.D.F. men were killed. Gunshots were fired on both sides," according to Marlin Fitzwater, White House press secretary. *New York Times,* January 1, 1990.

The presence of women on the frontlines in the Persian Gulf War has raised many of these same questions and will probably require the military to rethink its policy toward women.

55. *Michael M.,* 450 U.S. at 469 (quoting *Parham v. Hughes,* 441 U.S. 347, 354 (1979)).

56. Williams, "The Equality Crisis," pp. 182–83 n. 50.

57. Martha Minow, "Foreword: Justice Engendered," *Harvard Law Review* 101(1987), p. 40.

58. *Fiallo v. Bell,* 430 U.S. 787 (1977); *Quilloin v. Walcott,* 434 U.S. 246 (1978); *Parham,* 441 U.S. at 347; *Lehr v. Robertson,* 463 U.S. 248 (1983).

59. *Caban v. Mohammed,* 441 U.S. 380 (1979). In a later decision involving an unwed father and an illegitimate child, *Michael H. v. Gerald D.,* 109 S.Ct. 2333 (1989), the Court sustained a California law providing that a child born to a woman living with her husband was presumed to be the child of the husband. Decided on due process grounds, in a 5–4 vote the Court upheld the law despite evidence of a 98.07 percent probability that the plaintiff, who wanted the opportunity to prove his paternity, was the child's father.

60. *Parham,* 441 U.S. at 355.

61. Ann E. Freedman, "Sex Equality, Sex Differences, and the Supreme Court," *Yale Law Journal* 92(1983), pp. 944–45; Williams, "The Equality Crisis," pp. 182–83 n.50.

62. Leslie Goldstein argues that the decisions upholding the legislative classifications are

only "narrow exceptions" to the Court's general policy of opposition to sex discrimination. According to her, the Court has only sanctioned five kinds of laws: "(1) laws aimed at compensating women for socioeconomic discrimination, (2) laws related to the costs of child-bearing, (3) laws related to difficulties of proving paternity of illegitimate fathers, (4) statutory rape laws, and (5) laws implicating national security and foreign relations in general." Leslie Friedman Goldstein, "The ERA and the U.S. Supreme Court," *Law and Policy Studies* 1(1987), p. 150. Her categories are so inclusive that the exceptions threaten to overwhelm the rule.

63. Deborah L. Rhode, *Justice and Gender* (Cambridge: Harvard University Press, 1989); Catherine MacKinnon, *Feminism Unmodified* (Cambridge: Harvard University Press, 1987); Herma Hill Kay, "Models of Equality," *University of Illinois Law Review* (1985); Sylvia Law, "Rethinking Sex and the Constitution," *University of Pennsylvania Law Review* 132(1984).

2

Equal Employment Opportunity: Title VII— The Formative Years

The face of the American work force was irrevocably altered in the latter half of the twentieth century. While women had been employed outside the home as early as preindustrial America, the rate of their participation in the labor force began to change dramatically with the attack on Pearl Harbor on December 7, 1941. Not only were women necessary to replace men who went to war but they were also swallowed up by the overwhelming needs of the war production industries. By 1945, the number of women in the work force increased by more than 6 million, and rose to over 20 million, a jump of almost 50 percent since 1940.[1]

Following World War II, although two-thirds of wartime female workers wished to remain working, most were sent back to the kitchen, to wait to be summoned again if needed. "Rosie the Riveter" became "Henrietta Housewife."

The experience of women after the Second World War was similar to their experiences after the Civil War and the First World War. After each armed conflict, women were forced to abandon their newly acquired positions when the demand for war supplies declined and the men returned home to reclaim their jobs.[2]

Although most of the recently employed women were required to give up their jobs and return to their homes, they did not stay home long. Since the 1950s, there has been a steady increase in the participation rate of women in the labor force. By 1988, over half (56.6 percent) of women sixteen and over were in the work force. The participation rate in 1988 was slightly higher (58.0 percent) for African-American women and slightly lower (53.2 percent) for women of Hispanic origin. The most dramatic figures in increased labor force participation are among younger women: over 70 percent of women between 20 and 44 were in the work force in 1988.[3]

Title VII of the 1964 Civil Rights Act

The reemergence of women in the labor force after World War II was accompanied by a growing awareness among some of the need for government intervention against sex discrimination in employment. Although it did not begin that way, the Civil Rights Act of 1964 became an important vehicle for furthering equal employment opportunity for women.

In the 1960s, the energies of the civil rights movement were directed toward passage of a civil rights bill to alleviate racial discrimination in employment, education, and public accommodations, to mention only a few areas that needed immediate attention. The result was the 1964 Civil Rights Act, sent to Congress by President John Kennedy on June 19, 1963. Kennedy's bill was propelled forward by often bloody civil rights marches in Birmingham, Alabama, and the fight for desegregation at the University of Alabama. The bill sought equal access to public accommodations, additional federal guarantees of desegregation in public schools, protection of voting rights, and an end to employment discrimination. After Kennedy's assassination on November 22, 1963, President Lyndon Johnson exerted his considerable leadership skills to secure final passage of the bill. It was signed into law on July 2, 1964.

Controversial in many parts, the most far-reaching section of the Civil Rights Act was Title VII with its ban on employment discrimination in private industry. As originally proposed, Title VII of the 1964 act prohibited discrimination in employment on the basis of race, color, national origin, and religion. As the bill moved closer to passage, spurred by a coalition of Northern Democrats and Republicans, Southern Democrats stepped up their efforts to block it. Ironically, the prohibition against sex discrimination was inserted into the proposed legislation as a desperate, last-minute attempt to scuttle it entirely.

The bill that would eventually become the most important civil rights measure since the 1870s, H.R. 7152, was being debated on the floor of the House of Representatives when Judge Howard Smith, Democrat of Virginia and chair of the House Rules Committee, stood up: "'Mr. Chairman,' he drawled, 'I offer an amendment.'"[4]

These few words, uttered on the eighth day of House debate over H.R. 7152, were destined to change the lives of working women in the United States forever. Smith proposed to add the word *sex* to the employment discrimination section. He explained that his "amendment is offered to prevent discrimination against another minority group, the women, but a very essential minority group in the absence of which the majority group would not be here today."[5]

Smith's intentions were not benign; he offered his amendment "in a spirit of satire and ironic cajolery." In urging support for it, he quoted from a letter he received from a woman asking him what the government intended to do about the fact that there were 2,661,000 more women in this country than men, thereby "shutting off the 'right' of every female to have a husband of her own." The letter concluded by asking whether he had "any suggestions as to what course our Government might pursue to protect our spinster friends in their 'right' to a nice husband and family."

Judge Smith's support for the ban on sex discrimination in employment was disingenuous; he and his allies hoped the amendment would create enough controversy to prevent passage of the final bill. Exceeding his hopes, the amendment engendered more than controversy; it produced gales of laughter. In the spirit of hilarity that prevailed, the day became known as Ladies' Day.

The Democratic House leadership, including Representatives Emmanuel Celler of New York and Edith Green of Oregon, a member of the President's Commission on the Status of Women, spoke out against the amendment. In part, they were concerned that the amendment would threaten passage of the entire bill. They also feared that passage of the amendment would deprive women of legal protections they currently enjoyed, especially in areas of family law and employment.

Green reminded her colleagues of her credentials as a champion of women's rights and suggested that they reflect on the fact that the men supporting the amendment had been vehemently opposed to passage of last year's women's rights bill, the Equal Pay Act. She urged the members of the House to remember that the primary purpose of Title VII, indeed of the whole Civil Rights Act, was to battle racial discrimination, which was, in her view, a more serious problem. "For every discrimination that I have suffered," she proclaimed, "I firmly believe the Negro woman has suffered 10 times that amount of discrimination."

Despite the opposition by Green and Celler, a bipartisan coalition of women in the House joined forces to back Smith's tactical move. Representatives Frances P. Bolton, Republican of Ohio; Martha Griffiths, Democrat of Michigan; Edna F. Kelly, Democrat of New York; Catherine May, Republican of Washington; and Katherine St. George, Republican of New York, seized the opportunity provided by Smith to urge support of the ban on sex discrimination in employment. Griffiths herself had been planning to introduce an amendment extending the protections of Title VII to women. But in contrast to Smith, she was motivated by a genuine desire to combat sex discrimination against female workers. She waited until after Smith acted to take advantage of the votes from Southern Democrats who would follow his lead and would not have voted for the amendment otherwise.

Unlike other important pieces of legislation, no committee hearings were held on the meaning and potential impact of the Smith amendment — either in the Senate or the House. The amendment was accepted by the House in a 168–133 vote. Two days later, the Civil Rights Act passed the House by a vote of 290 to 130. Eventually, the Senate approved the civil rights measure after ending a Southern filibuster lasting over five hundred hours. The final Senate vote was 73–27.

Although the 1964 act did not banish all racial and sexual inequities in American employment, it provided an important impetus for equality in employment by forbidding discrimination in private employment and including sex within the ban on discrimination. The act also served as a model for equal employment statutes for other disadvantaged groups such as the aging and the disabled.

Title VII has had a dramatic impact on the status of women and minorities in the work force. Almost 2.5 million minority workers held better jobs in 1980 than they would have if they held the same kind of jobs they held in 1965; among women, 4 million were in higher status job categories in 1980 than they were in 1965. The wage income of minority workers was $9 billion higher in 1980 than it would have been if they held the kind of jobs they held in 1965; for women it was $22 billion higher.[6]

Administrative Policy-making

Section 706 of the Civil Rights Act created the Equal Employment Opportunity Commission (EEOC) and gave it the power to enforce the law's prohibition against employment discrimination. The EEOC is composed of five commissioners, not more than three of whom can be from the same political party, appointed by the president for a five-year term. The president designates one of the commissioners as chair, another as vice chair. A general counsel, with responsibility for litigation, is appointed by the president for a four-year term. The appointments of the commissioners and the general counsel must be confirmed by the Senate.

As originally constituted, the EEOC was authorized to respond to complaints of employment discrimination in several ways. If it did not believe discrimination had occurred, it would dismiss the charge, and individuals could file lawsuits on their own.[7] If the commission believed the charges were true, it could only try to persuade employers to abandon the discriminatory policies. If conciliation and negotiation failed, the EEOC was forced to refer cases to the Civil Rights Division of the Department of Justice for litigation.

The EEOC's weakened enforcement authority resulted from a number of compromises reached during passage of the Civil Rights Act. In the original version of the bill, the commission was empowered to issue cease and desist orders to employers found guilty of discrimination. Amended in the House Judiciary Committee, the bill was changed to permit the commission to sue on behalf of workers. This provision was also eliminated. The final, stripped-down version of the bill resulted from an amendment offered on the Senate floor.

Civil rights leaders objected to the attenuated bill, claiming it greatly reduced the EEOC's ability to enforce the new law. They wanted the EEOC to be able to combat discrimination rather than simply receive complaints, and they had more faith in administrative enforcement than judicial enforcement. The leaders were also aware that litigation required individual initiative and was expensive and time-consuming. Notwithstanding their objections, the political imperative of obtaining support from moderate Republicans to break the Southern Democrats' filibuster forced them to accept the compromise.[8]

The EEOC received almost 9,000 complaints of discrimination during its first year. In its first five years, it received a total of 52,000 charges of discrimination and recommended 35,445 for investigation. Of those recommended for investigation, about one-half complained of race discrimination, one-quarter of sex discrimination, and one-quarter of discrimination on the basis of religion or national origin.[9]

By 1969, the number of complaints had risen to 12,148 a year and then to 71,023 in 1975.[10] Not anticipating the large volume of complaints (only four regional offices had been established), the EEOC was unable to process them in a timely fashion and immediately fell behind. By 1975, a backlog of 106,700 unresolved cases had developed, and by the end of fiscal year 1976, the backlog had risen to 126,340.[11]

In a speech on the House floor in September 1971, Speaker of the House Carl Albert, Democrat of Oklahoma, attributed the EEOC's huge case backlog to two factors. First, he cited the EEOC's limited enforcement power. Because it could not take action on its own, its attempts to bring about conciliation from employers were largely ineffective. In 1970, for example, there were only 225 successful conciliations of 17,000 charges filed. Second, he charged, the EEOC's budget allocation was too low to allow it to hire a sufficient number of investigators to process complaints rapidly.[12]

While there was some sentiment in the House in 1971 to empower the EEOC to issue cease and desist orders to offending employers, this plan was put aside in the face of determined opposition. Instead, Congress attempted to deal with the deficiencies of EEOC enforcement by enacting the Equal Employment Opportunity (EEO) Act of 1972.

The 1972 act authorized the EEOC to file lawsuits against employers after unsuccessful attempts at voluntary conciliation.[13] In cases where state or federal government units were involved, however, the attorney general rather than the commission had to file suit. Also, beginning in 1974, authority to bring "pattern and practice" lawsuits (suits charging systemic discrimination on an industrywide or companywide basis) was transferred from the Civil Rights Division of the Department of Justice to the commission.[14] In addition to expanding the EEOC's power, the act also brought federal, state, county, and municipal workers as well as employees at educational institutions within reach of Title VII.

The EEOC came under attack from women's groups for its lack of vigor in filing suit against offending employers. But from 1972 to 1980, the commission filed legal actions against corporate giants that gained relief for millions of employees. And under the direction of Eleanor Holmes Norton, appointed by President Jimmy Carter, the EEOC virtually eliminated its backlog by encouraging settlement between parties and began to focus most of its attention on widespread employment discrimination through class action suits and pattern and practice cases.

In 1978, the commission's power was again increased under Carter's Reorganization Plan Number 1. Effective July 1, 1979, the reorganization established the EEOC as the "lead agency" in employment discrimination and transferred enforcement authority for the Age Discrimination in Employment Act and the Equal Pay Act from the Department of Labor to the EEOC.[15] Additionally, the EEOC was put in charge of enforcing equal employment opportunity for all federal employees.

After the 1980 election, with prompting from President Ronald Reagan's Justice Department, the EEOC changed direction under the leadership of Clarence Thomas, who became chair in May 1982. Reagan's appointment of Michael Connolly as general counsel also helped determine this new direction for the agency. Connolly announced to his staff, shortly after assuming office, that he would not focus on sexual harassment, equal pay, age discrimination, or class action suits.[16] Under Thomas's leadership at the agency, the policy of concentrating on class action suits and pattern and practice cases was replaced by a policy of focusing on cases with identifiable victims of discrimination. This new focus on individual cases was obviously less effective in combating patterns of widespread employment discrimination. According to Thomas, his "approach" to his role as chair of the commission was "more methodical, more cautious and certainly less noisy" than that of his predecessors.[17]

Thomas echoed the philosophy of other Reagan administration officials such as Attorney General Edwin Meese and Assistant Attorney General for Civil Rights William Bradford Reynolds. He charged that "those who insist on arguing that the principle of equal opportunity, the cornerstone of civil rights, means preferences for certain groups have relinquished their roles as moral and ethical leaders in this area." Comparing affirmative action to white racial superiority in South Africa, Thomas emphasized that he "bristle[d] at the thought . . . that it is morally proper to protest against minority [white] racial preferences in South Africa while arguing for such preferences here."[18]

Despite its nominal title as lead agency in employment discrimination, the EEOC deferred to the Justice Department during the Reagan administration years.[19] Specifically, in a 1983 case brought by African-American police officers against the city of New Orleans, the EEOC responded to pressure from the Justice Department and rescinded its decision to file a brief on the officers' behalf. The Justice Department claimed the EEOC had no jurisdiction in public employee cases. This was a novel interpretation of EEOC authority since it had consistently filed briefs in public employee cases in the past. The brief, subsequently filed by the Justice Department, argued against the African-American officers' position.

With Thomas expressing general approval of the Reagan administration's approach to civil rights policy, by the end of the 1980s the EEOC had substantially retreated from the battle against race and sex discrimination.

Sex Discrimination and the EEOC

The ridicule surrounding the passage of Smith's amendment to the 1964 act was also evident in the EEOC's attitude toward sex as a prohibited employment category. The first EEOC commissioners demonstrated indifference to, if not disdain for, the commission's role in fighting sex discrimination. Indeed, "EEOC commissioners and staff . . . expressed a general belief that the addition of *sex* to the law [Title VII] had been illegitimate — merely a ploy to kill the bill — and that it did not therefore constitute a mandate to equalize women's employment opportunities."[20]

When the commission was established in July 1965, it was chaired by Franklin Delano Roosevelt, Jr., and was composed of two other white men, one black man, and a black woman. Asked at his first press conference about his attitude toward sex, Roosevelt responded with "predictable wisecracks" and turned aside the question.[21]

The media joined in the fun as well. A *Wall Street Journal* article published in June 1965 "asked its readers to picture, if they could, 'a shapeless, knobby-kneed male "bunny" serving drinks to a group of stunned businessmen in a Playboy Club' or a 'matronly vice-president' chasing a male secretary around her desk."[22] The degree to which the commission would take Title VII seriously was also undermined when Executive Director Herman Edelsberg described the ban on sex discrimination as a "fluke . . . conceived out of wedlock."[23]

Provisions of Title VII

Because Title VII was hurriedly passed, there were no committee reports and little congressional debate to give courts clues to legislative intent. The essence of Title VII is found in section 703(a), which states that

it shall be an unlawful employment practice for an employer—

(1) to fail or refuse to hire or to discharge any individual, or otherwise to discriminate against any individual with respect to his compensation, terms, conditions, or privileges of employment, because of such individual's race, color, religion, sex, or national origin.

(2) to limit, segregate, or classify his employees or applicants for employment in any way which would deprive or tend to deprive any individual of employment opportunities or otherwise adversely affect his status as an employee, because of such individual's race, color, religion, sex, or national origin.[24]

Originally applicable to private employers with at least twenty-five employees, coverage was later expanded in the EEO Act of 1972 to employers with fifteen or more employees. The prohibition against discrimination was also applicable to twenty-five-member labor unions, and then after 1972, to fifteen-member unions.

Section 706(g) of the act gives courts authority to enjoin (stop) defendant employers or unions from engaging in unlawful employment practices. Courts could also "order such affirmative action as may be appropriate, which may include but is not limited to, reinstatement or hiring of employees, with or without backpay." When the act was amended in 1972, courts were further authorized to order "any other equitable relief as the court deems appropriate." These few words played a major role in sparking the battle over affirmative action in the 1980s.

Title VII Litigation

In the late nineteenth and early twentieth centuries, most states passed laws restricting women from entering certain occupations or regulating the conditions under which they could work. Such laws were ostensibly intended to protect women from harm in the workplace. Passage of Title VII led to immediate controversy over how it would affect state legislation that singled women out for protection. The Supreme Court's decision in *Muller v. Oregon,* 1908, upholding a law restricting women to a ten-hour day, had demonstrated the Court's willingness to allow states to impose conditions on female workers only.

By 1936, a majority of states, forty-three in all, had laws restricting the number of hours women could work.[25] In their book on women's employment rights, Barbara Brown and her coauthors argue that most of these laws were not prompted by protective instincts. Rather, they insist they "were based on stereotypes about women's transient and secondary role in the labor market and their weak physical condition as well as on the desire of male workers to reduce competition for higher paying jobs."[26]

A number of states repealed these laws after Title VII was enacted, but court challenges were required in others. The question for the courts to resolve was whether the laws could survive Title VII. In the brief debate over the sex discrimination amendment in the House, some members expressed concern that the bill would make it impossible to hire on the basis of sex for *any* reason—even when sex was relevant to job performance. Their concern was allayed when Congress voted to create an exception to the flat prohibition against sex discrimination.

The exception, included as section 703(e)(1) of the act, permitted employers to make distinctions "in those certain instances where religion, sex, or national origin is a bona fide occupational qualification reasonably necessary to the normal operation of that particular business or enterprise." Employers charged with sex discrimination could defend themselves by arguing that sex (or religion or national origin) was a bona fide occupational qualification (BFOQ) and that it was "necessary" to the business to hire on this basis.

BFOQs and Protective Legislation

The EEOC responded to the conflict between protective legislation and the BFOQ defense by firmly straddling the middle of the road. The EEOC argued that a truly protective law was acceptable as a bona fide occupational qualification; a discriminatory law violated Title VII.[27] The commission's ambivalence toward protective legislation reflected the views of some women's organizations as well as the Department of Labor and a number of labor unions.[28]

The EEOC's stance also found support in the Senate. In a written colloquy between Republican Senator Everett Dirksen of Illinois and Democrat Joseph Clark of Pennsylvania, Dirksen approved the prevalent pattern of sex discrimination in the United States. He described it as "a protective discrimination because we [in the United States] do not believe that women should do heavy manual labor of the sort which falls to the lot of some men."[29]

The first appellate opinion that explored the conflict between a BFOQ and a state protective law was *Weeks v. Southern Bell Telephone & Telegraph,* a Fifth Circuit case decided in 1969. Lorena Weeks brought suit against Southern Bell when the railroad refused to hire her as a "switchman" and gave the job to a man. Relying on a state labor commission rule,

Rule 59, that prohibited women from lifting over thirty pounds, Southern Bell argued that a reasonable state protective law serves as a bona fide occupational qualification within section 703(e). The district court agreed and ruled in favor of the company.

Georgia repealed Rule 59 while Weeks's appeal was pending, and Southern Bell was forced to rely on the district court's vague finding that the job of switchman was "strenuous" and therefore unsuitable for women. After carefully assessing the demands of a switchman's duties, the circuit court concluded that Southern Bell had not proven that sex was a bona fide occupational qualification for the job. To rely on a BFOQ defense, the court said, "an employer has the burden of proving that he had reasonable cause to believe, that is, a factual basis for believing, that all or substantially all women would be unable to perform safely and efficiently the duties of the job involved."[30] Southern Bell had introduced no evidence on women's capacity for lifting. Instead, it simply relied on the prevailing stereotype that women could not lift thirty pounds. And because its BFOQ defense was not accepted, the company was found guilty of violating Title VII.

Because Rule 59 had been repealed, the Fifth Circuit did not have an opportunity to rule on the validity of protective legislation under Title VII. But in *Rosenfeld v. Southern Pacific,* 1971, the Ninth Circuit took a strong stand against a California law restricting women from working more than ten hours a day and lifting over fifty pounds.

When Leah Rosenfeld applied for a transfer to the job of agent-telegrapher at Southern Pacific, she was denied because company policy excluded women from certain jobs. In defending against her Title VII suit, Southern Pacific argued that these jobs were too arduous for women and that it could not hire them because of state labor laws.

Southern Pacific maintained that sex was a valid BFOQ because women are not "physically" or "biologically" suited for the job for which Rosenfeld applied. The key question for the court was "whether employment restrictions based upon characterizations of a sex group's physical capabilities are, by their nature, capable of fitting within the BFOQ category."[31]

Ironically, although it accepted state protective legislation, the EEOC urged a narrow interpretation of the BFOQ defense. Commission guidelines stated that assumptions about women as a group (higher absenteeism); stereotypical notions about women's characteristics (less aggressive and less competent in mechanical skills); or preferences of customers, coworkers, or employers, do not fall within the BFOQ exception. The BFOQ exception, according to the guidelines, was only acceptable when "necessary for the purpose of authenticity or genuineness."[32]

Mindful of the EEOC's narrow construction of the BFOQ defense, the *Rosenfeld* court ruled that section 703(e) does not permit assumptions about the physical characteristics of the group as a whole to form the basis of employment decisions. The appellate court rejected the company's reliance on the California protective legislation. To rule otherwise, said the Fifth Circuit, would allow states to circumvent Congress's intent to prevent employers from basing employment decisions on group characteristics.

These federal court rulings made it clear that protective legislation was doomed because it could not withstand the assault of Title VII challenges. Following the lead of the courts, the EEOC finally reversed itself, and on August 19, 1969, revoked its earlier guidelines and announced its new position that Title VII superseded state protective legislation.[33] The year 1969 was a watershed year; no state protective labor law has survived a Title VII challenge since then.[34]

Customer Preferences

Diaz v. Pan American World Airways was another decision reinforcing a narrow interpretation of the BFOQ defense. In 1967, Celio Diaz filed suit against Pan American when he was rejected as a cabin flight attendant because he was male. He lost his case when the district court agreed that sex was a valid BFOQ for a flight attendant's job.

The Fifth Circuit reviewed the district court's findings that female flight attendants were better at performing nonmechanical tasks and that passengers preferred service from them, then ruled that Title VII only allows employers to use sex as a BFOQ when it is "reasonably necessary" to the operation of a business. The test, held the court, is "business *necessity,*" not "business *convenience.*" The court concluded that employers may only hire on the basis of sex "when the *essence* of the business operation would be undermined by not hiring members of one sex exclusively."[35]

Pan American presented expert psychiatric testimony to support its contention that accommodating the psychological needs of their customers required airlines to hire women. But the court found that assigning women to the cabins, even if they had a greater calming influence and their presence was desired by passengers, did not further the airline's major goal of safe transportation. And, said the court, it would be odd indeed if the company were allowed to defend a policy of sex discrimination on the basis of its customers' "preferences and prejudices" because Title VII was intended to eliminate those kind of biases in employment decisions.

While Pan American tried to persuade the court that women were better flight attendants, it did not argue that female flight attendants were essential to its continued financial success. In 1981, Southwest Airlines offered this argument in *Wilson v. Southwest Airlines Company.* In this case, a Texas federal district judge was asked to decide whether the airline's image of love (and sex?) in the air justified its refusal to hire men in customer service positions. By combining rules adopted in *Weeks* and *Diaz, Wilson* created a new test for interpreting the BFOQ exception.

Southwest Airlines began operations in 1971, and because of legal conflict with its competitors, immediately fell into serious debt. Trying to gain an edge in a fiercely competitive market, the airline created an advertising campaign based on its "love personality" in which it "projected[ed] an image of feminine spirit, fun, and sex appeal." The airline's slogan became "At Last There Is Somebody Else Up There Who Loves You." A few years later the slogan became "We're Spreading Love All Over Texas." Southwest dressed its flight attendants in hot pants and high boots and encouraged them to "entertain the passengers and maintain an atmosphere of informality and 'fun' during flights."[36]

Over the years, Southwest caught up with and surpassed its competitors. When sued for its refusal to hire men in public contact jobs, the airline argued that sex was a bona fide occupational qualification because its attractive female flight attendants were the single most important reason for its success.

The district court conceded that Southwest's image of love and feminine allure was important to the company but denied that it was so essential that it legitimized the company's refusal to hire men. Citing the congressional debate over the Smith amendment, as well as the EEOC guidelines, the court emphasized that the BFOQ exception must be narrowly interpreted to preserve the intent of Title VII.

Weeks and *Diaz*, explained the court, have given rise to a two-part BFOQ test that asks "(1) does the particular *job* under consideration require that the worker be of one sex only; and if so, (2) is that requirement reasonably necessary to the 'essence' of the employer's business." Under this test, an employer is permitted to hire employees of one sex only if a member of the opposite sex simply cannot do the job and if the business would be "undermined" if the "wrong" sex were hired.[37]

In applying the first part of the test, the court acknowledged that some jobs require at least a mixture of sex-linked and sex-neutral abilities, but unless the sex-linked skills predominate, the "opposite" sex can fill the job. In this case, concluded the court, because the job of flight attendant does not require service with love, men are capable of performing it. For the second part of the test, the court found that the task performed by female flight attendants (creating the illusion of sexuality) was not essential to the airline's primary business function of transporting passengers safely. In its final argument, Southwest contended that women were necessary to allow it to maintain its successful advertising campaign of love in the air. But the court ruled that "sex does not become a BFOQ merely because an employer chooses to exploit female sexuality as a marketing tool or to better insure profitability."[38]

The Supreme Court and Sex-plus Discrimination

In 1971, *Phillips v. Martin Marietta Corporation* became the first Title VII suit to reach the Supreme Court. The case, only a partial victory for female employees, arose when Ida Phillips sued the Martin Marietta Corporation after they rejected her application for the job of assembly trainee because she had preschool children. The company accepted men with preschool children for the same positions.

The district court dismissed her complaint of sex discrimination because almost 80 percent of the assembly trainee positions were held by women. The Fifth Circuit Court of Appeals affirmed the court below, agreeing that the company's refusal to hire Phillips was not sex discrimination. The appellate court found that Martin Marietta's refusal to hire her was "two-pronged": she was a woman, *and* she had preschool children. Because the company did not base its decision on sex alone, the court ruled there was no Title VII violation.

The Fifth Circuit found that Congress did not intend Title VII to ignore "differences between the normal relationships of working fathers and working mothers to their pre-school children," nor did it intend to force employers to hire men and women without regard to these differences.[39]

With Judge John Brown dissenting, the circuit court denied Phillips's petition for a rehearing. Brown thought the issue was a simple one: "A mother is still a woman. And if she is denied work outright because she is a mother, it is because she is a woman. Congress said that could no longer be done."[40]

He charged the majority with subverting the intention of Title VII through its "sex plus" test. As he explained it, by using a "sex plus" rule, an employer is only guilty of a Title VII violation by discriminating solely on the basis of a forbidden category such as race, sex, or religion. By adding another criterion to one of the prohibited categories, in this case, sex plus children, the employer escapes liability. "If 'sex plus' stands," he warned, "the Act is dead."[41]

In an unsigned (per curiam) opinion, the Supreme Court reversed the Fifth Circuit, ruling that Title VII does not allow a company to have one hiring policy for men and another for women. But the Court refused to rule out the possibility that stereotypical assumptions about women's roles could serve as a BFOQ. Although the company chose not to rely on a BFOQ defense, the high court remanded the case to the lower court to take evidence on whether sex was a bona fide occupational qualification for the job. If the company could show that having preschool children might significantly hamper a woman's job performance, it could refuse to hire women with small children.

Justice Thurgood Marshall, concurring, objected to the Court's reliance on stereotypical roles to determine bona fide occupational qualifications. He accused the Court of allowing employers to base job decisions on the belief that children interfere with women's jobs. By doing so, he said, the Court "has fallen into the trap of assuming that the Act permits ancient canards about the proper role of women to be a basis for discrimination."[42] Marshall insisted that Congress intended to eliminate stereotypical thinking as a basis for employment opportunities, not enhance it.

The Supreme Court and the BFOQ Defense

Then, in *Dothard v. Rawlinson,* 1977, the Supreme Court reinvigorated the BFOQ defense by allowing women to be excluded from the job of prison guard. *Dothard* was a setback for equal employment opportunity. By expressing special concern for women's safety, the Court ignored the danger that all guards face and that prisons must create credible threats of punishment to protect their employees and preserve order. The Court also ignored evidence that female guards performed satisfactorily in maximum security prisons in some states.

The lawsuit against the state arose when Dianne Rawlinson applied for the job of "correctional counselor" in an Alabama prison. She was initially rejected because she failed to meet the height and weight requirements. While her suit was pending in federal court, the prison authorities adopted Regulation 204 restricting "contact" positions in the prison wards to guards of the prisoners' sex. The state described a contact position as requiring "continual close physical proximity to inmates of the institution."[43] Rawlinson amended her complaint to include Regulation 204, and the prison claimed in its defense that sex was a bona fide occupational qualification permitted by section 703(e). Ruling that section 703(e) must be narrowly interpreted, the lower court rejected the state's argument.

Speaking for himself, William Rehnquist, Harry Blackmun, Lewis Powell, John Paul Stevens, and Warren Burger, Potter Stewart delivered the opinion of the Court. Agreeing in principle with the lower court's interpretation of the BFOQ exception, Stewart nevertheless concluded that Regulation 204 was valid.

Ordinarily, he acknowledged, women should be allowed to decide for themselves whether to accept dangerous jobs. But, in this case, the state's interest in prison security was more important. Denying that the Court was motivated by "romantic paternalism," Stewart said that a woman's ability to keep order in a maximum-security prison could be directly "*reduced by her womanhood.*" Because of overcrowded prison conditions, there was a "real risk" of danger to female guards from male prisoners, especially sex offenders, long deprived of the company of women.[44]

In dissent, Marshall and William Brennan objected to the majority's reasoning, arguing first that the prison conditions in Alabama were in constitutional violation and the Court's assent to the restriction on women prison guards was "justifying conduct that would otherwise violate a statute intended to remedy age-old discrimination."[45]

Prison authorities were not really afraid that female guards would be unable to maintain discipline, Marshall charged; their real concern was that women would provoke sexual attacks. "With all respect," he asserted, "this rationale regrettably perpetuates one of the most insidious of the old myths about women — that women, wittingly or not, are seductive sexual objects."[46] In his view, the Court should not sanction the deprivation of job opportunities on the basis of myths and unsupported forebodings.

In a footnote, Marshall commented on the irony of "state officials who have for years been violating the most basic principles of human decency" suddenly voicing interest in prisoners' rights. He doubted that their recent concern for these rights was anything "but a feeble excuse for discrimination."[47]

Marshall added that he hoped lower courts would perceive that the Court's opinion arose from the shocking conditions in the Alabama prison system and would continue to interpret the BFOQ defense narrowly.

In *International Union United Automobile, Aerospace, and Agricultural Implement Workers v. Johnson Controls*, 1991, in striking a sex-specific fetal protection policy, the Supreme Court reaffirmed its commitment to a narrow interpretation of the BFOQ defense.

Sex-segregated Advertising

In August 1965, the EEOC issued a guideline that condemned discrimination in newspaper advertising on the basis of race, religion, and national origin but was silent on the question of sex discrimination. It eventually required a Supreme Court case to abolish the practice of sexually defined advertisements.

After protests by women's groups, EEOC Chairman Roosevelt appointed an ad hoc committee to study the legal status of sex-segregated ads. The committee, dominated by advertising agencies and newspapers, determined that Title VII did not bar sex-segregated want ads. After receiving the committee report, the EEOC voted 3–2 in favor of allowing sex-segregated ads but required newspapers to insert disclaimers that they were not intended to deter job applicants of the other sex.

Despite this mild corrective to the press, the commission was heavily criticized by the media. The *New Republic,* a liberal journal, asked why "should a mischievous joke perpetrated on the floor of the House of Representatives be treated by a responsible administrative body with this kind of seriousness."[48] Finally, after declining to ban sex-segregated classified ads for three more years, in August 1968 the EEOC concluded that they were contrary to Title VII and issued a guideline against such advertising.[49]

Although some newspapers had voluntarily abandoned the practice of running separate want ads, many had not. The Supreme Court's ruling in *Pittsburgh Press v. Pittsburgh Commission on Human Relations,* 1973, finally made it official that want ads could not display sexual labels.

In keeping with the spirit of Title VII, the city of Pittsburgh adopted an ordinance mirroring the statute's prohibition on employment discrimination on the basis of sex except where sex was a bona fide occupational qualification.[50] Section 8(j) of the ordinance also made it illegal to "aid . . . in the doing of any act declared to be an unlawful employment practice." In October 1969, the National Organization for Women (NOW) filed a complaint with the Pittsburgh Commission on Human Relations charging that the Pittsburgh Press Company violated §8(j) by allowing prospective employers to place sex-designated ads for jobs in which sex was not a BFOQ.

In an apparent effort to comply with the law against discrimination, the *Press* placed this "Notice to Job Seekers" at the head of each column of ads.

> Jobs are arranged under Male and Female classifications for the convenience of our readers. This is done because most jobs generally appeal more to persons of one sex than the other. Various laws and ordinances — local, state, and federal, prohibit discrimination in employment because of sex unless sex is a bona fide occupational qualification. Unless the advertisement itself specifies one sex or the other, job seekers should assume that the advertiser will consider applicants of either sex in compliance with the laws against discrimination.[51]

NOW brought in noted psychologist Sandra Bem to testify to the effect of sex-segregated ads on women's employment. Bem reported that her survey of college women found that women were discouraged from applying for the jobs listed under the *Male-Interest* heading.[52]

The Human Relations Commission ruled that the *Pittsburgh Press* violated section 8(j) of the ordinance and ordered it not to print job advertisements under the labels *Male-Interest* and *Female-Interest* in the future. On appeal, the state court upheld the commission's order but specified that sex-designated advertisements for jobs were allowed where the employer was free to make sex-based hiring decisions.

The Supreme Court had to decide whether the ordinance, as interpreted by the Pennsylvania court, violated a newspaper's First Amendment right to publish free of government censorship. In a 5–4 decision with Powell, Brennan, Marshall, Byron White, and Rehnquist in the majority, the Court upheld the ordinance against the First Amendment challenge. Dissenting opinions by Burger, William Douglas, Stewart, and Blackmun objected to the majority's encroachment on the First Amendment. Acknowledging that First Amendment protections are especially valued, Powell emphasized that freedom of the press was not at issue because the law was not "undermining [the] institutional viability" of the press.[53]

The case largely revolved around the issue of whether the want ads could be regulated under the Court's commercial speech doctrine, which allowed states to impose limits on certain kinds of speech such as advertisements relating to commercial transactions.[54] Characterizing the ads as "classic examples of commercial speech," the Court rejected the *Press*'s argument that the newspaper's exercise of editorial judgment in placing the ads entitled them to full First Amendment protection. Additionally, Powell pointed out that the ads were not simply about commerce but about illegal commerce. "We have no doubt," he said, "that a newspaper constitutionally could be forbidden to publish a want ad proposing a sale of narcotics or soliciting prostitutes."[55]

By banning sex-specific help wanted ads, eliminating state protective legislation, and undermining the BFOQ defense, the federal courts eradicated many of the overt barriers to sex equality in employment in the 1970s. Despite these victories, women were forced to continue their legal battles for employment equality. In the next decade, they found the courts, especially the Supreme Court, increasingly hostile to their claims of employment discrimination and less willing to order changes in employment practices and policies.

NOTES

1. Ray Marshall and Beth Paulin, "Employment and Earnings of Women: Historical Perspective," in Karen Shallcross Koziara, Michael H. Moskow, and Lucretia Dewey Tanner, eds., *Working Women: Past, Present, Future* (Washington, DC: Bureau of National Affairs, 1987).

2. See Barbara Sinclair Deckard, *The Women's Movement* (New York: Harper & Row, 1975); Barbara R. Bergmann, *The Economic Emergence of Women* (New York: Basic Books, 1986); Betty Friedan, *The Feminine Mystique* (New York: Dell, 1963); June Sochen, *Herstory: A Women's View of American History* (New York: Alfred A. Knopf, 1974); Ethel Klein, *Gender Politics* (Cambridge, MA: Harvard University Press, 1984). See also Julianne Malveaux and Phyllis Wallace, "Minority Women in the Workplace," in Karen Shallcross Koziara, Michael H. Moskow, and Lucretia Dewey Tanner, eds., *Working Women: Past, Present, Future* (Washington, DC: Bureau of National Affairs, 1987) for differences in labor force participation between white women and women of color.

3. U.S. Bureau of Labor Statistics, *Employment and Earnings* (January 1989), Tables 3, 39.

4. Charles Whalen and Barbara Whalen, *The Longest Debate: A Legislative History of the 1964 Civil Rights Act* (New York: Mentor Books, 1985), p. 117.

5. See Carolyn Bird, *Born Female* (New York: Pocket Books, 1970), chapter 1, for the quotations from the House debate over the sex discrimination amendment. See also Francis

J. Vaas, "Title VII: Legislative History," *Boston College Industrial and Commercial Law Review* (1966), pp. 441–42.

6. Alfred Blumrosen, "The Legacy of *Griggs:* Social Progress and Subjective Judgments," *Chicago-Kent Law Review* 63(1987), p. 2.

7. Individuals can sue on their own after the EEOC issues a right-to-sue notice. Notice is issued for three possible reasons: 180 days have elapsed since the charge was filed with the EEOC, the agency determines there is no reasonable cause to believe there was discrimination, or (after 1972) the agency believes there was discrimination and, after unsuccessful attempts at conciliation, it decides not to file suit.

Litigants have within ninety days after receiving the right-to-sue notice to file suit in federal court. Dismissal of the individual's complaint by the EEOC does not prejudice the court case.

8. See Karen Maschke, *Litigation, Courts, and Women Workers* (New York: Praeger Publishers, 1989), chapter 3.

9. H. Rep. No. 238, 92d Cong., 2d Sess. 3 (1972).

10. David Rose, "Twenty-Five Years Later: Where Do We Stand on Equal Employment Opportunity Law Enforcement?," *Vanderbilt Law Review* 42(1989), p. 1136.

11. Richard Lehr, "EEOC Case-Handling Procedures: Problems and Solutions," *Alabama Law Review* 34(1983), pp. 243–44 n. 29.

12. 117 *Cong. Rec.* 32,088 (1971).

13. Individuals still retained the right to sue on their own behalf after 1972.

14. The EEOC has developed standards for determining when to bring charges against employers for systematic discrimination. See Note, "Factually or Statistically Based Commissioner's Charge: A New Approach to EEOC Enforcement of Title VII," *Boston University Law Review* 63(1983) for discussion of the EEOC's "pattern and practice" charges against employers.

15. Rose, "Twenty-Five Years Later," pp. 1148–49. See also Maschke, *Litigation, Courts, and Women Workers,* chapter 3.

16. B. Dan Wood, "Does Politics Make a Difference at the EEOC?," *American Journal of Political Science* 34(1990), p. 509. Wood's analysis of political change and the EEOC concluded that the commission "was dramatically invigorated" when Eleanor Holmes Norton assumed control and "dramatically enfeebled" after 1982 when Clarence Thomas was put in charge.

17. Clarence Thomas, "The Equal Employment Opportunity Commission: Reflections on a New Philosophy," *Stetson Law Review* 15(1985), p. 34.

18. Thomas, "The Equal Employment Opportunity Commission," p. 35.

19. This discussion of the Reagan administration and the EEOC is drawn from Eleanor Holmes Norton, "Equal Employment Law: Crisis in Interpretation—Survival against the Odds," *Tulane Law Review* 62(1988), pp. 704–07 and Norman Amaker, *Civil Rights and the Reagan Administration* (Washington, DC: Urban Institute Press, 1988), chapter 6.

20. Cynthia Harrison, *On Account of Sex: The Politics of Women's Issues, 1945–1968* (Berkeley: University of California Press, 1988), p. 187 (emphasis in the original).

21. Donald Robinson, "Two Movements in Pursuit of Equal Employment Opportunity," *Signs* 4(1979), p. 422.

22. Harrison, *On Account of Sex,* pp. 188–89.

23. Bird, *Born Female,* pp. 12–13.

24. Sections 703(a) (1–2) of the Civil Rights Act of 1964.

25. Maschke, *Litigation, Courts, and Women Workers,* p. 13.

26. Barbara Brown, Ann Freedman, Harriet Katz, and Alice Price, *Women's Rights and the Law* (New York: Praeger Publishers, 1977), p. 209.

27. 29 C.F.R. §1604.1(c) states that

> the Commission does not believe that Congress intended to disturb such laws and regulations which are intended to, and have the effect of, protecting women against exploitation and hazard. Accordingly, the Commission will consider qualifications set by such state laws or regulations to be bona fide occupational qualifications, and thus not in conflict with Title VII. Cited in *Weeks v. Southern Bell Telephone & Telegraph,* 408 F.2d 228, 233 (5th Cir. 1969).

28. Harrison, *On Account of Sex,* p. 186.
29. 110 *Cong. Rec.* 7217 (1964).
30. *Weeks,* 408 F.2d at 235.
31. *Rosenfeld v. Southern Pacific,* 444 F.2d 1219, 1224 (9th Cir. 1971).
32. 29 C.F.R. §1604.1, cited in *Rosenfeld,* 444 F.2d at 1224.
33. In 1970, the commission issued 29 C.F.R. §1604.1(b) (2), stating that

> the Commission [now] believes that such State laws and regulations, although originally promulgated for the purpose of protecting females, have ceased to be relevant to our technology or to the expanding role of the female worker in our economy. The Commission has found that such laws and regulations do not take into account the capacities, preferences, and abilities of individual females and tend to discriminate rather than protect. Accordingly, the Commission has concluded that such laws and regulations conflict with Title VII of the Civil Rights Act of 1964 and will not be considered a defense to an otherwise established unlawful employment practice or as a basis for the application of the bona fide occupational qualification exception.

34. Judith Baer, *The Chains of Protection* (Westport, CT: Greenwood Press, 1978), p. 167.
35. *Diaz v. Pan American World Airways,* 442 F. 2d 385, 388 (5th Cir. 1971) (emphasis in the original).
36. *Wilson v. Southwest Airlines,* 517 F. Supp. 292, 294–95 (N.D. Tex. 1981).
37. *Wilson,* 517 F. Supp. at 299 (emphasis in the original).
38. *Wilson,* 517 F. Supp. at 303.
39. *Phillips v. Martin Marietta Corporation,* 411 F.2d 1, 4 (5th Cir. 1969).
40. *Phillips v. Martin Marietta Corporation,* 416 F.2d 1257, 1262 (5th Cir. 1969) (Brown, J., dissenting).
41. *Phillips,* 416 F.2d at 1260 (Brown, J., dissenting).
42. *Phillips v. Martin Marietta Corporation,* 400 U.S. 542, 545 (1971) (Marshall, J., concurring).
43. *Dothard v. Rawlinson,* 433 U.S. 321, 325 (1977).
44. *Dothard,* 433 U.S. at 335 (emphasis added).
45. *Dothard,* 433 U.S. at 342 (Marshall, J., concurring in part and dissenting in part).
46. *Dothard,* 433 U.S. at 345 (Marshall, J., concurring in part and dissenting in part).
47. *Dothard,* 433 U.S. at 346 n. 5 (Marshall, J., concurring in part and dissenting in part).
48. Harrison, *On Account of Sex,* p. 188.
49. See Bird, *Born Female,* pp. 13–15; Robinson, "Two Movements," pp. 423–24.
50. Sex was added to the list of forbidden classifications in 1969.
51. *Pittsburgh Press v. Pittsburgh Commission on Human Relations,* 413 U.S. 376, 394 (1973) (Burger, C. J., dissenting).
52. Emily Kirby, *Yes You Can* (Englewood Cliffs: Prentice-Hall, 1984), p. 70.
53. *Pittsburgh Press,* 413 U.S. at 382.
54. In *Valentine v. Chrestensen,* 316 U.S. 52 (1942), the Supreme Court allowed a city to ban distribution of a handbill advertising a tour of a submarine.
55. *Pittsburgh Press,* 413 U.S. at 388.

3

Equal Employment Opportunity: Proving Discrimination

When Congress authorized litigation under Title VII of the 1964 Civil Rights Act, it offered virtually no guidance for judicial interpretation of the act. Ironically, the statute did not even include a legislative definition of the word *discrimination*. In the face of this void, the courts were forced to flesh out the contours of this momentous piece of legislation.

While the legislative and executive branches have contributed to the formulation of Title VII policy since 1964, the bulk of Title VII law has been molded by the judiciary. A primary focus of judicial attention has been on the allocation of the burden of proof in Title VII actions.

In discrimination law, as in all other areas of law, there are two sorts of burdens: the burden of proof (or persuasion) and the burden of production. The side bearing the burden of proof always has the more difficult task in the lawsuit: to produce evidence *and* to persuade the court that the evidence is true. The party with the burden of production merely has to produce the evidence. While the plaintiff traditionally bears the burden of proof for the whole trial, in some lawsuits the burden is shifted to the defendant during the trial. Civil suits are frequently won or lost depending on whether this shift occurs.

During the first decade of employment discrimination litigation, the courts began to identify two kinds of discrimination—intentional and unintentional. Intentional discrimination, reflecting the most common understanding of discrimination, exists when "people [are treated] less favorably than others because of their race, color, religion, sex, or national origin." The Supreme Court believed that Congress's primary motivation for enacting Title VII was to eliminate this "most easily understood type of discrimination."[1]

Intentional Discrimination: Disparate Treatment Theory

The key to winning a lawsuit for intentional discrimination, also known as disparate treatment, rests on being able to show that an employment policy or practice was motivated by discriminatory intent. In the 1973 case of *McDonnell Douglas v. Green,* followed by the 1981 case of *Texas Department of Community Affairs v. Burdine,* the Supreme Court formulated a three-stage process for courts to use in adjudicating a charge of intentional discrimination. With each side alternately presenting evidence to the court, the plaintiff retains the burden of proof at all times.

Because it is extraordinarily difficult for employees to obtain proof that they were victims of intentional employment discrimination, the courts do not require them to present direct evidence of discriminatory intent. Instead, at the first stage they have to demonstrate four facts to enable the judge to infer that there was discrimination. First, plaintiffs must be members of a class protected by Title VII; second, they must show they were qualified for the job; third, they have to demonstrate they applied for and were rejected for the job or denied the promotion; and fourth, they must prove the prospective employer continued to seek employees with their qualifications.[2] Once plaintiffs present these elements, they have established a prima facie case (a case with sufficient evidence to go to the jury) and the first part of the trial is over.

At the second stage, the employer has to rebut (or refute) the plaintiff's prima facie case by "articulat[ing] some legitimate, nondiscriminatory reason" for the decision not to hire or promote. Because the burden of proof stays with the plaintiff throughout the trial, employers have to offer a plausible reason for the employment decision but do not have to *prove* they actually relied on it.[3]

Then in the last stage of the case, the pretext stage, the plaintiff must persuade the court that the defendant's proffered reason was only a pretext for a discriminatory motive. Here, the court delves more deeply into the employer's asserted reason to ascertain whether it was the real reason for the decision.

The plaintiff can succeed at the third stage by persuading the court that the employer was more likely than not motivated by a discriminatory reason or that the employer's explanation is not credible. If the plaintiff successfully proves that the employer's asserted reason was not the actual one, the plaintiff has carried the burden of convincing the court that he or she was the victim of intentional discrimination.

Mixed Motive Cases

The *McDonnell Douglas-Burdine* theory was designed for a case in which an employee charges that intentional racial or sexual discrimination was the sole basis for an adverse job decision. Courts have had to develop a different approach for the more common situation where both legitimate and illegitimate motives are involved, the so-called mixed motive case. Here, the plaintiff has been able to show that race or sex played a role in the decision, but the employer can also show that the decision was motivated by legitimate reasons as well. Because the plaintiff demonstrates that the employer was at least partially influenced by discriminatory intent, the courts shift the burden of proof to the employer at the second stage of the trial.

Employees benefit from this shifting burden because while they may have proof that discrimination played a role in the employment decision, they rarely have enough information to know whether it was the *key* factor. As Justice Sandra Day O'Connor explained, "[P]articularly in the context of the professional world, where decisions are often made by collegial bodies on the basis of largely subjective criteria, requiring the plaintiff to prove that *any* one factor was the definitive cause of the decisionmakers' action may be tantamount to declaring Title VII inapplicable to such decisions."[4] Persuaded that pretext cases and mixed motive cases require different legal analyses, the Supreme Court created a new rule for the latter and no longer applies *McDonnell Douglas* to them.

The Court formulated its approach to mixed motive cases in the 1989 case of *Price Waterhouse v. Hopkins.* Resolving a conflict among appellate circuits, the Supreme Court's opinion was primarily devoted to the issue of which side should bear the burden of proof at the second stage of the trial.[5]

Ann Hopkins sued Price Waterhouse for refusing to promote her to a partnership position in the accounting firm. She claimed that the firm violated Title VII because sex stereotyping played a significant role in its decision-making process. First denying that its decision was based on sex, Price Waterhouse next argued that even if sex were a consideration, Hopkins should be required to *prove* she would have been promoted if there had been no discrimination. The Court disagreed, explaining that Title VII demands that sex "be irrelevant to employment decisions."[6]

William Brennan wrote an opinion for himself, Thurgood Marshall, John Paul Stevens, and Harry Blackmun. Byron White wrote separately to concur in the judgment as did O'Connor. Anthony Kennedy, joined by William Rehnquist and Antonin Scalia, dissented, charging that the creation of special rules for mixed motive cases unnecessarily causes "confusion" and "disarray" in Title VII law.

According to Brennan, the employee must initially show that the employer's decision was *motivated* by sex discrimination. And an employment decision is motivated by sex, he said, if the employer, responding truthfully, would admit that the employee's sex played a role. While generally agreeing with him, O'Connor and White would have required the employee to show that the employer was *substantially* motivated by discrimination.

All six majority justices agreed that once the plaintiff proved that her sex was a factor in the employment decision, the burden of proof shifted to the employer to show that it would have made the same decision in the absence of bias against her.[7] But unlike the pretext cases, the employer cannot simply articulate *a* legitimate reason for its decision. In essence, the Court required Price Waterhouse to satisfy the trial court that its refusal to promote Hopkins was based on *wholly* legitimate grounds. If Price Waterhouse were unable to prove its legitimate reason "standing alone" would have caused it to defer her promotion, the lower court could conclude that sex was a relevant factor and find that Price Waterhouse violated Title VII.

Unintentional Discrimination: Disparate Impact Theory

Title VII was enacted to "remov[e] artificial, arbitrary, and unnecessary barriers to employment when the barriers operate invidiously to discriminate on the basis of racial or other impermissible classification."[8] While those barriers are often intentionally erected, proving an employer's evil intent or motive is often an impossible task. The disparate treatment model was "premised on the overt discrimination of the 1960s" and possibly outlived its usefulness by the 1980s.[9] If Title VII were restricted to challenging employment practices where intent could be proven, employers would quickly learn to mask their intent more effectively, and Title VII would be vitiated.

Following the passage of Title VII, when employers were legally forbidden from discriminating against minorities and women, companies began to institute so-called objective criteria for job selection. While not overtly discriminatory, these facially neutral criteria had the *effect* of restricting job opportunities for women and minorities.[10] Soon such practices were challenged as discriminatory under Title VII. Recognizing that intentional discrimination was not alone responsible for racial and sexual barriers to employment, the Court was persuaded that Title VII must be interpreted to encompass employment policies that had a disproportionate impact on women and minorities. In the 1971 landmark decision of *Griggs v. Duke Power Company*, arguably the most significant Title VII case ever decided, the Supreme Court held that an employer could violate Title VII without harboring any intent to discriminate.[11]

Eleanor Holmes Norton, past chair of the Equal Employment Opportunity Commission (EEOC), testified to the power of this decision by claiming that "the *Griggs* Court, in announcing the disparate impact theory, defined the most important concept in modern employment discrimination work."[12] Similarly, former Chief of the EEOC Office of Conciliations Alfred Blumrosen claimed that "few decisions in our time—perhaps only *Brown v. Board of Education*—have had such momentous social consequences."[13]

In disparate (or adverse) impact cases, Title VII plaintiffs begin by identifying an employment policy or practice that disadvantages them; they do not have to prove the employer's intent to discriminate against them. Employers can justify employment barriers, such as written tests, height and weight limits, and high school diplomas, by showing there is a necessary business reason for these job selection criteria *and* there are no alternate selection policies with a lesser impact.

The Supreme Court's adoption of disparate impact theory in employment discrimination was not totally revolutionary. The 1965 Voting Rights Act (VRA) had outlawed voting mechanisms that had either the purpose or effect of discriminating on the basis of race. According to Drew Days III, assistant attorney general for civil rights during the Carter administration, the VRA's "emphasis on preventing discriminatory effects reflected the changing view of the nature of discrimination; namely, that discrimination flows not only from individuals but also from certain institutional arrangements which, whatever the motive for their establishment, disadvantage racial minority group members and women."[14]

Thus, the Court was not writing on a blank slate in *Griggs*. Speaking for a unanimous Court (Brennan took no part in the decision), Chief Justice Warren Burger explained that Title VII was designed

> to achieve equality of employment opportunities and remove barriers that have operated in the past to favor an identifiable group of white employees over other employees. Under the Act, practices, procedures, or tests neutral on their face, and even neutral in terms of intent, cannot be maintained if they operate to 'freeze' the status quo of prior discriminatory employment practices.[15]

Tests and Diplomas as Job Requirements

While Title VII makes it illegal to "classify employees" or "adversely affect their status" because of race or sex, the statute allows employers to rely on a "professionally developed ability test" as long as it is not used to discriminate. The question the Supreme Court had to resolve in *Griggs* was whether employers were forbidden from using professionally developed tests that were unrelated to job performance and disqualified a significantly higher number of black applicants.

The *Griggs'* plaintiffs were black employees of the Duke Power Company's Dan River Steam Station. They complained that the company violated Title VII by requiring a high school education or passage of a standardized general intelligence test for higher status jobs in the plant. Before Title VII, Duke Power had openly discriminated against its black employees by restricting them to the lowest paying department, the labor department. Other departments were exclusively white. The top wage in the labor department was $1.55 an hour — fourteen cents under the lowest hourly wage of white workers; top wages in the "white" departments ranged from $3.18 to $3.65 an hour.

In 1955, the company started requiring high school diplomas from all white employees hired after that year. When the Civil Rights Act went into effect in 1965, and all employees became legally eligible to work in previously all-white departments, the company created new hiring and transfer rules. Beginning employees in all departments other than labor had to pass two aptitude tests in addition to producing a high school diploma. Current employees wishing to transfer between departments were also required to show a high school diploma.

White employees protested the new transfer rule because it kept many of them out of the more desirable jobs. In response, the company changed the rule to permit employees to substitute a passing grade on two standardized intelligence tests for a high school diploma. Satisfactory scores on these tests were based on a national median grade of high school graduates. Neither test was related to ability to perform on the job.

The plaintiffs claimed that both the test and the high school diploma requirements disqualified blacks at a "substantially" higher rate than whites and kept them out of the higher paying jobs. Both district and appellate courts ruled in favor of Duke Power because there was no evidence that the company intentionally discriminated against the black employees. On the contrary, the company had even established a tuition reimbursement plan that helped undereducated employees attain their high school degrees.

Reversing the courts below in an expansive interpretation of Title VII, the Supreme Court held that the statute

> proscribes not only overt discrimination but also practices that are fair in form, but discriminatory in operation. The touchstone is business necessity. If an employment practice which operates to exclude Negroes cannot be shown to be related to job performance, the practice is prohibited.[16]

Duke Power lost the suit because it could not show that either the testing or the educational requirements were related to job performance.

Indeed, it had imposed these standards without even determining that they were related to work on the job. One of the vice presidents testified that they had been adopted "on the Company's judgment that they generally would improve the overall quality of the work force."[17] Based on these considerations as well as the fact that only 12 percent of black males but 34 percent of white males throughout North Carolina held high school diplomas, the Court ruled in favor of the employees.

Noting the lower courts' findings that there was no intent to discriminate, the Court held that "good intent or absence of discriminatory intent does not redeem employment procedures or testing mechanisms that operate as 'built-in headwinds' for minority groups."[18] And in what would prove to be a hotly contested issue eighteen years later, the Court ruled that "Congress has placed on the employer the burden of showing that any given requirement must have a manifest relationship to the employment in question."[19]

The Court was also persuaded by the EEOC's Guidelines on Employment Testing Procedures of 1966 and 1970. According to the guidelines, a "professionally developed ability test," specified in section 703(h) of the Civil Rights Act, is one that measures skills required for a job or gives the employer a chance to measure an employee's ability to perform a job.[20]

Burger noted that Title VII's legislative history supported the EEOC's interpretation. He cited a proposed amendment offered by Senator John Tower of Texas during floor debate over the bill. The amendment was defeated because Senate leaders were concerned that it would authorize the use of any test prepared by an expert, whether employment related or not. Title VII's final reference to job tests satisfied the senators that only job-related tests would be valid.

As a result of *Griggs,* and *Albemarle Paper Company v. Moody,* 1975, the Supreme Court created a test to determine when job selection procedures with a disproportionate or disparate impact on women and minorities violate Title VII.[21] Like the test for intentional discrimination, the disparate impact analysis consists of three stages. First, the plaintiff must establish a prima facie case by showing that a facially neutral employment policy has an adverse disproportionate impact on members of the protected class. The burden then shifts to the employer to demonstrate that the employment policy is justified as a business necessity. If the employer convinces the court the employment criteria is job related, the plaintiff then has an opportunity to demonstrate that less discriminatory alternatives are available to the employer.

As in disparate treatment cases, the allocation of the burden of proof is often the crucial element of the case. Also as in disparate treatment cases, the controversy centers on whether the burden of proof remains with the plaintiff at all times or whether it shifts to the defendant at the second stage of the trial.

Following *Griggs* and *Albemarle,* most lower courts ruled that the burden of proof shifts to the employer to show business necessity after the plaintiff demonstrates an adverse impact of employee tests or measures. There was disagreement, however, over what exactly had to be proved. The Supreme Court helped add to the confusion by its indiscriminate use of such phrases as "business necessity," "related to job performance," and "manifest relationship to the employment in question" in discussing the employer's burden.[22]

Height and Weight Requirements

Another example of a "neutral" employment requirement that was particularly effective in restricting women's employment opportunities was the height and weight requirement—most often found in police and fire departments or prisons. In 1977, the Supreme Court assessed the disparate impact of height and weight requirements on a female applicant for the job of correctional counselor, a prison guard.

The case of *Dothard v. Rawlinson* (also important for its ruling on the bona fide occupational qualification) arose when Dianne Rawlinson sued the Alabama state corrections department. She was rejected for the job of correctional counselor because she did not meet the statutory 120-pound minimum-weight requirement. The statute also imposed a minimum-height requirement of five feet two inches. Rawlinson claimed that the height and weight requirement had a disproportionate impact on women and therefore violated Title VII.[23] The district court agreed.

Rawlinson presented evidence that women fourteen years and over constituted 52.75 percent of the Alabama population and 36.89 percent of its total labor force, yet they hold only 12.9 percent of the correctional counselor positions. The district court found that the minimum-height requirement would exclude 33.29 percent of women in the United States between eighteen and seventy-nine years old, while less than 2 percent of men in the same age bracket would be excluded. The court also found that the minimum-weight requirement would exclude 22.29 percent of women and only 2.35 percent of men in the same age group. Combining the height and weight restrictions would exclude a little over 40 percent of the female population, while less than 1 percent of men would be excluded. Based on these findings, the district court found that Rawlinson had established a prima facie case of discrimination.[24]

The state argued that Rawlinson had not proved a prima facie case because her statistics were based on a national population sample and because she had introduced no figures for actual job applicants. Delivering the opinion of the Court, Potter Stewart noted that the statistics need not reflect the applicant pool because applicants below the minimum height or weight would have been discouraged from applying. Moreover, said Stewart, national figures are acceptable because there is no reason to assume that the physical characteristics of Alabaman men and women are different from those in the national population.

Alabama contended that height and weight were valid measures because they were related to strength, an essential of the job of prison guard. But the prison authorities offered no evidence to show that the height and weight requirements were correlated to "the requisite amount of strength thought essential to good job performance."[25] Reiterating an earlier theme, the Court noted that employers must "prov[e] that the challenged requirements are job related."[26] Because Alabama had not done so, it had not met its burden under Title VII.

By 1988, it was clear that the distinction between disparate impact and disparate treatment analysis revolved around the nature of the defendant's burden in the second stage of the trial. In disparate treatment cases, the employer's burden (of production) merely required it to articulate a legitimate reason; in disparate impact cases, the employer was required to prove that its reason was legitimate. This distinction was plain enough so that eleven of the twelve circuits joined the Supreme Court in maintaining different evidentiary rules for the two types of cases.[27]

Subjective Employment Criteria

Many employment decisions, especially at the professional or managerial level, are based on subjective judgments rather than objective criteria such as scores on a test or numbers on a height and weight chart. A woman seeking a traditional male-defined job is particularly vulnerable because an employer's decision may be influenced by unconscious stereotypes or prejudices about her proper role. The circuit courts were divided on whether they should employ a disparate impact model for subjective selection procedures or whether they should use the *McDonnell Douglas* intentional discrimination test. In part, the lower courts that opted for the disparate impact analysis were influenced by the difficulty of proving intentional discrimination when subjective measures were used to hire or promote employees.

The Supreme Court resolved the conflict among the circuits in 1988 by ruling in *Watson v. Forth Worth Bank and Trust* that challenges to subjective selection procedures could be brought under a disparate impact analysis.

Clara Watson, an African-American woman, filed a complaint against the Fort Worth Bank because she was denied promotion to a supervisory position four times within one year. The bank had no formal criteria for evaluating applicants for promotion. Its supervisors were allowed to use their own discretion in selecting employees to promote. Each time Watson applied, a white supervisor, using subjective judgment, rejected her application and offered the job to a white person.

Watson brought suit under both disparate treatment and disparate impact theories. The lower court dismissed the latter claim, ruling that disparate impact theory is not applicable to employment decisions using subjective judgments. The court also dismissed her charge of intentional discrimination because the bank offered legitimate nondiscriminatory reasons for passing over her. Watson could not persuade the court that these reasons were a pretext for discrimination against her.

The appellate court affirmed on appeal, and in an 8–0 decision (Kennedy did not participate), the Supreme Court reversed the courts below. Announcing the opinion of the Court, O'Connor reasoned that if subjective decision-making produces discriminatory results, it must be included within the reach of Title VII. She explained that an employer could easily escape responsibility under *Griggs* by adding interviews or other subjective factors to an objective (and illegal) selection process. She expressed concern for the future of disparate impact challenges if the Court were to adopt "a rule that allowed employers so easily to insulate themselves from liability under *Griggs*."[28]

New Questions about Disparate Impact Theory

Although the justices agreed on the principle of including subjective judgments within disparate impact analysis, the Court was sharply divided on the issue of proving discrimination. O'Connor, now speaking for a four-person plurality of herself, Rehnquist, White, and Scalia, proposed a new framework for disparate impact cases that would make it easier for the employer to rebut the plaintiff's prima facie case.

In *Watson,* the bank claimed that, unlike objective criteria, it was impossible to validate subjective measurements such as common sense, self-confidence, good judgment, or interpersonal skills. It warned that an employer's only defense in a disparate impact suit would be to create a preferential quota system with enough women or minorities in supervisory positions so that plaintiffs would not be able to establish a statistical prima facie case.

Sympathetic to the bank's argument, and noting that a racial or sexual quota system was directly contradicted by Title VII, O'Connor sought to allay the bank's fears by undertaking a "fresh and somewhat closer examination" of the "evidentiary standards" required in disparate impact cases.[29]

To establish a prima facie case, said O'Connor, a plaintiff must do three things: first, demonstrate a statistical disparity in the work force;

second, identify the specific discriminatory employment practice responsible for the disparity; and third, establish causation by offering statistical evidence that applicants of her (or his) race or sex have been excluded by this practice. While it is relatively easy, O'Connor warned, to identify objective measures or tests that discriminate, it is exceedingly difficult to identify discriminatory subjective measures.

The plurality justices demonstrated their discomfort with disparate impact analysis by urging the Court to adopt the disparate treatment approach for both impact and treatment cases. Moving away from the *Griggs-Albemarle* principle, they wanted a disparate impact plaintiff to carry the burden of proof throughout the trial; they would merely require the employer to articulate *a* legitimate business reason at the second stage of the trial. Collapsing the two models in this way would sharply "limit the utility of disparate impact analysis as a basis for Title VII claims."[30]

Blackmun, joined by Brennan and Marshall, pointed out that "the plurality's discussion of the allocation of burdens of proof and production that apply in litigating a disparate-impact claim under Title VII . . . is flatly contradicted by our cases."[31] Citing *Griggs, Dothard,* and *Albemarle,* Blackmun stressed that the Court had repeatedly used the word *prove* to describe the employer's burden of establishing the business necessity of a challenged policy.

The plurality, insisted Blackmun, appears to have confused the two types of Title VII analyses; in a disparate impact case, unlike an intentional discrimination case, the burden of proof has always shifted to the employer after the prima facie case is made. According to Blackmun, the reason for the difference in shifting burdens is that, in a disparate treatment case, the prima facie case only creates an inference of intent to discriminate. In a disparate impact claim, the plaintiff's prima facie case consists of direct proof that a particular employment practice has caused a significant numerical disparity. Permitting an employer merely to articulate rather than prove a nondiscriminatory justification in an impact case "is simply not enough to legitimatize a practice that has the effect of excluding a protected class from job opportunities at a significantly disproportionate rate."[32]

Stevens, concurring, agreed that the *Griggs* disparate impact test should be used for claims of discrimination on the basis of subjective criteria. But he reminded the Court that they were only asked to rule on this narrow question and to decide more at this time was unwise.

Watson indicated the likely direction the Supreme Court would take when all four Reagan-appointed justices, joined by the increasingly conservative White, ruled in future Title VII cases. Because Kennedy did not participate in *Watson,* the plurality view was short one vote on the burden of proof issue. With Kennedy participating in *Wards Cove Packing Company v. Atonio,* 1989, the matter of the shifting burden of proof was resolved. *Wards Cove* confirmed Blackmun's fear that the Supreme Court would adopt the *Watson* plurality's position on the employer's burden of proof in disparate impact cases.

A New Direction for Disparate Impact Theory

Wards Cove arose in 1974 when workers of color, primarily Filipinos and Alaskan natives, employed by two salmon canneries in Alaska filed a Title VII suit against their employers. They claimed they were being discriminated against because they held most of the unskilled cannery positions while white workers held most of the noncannery positions. The noncannery jobs, primarily skilled positions, paid more than the cannery jobs. Additionally, the workers claimed that their employers discriminated against them by maintaining separate—that is, segregated—housing and dining facilities for the two kinds of employees.

The situation at the salmon canneries prompted Blackmun to describe the industry as "a kind of overt and institutionalized discrimination [that] we have not dealt with in years: a total residential and work environment organized on principles of racial stratification and segregation which . . . resembles a plantation economy."[33]

Cannery workers were hired locally in Alaska while the noncannery workers were hired during the winter off-months from company offices in Washington and Oregon. Identifying these and other hiring and promotion policies, the workers filed suit under both disparate treatment and disparate impact theories. The district court dismissed both claims, and after remands and appeals, the Ninth Circuit ruled that plaintiffs had made out a prima facie case of disparate impact by presenting statistics showing a high percentage of minority workers in cannery jobs and a low percentage of minority workers in noncannery jobs. The appellate court remanded the case to the district court with an instruction that the burden of proof rested on the employer to prove business necessity. The *Watson* plurality of four was transformed into a majority of five as Kennedy joined White, O'Connor, Scalia, and Rehnquist. With White delivering the majority opinion, the Court reversed the appellate court.

White began his opinion by rejecting the circuit court's analysis of the statistical comparisons necessary to establish a prima facie case of disparate impact under Title VII. It is not sufficient, he said, to compare the number of white workers to workers of color in each kind of job. In disparate impact cases, the comparison must be "between the racial composition of the qualified persons in the labor market and the persons holding at-issue jobs."[34] An employer is not guilty of discrimination, White added, if no qualified minority applicants were available for the better jobs. But under the appellate court's approach, employers would be forced to defend against discrimination suits simply because they hired few minorities. The workers, he concluded, had not established a prima facie case of disparate impact.

Moreover, in addition to presenting the proper statistics, White continued, workers must do more than simply point to a "racial imbalance" in the work force. Citing O'Connor's opinion in *Watson*, he held that to establish a prima facie case of discrimination, plaintiffs must "demonstrate that it is the application of a specific or particular employment practice that has created the disparate impact under attack."[35] Employees had to show that each challenged practice led to the disparate impact at the focus of their complaint.

Despite the language in *Griggs* to the contrary, White proclaimed that in the second phase of the trial, once a plaintiff establishes a prima facie case of discrimination the employer "carries the burden of *producing* evidence of a business justification for his employment practice. The burden of *persuasion* [of proof], however, remains with the disparate-impact plaintiff."[36] Aware of the explosive effect this statement would have on his colleagues, as well as the civil rights community, White

> acknowledge[d] that some of our earlier decisions can be read as suggesting otherwise. . . . But to the extent that those cases speak of an employer's 'burden of proof' with respect to a legitimate business justification defense . . . they should have been understood to mean an employer's production — but not persuasion — burden.[37]

The Supreme Court remanded to the lower court to determine whether the company was guilty of employment discrimination under the majority's formulation of the disparate impact test.

In a bitterly worded dissent joined by Blackmun, Brennan, and Marshall, Stevens accused the majority of "retreat[ing]" from its long-established commitment to furthering the principles of equality and "turning a blind eye to the meaning and purpose of Title VII."[38] Claiming that the majority's cavalier treatment of "settled law" required a "primer" on Title VII case law, Stevens reviewed the eighteen-year history of disparate impact and disparate treatment analysis since *Griggs*.

Stevens focused on the majority's error in shifting the burden of proof to the plaintiff at the second stage of the inquiry. Distinguishing between disparate treatment and disparate impact cases, he explained that, in the former, when there is only indirect evidence of an intent to discriminate, the court utilizes the *McDonnell Douglas* analysis to explore the employer's motive. Because there is no Title VII violation until the discriminatory motive is established after the third stage of the trial, the burden of proving the discrimination remains with the plaintiff throughout the trial.

Because intent is irrelevant in disparate impact cases, the Title VII violation is established once the employees present a factual showing of a disproportionate impact on a Title VII protected class. With the Title VII violation settled, he said, the employer can only "justify the practice by explaining why it is necessary to the operation of business." Drawing on established legal principles, Stevens characterized the employer's burden in the second phase of a disparate impact case as "a classic example of an affirmative defense" (where the defendant bears the burden of proof).[39]

Stevens argued that the Court had always placed the burden *of proof* on the employer in disparate impact cases. He protested that he found the majority's "casual—almost summary—rejection" of the statutory construction that developed in the wake of *Griggs* most disturbing. "I have always believed," he added, "that the *Griggs* opinion correctly reflected the intent of the Congress that enacted Title VII. [And] even if I were not so persuaded," he continued, "I could not join a rejection of a consistent interpretation of a federal statute."[40]

Not bothering to mask his anger, Blackmun accused the majority of "tak[ing] three major strides backwards in the battle against race discrimination." He sarcastically asked "whether the majority still believes that race discrimination—or, more accurately, race discrimination against nonwhites—is a problem in our society, or even remembers that it ever was."[41]

The new formulation of the employer's burden in disparate impact analysis, Blackmun charged, makes it likely "that future plaintiffs would find it virtually impossible to prevail on a claim of disparate impact."[42] They will simply not have the resources (knowledge of the jobs, knowledge of testing procedures, or knowledge of necessary qualifications for the job) to be able to *prove* that the discriminatory practice is unjustified.

The Civil Rights Act of 1990

By changing the long-standing rules of disparate impact lawsuits, the Court undermined *Griggs* and sharply reduced the effectiveness of Title VII in battling employment discrimination. The congressional response to *Wards Cove* began with legislation introduced by Democratic Senator Howard Metzenbaum of Ohio and Republican Representative Tom Campbell of California. Their bills would have reinstated the *Griggs-Albemarle* rule and placed the burden of proof on the employer in the second phase of disparate impact cases. Metzenbaum's bill would have also exempted employees from having to show that a specific employment practice had a disparate impact on them.[43] When the first session of the 101st Congress adjourned in November 1989, neither bill received congressional approval.

In early February 1990, congressional civil rights supporters cosponsored legislation intended to modify or reverse five 1989 Supreme Court rulings in addition to *Wards Cove*. On behalf of thirty-seven Democratic and Republican cosponsors, Senator Edward Kennedy of Massachusetts and Representative Augustus Hawkins of California, both Democrats, introduced two companion bills, S. 2104 and H.R. 4000. Controversy over the bills focused on the reversal of the Court's ruling in *Wards Cove* and the proposed expansion of existing Title VII remedies.

On April 4, 1990, in an 11–5 vote, the Senate Labor and Human Resources Committee quickly approved S. 2104, known as the Kennedy-Hawkins bill. Reversing the Supreme Court, Senate bill S. 2104 would have (1) allowed suits for racial harassment in employment; (2) permitted employees to file discrimination suits when they are first made aware of being adversely affected by a seniority system rather than when the plan is adopted; (3) established the finality of consent decrees; (4) prohibited employers from using race, color, religion, sex, or national origin as motivating factors in employment decisions whether or not they can show they would have made the same decision for nondiscriminatory reasons; (5) required employers to prove a business need for practices that adversely impact minority and female workers and specified that employees do not have to pinpoint the specific practice that led to the adverse impact; and (6) allowed attorney's fees to be recovered from losing intervening parties as well as defendants.

The bill would have also expanded Title VII remedies by allowing compensatory damages (such as pain and suffering) for Title VII plaintiffs who proved intentional discrimination as well as punitive damages in egregious cases. If these remedies were sought, either side could demand a jury trial. Under an existing law (42 U.S.C. Section 1981), victims of racial discrimination are entitled to compensatory and punitive damages and jury trials. Because women and religious minorities are unable to file suit under Section 1981, they are restricted to Title VII suits where the only money damages available to them are back pay and attorney's fees.

In a letter to the committee after the vote, Attorney General Richard Thornburgh said that he and "other senior advisors" would recommend that President George Bush veto the bill. The administration, opposed to the bill's effect on four of the Court's decisions and the expansion of Title VII remedies, proposed instead a one-page bill that captured only the first two provisions of S. 2104. The administration version was unacceptable to civil rights advocates.[44]

On May 1, 1990, the House Education and Labor Committee began consideration of the bill and approved it a week later in a 23–10 vote.[45] During committee deliberation, in an attempt to make the bill more palatable to business interests and the White House, Hawkins proposed a change in the section of the bill relating to disparate impact suits. In the new version, instead of requiring employers to prove that the challenged practice is "essential to effective job performance," employers would have to show that the practice "bears a substantial and demonstrable relationship to effective job performance." Despite the amendment, business groups still opposed the bill, saying that the alteration was "at best cosmetic."[46]

The administration still objected to the disparate impact standard in the bill, arguing it would force employers to establish racial and sexual hiring and promotion quotas to avoid Title VII lawsuits against them. Supporters of the bill countered by saying that the bill merely restored the Court's ruling in *Griggs* which, they contended, had not led to companies adopting quotas to protect themselves against discrimination suits.

Following approval by the Senate and House committees, congressional supporters continued negotiations with the White House to try to arrive at language that would make the bill acceptable to the president. Anxious to maintain his high approval ratings among African-American voters, Bush insisted he wanted to sign the bill and urged the talks to continue. Retracting his threat of a veto, in a White House Rose Garden ceremony on May 17, 1990, Bush stated, "I want to sign a civil rights bill, but I will not sign a quota bill."[47]

Senate bill S. 2104 was brought to the Senate floor on July 10, 1990, after negotiations between the White House and congressional sponsors broke down. Amid bitter partisan debate, the bill was approved in a 65–34 vote. Ten Republicans joined with the fifty-five Senate Democrats to support the bill. The aye votes were two votes short of the sixty-seven votes needed to override the threatened presidential veto.[48]

On August 3, 1990, the House of Representatives approved the Kennedy-Hawkins bill in a 272–154 vote. The vote was twelve votes short of a veto override. Reflecting the same partisan imbalance as in the Senate vote, 240 Democrats and 32 Republicans voted in favor. Although substantially similar to the Senate's bill, the House version contained two additional amendments. The first took a firm stand against quotas by stating "nothing in . . . this act shall be construed to require an employer to adopt hiring or promotion quotas on the basis of race, color, religion, sex, or national origin." The other amendment put a cap on punitive damages at $150,000 or the amount of compensatory damages.[49] The White House reiterated its opposition to the bill after the House vote, characterizing it as a "quota bill that the President will have to veto if it is presented to him."[50]

Faced with the renewed threat of a veto, congressional leaders returned to the bargaining table with the White House. The talks, continuing throughout the summer of 1990, focused on two issues: compensatory and punitive damages in Title VII actions and the burden of proof in disparate impact cases.

After two separate Senate-House conferences, the conferees eventually agreed on a considerably watered-down bill. The new version limited punitive damages for intentional discrimination to $150,000, or compensatory damages plus back pay, whichever is greater. Such damages would only be available in cases of intentional discrimination. The conference version also stated that the bill should not be interpreted to "encourage quotas." Additionally, it eased the burden of proof on employers in showing business necessity and, as in *Wards Cove,* required plaintiffs to identify the specific employment practice that they claimed excluded them.[51]

On October 16, 1990, the Senate voted 62–34 to approve the bill presented to it; the vote was three less than the earlier Senate vote in July and five short of overriding an executive veto. Again, Bush objected to the bill, claiming it will force businesses to adopt quotas in hiring and promotion. He also predicted the bill will "foster divisiveness and litigation rather than conciliation and will do more to promote legal fees than civil rights."[52] Again, he promised to veto it. The next day, the House voted 273–154 to approve the conference bill.

It is not clear why the bill's supporters were unable to gather the widespread support needed to ensure a veto-proof bill. They blamed the president for falsely labeling the bill a "quota bill" and for his warnings that it will hurt business in a receding economy. They also believed that the technical nature of the bill (revolving around burdens of proof and damages) prevented them from gathering grass-roots support for it. Finally, they charged that the popularity of former Ku Klux Klan leader David Duke in a Louisiana senatorial primary caused members of Congress to wish to avoid associating with a bill perceived as favoring racial minorities.[53]

In a last-minute effort to avoid a veto, the administration attempted to break the impasse by proposing to substitute a substantially weaker bill for the congressional version. Led by Senator Kennedy, Congress rejected this attempt.

Events moved quickly thereafter. On October 22, 1990, Bush vetoed the bill, becoming the second president in the twentieth century to veto civil rights legislation; the first was Ronald Reagan in 1988. "Regret[ting] having to take this action with respect to a bill bearing such a title, especially since it contain[ed] provisions" that he "strongly endorse[d]," the president again urged Congress to take prompt action on his recently submitted civil rights bill.[54]

Two days later, the Senate failed to override the veto. With fifty-five Democrats and eleven Republicans voting to override, the vote was 66–34—just one vote short of the necessary two-thirds. David Duke, who had almost won the Louisiana primary election, watched the override vote from the Senate gallery. Civil rights leaders promised to introduce an even stronger bill in the next Congress.

While the Civil Rights Act of 1990 was a stunning defeat for racial minorities, it was a greater setback to equality for women. If passed, the bill would have extended employment discrimination remedies, primarily money damages, to women. This was one of the primary reasons for the administration's opposition to it. Trying to defend itself against the charge of inconsistency for favoring jury trials and money damages for victims of racial discrimination but not for victims of sexual discrimination, a White House official stated, "we fought a Civil War for blacks, we didn't fight a Civil War for women."[55] In adopting this position, the administration was signaling that it considered employment discrimination against women less harmful than other types of employment discrimination.

NOTES

1. *International Board of Teamsters v. United States,* 431 U.S. 324, 335 n. 15 (1977).
2. When the Supreme Court created this method of proof in *McDonnell Douglas v. Green,* 411 U.S. 792, 802 (1973), it was restricted to a race discrimination case. Since then, the *McDonnell Douglas* formula has been applied to suits based on sex, age, or disability discrimination. With some variation, the formula applies to suits alleging discrimination in hiring, promotion, and firing.
3. In *Texas Department of Community Affairs v. Burdine,* 450 U.S. 248, 254 (1981), the Supreme Court explained that establishing a prima facie case creates a presumption (a set of facts assumed to be true unless evidence to the contrary is presented) of intentional discrimination that the employer must refute to escape a finding of a Title VII violation.
4. *Price Waterhouse v. Hopkins,* 109 S.Ct. 1775, 1803 (1989) (O'Connor, J., concurring). This case is discussed in Chapter Nine.
5. The circuits were divided on their treatment of the allocation of the burden of proof in mixed motive cases. See Note, "Clearing the Mixed-Motive Smokescreen: An Approach to Disparate Treatment under Title VII," *Michigan Law Review* 87(1989).
6. *Price Waterhouse,* 109 S.Ct. at 1785.
7. Brennan differentiated between a pretext case such as *McDonnell Douglas* and a mixed motive case such as this and insisted that the law developed for pretext cases should not rule in mixed motive cases.
   Price Waterhouse succeeded on one significant issue in the case. The circuit court found Price Waterhouse liable for failure to prove by "clear and convincing evidence" the absence of discrimination. The Supreme Court reversed on that issue, ruling that a defendant was only required to prove the absence of discrimination by a "preponderance of the evidence." The latter standard, common for civil litigation, means that the defendant must satisfy the court that the reasons for its employment decision were "more likely than not" legitimate.
   Under the proposed 1990 Civil Rights Act, employers would have been liable for intentional discrimination even if the same decision would have been made for nondiscriminatory reasons.
8. *Griggs v. Duke Power Company,* 401 U.S. 424, 431 (1971).
9. Anita Allessandra, "When Doctrines Collide: Disparate Treatment, Disparate Impact, and *Watson v. Fort Worth Bank and Trust,"* *University of Pennsylvania Law Review* 137(1989), pp. 1778–79.
10. Alfred Blumrosen, "Strangers in Paradise: *Griggs v. Duke Power Co.* and the Concept of Employment Discrimination," *Michigan Law Review* 71(1972), p. 59.
11. In *Washington v. Davis,* 426 U.S. 229 (1976), the Supreme Court dealt a severe blow to civil rights plaintiffs when it held that proof of intentional discrimination was required in constitutional challenges to employment discrimination.
   Title VII did not become applicable to public employers until 1972, and because this suit was filed before 1972 plaintiffs were forced to rely on the Fourteenth Amendment's equal protection clause. Plaintiffs were a group of African-American applicants who applied for jobs as police officers in the District of Columbia. They were denied the jobs on the basis of a verbal skills test that they claimed had a disproportionate impact on African-Americans.

Under *Griggs*, their claim would have been decided under disparate impact analysis. The Supreme Court ruled, however, that claims of unconstitutionality cannot be judged under impact analysis but rather that the plaintiffs must demonstrate intentional discrimination. That is, they must prove that the tests were adopted by the District of Columbia for the *purpose* of keeping African-American applicants out of the jobs.

12. Eleanor Holmes Norton, "Equal Employment Law: Crisis in Interpretation — Survival against the Odds," *Tulane Law Review* 62(1988), p. 691 n. 41.

13. Alfred Blumrosen, "The Legacy of *Griggs*: Social Progress and Subjective Judgments," *Chicago-Kent Law Review* 63(1987), pp. 1–2.

14. Drew S. Days III, "The Courts' Response to the Reagan Civil Rights Agenda," *Vanderbilt Law Review* 42(1989), p. 1005.

15. *Griggs*, 401 U.S. at 429–30.

16. *Griggs*, 401 U.S. at 431.

17. *Griggs*, 401 U.S. at 431.

18. *Griggs*, 401 U.S. at 432.

19. *Griggs*, 401 U.S. at 432.

20. The EEOC guidelines were originally published in a pamphlet and then reprinted in a longer version in the Federal Register on August 1, 1970; they were codified in 1972 at 29 C.F.R. §§1607.1–.14. Blumrosen, "Strangers in Paradise," p. 60 n. 5. See also George Rutherglen, "Disparate Impact under Title VII: An Objective Theory of Discrimination," *Virginia Law Review* 73(1987), pp. 1316–29 for a discussion of the validation of testing devices used in employee selections. In 1978, the EEOC guidelines gave way to the Uniform Guidelines on Employee Selection Procedures formulated by the EEOC in conjunction with other federal agencies. The lower courts' reaction to these guidelines has been mixed, according them some deference but not total acceptance.

21. In *Albemarle Paper Company v. Moody*, 422 U.S. 405 (1975), the Court specified that once the defendant rebuts the prima facie case, the plaintiff has an opportunity to demonstrate that other tests, without such a disparate effect, would also serve the employer's needs.

22. Rutherglen, "Disparate Impact under Title VII," pp. 1312–13.

23. Rawlinson originally sued because of the height and weight requirement, but while the suit was pending, the Board of Corrections adopted a regulation limiting contact positions to men only. She amended her complaint to include the regulation, and the Court found it valid as a BFOQ in Title VII.

24. *Dothard v. Rawlinson*, 433 U.S. 321, 329–30 (1977).

25. *Dothard*, 433 U.S. at 331.

26. *Dothard*, 433 U.S. at 329.

27. Note, "*Watson v. Fort Worth Bank and Trust*: A Plurality's Proposal to Alter the Evidentiary Burdens in Title VII Disparate Impact Cases," *North Carolina Law Review* 67(1989), pp. 733–35.

28. *Watson v. Fort Worth Bank and Trust*, 108 S.Ct. 2777, 2786 (1988).

29. Section 703(j) of the Civil Rights Act of 1964 states that

> nothing in [Title VII] shall be interpreted to require any employer . . . to grant preferential treatment to any individual or to any group because of the race, color, religion, sex, or national origin of such individual or group on account of an imbalance which may exist with respect to the total number or percentage of persons of any race, color, religion, sex, or national origin employed by any employer . . . in comparison with the total number or percentage of persons of such race, color, religion, sex, or national origin in any community, State, section, or other area, or in the available work force in any community, State, section, or other area.

30. Allessandra, "When Doctrines Collide," pp. 1785–86.

31. *Watson*, 108 S.Ct. at 2792 (Blackmun, J., concurring).

32. *Watson*, 108 S.Ct. at 2794 (Blackmun, J., concurring).

33. *Wards Cove Packing Company v. Atonio*, 109 S.Ct. 2115, 2136 (1989) (Blackmun, J., dissenting).

34. *Wards Cove*, 109 S.Ct. at 2121.

35. *Wards Cove,* 109 S.Ct. at 2124.

36. *Wards Cove,* 109 S.Ct. at 2126 (emphasis added).

37. *Wards Cove,* 109 S.Ct. at 2126.

38. *Wards Cove,* 109 S.Ct. at 2127 (Stevens, J., dissenting).

39. *Wards Cove,* 109 S.Ct. at 2131 (Stevens, J., dissenting).

40. *Wards Cove,* 109 S.Ct. at 2132 (Stevens, J., dissenting).

41. *Wards Cove,* 109 S.Ct. at 2136 (Blackmun, J., dissenting).

42. Note, "*Watson v. Fort Worth Bank and Trust,*" p. 737. See also Merrill D. Feldstein, "*Watson v. Fort Worth Bank and Trust*: Reallocating the Burdens of Proof in Employment Discrimination Litigation," *American University Law Review* 38(1989).

43. *Congressional Quarterly,* November 11, 1989, pp. 3055–59.

44. *Congressional Quarterly,* April 7, 1990, pp. 1077–78; *Congressional Quarterly,* February 10, 1990, pp. 392–93.

45. On July 12, the House Judiciary Subcommittee on Civil and Constitutional Rights approved the House Education and Labor Committee version of H.R. 4000 in a 5–3 vote. The bill was sent to the full House Judiciary Committee for consideration. *Congressional Quarterly,* July 14, 1990, pp. 2225–26.

46. *Congressional Quarterly,* May 12, 1990, p. 1482.

47. *Congressional Quarterly,* May 19, 1990, p. 1563.

48. *Congressional Quarterly,* July 21, 1990, pp. 2312–16.

49. *Congressional Quarterly,* August 4, 1990, pp. 2517–18.

50. *New York Times,* August 4, 1990.

51. *Congressional Quarterly,* October 13, 1990, p. 3428.

52. *New York Times,* October 17, 1990.

53. *Congressional Quarterly,* October 20, 1990, pp. 3518–19.

54. *Congressional Quarterly,* October 27, 1990, p. 3654.

55. *New York Times,* October 26, 1990.

4

Equal Employment Opportunity: Remedies for Discrimination

Most Americans agree that equal opportunity is a desirable goal for a democratic society, yet there is sharp disagreement over what it entails and how it should be achieved. Phrases such as *affirmative action, reverse discrimination, quota, goal,* and *color blindness* have become part of the common parlance of the 1970s and 1980s, but the words mean different things to different people.

According to the Supreme Court, Congress intended Title VII of the 1964 Civil Rights Act to "make persons whole for injuries suffered on account of unlawful employment discrimination."[1] In the midst of debate over Title VII, some members of Congress asked whether the principle of nondiscrimination required employers to establish preferential hiring systems, or quotas, to achieve racial or sexual balance. They were assured that Title VII did not contemplate such a future: the goal of Title VII was a color-blind (and sex-blind) society.[2] Equal employment opportunity would be achieved because race and sex would no longer be relevant to employment decisions.

Title VII and the accompanying federal litigation removed many of the legal restrictions on women's employment opportunities, yet occupational and income disparities remain. Women are concentrated in support and service occupations and underrepresented in positions of executive, managerial, or skilled labor.[3]

Similarly, Title VII played an important role in opening up employment opportunities for minorities, but minority workers still lag behind white workers in holding professional, executive, and skilled occupations.

And the earnings of men and women of color are not on a par with those of white men and women of equal education, work experience, and occupation.[4]

Despite the advances of the last twenty-five years, race and sex still persist as obstacles to equal employment opportunity. While the laws helped diminish overt discrimination, they have been less successful in eradicating inequalities in employment.

The concepts of institutional racism and sexism are useful tools to analyze systemic inequities that persist in American society. Institutional racism and sexism exist when societal norms of behavior operate to the disadvantage of women and racial minority groups in a variety of social, economic, and political institutions.[5] The question is how to change norms that accord privilege to a favored group. One answer is affirmative action.

Affirmative Action

Affirmative action is based on the principle that employment opportunities should be directed toward individuals on the basis of their membership in a disadvantaged group. An affirmative action plan or program seeks to change racial and sexual patterns in the American labor force. Intended to remedy the effects of discrimination, the heart of an affirmative action plan is found in its "goals and timetables" approach. Employers are expected to repair the statistical imbalance in the work force within a prescribed time by taking sex and race into account in their employment decisions. Advocates of affirmative action argue that all employers have an obligation to correct these imbalances whether they were responsible for the discrimination or whether it derived from the widespread effects of societal discrimination.

Controversy over affirmative action has arisen because the imposition of numerical goals for women and minorities goes beyond compensating victims for past discrimination; it seeks to reorder the structural imbalance of the work force. Attempting to bring the labor force into greater equilibrium, affirmative action plans allow individuals who have not been identified as victims of discrimination to benefit simply because they share group characteristics with the victim.

Advocates of affirmative action agree that color blindness, and its corollary sex blindness, are desirable as long-term goals. But they contend that because discrimination has prevented women and minorities from achieving a competitive position in the labor force, ignoring race and sex in the hiring or promotion process maintains the relative differences between whites and people of color and men and women.

For them, it is not enough merely to *remove* obstacles to equal opportunity. They believe employers have an affirmative obligation to ensure equal distribution of employment opportunities. Fulfilling this obligation, they say, requires a commitment to racial or sexual preferences until redistribution is achieved. They argue that effectively combating the entrenched patterns of occupational segregation requires numerical formulas — based on sex and race — for hiring and promotion and includes setting goals and timetables for completing the task.[6] Affirmative action advocates insist that victim-specific remedies are insufficient to deal with widespread racial and sexual disparity in the workplace.

In a nutshell, its supporters proclaim that affirmative action is a logical — and necessary — outgrowth of Title VII's ban on discrimination. Without affirmative action, they argue, the vestiges of discrimination will linger indefinitely.

Affirmative Action and the Executive Branch

The major players in affirmative action policy-making have been the federal courts and the executive branch, particularly the Department of Justice. Ironically, Congress, after lighting the affirmative action fuse by enacting Title VII and the 1972 Equal Employment Opportunity Act, has been remarkably silent. While much of the attention of civil rights activists is typically focused on the Congress and the courts, the executive branch has played a major role in combating discrimination. Executive orders (directives from the president to the bureaucracy) have become part of the arsenal against employment discrimination in two ways: first, by requiring equal opportunity for federal employees, and second, by ensuring equal opportunity for employees of businesses that contract with the federal government (federal contractors).[7]

The modern era of the federal government's attack on discrimination began in 1961 when President John Kennedy established the Committee on Equal Employment Opportunity. Then, on September 24, 1965, President Lyndon Johnson issued Executive Order (EO) 11246 prohibiting federal contractors from discriminating on the basis of race, religion, or national origin. The secretary of labor was charged with overseeing the ban on discrimination. A year later, the Department of Labor established the Office of Federal Contract Compliance (OFCC) to ensure compliance with EO 11246.

Executive Order 11246, "which in ensuing years would be referred to as the Executive Order . . . remains the basis of the federal government's contractual compliance program"[8] Although the Executive Order did not mention sex, it was amended in 1967 by Executive Order 11375 to include sex discrimination as a prohibited category.

The Office of Federal Contract Compliance — which became the Office of Federal Contract Compliance Programs (OFCCP) in 1975 — was authorized by the Executive Order to increase opportunities for minority employment. Going beyond its mandate, it required self-evaluation and reporting by employers and imposed goals and timetables to remedy minority underrepresentation.[9]

In 1968, the OFCC promulgated regulations ordering all federal contractors with fifty employees or more and contracts of at least $50,000 to produce written affirmative action plans. A year later, under what became known as the Philadelphia Plan, government contractors were required to employ "good faith efforts" to remedy past discrimination against skilled minority workers in the construction industry by setting goals and timetables for increasing minority hiring. When challenged as a violation of Title VII, the plan was upheld by the Third Circuit Court of Appeals.[10]

Affirmative Action and the Reagan Administration

Opponents of affirmative action claim that an affirmative action plan that hires or promotes on the basis of sex or race violates Title VII by discriminating against white males.[11] Additionally, they contend, affirmative action is antithetical to the widely held belief in the U.S. value of individualism, the notion that success is a reward for merit.[12] These and other arguments against affirmative action were vigorously advanced by officials of the Reagan administration throughout the 1980s.

The intensified controversy over affirmative action was precipitated in large part by the 1980 presidential election campaign. Shortly after Ronald Reagan took office in January 1981, he set about changing the executive branch's role in enforcing civil rights laws.

> Propelled by his personal conviction as much as by his perception of his election mandate, the president adopted policies designed to facilitate the change he and his advisers believed was needed and, in so doing, reversed many of the existing policies in a manner often described as 'turning back the clock' of civil rights enforcement.[13]

Proclaiming that intentional discrimination is the primary evil, the administration sought to cut back on disparate impact litigation with its emphasis on large groups and race-conscious remedies.[14] The major impetus for the changes in civil rights policy came from the Department of Justice. Title VII authorizes the Justice Department to file practice and pattern suits against public employers and to intervene in private litigation of "general public importance." With the department's key role in Title VII litigation, it had ample opportunity to advocate its position on civil rights policy, particularly on affirmative action.

The Reagan Justice Department argued that numerical hiring and promotion goals were unacceptable remedies for employment discrimination. The department took primary aim at the goals and timetables strategy that courts and executive agencies such as the Equal Employment Opportunity Commission (EEOC) and OFCCP had used for over a decade to monitor compliance with affirmative action plans. In briefs before the Supreme Court, the Justice Department urged the elimination of goals and timetables. Most of the major affirmative action cases during the Reagan era were accompanied by Justice Department briefs arguing against widespread race-conscious remedies and for limiting compensation to identified victims of discrimination.

In scholarly writings, in congressional testimony, and in appellate briefs to the judiciary, representatives of the Reagan Justice Department denounced affirmative action by labeling efforts to redress the racial and sexual imbalance in the work force as discrimination. Administration officials accused civil rights leaders, aided by academia, the media, and the courts, of distorting the principle of nondiscrimination.

Early in the Reagan administration, Assistant Attorney General William Bradford Reynolds testified before a House subcommittee that "the Justice Department will not urge or support in any case 'the use of quotas or any other numerical or statistical formulae designed to provide to non-victims of discrimination preferential treatment based on race, sex, national origin, or religion.'"[15] Later, writing in 1989, Reynolds warned that "negative preference had wormed its way into the policy of 'affirmative action' and threatened everything sacred to the American ideal of equality of opportunity."[16]

The dispute between the Reagan administration and the civil rights community centered around the administration's view that affirmative action constituted unlawful discrimination against white males. "The intent of the law [Title VII] is to insure that those who were victims are made whole," Reynolds said, it was not to permit "discriminat[ion] against those who were innocent victims."[17]

The administration argued that extending preferential treatment to racial or sexual groups to redress a statistical imbalance not of the employer's making was contrary to Title VII. Its opposition took on greater intensity as it insisted that even when employers were found guilty of prior discrimination, the remedy must be as narrow as possible and limited to those who could prove they personally suffered discrimination.

In 1984, the White House came closest to achieving judicial endorsement for its position that Title VII relief must be limited only to minority group members identified as victims of past discrimination. In *Firefighters Local Union #1784 v. Stotts,* decided that year, the Supreme Court reversed a lower federal court decree that ordered white Memphis firefighters to be laid off first to protect the jobs of African-Americans hired more recently under a court-approved affirmative action plan.[18]

The Reagan administration applauded the decision, interpreting it as support for its position against affirmative action plans not limited to victims of discrimination. Following *Stotts,* the Justice Department raised challenges to existing minority hiring plans in over fifty cities across the United States.[19] The sense of victory was short-lived. Two years later, in two 1986 cases, *Local 28 of the Sheet Metal Workers v. EEOC* and *Local Number 93 v. Cleveland,* the Court ruled that Title VII relief was not restricted to victims only.[20]

Reagan's civil rights posture was also reflected in EEOC policy. Following the lead of the Justice Department, EEOC chair Clarence Thomas expressed opposition to the goals and timetables approach. In testimony before the Subcommittee on Employment Opportunities of the House Committee on Education and Labor, in March 1986 Thomas reported EEOC "skepticism about the values of goals and timetables, relative to the value of other available remedies in providing equal employment opportunities and eradicating discrimination."[21] Subsequently, the acting general counsel instructed regional staff attorneys to exclude goals from settlement agreements with employers. Despite its antipathy to goals and timetables, the EEOC continued to require affirmative action plans from federal agencies that included numerical goals and timetables.[22]

The administration took further aim at administrative enforcement by seeking to revise the regulations enforcing Executive Order 11246. The proposed plan would have eased requirements for filing affirmative action plans with the OFCCP by eliminating the use of goals and timetables in such plans. This attempt to weaken the Executive Order led to conflict among members of the cabinet, with Secretary of Labor William Brock III opposed to the change and Attorney General Edwin Meese III arguing for it.[23] Although the existing regulations remained in force, the effectiveness of the OFCCP in monitoring compliance by federal contractors diminished sharply. Between 1981 and 1986, there were only two instances of federal funds being withheld from noncompliant companies.[24]

Changes in civil rights policy were also evident at the Civil Rights Commission, an independent agency created by the Civil Rights Act of 1957. The commission, an outspoken advocate of affirmative action policy before Reagan came into office, soon found itself on a collision course with the newly elected president.[25]

Utilizing his appointment powers, Reagan sought to mold the commission in his own image by naming Clarence Pendleton and Linda Chavez, opponents of affirmative action, as chair and staff director. Reagan also sought to impose his imprint on the commission by trying to fire most of its current members, a matter of questionable legality.

Eventually, the president and Congress worked out a compromise with the president naming four commissioners and the House and Senate majority and minority leaders appointing one each. When the dust settled, Reagan had a 5–3 majority in favor of his civil rights position and had effectively silenced the commission as an advocate for civil rights. "Because of bitter clashes among the appointees, the Commission since 1983 has been known more for its contentious nature than for its civil rights work."[26] Once known as the "duly appointed conscience of the government in regard to civil rights," during the Reagan administration the commission became an outspoken opponent of many of the goals of the civil rights community, particularly affirmative action.[27]

Finally, the president's power over judicial appointments gave him an opportunity to seat like-minded judges on the federal courts. By 1988, almost half the members of the federal bench were appointed by Reagan. He had named 78 of the 160 full-time appellate court judges and 292 of the 556 full-time district court judges.[28] With the appointment of Sandra Day O'Connor in 1982, Reagan had his first opportunity to place his imprimatur on the Supreme Court. Later appointments of Antonin Scalia and Anthony Kennedy and the elevation of William Rehnquist to chief justice made it more likely that the Reagan image of equal opportunity would prevail. Frequently joined by Byron White, the Reagan justices could look forward to increasing victories on the Court.

Affirmative Action Litigation

Title VII law developed as the result of employment discrimination suits brought by women and ethnic and racial minorities, primarily the latter. For the most part, employers were forbidden from considering race or sex as criteria for employment. Ironically, this put Title VII on a collision course with itself as court-ordered remedies for employment discrimination fostered a new round of suits by white males. Called affirmative action suits, these cases sorely tested the judiciary's ability to provide an even-handed interpretation of Title VII.

Affirmative action cases are typically brought to the federal courts by white males arguing that their employer's preferential treatment of women and minorities is illegal. The courts must determine whether the preferential treatment is a permissible remedy for past discrimination against women or minorities or whether it has transcended remedy into discrimination against white males.

In part, the court's decision depends on the origins of the preferential treatment plan. Affirmative action plans generally arise for three reasons: as a voluntary action by an employer to remedy discrimination; as a result of a consent decree (an agreement between parties arising out of a discrimination suit by a woman or minority-group member), or pursuant to a court order (following a judicial ruling at trial). In general, voluntary actions and consent decrees are more likely to be accepted under Title VII.

To complicate the law further, affirmative action cases may arise under Title VII and/or constitutional equal protection theory. Voluntary affirmative action plans of private employers are unique in that they are solely governed by Title VII. But both Title VII and the Constitution apply to voluntary preferential treatment plans adopted by public employers. Both may also apply to public and private employer plans imposed by judicial order or consent decree.[29]

Affirmative Action and the Supreme Court

With the exception of the 1987 case of *Johnson v. Transportation Agency of Santa Clara,* affirmative action cases were based on charges of racial discrimination in employment. Because *Johnson* alone focuses on preferential treatment for women, it makes sense to delve more deeply into the Court's opinion in this case. But before turning to *Johnson,* it is necessary to take a brief look at affirmative action case law.

Perhaps no other area of law has spawned as many diverse judicial viewpoints as affirmative action. In eight employment-related affirmative action cases (from 1979 to 1987), there have been thirty-five majority, concurring, or dissenting opinions, occupying over six hundred written pages.[30] Perhaps no other area of law has engendered as much division on the Court. With one exception, all the employment-related cases (from 1979 to 1989) have been decided by votes of 5–4 or 6–3; the exception was a 5–2 decision with two justices not participating.[31]

The Supreme Court entered the debate over affirmative action in 1978 in *Regents of the University of California v. Bakke.* In a highly fragmented plurality opinion, the Court announced that the University of California at Davis Medical School could not establish a separate admissions policy for racial minorities but that it could take race into account in its admissions decisions. Lewis Powell's opinion shed little light on the debate over university admissions policies and even less light on the struggle over affirmative action in employment.[32]

The Supreme Court has approved affirmative action plans as part of a judicial order to remedy past discrimination against minorities, and in general, it has rejected the Reagan administration argument that preferential treatment must be limited to identified victims of discrimination. The Court allows employers (both public and private) to voluntarily adopt affirmative action plans to redress societal discrimination—that is, an imbalance in the work force not of their making. But in other cases, it insists on evidence of past discrimination by the employer and stops short of approving preferential treatment by employers who have not been found guilty of past discrimination.

The confusion in affirmative action law is partly attributable to the Court's application of Title VII to some employment situations and of constitutional equal protection to others. In general, when Title VII is applied to an affirmative action plan, it is more likely to be upheld. And when the constitutional test—with its more exacting scrutiny—comes into play, the plan is less likely to be approved. The Court's acceptance of societal discrimination to justify affirmative action under Title VII but not under equal protection theory illustrates the dichotomy between the two kinds of legal analyses.

Despite inconsistencies, it is possible to isolate two major principles that have guided the justices in deciding most affirmative action cases: first, the burden placed on "innocent" parties (white males) must not be too onerous; second, there must be some evidence of past discrimination, or at least a significant imbalance in the employer's work force, to justify the preferential treatment.[33]

Balancing these considerations, the Supreme Court has permitted race-conscious recruitment in an apprenticeship training program.[34] It has approved preferential treatment in promotions.[35] It has upheld court-ordered quotas for minority union memberships.[36] It has accepted a federal public works set-aside program.[37] And, in the 1989–90 term, the Court upheld two Federal Communications Commission (FCC) preference programs that aided women and minorities in obtaining broadcast licenses.[38]

In limiting affirmative action remedies, the Court has refused to allow affirmative action plans that protect the jobs of minority employees at the expense of more senior white employees when layoffs are instituted.[39] And it rejected a plan by a municipal government to create a minority set-aside program in the absence of evidence of past discrimination by the city.[40] More recently, the Court ruled that white firefighters may challenge preferential promotion and hiring decisions made on the basis of a consent decree between the city and minority firefighters.[41]

An Affirmative Action Plan for Women

In *Johnson*, the first case in which the Court ruled on preferential treatment of women, Paul Johnson sued Santa Clara County for sex discrimination. An employee of the Transportation Agency, Johnson applied for a road dispatcher job and was passed over in favor of Diane Joyce, a female employee. Joyce, perhaps slightly less qualified than Johnson because of a lower score on her interview, got the job because the agency was following a voluntarily adopted affirmative action plan to increase the number of women in certain job categories.

In 1978, the agency responded to a scarcity of women and minorities in its work force by creating a plan with the "long-term goal" of achieving "a work force whose composition reflected the proportion of minorities and women in the area labor force."[42] No fixed percentage of women or minority workers was specified. But because women comprised about 36 percent of the area labor market, the agency hoped eventually to fill its roster with roughly the same proportion of female workers. At the time of the competition between Joyce and Johnson, women were severely underrepresented in professional and administrative positions, and in the 238 skilled-craft jobs, one of which was road dispatcher, there were *no* women at all.

When the road dispatcher position opened up in December 1979, twelve employees, including Johnson and Joyce, applied. Both had the necessary experience of road maintenance worker. Nine employees were interviewed, and seven scored above the required seventy points. Johnson was tied for second place with a score of seventy-five, Joyce came in next with a score of seventy-three. After a second round of interviews, Johnson was recommended to the director of the agency for the promotion. Both were ranked well-qualified for the job, and Joyce was recommended for the position by the agency's affirmative action coordinator. After deliberating over the appointment by "try[ing] to look at the whole picture," the head of the agency named Joyce for the job.[43]

Johnson sued, claiming that the agency's affirmative action plan violated Title VII. He won at the district court level. The Ninth Circuit Court of Appeals reversed, and the Supreme Court affirmed the appellate court.

The key to this decision, announced William Brennan, speaking for himself, Thurgood Marshall, Lewis Powell, John Paul Stevens, and Harry Blackmun, was to assess the agency's plan according to standards developed in *United States Steelworkers v. Weber. Weber,* said Brennan, "was grounded in the recognition that voluntary employer action can play a crucial role in furthering Title VII's purpose of eliminating the effects of discrimination in the workplace, and that Title VII should not be read to thwart such efforts."[44] It was not material to the Court's analysis of Title VII that *Weber* involved a private employer and *Johnson* a public employer.[45]

In *Weber,* a white male employee filed a Title VII race discrimination complaint against his employer, Kaiser Aluminum and Chemical Corporation of Louisiana. Kaiser had entered into a collective bargaining agreement with the Steelworkers Union in 1974 in which the company created training programs in three skilled-craft positions. The programs were open to all employees on the basis of seniority, but 50 percent of the openings were reserved for minority workers.

Kaiser's agreement with the union was voluntary. The company had never been found guilty of discrimination against black workers but it was motivated to enter into the agreement by the low percentage of blacks in its craft positions. Black employees at the plant comprised less than 2 percent of the skilled work force yet equalled 39 percent of the area labor force.

The scarcity of black employees was attributable to prior discrimination by the craft unions. Kaiser only hired workers with craft experience, and blacks did not have the experience required for the jobs. Afraid of a Title VII lawsuit from its black employees, Kaiser decided to institute a training program to make them eligible for its craft jobs.

Brian Weber, a white employee with six years' experience at the plant, was denied admittance into the training program despite higher seniority than two black workers admitted to it. He argued that the apprenticeship program violated section 703(j) of the Civil Rights Act, which stated that "nothing in this title shall be interpreted to require" preferential treatment on the basis of race, sex, or national origin.

In a 5–2 vote (with Powell and Stevens not participating), the Supreme Court rejected Weber's argument and held that Title VII allowed employers to create a preferential program "designed to break down old patterns of racial segregation."[46] Speaking for the majority, Brennan ruled that Congress intended Title VII to encourage voluntary action by private employers. He reasoned that while section 703(j) prohibits courts from requiring employers to create preferential hiring plans, it does not ban voluntary efforts.

Weber created a two-part test for voluntary affirmative action plans. First, the plan had to be justified by "manifest racial imbalances in traditionally segregated job categories."[47] Then, the plan must not "unnecessarily trammel the interests of the white employees." The latter would be determined by whether the plan was temporary, whether it led to "the discharge of white workers and their replacement with new black hirees," whether it created "an absolute bar to the advancement of white employees," and whether it was intended to "maintain racial balance" or designed as a short-term effort to "eliminate a manifest racial imbalance."[48]

Using *Weber* as the yardstick, Brennan found that the Santa Clara Agency had made a reasonable assessment that there was "manifest imbalance" in the work force. Because of its commitment to changing this imbalance, the agency could consider Joyce's sex in the promotion decision. There was no need, said Brennan, to find that the agency had been guilty of sex discrimination in the past.

The plan also conformed to the *Weber* standards because, as in *Weber,* it did not require men to be fired and replaced by women, it did not create an absolute obstacle to advancement by men, and it was only temporary. The Court therefore concluded that, like the Kaiser program, the Santa Clara plan did not unduly burden the white male employees. (Johnson became a road dispatcher when an opening appeared in 1983.)

In sum, Brennan stated, with its goal of gradually improving the sexual imbalance in the work force, the agency followed a "moderate, flexible" approach to affirmative action in which sex was a relevant factor in a promotion decision. The plan was "fully consistent with Title VII, for it embodie[d] the contribution that voluntary employer action can make in eliminating the vestiges of discrimination in the workplace."[49]

Scalia, joined by Rehnquist and White, dissented from the Court's decision and expressed displeasure at affirmative action policy. "We effectively replace the goal of a discrimination-free society with the quite incompatible goal of proportionate representation by race and by sex in the workplace." He accused the Court of "converting this [Title VII] from a guarantee that race or sex will *not* be the basis for employment determinations, to a guarantee that it often *will*."[50]

Scalia first expressed dismay that the majority was applying *Weber*, a private employer case, to a public employer, without acknowledging the leap of judicial logic. But recognizing that the language of Title VII does not distinguish between public and private employers, Scalia argued that rather than merely limiting *Weber* to private employers, the Court should instead overrule it. *Weber* should be abandoned, Scalia said, because it "rewrote the statute it purported to construe."[51] Contrary to congressional intent, it permitted employers to discriminate.

Scalia was most troubled by the far-reaching implications of the majority opinion. The Court allowed preferential treatment for women without a finding of past discrimination against the employer. Indeed, in his view, the situation at the agency did not even constitute societal discrimination against women. "The most significant proposition of law established by today's decision," he said, "is that racial or sexual discrimination is permitted under Title VII when it is intended to overcome the effect, not of the employer's own discrimination, but of societal attitudes that have limited the entry of certain races, or of a particular sex, into certain jobs."[52]

In *Weber*, Kaiser itself had not been guilty of past discrimination, but it was trying to redress the effects of "conscious, exclusionary discrimination" against African-American workers. Here, there was no evidence of discrimination against women. It was "absurd," Scalia said, to think that road crew positions were "traditionally segregated" because of "systematic" discrimination against women "eager to shoulder pick and shovel."[53] He insisted that women did not occupy the skilled-craft jobs because they viewed them as undesirable jobs.

Scalia predicted that as a result of this decision employers will be required to establish preferential treatment plans to protect themselves against lawsuits by minorities and women. He also predicted that men and white workers will be precluded from filing Title VII suits of their own when they are subject to discrimination. He concluded by pointing out that the Court's decision will be welcome to politicians pandering to organized interests and to employers seeking to hire less qualified workers for less pay. "The only losers in the process," he said, "are the Johnsons of the country, for whom Title VII has been not merely repealed but actually inverted."[54]

The Conflict Continues

The Reagan administration had entered office with a desire to alter the nation's approach to civil rights policy. Focusing primarily on administrative and judicial enforcement of the civil rights laws, the administration "pursued its agenda with a single-mindedness that perhaps was unequaled by any of its recent predecessors."[55]

In 1986, President Reagan reiterated his commitment to "a color-blind society. The ideal," he said, "will be when . . . nothing is done to or for anyone because of race differences or religion or ethnic origin."[56] Although the administration's views did not entirely prevail during Reagan's tenure in office, they began to find favor on the Supreme Court, especially during his second term in office.

The focus of the debate surrounding affirmative action on the Supreme Court has been the extent to which racial and sexual preferences can be used to remedy imbalances in the work force caused by societal discrimination, such as exclusion from craft unions, job-training programs, or educational benefits, rather than the employer's own discriminatory actions.[57] Opponents of affirmative action on the Court, such as Scalia, Kennedy, Rehnquist and, increasingly, White, argue that Title VII and the Constitution foreclose race- or sex-conscious treatment to cure societal discrimination.

Among those who find affirmative action palatable, two positions have emerged. The more far-reaching view of affirmative action, posited by Brennan, Marshall, Stevens, and Blackmun, holds that even employers innocent of past discrimination themselves can remedy statistical imbalances *resulting from societal discrimination* with preferential treatment plans. A more limited view of affirmative action, typically put forward by O'Connor, is that employers can create narrowly tailored preferential treatment plans when necessary to cure past acts of discrimination.

The Supreme Court's 1988–1989 term brought accusations of surrender to anti–civil rights forces from members of the civil rights community. The civil rights cases decided this term suggested that a new majority was emerging, and civil rights advocates feared this coalition would dismantle the structure of rights erected over the years. Their fears were not illusory. The divisions on the Court reflected society's discomfort with affirmative action, and the conflict was forcing a reexamination of the nation's commitment to equal opportunity.

NOTES

1. *Albemarle Paper Company v. Moody,* 422 U.S. 405, 418 (1975).
2. The phrase *color-blind* arose in Justice John Marshall Harlan's dissenting opinion in *Plessy v. Ferguson,* 163 U.S. 537 (1896). Harlan argued that the Constitution forbids racial classifications because it is color-blind.

3. Francine D. Blau and Marianne A. Ferber, "Occupations and Earnings of Women Workers," in Karen Shallcross Koziara, Michael H. Moskow, and Lucretia Dewey Tanner, eds., *Working Women: Past, Present, Future* (Washington, DC: Bureau of National Affairs, 1987); Ray Marshall and Beth Paulin, "Employment and Earnings of Women: Historical Perspective," in Karen Shallcross Koziara, Michael H. Moskow, and Lucretia Dewey Tanner, eds., *Working Women: Past, Present, Future* (Washington, DC: Bureau of National Affairs, 1987).

4. Jennifer L. Hochschild, "Race, Class, Power, and Equal Opportunity," in Norman E. Bowie, ed., *Equal Opportunity* (Boulder: Westview Press, 1988).

5. Joe E. Feagin and Clairece Booher Feagin, "Theories of Discrimination," in Paula Rothenberg, ed., *Racism and Sexism: An Integrated Study* (New York: St. Martin's Press, 1988). The concept of institutional racism was first identified in Charles Hamilton and Stokeley Carmichael, *Black Power* (New York: Random House, 1967). See also Louis L. Knowles and Kenneth Prewitt, eds., *Institutional Racism in America* (Englewood Cliffs: Prentice-Hall, 1969).

6. See Drew S. Days III, "The Courts' Response to the Reagan Civil Rights Agenda," *Vanderbilt Law Review* 42(1989).

7. See Norman Amaker, *Civil Rights and the Reagan Administration* (Washington, DC: Urban Institute Press, 1988), chapter 6.

8. Amaker, *Civil Rights and the Reagan Administration,* p. 20.

9. Gary Bryner, "Congress, Courts, and Agencies: Equal Employment and the Limits of Policy Implementation," *Political Science Quarterly* 96(1981), p. 419.

10. James E. Jones, Jr., "The Origins of Affirmative Action," *University of California, Davis Law Review* 21(1988), p. 401.

11. See Eleanor Holmes Norton, "Equal Employment Law: Crisis in Interpretation—Survival against the Odds," *Tulane Law Review* 62(1988); Days, "The Courts' Response to the Reagan Civil Rights Agenda"; Jones, "The Origins of Affirmative Action."

12. Andrea Giampetro and Nancy Kubasek, "Individualism in America and Its Implications for Affirmative Action," *Journal of Contemporary Law* 14(1988).

13. Amaker, *Civil Rights and the Reagan Administration,* p. 3.

14. Days, "The Courts' Response to the Reagan Civil Rights Agenda," p. 1008.

15. Amaker, *Civil Rights and the Reagan Administration,* p. 124.

16. William Bradford Reynolds, "The Reagan Administration's Civil Rights Policy: The Challenge for the Future," *Vanderbilt Law Review* 42(1989), p. 995.

17. *New York Times,* February 26, 1986.

18. *Firefighters Local Union #1784 v. Stotts,* 467 U.S. 561 (1984).

19. Norton, "Equal Employment Law," p. 703 n. 93.

20. *Local 28 of the Sheet Metal Workers v. EEOC,* 478 U.S. 421 (1986); *Local Number 93 v. Cleveland,* 478 U.S. 501 (1986).

21. *Equal Employment Opportunity Commission Policies regarding Goals and Timetables in Litigation Remedies: Hearings before the Subcommittee on Employment Opportunities of the House Committee on Education and Labor,* 99th Cong., 2d Sess. (1986), p. 25.

22. United States Commission on Civil Rights, *Federal Enforcement of Equal Employment Requirements,* Clearinghouse Publication, July 1987, pp. 21–22.

23. *Congressional Quarterly,* February 15, 1986, p. 315.

24. *Washington Post National Weekly Edition,* January 27, 1986, p. 29.

25. Amaker, *Civil Rights and the Reagan Administration,* Appendix A.

26. *Congressional Quarterly,* November 18, 1989, p. 3168.

27. Amaker, *Civil Rights and the Reagan Administration,* p. 167.

28. *Congressional Quarterly,* November 26, 1988, p. 3392.

29. George Rutherglen and Daniel R. Ortiz, "Affirmative Action under the Constitution and Title VII: From Confusion to Convergence," *UCLA Law Review* 35(1988), pp. 469–70.

30. Maureen E. Lally-Green, "Affirmative Action: Are the Equal Protection and Title VII Tests Synonymous?," *Duquesne Law Review* 26(1987), pp. 295–96.

31. See *Congressional Quarterly,* November 15, 1986, p. 2899 for votes in cases through 1986; information on the later decisions was obtained from analysis of the cases.

32. *Regents of the University of California v. Bakke,* 438 U.S. 265 (1978). The *Bakke* opinion is long and complex, with Powell joining Burger, Stewart, Rehnquist, and Stevens in striking down a separate minority admissions policy and ordering Allen Bakke admitted into the medical school. Powell also joined Brennan, Marshall, White, and Blackmun in ruling

that race may be taken into account as *one* of the factors of admission. Powell also pro-claimed that racial classifications, even benign ones established to improve the status of minority group members, should be analyzed under strict scrutiny rather than the interme-diate scrutiny urged by Brennan. This position was adopted by a majority of the Court about ten years later.

33. Rutherglen and Ortiz, "Affirmative Action under the Constitution and Title VII," pp. 468–71.

34. In *United Steelworkers of America v. Weber,* 443 U.S. 193 (1979), its first affirmative action employment case, the Supreme Court ruled that private employers may voluntarily adopt affirmative action plans to correct past discrimination in their labor forces even though they were not found guilty of past discrimination. The Carter Justice Department supported the company's position that its affirmative action plan was permitted under Title VII because it conformed with congressional intent of the 1964 Civil Rights Act.

35. In *Local Number 93,* 478 U.S. at 501, the Court ruled that under Title VII a city may enter into a settlement agreement to use race-conscious promotions even though the courts may not have ordered the employer to create the preferential system. Cleveland entered into a consent decree to settle a racial discrimination suit brought by African-American and His-panic firefighters. The city of Cleveland had admitted a long history of racial discrimination in the past.

The agreement included a provision with specific goals that required the fire depart-ment to promote minority firefighters as a remedy for past discrimination. In a 6–3 decision, the Court upheld the promotion policy, saying that lower court judges have broad discretion to approve settlement agreements in which the city establishes a preferential treatment plan to hire or promote members of minority groups. As in *Local 28,* 478 U.S. at 421, the Court made it clear that relief was not limited to specific victims of discrimination.

In *United States v. Paradise,* 480 U.S. 149 (1987), the Court approved a court-ordered racial quota in the Alabama State Police. In a 5–4 vote, the Court let stand a lower court ruling that the state police must promote one black for every white promoted until blacks make up 25 percent of all officers above the rank of trooper. *Paradise* was decided under equal protection with the Court ruling that there was a compelling state interest in a one-for-one promotion policy because of the need to remedy the "egregious" discrimination commit-ted by the state.

Relying on *Weber,* in *Johnson v. Transportation Agency,* 480 U.S. 616 (1987), the Court ruled that public employers may voluntarily implement affirmative action promotions plans to correct "manifest imbalances" in the work force.

36. In *Local 28,* 478 U.S. at 421, in a 5–4 decision, the Court let stand a court-ordered affirmative action plan in which a local union was ordered to meet a 29 percent minority membership goal to remedy racial discrimination. After more than a decade, and several court decisions, the Supreme Court was asked to decide whether the lower court had the authority to order the numerical goal (and also to impose fines in a contempt citation against the union). The Court based its opinion on the Union's "longstanding [and] egregious discrimination." The opinion stressed that Title VII did not mandate that preferential relief be limited to specific victims of discrimination.

37. In *Fullilove v. Klutznick,* 448 U.S. 448 (1980), in a 6–3 vote the Supreme Court upheld a set-aside program that the federal government established to reserve 10 percent of federal construction grants for minority business enterprises. The Court held that Congress had adequate authority to use race-conscious remedies to redress patterns of racial discrimi-nation in the construction industry with a narrowly tailored program.

38. In *Metro Broadcasting v. FCC,* 110 S.Ct. 2997 (1990), in a 5–4 decision the Supreme Court relied on its 1980 ruling in *Fullilove* to allow Congress to endorse affirmative action programs at federal agencies. The FCC adopted the affirmative action policies to promote diversification of programming. Citing *Fullilove,* the Court said that it owes deference to congressional judgment. Thus, because the FCC policy was approved by Congress, the Court declined to use strict scrutiny saying that Congress has the authority to create benign race-conscious measures—even if they are not designed to remedy past discrimination. Using intermediate scrutiny, the Court found that the FCC program does not violate the equal protection clause because it served an important government objective and was substantially related to achieving the government's interest in broadcast diversity.

39. In *Stotts,* 467 U.S. at 561, the Supreme Court held that a valid seniority system protects the jobs of white workers even at the expense of newly hired minority workers who will be laid off. The city of Detroit and minority firefighters entered into a consent decree that included a commitment by the city to increase minority hiring and promotion but did not mention layoffs. When the city began to lay off firefighters in response to a budget crisis, the layoffs were conducted under the traditional last-hired, first-fired rule of seniority.

The lower courts enjoined layoffs that would decrease the percentage of African-Americans in the department. In a 6–3 decision, the Supreme Court reversed, holding that affirmative action must give way to a valid seniority system, even though the racial composition of the work force would revert to the pre–affirmative action time. The district court could not grant retroactive seniority to African-American employees because there was no finding that any of the African-American employees protected from layoffs had been victims of discrimination.

In *Wygant v. Jackson Board of Education,* 476 U.S. 267 (1986), pursuant to an agreement between the Board of Education and the teachers' union, the board laid off nonminority teachers with more seniority than minority teachers. In a 5–4 vote, using strict scrutiny the Court found that the board did not have a compelling interest in preserving the jobs of the black employees. The Board had argued that it had a compelling interest in remedying societal discrimination by providing role models for minority youngsters.

Although *Stotts* was a Title VII case and *Wygant* an equal protection case, the Court ruled against the affirmative action layoffs in both cases. The common denominator of the cases was the seniority enjoyed by the white employees; the Court was unwilling to accept affirmative action plans that undercut seniority rights.

40. In *Richmond v. J. A. Croson,* 109 S.Ct. 706 (1989), the issue was an ordinance adopted by Richmond, Virginia, in 1983 requiring that 30 percent of its public works contracts be awarded to minority-owned companies. The ordinance was adopted by the Richmond City Council to combat what it considered long-standing pervasive discrimination in the construction industry. The council cited evidence that although African-Americans and other minorities comprise half the city's population, less than 1 percent of the $124 million in construction contracts were awarded to minority-owned businesses in the previous five years.

In 1987, the J. A. Croson Company brought suit, claiming the ordinance was unconstitutional. The Supreme Court agreed in part because there was no proof that the city had engaged in past discrimination against minority contractors. Using strict scrutiny, O'Connor's opinion stressed that before a government can impose a racial preference, there must be evidence of specific acts of discrimination either by the municipality itself or by others and passively accepted by the municipality. Voluntary efforts to remedy societal discrimination are constitutionally unacceptable. If there is evidence of past discrimination, a racial remedy must be "narrowly tailored," that is, it is not permitted unless there is no alternative race-neutral remedy available. This decision did not affect the Court's *Fullilove* decision of 1980 because that program was allowed under Congress's Fourteenth Amendment power.

Croson, decided by a 6–3 vote, was the first case in which a majority of the Court agreed to apply strict scrutiny to benign racial classifications.

41. In *Martin v. Wilks,* 109 S.Ct. 2180 (1989), a group of white firefighters filed suit against an eight-year-old consent decree negotiated by the city of Birmingham, the federal government, and black firefighters. The suits against the city leading to the consent decree were filed in the early 1970s. As in *Paradise,* the city had agreed to a one-for-one promotion policy with a black firefighter promoted for every white. The white firefighters charged that the hiring decisions violated their rights under Title VII and the Constitution.

In a 5–4 decision, largely based upon an analysis of the Federal Rules of Civil Procedure, the Court ruled that the plaintiffs were not bound by a consent decree to which they had not been a party. Under the proposed 1990 Civil Rights Act, a consent decree would have been final as long as all potentially affected individuals were notified that it was being negotiated.

42. *Johnson,* 480 U.S. at 621–22.

43. *Johnson,* 480 U.S. at 625.

44. *Johnson,* 480 U.S. at 630.

45. *Johnson* was decided under Title VII because the parties had inexplicably failed to raise the constitutional issue.

46. *Weber,* 443 U.S. at 208.

47. *Weber,* 443 U.S. at 197.

48. *Weber,* 443 U.S. at 208.

49. *Johnson,* 480 U.S. at 642.

50. *Johnson,* 480 U.S. at 658 (Scalia, J., dissenting) (emphasis in the original).

51. *Johnson,* 480 U.S. at 670 (Scalia, J., dissenting).

52. *Johnson,* 480 U.S. at 664 (Scalia, J., dissenting).

53. *Johnson,* 480 U.S. at 668 (Scalia, J., dissenting).

54. *Johnson,* 480 U.S. at 677 (Scalia, J., dissenting).

55. Days, "The Courts' Response to the Reagan Civil Rights Agenda," p. 1010.

56. *Congressional Quarterly,* February 15, 1986, p. 315.

57. Note, "Finding a 'Manifest Imbalance': The Case for a Unified Statistical Test for Voluntary Affirmative Action under Title VII," *Michigan Law Review* 87(1989), p. 1989 n. 13.

5

Wage Discrimination: From Equal Pay to Comparable Worth

Passage of the 1963 Equal Pay Act (EPA), an act requiring employers to pay men and women performing equal work an equal salary, "marked the entrance of the federal government into the field of safeguarding the right of women to hold employment on the same basis as men."[1] Prior to 1963, there was no federal ban on sex discrimination in employment.

This history of equal pay legislation in the United States dates back to the early part of the twentieth century when Michigan, Montana, and Texas adopted equal pay laws in 1919. The issue drew national attention during World War II when the National War Labor Board required employers to pay equal wages for comparable work.

Bills requiring equal pay for comparable work were unsuccessfully introduced in Congress as early as 1945. By the 1960s, increased urgency for an equal pay bill mounted. The drive for equal pay legislation was spearheaded by Esther Peterson, head of the Department of Labor's Women's Bureau. In 1963, Congress approved the Equal Pay Act; it was signed into law by President John Kennedy on June 10, 1963, and went into effect a year later on June 11, 1964.

The 1963 act was a compromise bill limited to requiring equal pay for equal work. During House debate over the bill, members of Congress objected to the phrase "equal pay for comparable work" as too far-reaching, even though virtually all state laws at the time applied the equal pay standard to comparable jobs. Supporters of the "equal pay for comparable work" language feared that an "equal work" standard would be restricted to "identical" work and minor differences between jobs could be used to defeat the act.

Seeking to expedite passage of the bill, Republican Representative Katherine St. George of New York offered an amendment to substitute the phrase "equal pay for equal work" for the proposed "equal pay for comparable work." Her amendment passed in a 138–104 vote. Congress's retreat from comparable work to equal work would have lasting legal and economic implications for female workers.[2]

Equal Pay Act Enforcement

The Equal Pay Act, giving rise to the slogan "equal pay for equal work," prohibits employers from discriminating

> between employees on the basis of sex by paying wages to employees . . . at a rate less than the rate at which he pays employees of the opposite sex . . . for equal work on jobs, the performance of which requires equal skill, effort, and responsibility, and which are performed under similar working conditions, except where such payment is made pursuant to (i) a seniority system; (ii) a merit system; (iii) a system which measures earnings by quantity or quality of production; or (iv) a differential based on any other factor other than sex: *Provided*, That an employer who is paying a wage rate differential in violation of this subsection shall not, in order to comply with the provisions of this subsection, reduce the wage rate of any employee.[3]

The EPA was passed as an amendment to the Fair Labor Standards Act (FLSA), which at the time of passage covered approximately 27,500,000 employees.[4] Originally restricted to workers covered by the FLSA, with the passage of the 1972 Education Amendments the EPA applied to executive, administrative, and professional employees. Subsequent passage of the Fair Labor Standards Amendments of 1974 extended equal pay protection to federal, state, and municipal workers.[5]

While the Equal Pay Act permitted women to file lawsuits on their own, the secretary of labor assumed most of the responsibility for enforcing the provisions of the act. In 1978, President Jimmy Carter's Civil Rights Reorganization Plan transferred enforcement authority to the Equal Employment Opportunity Commission (EEOC), and the EEOC assumed the responsibility for bringing EPA cases.

To win an Equal Pay Act suit, plaintiffs must show that employees of the other sex are being paid higher wages for equal work. Although the act applies to either sex, the vast majority of suits are brought by, or on behalf of, women. Because the act was intended to remedy deep-seated wage disparities between men and women, the courts have only required plaintiffs to show that the skill, effort, responsibility, and working conditions of the jobs are "substantially equal"; the jobs must be more than similar but not identical.

Once plaintiffs meet the "substantially equal" test, the employer has an opportunity to show that the wage difference is based on one of the four reasons specified in the statute. Based on the exceptions authorized under the act, if the employer convinces the court that the wage differences are based on a merit system, a seniority system, a difference in productivity, or "a factor other than sex," the plaintiffs lose. Plaintiffs initially bear the burden of proof in showing that men and women are paid differently for equal work. The burden then shifts to the employer to prove that the differential is justified by one of the four exceptions permitted by the act.[6]

Substantially Equal Jobs

Schultz v. Wheaton Glass Company, 1970, was the first Equal Pay Act case decided by an appellate court. In holding that jobs meriting equal pay need not be "identical," but only "substantially equal," the Third Circuit paved the way for other circuits to construe the EPA, as it did, "as a broad charter of women's rights in the economic field." In the circuit court's view, Congress intended the act to "overcome the age-old belief in women's inferiority and to eliminate the depressing effects on living standards of reduced wages for female workers and the economic and social consequences which flow from it."[7] *Wheaton Glass* also demonstrated that courts must examine the duties performed by the male and female workers, rather than simply rely on company job descriptions in determining whether men should be paid a higher salary.

The Wheaton Glass Company plant in New Jersey made glass containers to special order and required visual inspection of the finished product. The plant's bottle inspection department hired selector-packers who selected the glass products as they came from the ovens and sent them to the next department for further inspection. The department also employed "snap-up boys" who cleaned the area, moved crates, and performed other unskilled work. Before 1956, only men were hired as selector-packers. After 1965, because of a shortage of men, women were hired as selector-packers, with a company rule restricting them from lifting anything over thirty-five pounds.

At the time of the trial, Wheaton paid its male selector-packers $2.35 an hour and its female selector-packers $2.14 an hour; "snap-up boys" were paid $2.16 an hour. The company argued that even though the inspecting work was equal, because men also moved and stacked boxes and crates and cleaned the work area, the jobs did not fall within the EPA's requirement of "equal work."

The company argued that there was no EPA violation, even if the jobs were equal, because the wage difference was based on a "factor other than sex." Because it was necessary to shut the ovens down between special-order jobs, the female selector-packers were sent to another inspection and packing area. Although men were sent there as well, some were assigned to do the "snap-up boy" jobs during the hiatus. The lower court ruled in favor of Wheaton Glass, finding that men merited higher wages because their greater flexibility in work assignments benefited the company.

Reversing the court below, the Third Circuit held that Wheaton Glass's payment scheme was motivated by a desire to "keep women in a subordinate role rather than to confer flexibility on the company."[8] The court pointed out that it was irrational to pay men 21½ cents an hour more for occasionally performing extra work — essentially unskilled labor — that paid only 2 cents more than the women's hourly wage. The court did not rule out the possibility that an economic benefit could justify a pay differential but, it said, in this case, the company did not show that the economic benefit was worth a 10 percent wage differential. Moreover, said the court, there was no reason why women could not also work as "snap-up boys" and thereby increase their value to the company.

Equal Skill, Effort, and Responsibility

Later that year, in *Hodgson v. Brookhaven General Hospital*, the Fifth Circuit carefully examined the hospital's claim that its male orderlies were entitled to higher salaries than its female aides because the orderlies' jobs involved greater "skill, effort, and responsibility." The court outlined a test for assessing whether an employer's wage policy violates the Equal Pay Act.

Conceding that orderlies and aides were at the same level of skill, effort, and responsibility in their primary jobs, the hospital argued that orderlies frequently performed additional tasks requiring greater skill, effort, and responsibility, while the aides rarely did. Moreover, orderlies were assigned to handle intimate jobs that male patients preferred to have men do. The trial court judge found, and the appellate court concurred, that the levels of skill and responsibility between the aides and orderlies were substantially equal and the decisive issue was whether there was a difference in effort.

The circuit court explained that a difference in pay between jobs with overlapping duties is only justified if one job demands extra effort for a "significant amount" of time from all those performing the job and provides economic value to the employer in line with the pay difference. "Employers," the court continued, "may not be permitted to frustrate the purposes of the [Equal Pay] Act by calling for extra effort only occasionally, or only from one or two male employees."[9]

The hospital argued that while orderlies and aides were responsible for approximately the same number of patients, orderlies were more frequently required to perform the nonroutine patient-care chores. When finished with their extra tasks, the orderlies have to complete their regular duties. Because of their extra effort, they deserve higher pay. Since the trial judge made no findings of fact on this crucial issue, the appellate court did not have the information necessary to rule on Brookhaven's defense.

On remand, the trial court ruled against the hospital once more and ordered it to give the aides back pay and raise their salaries to match the orderlies' wages.[10]

Factor Other Than Sex

In *Hodgson v. Robert Hall Clothes*, 1973, the Third Circuit disappointed EPA plaintiffs by broadly defining the catchall defense, "factor other than sex." This ambiguously phrased exception to the Equal Pay Act has been the subject of more litigation than the other three combined.[11]

The case began when the secretary of labor filed a suit against Robert Hall, a clothing store in Wilmington, Delaware, for paying its saleswomen less than its salesmen.[12] Women were restricted to selling women's clothes and men to men's clothes. Because the men's clothes were of a higher quality and price, the department yielded more sales dollars and a greater profit.

After a trial in 1970, the district court found that the sex segregation was based on a valid business reason (physical intimacy between sales staff and customers). It also found that men and women at Robert Hall performed equal work. Nevertheless, the court ruled in the company's favor, accepting its argument that the higher profitability of the men's department justified higher wages to employees within that department.

On appeal, the secretary argued that the "factor other than sex" phrase should not be construed as an open-ended invitation for pay disparity but should be limited to factors "related to job performance or . . . typically used in setting wage scales."[13] The company contended that a legitimate business reason is a valid "factor other than sex." Because the men's department was more profitable, Robert Hall claimed it was entitled to pay employees who sold men's clothes more than employees who sold women's clothes.

The appellate court agreed that a difference in "economic benefits" to the employer can justify wage differences between the sexes, and thus Robert Hall can reward employees who earn more money by paying them a higher salary. Moreover, the court allowed the store to base its wage policy on the average earnings of the department as a whole; it was not forced to show a relationship between wages and individual job performances.

The Third Circuit's broad interpretation of the "factor other than sex" exception in *Robert Hall* is at odds with the remedial purpose of the Equal Pay Act. The legislative history of the act shows that Congress intended to allow employers to base wage differentials on job requirements or job performance measures only. In allowing the unequal pay policy to stand, despite the lower court's finding that women and men performed equal work for the company, the appellate court was undermining the effectiveness of the act and perpetuating the sex-based wage differences the act was designed to eliminate.[14]

The appellate court also ignored the fact that Robert Hall organized its labor force so that men provided a greater economic benefit to the company. The evidence in the case showed that the man's department generated more income because it sold more expensive merchandise. Because women were restricted to the less profitable women's clothing department, their work would always provide less economic benefit to the employer. The court was allowing the store to justify its sex-based wage policy on the basis of its own decision to segregate employees by sex.

The Supreme Court Rules on Equal Pay

In *Corning Glass Works v. Brennan*, 1974, the first Equal Pay case to reach the Supreme Court, the Court was asked to determine whether men who worked the night shift could be paid more than women who worked on the day shift because the working conditions were not similar. In a 5–3 decision, with Thurgood Marshall, William Douglas, William Brennan, Byron White, and Lewis Powell in the majority, and Warren Burger, Harry Blackmun, and William Rehnquist dissenting, the Court ruled that the men and women at Corning performed equal work and merited equal pay.[15]

Before 1925, only women inspected the finished glass products at the plant. Then, when it created a nighttime inspection shift, Corning hired men because women were barred from night work by New York State law. The new inspectors, men who transferred from higher paying jobs within the plant, were paid more than the women daytime inspectors even though the work was the same.

Aside from the inspecting jobs, there were no wage differences between nighttime and daytime workers until 1944, when the company established such a pay differential. The male inspectors, working at night, were able to add this extra increase to their already existing higher salary. In 1966, Corning allowed women to work at night and to compete for the higher paying night inspection jobs. Three years later, in 1969, the plant eliminated the day-night pay differential for inspectors hired after that year; male nighttime inspectors hired before 1969 continued to receive a higher wage that perpetuated the day-night wage distinction.

Speaking for the Court, Marshall explained that the EPA prohibits pay disparity for equal work in jobs performed under similar working conditions. Corning's own job evaluation scheme indicated that working conditions differed by "surroundings" and "hazards," not by time of day. He ruled that Corning's differential pay for male nighttime and female daytime inspectors violated the Equal Pay Act, and that simply allowing women to become nighttime inspectors when openings occurred was not an adequate remedy as long as men continued to receive higher wages than women for doing the same job. He concluded that Corning could only cure the violation by "equalizing the base wages of female day inspectors with the higher rates paid the night inspectors."[16]

Inadequacy of the Equal Pay Act

In 1963, women earned sixty cents for every dollar men earned. Twenty-three years after passage of the Equal Pay Act, women were earning sixty-four cents for every dollar men earned.[17] And a study by the Rand Corporation predicts that by the year 2000, women would earn only seventy-four cents for every dollar men earn.[18]

Although women won millions of dollars in increased wages in EPA suits, the act's equal work requirement has meant that it can "contribute only modestly to closing the salary gap."[19] The EPA has not been able to solve the problem of the earnings disparity between the sexes because it can only be used in situations in which men and women work at substantially equal jobs. And most women in the United States work in sex-segregated occupations—that is, occupations predominantly held by members of one sex.

Sex Segregation

The pervasiveness of sex segregation in the work force is illustrated by the fact that, in the early 1980s, over half the women employed held clerical or service jobs. U.S. Labor Department statistics show that, as late as 1988, over 99 percent of all secretaries were women as were almost 95 percent of registered nurses and 99 percent of dental assistants.[20] The challenge for women was to fight for equal pay in a sex-segregated work force while staying within the bounds of acceptable legal theory. In the 1980s, this strategy became known as the fight for comparable worth or pay equity.

The struggle for comparable worth became part of the ideological battle over women's rights in the 1980s. Reflecting the Reagan administration's opposition, during the 1984 presidential election campaign a member of Reagan's Council of Economic Advisors, William Niskanen, called comparable worth a "truly crazy proposal." After the election, the head of the Civil Rights Commission, Clarence Pendleton, referred to comparable worth as the "looniest idea since Looney Tunes came on the screen."[21] Writing in 1986, Assistant Attorney General William Bradford Reynolds charged that comparable worth advocates have "revolutionary" aims to bring about a "redistribution of wages and salaries in this country along preconceived notions of a properly ordered society."[22]

The controversy over comparable worth often centers on the extent to which discrimination causes the discrepancies between male and female earnings. After analyzing the debate over the role of labor market discrimination, Henry Aaron and Cameran Lougy concluded that they "support the commonsense notion that women have suffered extensive and damaging discrimination in the labor market."[23] In their study of comparable worth, Joseph and Timothy Loudon agree that "the higher wages paid to tree trimmers (a male-dominated job category) as compared to nurses (a female-dominated job category) is the result of a discriminatory compensation system that simply perpetuates historical discrimination."[24]

A 1985 report issued by the Civil Rights Commission reached the opposite conclusion. According to the commission, the wage gap between men and women "result[ed], at least in significant part from a variety of things having nothing to do with discrimination by employers." The report identified three reasons for women's lower paying jobs: lower job expectations, educational choices leading to jobs that can accommodate their childbearing and child-rearing functions, and interrupted labor force participation.[25]

Similarly, Reynolds contended that "comparable worth has very little to do with gender-based discrimination and even less to do with pay equity."[26] He echoed the commission's findings that the wage gap between men and women can be attributed to women choosing to accommodate their family responsibilities with their work. Their desire to combine family and work responsibilities causes women to enter the job market later than men, take time out for raising children, work part-time, and refuse to work overtime. Reynolds defined discrimination as deliberate exclusion from male-dominated occupations or unequal compensation for the same job. In his view, the Equal Pay Act and Title VII are sufficient to combat it.

The commission's findings are contradicted by studies showing that the concentration of women in female-dominated occupations is not explained by their family obligations. Neither parental nor marital status, race, nor age affects the likelihood of women occupying jobs outside traditional sex-role occupations. By claiming that women lack interest in higher-paid male-dominated occupations and prefer lower-paid female-dominated jobs, policy-makers conveniently ascribe the blame to women themselves. But "contrary to conventional wisdom, sex segregation does not persist because women's commitment to the family leads them to 'choose' to consign themselves to lower-paid, female dominated occupations."[27] Blaming women for sex segregation denies that labor market forces, particularly discrimination, affect women's job status.

Comparable Worth

Comparable worth policy is intended to bypass the equal work requirements of the Equal Pay Act. It is based on the premise that men and women working in jobs of comparable skill, effort, responsibility, and conditions merit comparable pay. Relying on the assumption that the value of a job can be objectively measured, implementation of a pay equity policy requires a detailed evaluation of jobs within a company or organization.[28] Following the evaluation, every job classification is given an overall score based on factors such as responsibilities, skills, and working conditions. In this way, different jobs such as secretary and truck driver, nurse and physical-plant worker, are evaluated and compared.

Comparable worth advocates contend that because job classifications with equal scores have equal value to the employer, they should claim the same wage—seniority and merit being equal. According to Barbara Nelson and Sara Evans, comparable worth policy is needed to attain equity between male and female wages because

> a large number of studies have shown that if two job classifications have the same value according to the job evaluation system, but one is held primarily (i.e. 80% or more) by men and the other held primarily (i.e. 70% or more) by women, the job held by men usually pays more.[29]

Opponents of comparable worth theory reject it, arguing that employers do not base salary decisions solely upon job classification scores. Rather, they say, salaries are determined in large part by an assessment of the demand for, and supply of, the type of labor needed. Relying on prevailing market rates, they contend, is a neutral, nondiscriminatory wage mechanism based on supply and demand.[30]

Comparable worth proponents claim that sex segregation in the work force is one of the primary reasons for the salary gap between men and women.[31] They argue that women are channeled into a small number of low-paying and low-prestige job categories. Economist Ruth Blumrosen maintains that the pay differential between the sexes arises because occupations in which women predominate are undervalued. She asserts that

> wherever there is job segregation, the same forces which determine that certain jobs or job categories will be reserved for women or minorities also and simultaneously determine that the economic value of those jobs is less than if they were 'white' or 'male' jobs.[32]

The courts' reluctance to find merit in comparable worth claims arises from their unwillingness to interfere with the principle of market-set rates that they perceive as natural and nondiscriminatory. Comparable worth plaintiffs lose because courts have ruled that market conditions, such as the supply of available workers, the wages workers can command from other employers, and the rate of unionization of workers, are nondiscriminatory. Believing that employers did not create the sex disparity in market wage rates, the courts refuse to require them to eliminate wage disparities not of their making.

Pay Equity and Title VII

Because of the limitations of the EPA, women claiming sex-based wage discrimination were forced to sue under Title VII, with the battle cry changing from "equal pay for equal work" to "equal pay for jobs of comparable worth."

Title VII did not easily lend itself to wage discrimination claims because some courts interpreted it to require plaintiffs to satisfy the equal work standard in their Title VII action. In *County of Washington v. Gunther*, 1986, the Supreme Court removed a major hurdle to Title VII wage disparity suits: section 703(h) of the 1964 Civil Rights Act, the Bennett amendment. Section 703(h), a hastily enacted provision of Title VII, allowed wage differences on the basis of sex if "such differentiation is authorized" by the Equal Pay Act.

The Bennett Amendment

Part of the confusion over interpretation of the Bennett amendment arose from unusual post-enactment attempts by its sponsor to explain its original intent.

On June 12, 1964, during the stormy passage of the 1964 Civil Rights Act (after cloture had been invoked), Republican Senator Wallace Bennett of Utah offered an amendment to Title VII that he described as a "technical correction." He described the Equal Pay Act as the culmination of "many years of yearning by members of the fair sex in this country." And, he said, he merely wanted to ensure that if conflicts arose between the equal employment provisions of Title VII and the Equal Pay Act, the "provisions of the Equal Pay Act shall not be nullified."[33]

Almost one year later, on June 11, 1965, Bennett introduced a memorandum into the *Congressional Record* that purported to clarify the amendment's intent. Responding to a law review article questioning its meaning, Bennett replied that the Senate had understood the amendment was intended to ensure "that discrimination in compensation on account of sex does not violate Title VII unless it also violates the Equal Pay Act."[34] According to Anne Draper, head of the National Committee for Equal Pay, this revisionist interpretation would have nullified Title VII for claims of discrimination in compensation and "leave the Equal Pay Act as the only applicable Federal statute in the field."[35]

The Bennett amendment lent itself to two conflicting interpretations. The narrow one, exemplified in *Christensen v. Iowa*, 1977, and *Lemons v. City and County of Denver*, 1980, imposed an equal work requirement on Title VII wage claims. This approach "incorporate[d] into Title VII the Equal Pay Act's rejection of the comparable work approach."[36]

The Narrow Interpretation of the Bennett Amendment

The *Christensen* case arose when clerical workers at the University of Northern Iowa objected to the university's wage policy. Full of good intentions, in 1974 the university had adopted a wage scheme that rated the nonprofessional jobs within the university. They were divided into labor grades based on an "objective evaluation of each job's relative worth to the employer regardless of the market price."[37] Prior to 1974, the pay for each job was determined by its value in the labor market outside the university.

Most of the physical-plant employees were male; all of the clerical staff were female. Despite their common grade, however, physical-plant workers started at higher salaries than clerical workers. The university attributed this difference to disparities in the local job market. The clerical workers brought suit under Title VII claiming that the wage disparity is a "continuation of a long history of sex discrimination in the local job market."[38]

The district court dismissed their claim, citing the narrow interpretation of the Bennett amendment. The court of appeals affirmed, also accepting the university's argument that the local job market created upward pressure on the salaries of the physical-plant workers. The appellate court doubted that "Congress intended to abrogate the laws of supply and demand or other economic principles that determine wage rates for various kinds of work."[39] Because the university had made a good faith effort toward equalizing wages, the court did not consider the remaining wage disparity a Title VII violation.

In *Lemons*, the Tenth Circuit also upheld the law of supply and demand by dismissing a suit brought by Denver nurses who claimed that the city's pay scale violated Title VII. The city denied the Title VII charge by pointing out that its wage structure was comparable to the private sector's. The nurses argued that because nurses are almost exclusively female, they are historically undervalued and underpaid. And basing city nurses' salaries on those in the private sector perpetuates the low wage status of public employees.

The nurses lost when the court ruled that a Title VII action, like an Equal Pay Act action, depended on a showing of equal work. More fundamentally, the judge also expressed concern about the propriety of courts interfering in market relationships. He said, "[T]he courts under existing authority cannot require the City . . . to reassess the worth of services in each position in relation to all others, and to strike a new balance and relationship."[40]

A Broad Interpretation of the Bennett Amendment

The circuit courts did not uniformly accept the restrictive view of the Bennett amendment. In another 1980 case, *International Union of Electrical, Radio and Machine Workers v. Westinghouse Electric Company*, the Third Circuit reached the opposite conclusion and refused to require plaintiffs to demonstrate equal work in their Title VII suits. Instead, it interpreted the Bennett amendment as only incorporating the four affirmative defenses of the Equal Pay Act into Title VII. This allowed employers to defend themselves against Title VII wage claims with proof that the wage disparity was attributable to a merit or seniority system, a production scale, or a factor other than sex.

The International Union of Electrical, Radio and Machine Workers (IUE) filed suit against Westinghouse for setting the wages in female-dominated job classifications lower than male-dominated job classifications. The company initially established a separate wage scale for men and women in the 1930s. All jobs within the plant were given points and assigned a grade based on the totals; salaries were determined by the grade. Under this plan, the women's rates of pay were lower than the men's even when the jobs were equally ranked on the basis of knowledge, training, demands, and responsibility.

In 1965, the two pay scales were combined, but the women's jobs were given a lower grade than the men's jobs—even though they had been at equal grades in the old system. Under the new plan, with just one exception, all workers in the four lowest grades were women and no women were in the highest four grades. In bringing suit, the union claimed that "the new wage scale . . . embodies the deliberately discriminatory policy of the prior plan."[41]

Citing the Bennett amendment, the district court dismissed the suit because the IUE had not claimed that the men and women performed equal work. Following an extensive analysis of the language and legislative history of Title VII and the passage of section 703(h), the appellate court reversed.

The court pointed out that placing an equal work limit on a Title VII sex discrimination claim allowed employers to discriminate on the basis of sex where they could not on the basis of race, religion, or national origin. The court questioned why sex-based wage claims should be treated differently from other Title VII wage claims. Commenting that "the legislative materials on the Bennett amendment are remarkable only for their equivocacy and turbidity," the court concluded that, on balance, the broader interpretation was the one Congress intended.[42]

After the case was remanded to the district court, the parties settled, with Westinghouse agreeing to pay $75,000 to the six hundred plaintiffs; the company also promised to raise the jobs of about eighty-five women to a higher grade.[43]

The Supreme Court Decides *Gunther*

Prior to the *Gunther* decision, federal courts tended to dismiss wage discrimination Title VII actions for two reasons: they held that (1) plaintiffs failed to satisfy the Bennett amendment's requirement of equal work, and (2) plaintiffs failed to prove sex discrimination. The *Gunther* opinion eliminated the first as a valid reason for dismissal; the second remains the major obstacle to comparable worth actions.

Gunther arose when female jail guards in Washington County, Oregon, filed a Title VII action, complaining that they were paid less than male guards for performing substantially equal work. They also charged that the pay difference was a result of intentional discrimination.[44]

The district court dismissed their claim because they had not satisfied the equal work requirement. The Ninth Circuit reversed. In a narrowly focused opinion, with Brennan, Marshall, White, Blackmun, and John Paul Stevens in the majority, the Supreme Court upheld the appellate court.

Far from endorsing comparable worth theory, the high court pointedly noted that the guards' claim was based on intentional discrimination, not comparable worth. Speaking for the 5–4 majority, the Court limited its ruling to proper interpretation of the Bennett amendment by deciding the narrow question of whether the guards' inability to comply with the equal work requirements of the Equal Pay Act invalidated their Title VII claim. Basing its decision on language and legislative history, the Court adopted the broad interpretation of the amendment. Brennan cited the remedial purposes of Title VII and the Court's desire to "avoid interpretations of Title VII that deprive victims of discrimination of a remedy, without clear congressional mandate."[45]

In dissent, speaking for himself, Burger, Potter Stewart, and Powell, Rehnquist charged that the Court's broad interpretation of the Bennett amendment misconstrued congressional intent. Delving into the debate surrounding passage of the act, Rehnquist argued that the legislative history shows that "Congress was unwilling to give either the Federal Government or the courts broad authority to determine comparable wage rates."[46]

He also criticized the decision because it provided "little guidance to employers and lower courts as to what types of compensation practices might now violate Title VII."

> All we know, [he said,] is that Title VII provides a remedy when, as here, plaintiffs seek to show by *direct* evidence that their employer *intentionally* depressed their wages. And, for reasons that go largely unexplained, we also know that a Title VII remedy may not be available to plaintiffs who allege theories different than that alleged here, such as the so-called 'comparable worth' theory.[47]

Comparable Worth after *Gunther*

Gunther sparked a debate about whether plaintiffs should rely on disparate treatment or disparate impact theory in bringing Title VII wage discrimination claims to court. The debate was short-lived as plaintiffs were unable to prevail in disparate treatment cases because they had no evidence of discriminatory intent and the majority of courts rejected wage-based claims brought under disparate impact theory. Thus, while *Gunther* was hailed as a victory by women's rights advocates, it proved to be an ephemeral one. In opening the door to Title VII suits for wage discrimination, the Supreme Court had cautioned that it was not deciding "the precise contours of lawsuits challenging sex discrimination in compensation under Title VII."[48] Following *Gunther*, the door began to close as lower courts rejected disparate impact analysis, demanded proof of intentional discrimination, and accepted market-based salary structures as defenses.[49]

Two Ninth Circuit cases decided after *Gunther* dealt a major blow to comparable worth litigation. The first, *Spaulding v. University of Washington*, 1984, was brought by nursing faculty in the School of Nursing; the second, *American Federation of State, County, and Municipal Employees (AFSCME) v. Washington*, 1985, was filed on behalf of 15,500 female employees of Washington. These two cases highlight the problems comparable worth suits face in court. Fearing that courts would become overwhelmed by comparable worth claims, and that remedies would require sweeping economic changes, the judiciary has been unreceptive to comparable worth actions.

Disparate Impact and Comparable Worth

Spaulding arose when nursing faculty filed Title VII and Equal Pay actions against the university for sex-based wage discrimination; the lower court dismissed both claims. On appeal, the circuit court also rejected the EPA claim, holding that the nurses were unable to prove that their jobs and the jobs of male faculty in male-dominated departments and schools of the university were substantially equal.

The nursing teachers relied on both disparate treatment and disparate impact theories in their suit. The first theory failed because the appellate court refused to "infer intent merely from the existence of wage differences between jobs that are only similar."[50] The court assessed plaintiffs' evidence of discriminatory intent, consisting primarily of attitudes among university administrators, but also including statistical evidence. Unconvinced, the court concluded that they failed to establish that discrimination motivated the university's wage system.

The faculty's disparate impact theory was premised upon the university's adoption of a market-priced wage policy. The court framed the question as one of deciding whether "the disparate impact model is available to plaintiffs who . . . make a broad-ranging sex-based claim of wage discrimination, based on comparable worth."[51]

Stressing that *Gunther* was a disparate treatment case, and pointing out that "other courts have compellingly rejected the comparable worth theory in sex-based wage discrimination claims under an impact theory," the court answered the question with a resounding no. Aligning this case squarely with *Lemons*, in which city-employed nurses also complained of market-based salary policy, the court added in a footnote that "courts are not competent to engage on a sweeping revision of market wage rates."[52]

Another setback for comparable worth litigants occurred the following year — again in the Ninth Circuit. In the suit brought by the American Federation of State, County, and Municipal Employees (AFSCME), the union charged that the state's own studies showed that women earned about 20 percent less than men for comparable work. It claimed that the wage system had a disparate impact on predominantly female job classifications and that failure to correct the pay disparities amounted to intentional discrimination on the basis of sex. District Court Judge Jack Tanner agreed on both counts. Tanner's decision allowing plaintiffs to proceed under a disparate impact theory represents the only successful attempt to apply this theory to a Title VII comparable worth claim.[53] Tanner was reversed by the Ninth Circuit.

The union contended that Washington's reliance on prevailing market rates to determine wages had an adverse impact on women who received lower wages than men. But the appellate court ruled that AFSCME had not made a valid claim under disparate impact theory. "Disparate impact analysis," explained Judge, now Justice, Anthony Kennedy, "is confined to cases which challenge a specific, clearly delineated employment practice applied at a single point in the job selection process." Because the state based its compensation decisions on a large number of complex factors, there was no "single practice . . . to support a claim under disparate impact theory."[54]

Turning to the disparate treatment charge, the court ruled that the plaintiffs failed to prove intentional discrimination against women. AFSCME argued that the state's intent could be inferred from its perpetuation of a discriminatory market rate. Again, Kennedy rejected the union's position. In a decisive attack on comparable worth theory, he emphasized that

> neither law nor logic deems the free market system a suspect enterprise. Economic reality is that the value of a particular job to an employer is but one factor influencing the rate of compensation for that job. . . . Nothing in the language of Title VII . . . indicate[s] Congress intended to abrogate fundamental economic principles such as the laws of supply and demand or to prevent employers from competing in the labor market. . . . Title VII does not obligate . . . [a company] to eliminate an economic inequality which it did not create.[55]

Moreover, said Kennedy, the state was not obligated to implement the job evaluation study simply because it commissioned the study to be performed.

Disparate Treatment and Comparable Worth

Forced to use disparate treatment theory in comparable worth claims after *Spaulding* and *AFSCME*, employees had to prove that sex-based wage differences resulted from intentional sex discrimination.[56] But in accepting market-based rates as a legitimate basis for male-female wage differences, courts make it virtually impossible for comparable worth suits brought under disparate treatment theory to succeed. The courts rule that because employers are not responsible for market rates, they are not guilty of intentional sex-based wage discrimination.

American Nurses' Association v. Illinois, 1985, illustrates what kind of proof might be required to make a successful claim of intentional wage discrimination under Title VII. The case was brought on behalf of all female employees working for the state in predominantly female job classifications. The plaintiffs claimed that men in predominantly male jobs were paid a higher wage not justified by the relative worth of the jobs. Moreover, they argued that the state did not implement its own job evaluation study that showed that women were underpaid.

The district court dismissed the nurses' complaint, ruling that plaintiffs do not have a claim under Title VII because the state does not act on the findings of a job evaluation study. The Seventh Circuit, in an opinion written by Judge Richard Posner, reversed and remanded the case, with instructions to plaintiffs about what kind of evidence they needed to present to win a Title VII claim of intentional sex-based wage discrimination.

Proof of intent to discriminate cannot be inferred merely from a state's inaction, Posner noted. Citing *AFSCME*, he pointed out that a state does not violate Title VII by failing to implement a job evaluation study and to eliminate existing wage disparities. He explained that "the critical thing lacking in *AFSCME* was evidence that the State decided not to raise the wages of particular workers *because* most of those workers were female."[57] Inferring a Title VII violation every time a state commissions a wage study would discourage such studies.

Because the case was dismissed at the complaint stage, before plaintiffs were able to present proof of discrimination, the appellate court remanded the case to the lower court to give them this opportunity. The court suggested that plaintiffs could make out a claim for intentional discrimination if they could show that Illinois deliberately kept women out of male-dominated jobs or that Illinois departed from market rates only for the male-dominated jobs—because the jobs were held by men. The judge concluded, however, by warning that the court did "not want to arouse false hopes; the plaintiffs have a tough row to hoe."[58]

Posner understated the difficulty ahead for comparable worth plaintiffs. One scholar looking at the future of comparable worth litigation predicted that "the judiciary has been and, apparently, will continue to be unreceptive to the doctrine of comparable worth as a viable legal theory under Title VII."[59]

Comparable Worth Legislation

With comparable worth litigation meeting with little success in the federal courts, comparable worth advocates turned their attention to state and local governments. And most of the wage adjustments at these levels are attributable to political, rather than judicial, prompting.

The demand for comparable worth legislation was largely initiated by women's organizations within state governments such as Commissions on the Status of Women. State employee organizations with large female constituencies, such as nurses' and clerical workers' unions, added their voices as well. Responding to this pressure, between 1981 and 1983, comparable worth bills were introduced in thirteen state legislatures.[60]

As a result of collective bargaining agreements with state employee unions, as well as equity legislation, state and local governments began to adopt comparable worth policies. In July 1981, after a nine-day strike, the city of San Jose, California, reached a settlement with AFSCME workers and agreed to pay $1.45 million over a two-year period as comparable worth pay adjustments.

On a statewide level, in 1982 Minnesota adopted legislation affecting nine thousand state employees. It called for a job evaluation study for civil service positions every two years. Over $20 million was appropriated for pay adjustments during 1983–1984. Minnesota also enacted legislation to mandate equal pay for comparable work at the municipal level in 1984. Diverse states such as Iowa and New Mexico appropriated money in 1983 and 1984 to increase salaries of workers found to be undercompensated.[61]

Pay equity actions range from research and data collection, to creating task force commissions, to performing job evaluation studies, to implementing pay equity plans by making salary adjustments. By 1987, twenty states, including Washington — site of *Spaulding* and *AFSCME* — were in the process of implementing pay equity plans. Four states — Arkansas, Delaware, Georgia, and Idaho — had undertaken no comparable worth action at all. Only one state — Minnesota — had completed the pay equity wage adjustments for its state employees.[62]

NOTES

1. Cynthia Harrison, *On Account of Sex: The Politics of Women's Issues, 1945–1968* (Berkeley: University of California Press, 1988), p. 104.
2. Harrison, *On Account of Sex*, pp. 96–97; see Virginia Dean, "Pay Equity/Comparable Worth" in Carol Lefcourt, ed., *Women and the Law* (New York: Clark Boardman, 1987).
3. The Equal Pay Act, 29 U.S.C. §206(d) (1).
4. H. Rep. No. 309, 88th Cong., 1st Sess. 2 (1963).
5. In *National League of Cities v. Usery*, 426 U.S. 833 (1976), the Supreme Court struck down the extension of the FLSA's provision on wages and hours to state and local employees. In 1985, in *Garcia v. San Antonio Metropolitan Transit Authority*, 469 U.S. 528 (1985), the Supreme Court overruled *National League of Cities* on the issue of state and local government workers. Even before *Garcia*, the majority of lower federal courts limited *National League of Cities* to wages and hours provisions and allowed Equal Pay Act claims against state and local governments. See Joel Friedman and George Strickler, Jr., eds., *The Law of Employment Discrimination* (Mineola: Foundation Press, 1987), p. 575.
6. In *Corning Glass Works v. Brennan*, 417 U.S. 188, 196 (1974), the Supreme Court approved this shifting burden of proof procedure that had been followed by most lower federal courts.
7. *Schultz v. Wheaton Glass*, 421 F.2d 259, 265 (3d Cir. 1970).
8. *Wheaton Glass*, 421 F.2d at 264.
9. *Hodgson v. Brookhaven General Hospital*, 436 F.2d 719, 725 (5th Cir. 1970). In *Schultz v. American Can Company*, 424 F.2d 356 (8th Cir. 1970), the Eighth Circuit also ruled that the work of male and female machine operators was "substantially equal" even though the men loaded the machines with heavy rolls of paper.
10. Diana Stone, *Pay Equity Sourcebook* (San Francisco: Equal Rights Advocates and Washington, DC: National Committee on Pay Equity, 1987), p. 195.
11. Charles A. Sullivan, "The Equal Pay Act of 1963: Making and Breaking a Prima Facie Case," *Arkansas Law Review* 31(1978), pp. 592–606. The courts have generally refused

to allow participation in training programs or shift differentials as a valid "factor other than sex."

12. Robert Hall was not the only company that paid women less than men. As a whole, women sales personnel earned much less than men. In 1985, the median income of male year-round, full-time workers in sales was $25,445; for women the median income for year-round, full-time workers in sales was $12,682. U.S. Department of Commerce, Bureau of the Census, *Current Population Reports*, Series P-60, No. 156(1985).

13. *Hodgson v. Robert Hall Clothes*, 473 F.2d 589, 593 (3d Cir. 1973).

14. See Note, "Not Just Any 'Factor Other Than Sex': An Analysis of the Fourth Affirmative Defense of the Equal Pay Act," *George Washington Law Review* 52(1984), p. 335; Sullivan, "The Equal Pay Act of 1963," p. 599.

15. This case came to the Supreme Court from two circuits. The Court of Appeals for the Second Circuit ruled against Corning in a case involving several Corning plants in New York. The Court of Appeals for the Third Circuit ruled in favor of Corning on the same issue. The Supreme Court accepted the case to resolve the conflict among the two circuits. Potter Stewart took no part in the consideration or decision of the cases.

16. *Corning Glass*, 417 U.S. at 206.

17. Stone, *Pay Equity Sourcebook*, p. 4. In 1988, women in sales occupations earned only 54.1 percent of men's earnings. Women's earnings compared to men were generally better in more skilled occupations. Female engineers earned 87.1 percent of the salaries of male engineers. Women, however, constituted only 7 percent of engineers in the country. U.S. Department of Labor, Bureau of Labor Statistics, *Current Population Survey*, 1988 Annual Averages, Table 5.

18. Mary Frances Berry, *Why ERA Failed* (Bloomington: Indiana University Press, 1986), p. 112.

19. Barbara Bergmann, *The Economic Emergence of Women* (New York: Basic Books, 1986), p. 186.

20. U.S. Department of Labor, Bureau of Labor Statistics, *Employment and Earnings* (January 1989), Table 22.

21. Quoted in Berry, *Why ERA Failed*, p. 111.

22. William Bradford Reynolds, "Comparable Worth: Bad Policy and Bad Law," *Harvard Journal of Law & Public Policy* 9(1986), p. 90.

23. Henry Aaron and Cameran M. Lougy, *The Comparable Worth Controversy* (Washington, DC: Brookings Institution, 1986), p. 15.

24. Joseph P. Loudon and Timothy D. Loudon, "Applying Disparate Impact to Title VII Comparable Worth Claims: An Incomparable Task," *Indiana Law Journal* 61(1986), p. 165.

25. Judith Brown, Phyllis Tropper Baumann, and Elaine Millar Melnick, "Equal Pay for Jobs of Comparable Worth: An Analysis of the Rhetoric," *Harvard Civil Rights-Civil Liberties Law Review* 21(1986), pp. 127–34.

26. Reynolds, "Comparable Worth: Bad Policy and Bad Law," p. 89.

27. Vicki Schultz, "Telling Stories about Women and Work," *Harvard Law Review* 103(1990), pp. 1816–24.

28. Although opponents of comparable worth stress the difficulty of measuring the worth of jobs, the theory and practice of job evaluation has been used in American industry for decades; unions have relied on job evaluation studies with some success for public sector jobs. Brown et al., "Equal Pay for Jobs of Comparable Worth," pp. 132–33; Aaron and Lougy, *The Comparable Worth Controversy*, pp. 24–36.

29. Sara Evans and Barbara Nelson, "Comparable Worth: The Paradox of Technocratic Reform," *Feminist Studies* 15(1989), p. 173. See also Jane Bayes, "Women, Labor Markets, and Comparable Worth," *Policy Studies Review* 5(1986), p. 797.

30. A primary difference between an equal pay action and a comparable worth action lies in the employer's ability to use market wages as a defense in the latter. In an EPA suit, employers are not permitted to use prevailing market rates to justify less pay for female workers.

31. Donald Treiman and Heidi Hartmann, eds., *Women, Work, and Wages: Equal Pay for Jobs of Equal Value* (Washington, DC: National Academy Press, 1981). See also Roslyn Feldberg, "Comparable Worth: Toward Theory and Practice in the United States," *Signs* 10(1984); Bayes, "Women, Labor Markets, and Comparable Worth."

The American labor force is also highly segregated by race, a fact that helps to explain wage gaps between the races. See National Committee on Pay Equity, *Pay Equity: An Issue of Race, Ethnicity and Sex* (Washington, DC: National Committee on Pay Equity, 1987); Mary Corcoran and Greg Duncan, "Work History, Labor Force Attachment, and Earnings Differences between the Races and Sexes," *Journal of Human Resources* 14(1979).

32. Ruth Blumrosen, "Wage Discrimination, Job Segregation, and Title VII of the Civil Rights Act of 1964," *University of Michigan Journal of Law Reform* 12(1979), p. 401.

33. 110 *Cong. Rec.* 13,647 (1964).

34. 111 *Cong. Rec.* 13,359 (1965).

35. 111 *Cong. Rec.* 18,263 (1965).

36. *International Union of Electrical, Radio and Machine Workers v. Westinghouse Electric Company*, 631 F.2d 1094, 1110 (3d Cir. 1980) (Van Dusen, J., dissenting).

37. *Christensen v. Iowa*, 563 F.2d 353, 354 (8th Cir. 1977).

38. *Christensen*, 563 F.2d at 355.

39. *Christensen*, 563 F.2d at 356.

40. *Lemons v. City and County of Denver*, 620 F.2d 228, 229 (10th Cir. 1980).

41. *Westinghouse*, 631 F.2d at 1097.

42. *Westinghouse*, 631 F.2d at 1101–102.

43. Stone, *Pay Equity Sourcebook*, p. 121.

44. Plaintiffs were forced to file suit under Title VII because the Equal Pay Act did not apply to municipal employees until the Fair Labor Standards Act Amendments of 1974.

45. *County of Washington v. Gunther*, 452 U.S. 161, 178 (1981).

46. *Gunther*, 452 U.S. at 188 (Rehnquist, J., dissenting).

47. *Gunther*, 452 U.S. at 183 (Rehnquist, J., dissenting) (emphasis in the original).

48. *Gunther*, 452 U.S. at 181.

49. Brown et al., "Equal Pay for Jobs of Comparable Worth," p. 143.

50. *Spaulding v. University of Washington*, 740 F.2d 686, 700 (9th Cir. 1984).

51. *Spaulding*, 740 F.2d at 705.

52. *Spaulding*, 740 F.2d at 706, n.11.

53. Loudon and Loudon, "Applying Disparate Impact to Title VII Comparable Worth Claims," p. 174.

54. *American Federation of State, County, and Municipal Employees (AFSCME) v. Washington*, 770 F.2d 1401, 1405–06 (9th Cir. 1985).

55. *AFSCME*, 770 F.2d at 1407.

56. In applying Title VII case law to comparable worth claims, courts demand that plaintiffs establish a prima facie case of employment discrimination. Ruth Blumrosen has argued that a plaintiff should merely have to show that her job is segregated on the basis of sex to raise a prima facie case of discrimination because "evidence of segregated jobs justifies an inference of discrimination in compensation." Blumrosen, "Wage Discrimination, Job Segregation and Title VII," p. 465. Blumrosen's theory was explicitly rejected in *Briggs v. City of Madison*, 536 F.Supp. 435, 444–45 (W.D. Wis. 1982). See also Loudon and Loudon, "Applying Disparate Impact to Title VII Comparable Worth Claims," pp. 171–72.

57. *American Nurses' Ass'n v. Illinois*, 783 F.2d 716, 722 (7th Cir. 1986) (emphasis in original).

58. *American Nurses' Ass'n*, 783 F.2d at 730. The lower court opinion was reversed because, by construing their complaint liberally, the circuit court determined that the plaintiffs had sufficiently pleaded a claim of intentional discrimination.

59. Tina L. Speiser, "The Future of Comparable Worth: Looking in New Directions," *Syracuse Law Review* 37(1987), p. 1207.

60. See Keon Chi, "Comparable Worth in State Government: Trends and Issues," *Policy Studies Review* 5(1986), for factors associated with adoption of comparable worth policy in the states.

61. Aaron and Lougy, *The Comparable Worth Controversy*, pp. 37–38.

62. Stone, *Pay Equity Sourcebook*, pp. 461–66.

6

Pregnancy and Employment

In the late 1980s, the majority of women in the labor force (more than 70 percent) were in the prime childbearing ages of sixteen to forty-four; an even greater number (93 percent) of women in this group was likely to have one child during those years.[1]

Despite the high incidence of pregnancy among women in the work force, U.S. policy-makers, for the most part, seemed unconcerned about its economic, social, and political impact and made few attempts to alleviate the burdens of pregnancy on working women. On the contrary, states typically enacted pregnancy legislation that was "synonymous with unfavorable treatment."[2] When challenged in court, such laws were usually upheld by judges who failed to perceive "that some of the legal rules restricting the activities of pregnant women were not required by physiology, but resulted from a social order built on patriarchal principles, designed to protect the family as a reproductive institution."[3]

Restrictions on the work of pregnant women stemmed from assumptions about women's role in the work force and in the family. Pregnancy legislation was prompted by the perception that working women were primarily wives and mothers and therefore loosely committed to their work. Seeking to correct this perception, noted labor historian Alice Cook argues that the number of women who work because they have to is very high, not just in the United States but throughout the world. Most women work for the same reasons men do, to support themselves and their families.[4]

More recently, the impact of pregnancy on women in the labor force has been recognized, but because of conflicting goals and standards, the government has sent pregnant women contradictory messages based on a variety of legal criteria. Thus, today, despite the advances of the last ten years, pregnancy policy remains in disarray. Not surprisingly, government policy reflects society's ambivalence toward pregnancy and the role of women in the workplace.[5]

Public policy-making regarding pregnancy can be divided into three eras. The first, revolving around state and local laws based on presumptions about a pregnant woman's inability to work, ended in 1974 when the Supreme Court ruled that such presumptions violated due process rights.

The second era, ending around 1977, consisted of cases arising because pregnant women were deprived of a variety of fringe benefits and employment rights, primarily disability compensation. These cases were adjudicated under both constitutional equal protection and Title VII with the Supreme Court approving the pregnancy exclusions.

The third era, the current one, is characterized by the debate over whether pregnant working women are better served by equal treatment or preferred treatment. Equal treatment, its advocates argue, is consistent with the women's equality movement and does not have the negative connotations of the "protective" legislation of the early 1900s. Preferred treatment, its proponents urge, is necessary to achieve equal opportunity in the workplace.

The Executive Branch and Pregnancy Policy

The first era of policy-making in the area of pregnancy and employment began in the early 1970s when the federal government began to pay attention to pregnancy. In 1970, the Citizens' Advisory Council on the Status of Women, a council consisting of twenty private citizens established at the recommendation of the President's Commission on the Status of Women, adopted a Statement of Principles on pregnancy and the workplace. Council members recommended that employers and health insurers treat pregnancy and childbirth as any other temporary disability. In their view "no additional or different benefits or restrictions should be applied to disability because of pregnancy and childbirth, and no pregnant woman employee should be in a better position in relation to job-related practices or benefits than an employee similarly situated suffering from other disability."[6]

The Office of Federal Contract Compliance, charged with administering executive orders on equal employment opportunity, took the opposite tack and required employers subject to its rules to grant leaves of absence for pregnancy even if such leaves were not available to other employees.[7]

In contrast, the Equal Employment Opportunity Commission (EEOC) showed little concern for the plight of the pregnant working woman. In 1965, when the EEOC was generally indifferent, if not hostile, to women's concerns — its guidelines made no mention of pregnancy disability. A year later the agency took a stance on pregnancy disability, exemplified in an opinion letter from the general counsel's office.

> The Commission's policy with respect to pregnancy does not seek to compare an employer's treatment of illness or injury with his treatment of maternity, since maternity is a temporary disability unique to the female sex and more or less to be anticipated during the working life of most woman employees. Therefore, an insurance or other benefit plan may simply exclude maternity as a covered risk, and such exclusion would not in our view be discriminatory.[8]

The EEOC followed this policy for the next five years when it abruptly reversed itself without explanation in a March 1971 decision. New guidelines reflecting this change were published in 1972 and were "heavily influenced by the Citizen's Advisory Council's equality concept."[9]

The 1972 guidelines, making pregnancy disability equal to other temporary disabilities, contained three parts. The first section prohibited employers from refusing to hire qualified women because they were pregnant or *might become* pregnant. The second part required employers to treat pregnancy like other temporarily disabling conditions. The third section prohibited employers from disproportionately firing women for absences from the job due to pregnancy unless justified by business needs.[10]

Judicial reaction to the guidelines was mixed. Noting that they were not legally binding, a number of courts, including the Supreme Court, rejected the EEOC's view that denial of pregnancy disability benefits amounted to a Title VII violation.[11]

Forced Maternity Leaves

Supreme Court decision-making during the first era was characterized by cases involving forced maternity leaves. In the "old" days, it was often recommended that pregnant women cease working after their sixth month, and most quit their jobs well before their delivery date. Today, the medical establishment says that unless the work involves heavy physical labor, women should be able to stay on their jobs until their labor pains start. Statistics collected in 1980 show that almost half (41 percent) of women holding white-collar jobs continued working into their last month of pregnancy.[12] The Supreme Court's recognition of the changing times was reflected in two cases decided in the mid-1970s.

The first case, *Cleveland Board of Education v. LaFleur*, 1974, arose in 1971 when Jo Carol LaFleur and Ann Nelson, two Cleveland junior high school teachers, were forced to take maternity leave in March; their babies were born in July and August respectively.

Cleveland policy required pregnant schoolteachers to take maternity leave at least five months before their child was due and to stay out of the classroom until the child was at least three months old. To return to work, they needed a doctor's certificate, and, in some cases, a physical examination. Not following these rules could lead to dismissal, but compliance did not guarantee rehiring; it merely entitled them to a priority reassignment as positions became available. Teachers with less than one year seniority were simply dismissed at the beginning of their fifth month.

LaFleur and Nelson filed suit against the school but lost their case in the lower court. They won on appeal when the Sixth Circuit held that the school policy violated the equal protection clause of the Fourteenth Amendment. The Supreme Court affirmed but declined to rest its decision on equal protection grounds.[13] Instead, with Potter Stewart speaking for the majority, the Court based its opinion on the Fourteenth Amendment's due process clause. In a 7–2 vote, the Court held that the mandatory leave rules unduly burdened a teacher's fundamental right to bear a child by creating an irrebuttable presumption (a conclusion that cannot be refuted) that all pregnant women were unfit to work after an arbitrarily selected date.[14]

The Court felt that because there was no "individualized determination" of a teacher's fitness, the rules "sweep too broadly." In legal terms, the Court explained that the rules are invalid because they contain "an irrebuttable presumption of physical incompetency, and that presumption applies even when the medical evidence as to an individual woman's physical status might be wholly to the contrary."[15] Because a teacher is not given an opportunity to show she is fit after the predetermined date, the presumption violates due process. Despite the schools' argument that it was too burdensome to make an "individualized" determination of fitness for each teacher, Stewart said that "administrative convenience alone is insufficient to make valid what otherwise is a violation of due process of law."[16]

A year later, in *Turner v. Department of Employment Security*, the Court also relied on the due process clause in striking down a Utah law that denied pregnant women unemployment benefits from twelve weeks before the expected date of delivery to six weeks after birth.[17]

Mary Ann Turner lost her job in November 1972 and collected unemployment benefits until March 1973, twelve weeks before her child was due. Like the statutes of most states, Utah's unemployment compensation law required recipients to be able to work. Also, as in most states, pregnant women were unable to receive benefits for a period of time during, and shortly after, their pregnancy. Relying on its decision in *LaFleur*, in a per curiam opinion the Court held that the Utah statute violated due process of law by creating an irrebuttable presumption that all women were unfit to work during the latter stages of pregnancy.

In striking the law on due process grounds, the Court was able to avoid subjecting the pregnancy classification to the more rigid equal protection analysis adopted in *Reed v. Reed* in 1971. Under equal protection law, the Court would have compared the state's treatment of pregnancy with its treatment of other disabling conditions. Instead, by analyzing pregnancy apart from other disabilities, the Court accepted the premise that pregnant women can be subject to special restrictions—as long as they are not too onerous or unreasonable. With the Court's approach, "pregnancy could still create a presumption of unfitness, albeit a rebuttable one."[18] Thus, despite the rulings in *LaFleur* and *Turner*, women's equality was only marginally advanced.

The *LaFleur* and *Turner* rulings left open the question of whether states may draw lines on the basis of pregnancy. There was hope that the court would eventually turn to the equal protection clause to invalidate discriminatory state laws regarding pregnancy. But in 1974, the Court made it clear that it did not accept the widely held belief that pregnancy classifications implicate sexual equality.

Pregnancy Disability and the Equal Protection Clause

The second era of public policy-making in the area of pregnancy and working women began with the Supreme Court's ruling in *Geduldig v. Aiello*, 1974, when the Court rejected a challenge to a California disability insurance plan that was designed to pay benefits to private (nonstate) disabled employees. The plan was self-supporting and financed by contributions of 1 percent of workers' salaries (up to a maximum of $85.00 a year); payments were available for up to twenty-six weeks.

Under the California plan, employees were protected against income loss arising from a wide variety of mental and physical disorders. Virtually the only disability not covered was pregnancy.[19] Three women, disabled by complications arising during their pregnancies (two required surgery and one suffered a miscarriage), brought suit charging that the state plan violated the equal protection clause. A fourth woman, healthy but temporarily unable to work because of her pregnancy, joined in their action. The three-judge district court ruled in their favor, finding that discrimination on the basis of this sex-linked characteristic constituted sex discrimination.[20]

On appeal, the Supreme Court focused on the solvency of California's social insurance plan, explaining that the maintenance of the program under current fiscal conditions was a "policy determination by the State." And the Court had to decide "whether the Equal Protection Clause requires such policies to be sacrificed or compromised in order to finance the payment of benefits to those whose disability is attributable to normal pregnancy and delivery."[21]

Delivering the opinion of the Court for himself, Byron White, Harry Blackmun, Lewis Powell, William Rehnquist, and Warren Burger, Stewart ruled in favor of the state. The California plan was consistent with the equal protection clause, he said, because the exclusion was based on pregnancy, not sex. And because sex discrimination was not at issue, the Court subjected the law to the minimal scrutiny normally accorded economic and social welfare legislation. Under this analysis, the Court found that the pregnancy exclusion was rationally related to the state's interest in maintaining the plan under its current fiscal constraints.

Stewart explained that the equal protection clause does not require a state to provide a fully comprehensive disability plan. He accepted California's argument that its 1 percent contribution rate was designed to "provide the broadest possible disability protection that would be affordable by all employees, including those with very low incomes."[22] To include normal pregnancy within the plan would be "extraordinarily expensive" and force a drastic restructuring of the program—either by raising the contribution rate or by reducing benefits. By excluding pregnancy, the disability plan could remain self-sufficient.[23]

The most memorable part of the decision was Stewart's portrayal of pregnancy as a unique physical characteristic unrelated to sex. In the widely quoted Footnote 20, he declared that the California plan does not exclude women on the basis of sex. The state merely selected among risks and omitted the risk of pregnancy as a covered disability; the unique features of pregnancy justify the exclusion. Sex was not used as a dividing line in the plan because "there is no risk from which men are protected and women are not. Likewise, there is no risk from which women are protected and men are not."[24]

Acknowledging that "only women can become pregnant," Stewart denied what was for many an inevitable connection between pregnancy and sex. But sex is not at issue, Stewart said, because the California scheme "divided potential recipients into two groups—pregnant women and nonpregnant persons. While the first group is exclusively female, the second includes members of both sexes."[25] Since the benefits available to nonpregnant persons are equal, the plan does not discriminate on the basis of sex by denying benefits to pregnant persons—even though they are exclusively female. Footnote 20 thus conveniently disposed of the linkage between pregnancy and sex.

William Brennan, joined by William Douglas and Thurgood Marshall, criticized the majority for closing its eyes to the tie between pregnancy and sex and analyzing the California plan under minimal scrutiny. He found Stewart's logic unpersuasive. In his view, pregnancy discrimination equated to sex discrimination and the disability plan therefore demanded the more searching scrutiny of sex-based classifications. Using the strict scrutiny approach urged by the four-justice plurality in *Frontiero v. Richardson* a year before, he argued that the state's desire to maintain the fiscal status quo did not justify the exclusion of pregnancy benefits.

Brennan reminded the Court that the disability program was intended to serve "broad humanitarian goals." Toward this end, it provided a wide range of benefits for costly disabilities (e.g., heart attacks), voluntary disabilities (e.g., cosmetic surgery and sterilization), sex- and race-specific disabilities (e.g., prostate operations and sickle-cell anemia), preexisting conditions (e.g., arthritis or cataracts), and so-called normal disabilities (e.g., impacted wisdom teeth). By singling out pregnancy disability, he said, the state placed limits on benefits for disabilities pertinent to women but placed no limits on benefits for disabilities pertinent to men. "In effect," he charged, "one set of rules is applied to females and another to males."[26]

Differentiating between men and women on the basis of a physical characteristic unique to one sex, Brennan insisted, is sex discrimination. This reality does not change just because the characteristic is not found among *all* members of the affected sex. Brennan also pointed out that the Court's decision contradicted the EEOC's 1972 guidelines on pregnancy benefits, a fact that the majority had ignored.

The most enduring effect of the *Geduldig* decision was the Court's surprising declaration of the distinction between pregnancy and sex. But in addition to the Court's verbal gymnastics, a more serious indictment of the opinion is that it indicates a cavalier approach to female workers. By ignoring the effect of the pregnancy disability exclusion on women's employment opportunities, the Court appeared to accept the stereotypical view of women as marginal workers.[27]

Pregnancy and Title VII

Geduldig made it clear that plaintiffs should rely on Title VII, when possible, to challenge pregnancy discrimination in the workplace. And, for a number of reasons, Title VII suits were likely to yield better results. First, the equal protection doctrine allows a state to plead that its sex-based classification is reasonably (or, after 1976, substantially) related to its goal. Title VII imposes a "standard of absolute equality" without permitting reasonableness as a defense. Second, cost does not justify discrimination under Title VII; employers are limited to bona fide occupational qualification and business necessity defenses only.[28] Finally, equal protection requires evidence of intentional discrimination. A Title VII case can be won by showing that a pregnancy exclusion has an adverse impact on women. Since most pregnancy disability cases arise in the employment context, it was reasonable to hope that *Geduldig* could become a footnote to judicial history with little practical impact.

A contrary scenario was also possible. Given the Court's view that pregnancy distinctions did not implicate sex, women attempting to sue for pregnancy discrimination under Title VII might be told they lack grounds for suit since Title VII requires a showing of sex discrimination.[29]

Ironically, after *Geduldig*, at the low point of Supreme Court decision-making on pregnancy, progress was being made on other fronts. Through legislation, state judicial decisions, and the rulings of state attorneys general, a number of states were expanding women's rights, especially with respect to disability insurance.[30]

Meanwhile, as well, the EEOC continued to argue that Title VII required pregnancy to be treated like other disabilities. The lower federal courts agreed and refused to apply *Geduldig* to Title VII suits. By 1976, six circuits and eighteen district courts ruled that *Geduldig* only controlled in equal protection cases. In accordance with the guidelines, they held that a pregnancy exclusion violated Title VII's ban on sex discrimination.[31]

In one of those cases, *Gilbert v. General Electric Company*, the lower court held that the pregnancy exclusion in General Electric's (GE) disability benefits plan was an unlawful employment practice under Title VII. The judge found that the inequality of the plan was "'inextricably sex-linked' in consequences and result."[32]

On appeal, in *General Electric Company v. Gilbert*, 1976, the Supreme Court reversed the lower court, approving General Electric's pregnancy exclusion. In reaching this decision, the Court appeared to be guided less by legal principle and logic and more by societal attitudes towards women. Feminist legal scholar Ann Scales asserts that the Court allowed GE to exclude pregnancy "because the Justices perceived that a woman's role is to bear children and that women should bear the cost of childbearing just as they have always done."[33]

Gilbert demonstrated the Court's continued ostrichlike approach to pregnancy. By refusing to equate pregnancy to other disabilities requiring brief interruptions from work, the Court ignored the financial burden of pregnancy on women's employment opportunities.

Pregnancy Disability and Title VII

General Electric provided its employees with a far-reaching disability plan. As in *Geduldig*, employees were covered for diseases, disabilities, and illnesses regardless of the effect, the voluntariness, the predictability, or the cost. The plan included circumcisions and prostatectomies, conditions unique to men. The only excluded disabilities were those arising from pregnancy, miscarriage, or childbirth. Even unrelated illnesses that surfaced during pregnancy were excluded.

The lawsuit against General Electric arose after female employees applying for disability benefits were denied on the basis of the company exclusion. In their suit, the women presented several arguments, inviting the Court to accept one. First, they claimed that the pregnancy exclusion was explicit sex-based discrimination. Alternatively, they wanted the Court to find that the exclusion was a pretext for discrimination against women. Finally, they argued that the plan had a disparate impact on women. They also asserted that GE's policy contravened the EEOC guidelines.

In a 6–3 decision, with Rehnquist announcing the opinion of the Court, plaintiffs' arguments were wholly rejected. Stewart and Blackmun filed concurring opinions while Brennan, Marshall, and John Paul Stevens dissented. The decision was premised on *Geduldig*'s distinction between pregnancy and sex. Because Title VII did not contain a definition of discrimination, the Court elected to adopt the principles of constitutional equal protection outlined in *Geduldig*.[34]

Reiterating the theme of *Geduldig*, Rehnquist denied that the GE plan constituted sex discrimination. This case was about the classification of risks, he said, not the exclusion of persons or groups. Under the General Electric plan, both men and women were entitled to disability insurance for risks they shared in common. A plan that removed a condition only affecting women was not discriminatory. Because both men and women belonged to the class of nonpregnant persons, it was not discriminatory to exclude pregnancy.

Brushing aside evidence of GE's record of discrimination against women, the Court rebuffed plaintiffs' argument that the plan was a pretext for discrimination against women. Because pregnancy was sufficiently different from other disabilities, the company was entitled to treat it differently.

Noting that the average cost of the plan was still higher for women than for men, Rehnquist rejected the plaintiffs' disparate impact argument with these words:

> As there is no proof that the package is in fact worth more to men than to women, it is impossible to find any gender-based discriminatory effect in this scheme simply because women disabled as a result of pregnancy do not receive benefits; that is to say, gender-based discrimination does not result simply because an employer's disability-benefits plan is less than all-inclusive. For all that appears, pregnancy-related disabilities constitute an *additional* risk, unique to women, and the failure to compensate them for this risk does not destroy the presumed parity of the benefits accruing to men and women alike, which results from the facially evenhanded *inclusion* of risks.[35]

Finally, said Rehnquist, the EEOC guidelines were not binding on the Court for two reasons. First, although helpful in assessing legislative intent, they were not entitled to as much weight as administrative regulations. Second, the guidelines were not issued until 1972—eight years after Title VII was enacted. And, they were inconsistent with the EEOC's original policy toward pregnancy disability that followed soon after the law was passed.

Brennan, in dissent, criticized the majority for ignoring the lower court's findings that GE had a long history of discrimination against women. He argued that the plan was sex-based because it insured all male-specific disabilities and all female-specific disabilities—except the most common, pregnancy.

In his dissent, Stevens also pointed out that the classification of pregnancy was not sex-neutral. "It is the capacity to become pregnant which primarily differentiates the female from the male." In a footnote he rejected the Court's reliance on the famous *Geduldig* formulation of "pregnant women and nonpregnant persons." This categorization is inappropriate, he said; the proper one "is between persons who face a risk of pregnancy and those who do not."[36]

Within the next two years, there were two more Title VII decisions that left people even more befuddled about interpreting the statute's prohibition on sex discrimination. First, in *Nashville Gas Company v. Satty*, 1977, the Supreme Court handed down a partial victory for women. The case arose when Nora Satty, required by company policy to take pregnancy leave, was denied her accumulated seniority on her return to work. She was also denied sick-leave pay even though other employees who were out sick were entitled to it. Satty claimed the policy was discriminatory because she was being treated differently from employees absent from work for other reasons; the others not only retained their seniority but continued to accrue it during the time they were out.

With Rehnquist again delivering the opinion, the Court held that the company's seniority policy violated Title VII. This case was unlike *Gilbert*, he said, because there had been no evidence that General Electric's policy "favored men over women." Here, the company "has not merely refused to extend to women a benefit that men cannot and do not receive, but has imposed on women a substantial burden that men need not suffer."[37] On the other hand, the Court rejected Satty's view of the company's sick-leave policy because it was virtually identical to the GE plan upheld by the Court in *Gilbert*.

Shortly after *Satty*, in *Los Angeles Department of Water & Power v. Manhart*, 1978, the Court found the city violated Title VII by requiring women to make higher contributions than men to the pension fund. The city claimed its policy was justified because women live longer than men and would receive benefits for a longer time.

Delivering the opinion of the Court, Stevens distinguished *Gilbert* by explaining that "on its face, this [the Los Angeles] plan discriminates on the basis of sex whereas the General Electric plan discriminated on the basis of a special physical disability."[38] Title VII forbids treating an individual on the basis of a generalization — even a true one — about the group. While women as a class live longer than men as a class, any one woman could die at the same age as a man and would have contributed more money into the pension plan. Because men and women who could die at the same age were similarly situated, they must be treated alike.

The PDA Reverses *Gilbert*

The onset of the third era of public policy-making concerning pregnancy began with the enactment of the Pregnancy Discrimination Act (PDA) of 1978. Within days of the Supreme Court's decision in *Gilbert*, a coalition of over three hundred groups, called the Campaign to End Discrimination against Pregnant Workers, formed to lobby Congress to reverse the Court's decision. Primarily composed of union groups, the campaign also included members of the National Organization for Women, the National Women's Political Caucus, and the Women's Equity Action Alliance.[39]

Congressional response to *Gilbert* was also swift. On October 31, 1978, Congress enacted the PDA by amending Title VII to include a section stating that "women affected by pregnancy . . . shall be treated the same for all employment-related purposes . . . as other persons not so affected but similar in their ability or inability to work."[40] The House committee report accompanying the bill noted that *Gilbert* had been wrongly decided and that "the dissenting Justices [had] correctly interpreted the Act."[41]

At the time of the PDA's passage, almost half the nation's women were already protected by the principle of nondiscrimination through state action. About twenty-two states required some disability coverage for pregnant women, primarily through state fair employment practices laws.[42] By providing a uniform interpretation of employment discrimination, the PDA ended this piecemeal approach to pregnancy policy-making. In enacting the PDA, Congress corrected the Court's error in *Gilbert* and adopted an evenhanded approach to pregnancy that placed it on a par with other disabilities. It did not intend to create a preferred status for pregnancy by requiring an employer "who does not provide disability benefits or paid sick leave to other employees to provide them for pregnant workers." And to establish that the bill was aimed only at the physical needs of childbearing, Congress restricted benefits to women "medically unable to work."[43]

Despite the nondiscrimination principles of the act, there was also evidence that Congress was concerned about promoting equal opportunity for women and perceived of the PDA as another step toward parity in the work force. In the words of one of its cosponsors in the Senate, Democrat Alan Cranston of California, the act "is fully compatible with the underlying objectives of Title VII to assure equality of employment opportunity and to eliminate those discriminatory practices which pose barriers to working women in their struggle to secure equality in the workplace."[44]

Enacting the PDA

The move to amend Title VII began on March 15, 1977, about three months after *Gilbert* was decided, when Representative Augustus Hawkins, Democrat of California, introduced H.R. 5055 in the House. The bill was subsequently amended and reintroduced as H.R. 6075 with 119 cosponsors; hearings were held on it during April and June 1977. On February 2, 1978, the bill was approved with amendments by the House Subcommittee on Employment Opportunities.

The bill was favorably reported to the House by the Committee on Education and Labor with an amendment exempting employers from paying for abortions unless the mother's life were endangered. The amendment was added because of concerns that an employer with moral or religious objections to the abortion procedure, like a church organization for example, would be obligated to fund it. The final committee vote was 25–6.

The Senate version of the bill, S. 995, approved by the Committee on Labor and Human Resources, omitted the abortion exception. When the bill went to conference, the House side prevailed and the final bill included the abortion exclusion.[45] Despite this exclusion, the conference report stressed that complications arising from abortions were still fully insured under disability or sick-leave provisions. And the bill also prohibited employers from discriminating against women exercising their right to abortion.

The Debate Begins

A new debate over pregnancy policy emerged in 1978 with passage of the PDA. With guarantees of equal treatment secured through federal statute, litigation over pregnancy took a new turn. While the subject of dispute in the early cases had been over whether pregnant women at work should be treated differently—and worse—than men at work, the question now was whether pregnant women could (and should) be treated differently—and better—than men.

Although this debate has deeply divided feminists, it is important to remember that it arose on the heels of their success in establishing the principle of nondiscrimination in pregnancy policy. It is only recently that women have had the luxury of debating the best approach to pregnancy among themselves because it was not so long ago that they were fighting against pregnancy discrimination in hiring, firing, promotion, disability, seniority, pensions, sick pay, and unemployment compensation. The PDA's evenhanded approach would end the discriminatory treatment but would it also proscribe more favorable treatment?

The debate over the status of pregnancy in the workplace was partially fueled by ambiguities in the PDA. Intended to prohibit discrimination, the statute required pregnancy to be treated like other disabilities. However, by reversing *Gilbert*, Congress emphasized that protecting women against the financial burdens of pregnancy is an important factor in securing their equality in the workplace. The relationship of the act to existing and future state laws mandating special treatment for pregnant women was also left open.

The Supreme Court and the PDA

The first PDA case to reach the Supreme Court was *Newport News Shipbuilding & Dry Dock Company v. EEOC*, 1983. At issue was the company's hospitalization plan that offered pregnancy benefits to its female employees but provided less extensive pregnancy benefits to the wives of its male employees. John McNulty, an employee of the shipbuilding company, filed a discrimination charge with the EEOC in 1979, claiming that the hospitalization plan discriminated against him. A month later the United Steelworkers Union filed a similar charge on behalf of the other male employees in the company.

Although the company argued that the PDA was intended to protect female employees only, the Supreme Court disagreed. In a 7–2 decision, with Powell and Rehnquist dissenting, Stevens stressed the PDA's evenhanded approach that bars employers from treating pregnancy differently from other medical conditions. "For all Title VII purposes," he said, "discrimination based on a woman's pregnancy is, on its face, discrimination because of her sex."[46] The Newport News Company plan was unacceptable because it employed a pregnancy classification that disadvantaged married male employees.

It is ironic the Supreme Court's first PDA opinion struck down a pregnancy distinction because it discriminated against men.

The Supreme Court Approves
Preferential Treatment

During the 1970s, some states, such as Montana, Connecticut, and Massachusetts, enacted laws mandating reasonable periods of time for pregnancy leave, reasonable guarantees of reinstatement, and protection of fringe benefits.[47] And then shortly before the PDA was passed, California followed the lead of these states by amending its Fair Employment and Housing Act to require employers to provide female employees covered by Title VII up to four months of unpaid pregnancy disability leave and a qualified guarantee of reinstatement.

Lillian Garland worked as a receptionist for the California Federal Savings and Loan Association (Cal Fed) for several years. When she became pregnant, she took a disability leave for three months. Cal Fed allowed employees to take unpaid leaves of absence and promised to try to reinstate them in their jobs if possible. When Garland wanted to return to work, the bank told her there were no openings for receptionists. (She was eventually rehired seven months later.)

She filed a complaint with the California Fair Housing and Employment Commission, charging that Cal Fed violated the statute. Before the commission acted on her complaint, the bank, joined by the Merchants and Manufacturers Association and the California Chamber of Commerce, went to federal court to ask that the California statute be declared invalid under Title VII. The court agreed, holding that it discriminated against disabled men. The Ninth Circuit reversed, ruling that the federal law was a minimum standard of protection for pregnant women. The PDA, the court said, serves as "a floor beneath which pregnancy disability benefits may not drop—not a ceiling above which they may not rise."[48]

The question before the courts was whether the California preferential treatment law conflicted with the PDA's principle of nondiscrimination. According to Martha Minow, "[T]he dilemma in the case . . . was whether women could secure a benefit that would eliminate a burden connected with their gender, without at the same time reactivating negative meanings about their gender."[49]

The major legal issue presented by the case was whether the California law was preempted by the PDA. Under the supremacy clause of the U.S. Constitution, a state law is invalid if preempted by federal statute. And in deciding whether a state law is preempted or not, courts look to the intent of Congress. Preemption can be either explicit (when specified by Congress) or implicit (when the federal law is so comprehensive that it is reasonable to infer that Congress "left no room" for states to act).

When neither condition prevails, a state law is preempted if it conflicts with federal law. Laws conflict "either because 'compliance with both federal and state regulations is a physical impossibility' . . . or because the state law stands 'as an obstacle to the accomplishment and execution of the full purposes and objectives of Congress.'"[50]

The resolution of the preemption issue had far-reaching implications for pregnancy policy. If Title VII preempted the California law, all state preferential treatment laws were doomed. A finding of no preemption meant that state legislation recognizing the special needs of pregnant women through guarantees of leaves of absence and job reinstatement could be reconciled with the nondiscrimination principles of the PDA.

In 1987, in a 6–3 opinion in *California Federal Savings and Loan v. Guerra* (*Cal Fed*), Marshall announced the opinion of the Court, joined by Brennan, Blackmun, Stevens, and Sandra Day O'Connor. Stevens and Antonin Scalia also filed separate concurring opinions. White, joined by Rehnquist and Powell, dissented.

Rejecting Cal Fed's argument that the nondiscrimination language of the PDA mandated a decision striking down the California law, Marshall articulated an expansive interpretation of the act. He said that it did not "require" preferential treatment but neither did it "prohibit" it. Congress was aware of preferential treatment statutes when deliberating passage of the PDA, and there was no indication that it intended to ban them.

Recalling the legislative history of Title VII, Marshall pointed out that it, and by extension the PDA, was intended to remove barriers to allow women to "'participate fully and equally in the workforce, without denying them the fundamental right to full participation in family life.'"[51] The California statute has the same objective. "By 'taking pregnancy into account,' California's pregnancy disability-leave statute allows women, as well as men, to have families without losing their jobs."[52]

Finally, said Marshall, it was possible for an employer to comply with the two laws at the same time. Both the California law and the nondiscrimination requirements of the PDA could be satisfied if the employer merely extended the pregnancy leave and reinstatement benefit to nonpregnant workers. Because there is no conflict between the two statutes, the Court concluded, Title VII does not preempt the California law.

Stevens's and Scalia's concurring opinions expressed concern that the Court's ruling would be interpreted as giving blanket approval to all state preferential treatment laws. Stevens pointed out in a footnote that "the Court has not yet had occasion to explore the exact line of demarcation between permissible and impermissible preferential treatment under Title VII."[53]

Writing for the three dissenters, White wrote that the language of the PDA "leaves no room for preferential treatment of pregnant workers."[54] The legislative history, he added, clearly supports his interpretation of the act.

White noted that Congress was concerned with discrimination *against* pregnant women and did not consider the possibility of discrimination in their favor. Congressional silence on preferential treatment, he concluded, "cannot fairly be interpreted to abrogate the plain statements in the legislative history, not to mention the language of the statute, that equality of treatment was to be the guiding principle of the PDA."[55]

The Supreme Court Rejects Preferential Treatment

In *Wimberly v. Labor and Industrial Relations Commission*, 1987, shortly after *Cal Fed*, the Court shied away from a preferential treatment approach to pregnancy. The case revolved around interpretation of the Federal Unemployment Tax Act (FUTA). The Court had to decide whether FUTA's prohibition against denying unemployment compensation "solely on the basis of pregnancy or termination of pregnancy" required states to accommodate women who leave work because they are pregnant.

Upon returning from her pregnancy leave, Linda Wimberly was told there were no positions available at J. C. Penney, her employer for three years. When she applied for unemployment compensation, her claim was denied because she left work voluntarily. Under Missouri law, unemployment compensation was available only for persons who quit their jobs for "good cause," that is, reasons related to the job or the employer. Leaving for any other reason, including childbirth, was not "good cause."

Although Wimberly argued that Missouri law contravened FUTA, the Supreme Court upheld the Missouri statute. In a 8–0 decision (with Blackmun not participating), the Court ruled that FUTA is intended "only to prohibit states from singling out pregnancy for unfavorable treatment."[56] Because pregnancy was only *one* of any number of reasons for denying her claim for unemployment compensation, the state could have withheld her benefits without knowing about the pregnancy.

Speaking for the Court, O'Connor pointed out that there is a great deal of variation among states with respect to pregnancy and unemployment compensation. The FUTA's ban on pregnancy discrimination was intended to forbid unemployment compensation schemes like the one in Utah, the one struck down in *Turner*. It was not intended to obligate a state to accommodate a worker's pregnancy. The language in FUTA, she explained, should be construed "as prohibiting disadvantageous treatment, rather than as mandating preferential treatment."[57]

In her brief to the Supreme Court, Wimberly argued that "the word 'solely' in the context of the statute meant that a state could not 'deny compensation to an *otherwise eligible* woman' simply because 'she left her job because of pregnancy.'"[58] But in construing the federal tax act so narrowly, the Court held that FUTA allowed states to deny unemployment benefits to "otherwise eligible women" who left work because of pregnancy.

Wimberly was relying on a 1981 Fourth Circuit opinion, *Brown v. Porcher*, in which the circuit court ruled that FUTA prohibited states from denying unemployment benefits to "otherwise eligible" pregnant women who left their jobs. The court held that it did not matter how the claims of other disabled workers were treated; the state could not deny benefits to women unable to work because of pregnancy.[59]

In *Wimberly*, unlike the Fourth Circuit, the high court chose to disregard the fact that the Missouri unemployment compensation law had a disproportionate effect on female workers. Once again, as in *Geduldig*, the Court ignored the financial burdens imposed by the state on female workers. By refusing to alleviate the conflict that often arises between pregnancy and work, the Court again seemed to lend support to the stereotypical notion of women as marginal workers.

Another Look at Preferential Treatment

On January 20, 1987, a week after *Cal Fed* was decided, the Supreme Court refused to decide on the validity of the 1975 Montana Maternity Leave Act (MMLA), which prohibited employers from firing a pregnant woman and from refusing to grant her "a reasonable leave of absence for such pregnancy."[60] Instead, in *Miller-Wohl Company v. Commissioner of Labor and Industry*, the Court remanded the case to the Montana Supreme Court for review.[61] *Miller-Wohl* drew the attention of the nation's feminists by sparking a controversy about accommodating pregnancy in the workplace.

Tamara Buley was a sales clerk at the Three Sisters store in Great Falls, Montana, for less than one month when she began missing work because of morning sickness. Company policy at the time entitled all full-time employees with *one year of seniority* to five paid days of sick leave per year and unpaid leaves of absence for longer illnesses. Because she was not eligible for sick days or a leave of absence, she was fired. There was no evidence that the company treated women differently from men.

Buley filed a complaint with the Montana Labor and Industry Commission, claiming her employer violated the MMLA. The commission ruled in her favor, and the company sought judicial review of the commission's decision in the Montana state district court.[62] The state court judge ruled in favor of Miller-Wohl, finding that the MMLA discriminated against nonpregnant women and men and was preempted by Title VII. On appeal, the Montana Supreme Court reversed.

Announcing its decision in December 1984, the Montana high court upheld the commission's decision. Three alternative positions had been argued to the court. The state of Montana, supported by briefs from the state of California and California feminist organizations, urged the court to uphold the MMLA, arguing that preferential treatment is consistent with Title VII.

In their joint brief, the American Civil Liberties Union, the National Organization for Women, and the League of Women Voters argued that the MMLA was inconsistent with the PDA and asked the court to order it extended to all workers.

Miller-Wohl simply argued that the MMLA was invalid because it was preempted by the PDA.

The Montana Supreme Court found that though the no-leave rule "was facially neutral, it nonetheless subjected pregnant women to job termination on a basis not faced by men."[63] Therefore, even without an MMLA, Miller-Wohl's policy violated the PDA. Additionally, the court ruled, because employers could comply with both laws by simply extending leaves to both sexes, the PDA did not preempt the MMLA.

The Montana court also had a message for the Montana legislature, scheduled to meet shortly. It suggested that further debate over preferential treatment of pregnancy could be halted by expanding the provisions of the MMLA to all employees.

On appeal, the U.S. Supreme Court vacated the Montana Supreme Court's ruling without explanation and remanded the case to the state high court for reconsideration in light of *Cal Fed*. Confessing itself unclear as to why the Supreme Court vacated its decision, the Montana court reinstated its judgment in Buley's favor.

Pregnancy Policy-making

The Supreme Court's pregnancy policy-making to date has ranged from minimal endorsement of a preferential treatment law in *Cal Fed*, to refusal to express an opinion on a more far-reaching maternity leave law in *Miller-Wohl*, to narrow construction of a federal statute banning discrimination on the basis of pregnancy in *Wimberly*.

The decisions show that the Court is unable, or unwilling, to articulate a consistent approach to pregnancy in the workplace. The Court's uncertainty about pregnancy is mirrored in the actions (and inactions) of state and federal lawmakers. Perhaps one of the root causes behind the lack of national pregnancy policy is that policy-makers, including the courts, have not yet decided the extent to which pregnancy should be treated like other disabilities and the extent to which pregnancy, because it is different from other disabilities, requires special treatment. Women's rights advocates, themselves caught up in the special treatment/equal treatment debate, must also accept part of the responsibility for this policy vacuum because they have not presented a clear set of demands to policy-makers.

To some extent, the debate over equal treatment/special treatment has diverted feminists from the task of formulating a politically feasible pregnancy policy. The fault is not all theirs, however, because the proposals they have made have largely fallen on deaf ears.

The Equality Model

Concerned about the implications of a special treatment approach, some feminists argue that the legislation tested in *Miller-Wohl* renews visions of protectionist laws finally laid to rest in the 1960s. Maternity leave provisions, they say, represent a step backward for women's employment equality. They "tend to encourage stereotyping and hierarchy, and thus operate as *Muller [v. Oregon]* did, though far less offensively."[64]

Wendy Williams, one of the foremost proponents of the equality approach, urges laws based on an "assimilationist" model of equality. The model contemplates an equality arising from the joinder of men's and women's interests in the workplace.[65] Following this model, Williams believes that considerations of sex should be kept to a minimum in the policy-making process because one cannot make principled distinctions between special treatment in favor of pregnant women and special treatment against them. Because pregnancy legislation has restricted women's employment opportunities in the past, pregnancy should be treated like other physical conditions affecting workers.

Aside from the risks of restrictive legislation, Williams and other advocates of the equality model believe that special treatment for pregnant workers draws attention away from demands for labor reform such as eliminating toxins in the workplace and creating viable sick-leave and disability plans for all employees. Even worse, they argue, attention that should be focused on employers with inadequate sick-leave policies will become displaced by resentment against pregnant employees.

A Critique of the Equality Model

While the equal treatment model has superficial appeal, it ignores the needs of too many pregnant workers: the nonunion employee in the North Carolina textile factory and Tennessee chicken ranch, the nurse's aide in a small private hospital, the lone secretary working for a small business, or the waitperson serving meals in a roadside diner.

Equal treatment proponents play an important role in advancing women's rights by advocating the goal of equality in the work force. But they lose sight of the fact that equality affects female and male workers differently because of the differential burdens of pregnancy. Insisting on equality or parity of treatment between men and women ignores the effects of pregnancy on employment, an effect that falls disproportionately on female employees. Failing to accommodate the needs of pregnant workers affects their ability to compete in the workplace and leaves the impression that pregnancy and employment are incompatible. Preferential treatment of pregnancy sends the opposite message.

The Preferential Treatment Model

Taking heart from the Montana Supreme Court's decision in *Miller-Wohl*, proponents of a special treatment model argue that a positive action or "reasonable accommodation" approach to pregnancy is necessary to overcome structural inequities in the work force. The equality approach, they assert, is premised on a workplace adapted to the male experience of reproduction and family life. Merely treating pregnant women like "disabled" men will not ensure equality in the labor force; only positive action that recognizes the special needs of pregnant women will serve.

Special treatment advocates Linda Krieger and Patricia Cooney contend that the nondiscrimination principles of the PDA will not overcome sex discrimination in the workplace because they merely require women to be treated like similarly situated men. Because women tend to be concentrated in female-dominated occupations, there are often no similarly situated men to compare them to. And since women are more likely to hold nonunion, part-time, or temporary jobs entitling them to few fringe benefits, they are less likely to have sufficient bargaining power to demand disability rights on their own.

In their article on the *Miller-Wohl* case, Krieger and Cooney deny that the Montana legislation raises the evil specter of protective legislation. The Montana law is different from the old protective laws, they maintain. Furthermore, they argue, it is easy to distinguish between Montana's statute and restrictive laws based on stereotypical assumptions about women's capacities. The MMLA "does not provide women with an additional benefit denied to men; it merely prevents women from having to suffer an additional burden which no male would ever have to bear."[66]

Attacking the equal treatment approach, they assert that a no-leave policy such as Miller-Wohl's violates Title VII's adverse impact doctrine. To support their argument, they cite a 1981 ruling by the District of Columbia Circuit Court in which the court invalidated an employer's flat ten-day disability leave policy because it "portended a drastic effect on women employees of childbearing age—an impact no male would ever encounter."[67]

Responding to the argument that the language of the PDA precludes a preferential status for pregnancy, Krieger and Cooney maintain that a literal interpretation of the PDA would vitiate the disparate impact theory of sex discrimination. And they insist "there is no reason to believe that Congress intended such a result."[68]

Reconciling the Debate

With their victory over the Supreme Court in 1978, women were faced with the difficult task of formulating an approach to pregnancy that was consistent with equality theory, could be justified legally, and was politically realistic. Unfortunately, the controversy of whether pregnant women must receive the same benefits as disabled workers—no more and no less—often diverted attention from this task and retarded achievement of the goal.

Realizing the futility of debating among themselves, some have attempted to reconcile the two approaches to pregnancy legislation. On a theoretical level, recognizing that it is contradictory to insist that men and women are equal while at the same time demanding special treatment, Herma Hill Kay argues that traditional equality theory, based on the assumption that equality requires the same treatment, is inapplicable to the issue of pregnancy in the workplace. The formal model of equality, she points out, ignores the fact that where people are different, to treat them alike is to treat them unequally.

Instead, she proposes equality of opportunity theory as the appropriate framework for analysis because it "offers a theoretical basis for making unequals equal in the limited sense of removing barriers which prevent individuals from performing according to their abilities."[69] Equality of opportunity theory justifies modification of the workplace rules for short periods of time so that women are not adversely affected by pregnancy.

Concerned about the effect of labeling pregnancy as a women's issue, but anxious to promote equal opportunity for women in the labor force, Kay advocates a limited role for sex-based classifications. She suggests a pregnancy policy in which "biological reproductive sex differences" are assigned legal significance "only when they are being utilized for reproductive purposes."[70] The "episodic analysis" she proposes requires policies that accommodate working women in jobs where their performance is adversely affected by their pregnancy. Unless such policies are instituted, she warns, a woman "will experience employment disadvantages arising from her reproductive activity that are not encountered by her male co-worker."[71]

While rejecting the equality model, advocates of special treatment fear that their approach might lead to the further entrenchment of women in the *childrearing* role. They recognize that if leaves of absence extend beyond the time needed to compensate the physical needs of pregnancy, they perpetuate the image of women as the primary child caretaker. This can be avoided, they say, by limiting pregnancy leaves to the medical aspects of pregnancy.

Ann Scales, another critic of the equal treatment approach, argues that a preferential status for pregnancy must be accompanied by reform of the workplace to encourage egalitarian child-rearing responsibilities. Specifically, she believes it necessary to make part-time work more attractive and accessible to all workers and to allow greater flexibility in the workday schedule so that both men and women can perform their dual roles of parent and worker.[72]

Also attempting to bridge the gap between the equal treatment/special treatment models, Lucinda Finley urges a unified focus on the "responsibilities" and "interconnectedness" of all workers. She criticizes the equality approach because it is premised on the belief that "whatever is male is the norm." But she also rejects the special treatment approach because it furthers the stereotypical notion that pregnancy is a "woman's problem."[73]

What is needed, she asserts, is to transcend equality analysis and transform the workplace into a place that promotes human responsibilities. This can be done by recognizing the interdependence of home and job for both male and female workers. Finley believes that state maternity-leave laws, such as California's, have made a good start in the direction of equality. And rather than criticize these laws as special treatment, she feels they should be extolled as benefits to both sexes and their scope expanded.

Agreeing with this principle, Christine Littleton identifies two versions of sexual equality: symmetrical and asymmetrical. The first, urging men and women to be similarly treated, has two models—the assimilationist model (where social institutions are urged to treat women as they already treat men) and the androgynous model (where social institutions are urged to treat men and women according to a norm patterned on a middle ground of behavior of the two sexes). She rejects both models, and indeed, the entire symmetrical approach, as infeasible and undesirable.

The asymmetrical approach she urges recognizes biological and cultural differences between the sexes. She wants society to adopt an asymmetrical "acceptance" model which accommodates these differences. In her view, society must learn to accept the different behaviors of men and women and cease to rely on these differences to justify inequality. Society must recognize that women are the primary caretakers of children and should learn "how to assure that equal resources, status, and access to social decisionmaking flow to those women (and few men) who engage in this socially female behavior."[74]

National Maternity Policies

Despite the differences of opinion, there is a good deal of commonality among these views. Anxious to make clear distinctions between childbearing and child-rearing, all share the goal of restructuring the workplace so that men and women share responsibilities for work and family. And they agree that energy must be redirected from debate among themselves to a combined effort to place pregnancy policy on the political agenda.

The task of agenda setting must begin with the recognition that currently among industrialized nations, the United States is virtually alone in failing to provide job protection for pregnant employees. Among twenty-six industrialized nations in the world, the United States, joined only by the Republic of South Africa, has no national maternity leave law. Altogether more than 100 countries (117 to be precise) guarantee women childbirth leave with job protection and at least some form of income replacement during their leaves.[75]

First established in Germany in the late 1800s as a social insurance benefit, paid leave and job reinstatement for pregnant workers soon spread to the rest of Europe. Part of the impetus for the commitment to national maternity policies in Europe came from the International Labor Organization's (ILO) Convention on Maternity Protection for Working Women in 1919. Revised in 1952, the convention established fourteen weeks (six weeks before birth and eight after) as the standard for pregnancy leave.

A survey of national maternity and parental leave policies published in 1986 compared benefits provided in selected Western European countries, Canada, Chile, and the United States. Based on variations of the ILO model, benefits range from fifty-two weeks of leave in Sweden and Austria to eighteen weeks in Chile to none in the United States. Income replacement ranges from 100 percent of pay for thirty-five weeks in Finland to 60 percent of pay for fifteen weeks in Canada to none in the United States. Finally, with the exception of the United States, all countries guarantee job security during the leave. Somewhat disturbing though is the fact that, except for in Sweden and Finland, only women are eligible for childcare leave.[76]

Adopting a national pregnancy policy "reflects a view of maternity as contributing to the needs of the society as well as those of individual adults and families, and a view of income loss at the time of maternity as a social risk against which the society as a whole should provide protection."[77] The U.S. reluctance to initiate such limited measures as short-term guaranteed leaves and qualified reinstatement show that it is far from adopting this view of maternity.

State Maternity Policies

In contrast to so many other nations in the world, the United States has not yet developed a national policy to deal with the increasing numbers of women in the work force. Rather, the U.S. experience has been to deny its collective responsibility for pregnancy in the workplace. The major legislation to date, the PDA, has taken only a minimalist stance on maternity policy. In part, the decentralized nature of American public policy-making, exacerbated by the federalist system and the state's primary role in legislating for public health and safety, has retarded efforts towards a national policy on the ILO model.[78]

To date, the primary locus of pregnancy policy-making has been at the state level. State laws affecting pregnancy can be divided into three categories. A few statutes, such as the ones in Maryland and Maine, are based on the equality model and mirror the PDA's nondiscrimination principle of treating pregnancy like other disabilities.[79] Thirteen states distinguish pregnancy from other disabling conditions by mandating affirmative rights for pregnant women. With one exception, all are similar to the one upheld in *Cal Fed.*[80] There is no uniformity among these laws as they differ with respect to coverage of full-time or part-time employees, mandatory waiting periods for eligibility, the minimum number of employees required before an employer is covered by the statute, the permissible length of the leaves, and allowable reasons for an employer's refusal to reinstate women seeking to return to their jobs.

Only four states currently have parental leave acts that allow either one or both parents to take unpaid childcare leave. Again, conditions vary with respect to length of leave, type of employee, size of company, reinstatement rights, and waiting period for eligibility.[81]

Because of the diversity among, and the limited geographic impact of, state laws, pregnancy policy-making requires more than a piecemeal state-by-state approach. But while it is clear that the federal government must take the lead, Congress has not yet successfully devised a national policy to deal with pregnancy in the work force. And indications to date are that the U.S. version of such a policy, if enacted as currently proposed, will be a far cry from the ILO model.

The Family and Medical Leave Act

While some attempts to accommodate pregnancy already exist at the state level, a national policy is critically needed to allow women to become fully integrated members of the work force. A federal parental leave bill could advance equal employment opportunity by addressing the needs of pregnant women on the job and, if sex-neutral, would be an important first step in promoting equal parenting. Such a law could also put an end to the special treatment/equal treatment debate. However, even if the bill under consideration is eventually approved by Congress and the president, given its limited reach, it is unlikely to satisfy feminist demands—of any perspective—for an acceptable pregnancy policy.

For the past four years, Congress has been deliberating over a proposed Family and Medical Leave Act. First introduced in 1986, H.R. 4300 would have required public and private employers with fifteen or more workers to grant up to eighteen weeks of unpaid "family" leave to employees (male or female) for a variety of circumstances, including birth, adoption, or serious illness of a child or dependent parent. Employees would have been permitted to take up to twenty-six weeks of unpaid disability leave for medical reasons. The bill would have required employers to continue health insurance benefits during the leave time and would have allowed employees to reclaim their jobs with seniority and other benefits intact. The bill also would have created a commission to study the issue of income replacement during leaves.

Supported by labor, women's rights, and health groups, the bill faced strong opposition from the business community, who objected to it as anticompetitive and expensive. A letter to members of Congress from the Chamber of Commerce and other business groups argued that the proposed legislation "is contrary to the voluntary, flexible and comprehensive benefit system that the private sector has developed."[82] Despite opposition, H.R. 4300 was approved in a voice vote by the House Education and Labor Committee on June 24, 1986, but never reached the House floor.

In the 100th Congress, on February 3, 1987, Democratic Representatives William Clay of Missouri and Patricia Schroeder of Colorado made another attempt at enacting a family leave act by introducing H.R. 925, an updated version of the 1986 bill. Approved by the House Subcommittee on Labor-Management Relations, the bill was later dramatically reshaped by the full Education and Labor Committee.

H.R. 925 was accompanied by intense lobbying on both sides. Supporting the bill were members of the National Organization for Women, who sent more than twenty-five thousand Mother's Day cards to congressional leaders. Testifying against the bill at a Senate subcommittee hearing, a member of the Chamber of Commerce gloomily predicted that the legislation would cost over $27 billion a year. The General Accounting Office (GAO) rejected this figure, saying that the Chamber's estimates were based on "unrealistic assumptions." The GAO placed the amount at $188 million with a fifty-employee cutoff and $212 million at the thirty-five-employee level.[83]

The final House committee-approved version of H.R. 925 set the threshold size of a covered business at fifty employees, the number dropping automatically to thirty-five after three years unless Congress took affirmative steps against the decrease.[84] Employees would be permitted to take leaves of absence to care for others, including children and ill parents, for ten weeks over a two-year period; personal disability leaves would be limited to fifteen weeks per year. To be eligible for leave, employees had to work for a minimum of twenty hours a week for at least a year. Employers were given the right to refuse to reinstate the highest-paid 10 percent of their work force.[85]

Although the bill was approved by a House committee in November 1987, it failed to pass out of Congress that year. The next year a Senate version became stalled in a filibuster, and although parental leave became part of a congressional pro-family package along with childcare and a crackdown on child pornography, it did not clear Congress in 1988.

Then in February 1989, parental leave legislation was again introduced in both the Senate and House. Both bills required companies to provide up to ten weeks every two years to new parents and workers with ill parents or children. The bills differed slightly in that the House version, H.R. 770, covered businesses with fifty or more workers and allowed fifteen weeks of medical leave. To qualify for the benefit, workers would have to be employed by the company for at least one year and have worked at least one thousand hours (nine hundred hours for the Senate version) in the year before taking a leave. The Senate measure, S. 345, covered businesses with twenty or more workers and allowed thirteen weeks of individual medical leave in a year for a serious illness.

Both House and Senate bills were approved by a total of four congressional committees during March and April 1989.[86] Shortly thereafter, in a letter to Utah Senator Orrin Hatch, ranking Republican on the Labor and Human Resources Committee, Labor Secretary Elizabeth Dole indicated that she would advise President George Bush to veto the bill. She stated "we strongly believe this [benefit program] can be best achieved voluntarily; therefore, the administration strongly opposes the mandated approach to employee benefits."[87]

The House passed H.R. 770 in a 237–187 vote on May 10, 1990. Just before the House vote, White House Chief of Staff John Sununu told business leaders at a White House meeting that "if Congress passed a measure requiring parental leave, Mr. Bush would veto it because he opposed Government's dictating fringe benefits."[88] The bill was approved in a voice vote by the Senate on June 14, 1990.

In the final bill H.R. 770, employers with fifty or more employees would have to offer twelve weeks of unpaid medical or parental leave. Only one parent could take parental leave at a time. Medical leave could be used to provide care for an ill child, parent, or spouse. Workers would be eligible for the released time if they worked in the job for at least one thousand hours over the course of a year. Employers would have to continue health coverage for employees on leave and place returning employees in their previous jobs or equivalent positions.[89]

In response to the congressional vote on the Family and Medical Leave Act of 1990, the Office of Management and Budget released a statement restating the administration's opposition to the bill, saying the White House favored the goal of parental and medical leave but wanted to leave it in the hands of the private sector.[90]

On June 29, 1990, as promised, Bush vetoed the legislation. In his veto message, he said, "I want to emphasize my belief that time off for a child's birth or adoption or for family illness is an important benefit for employers to offer employees. I strongly object, however, to the Federal Government mandating leave policies for America's employers and work force. H.R. 770 would do just that."[91]

Almost one month later, on July 25, 1990, the House of Representatives failed to override the president's veto in a 232–195 vote, fifty-four votes shy of the necessary two-thirds. Reacting to the vote, a White House official said, "We're very pleased that the President was able to sustain the veto. . . . We feel that we will be able to realize sensible parental leave policies, but without it being mandated by Washington."[92]

Although the measure failed this time, members of Congress promised to keep presenting family leave legislation to the president until they succeeded in its passage. Ironically, even if the bill had passed, the U.S. family would still lag far behind the European family in family and pregnancy leave protection.

NOTES

1. Note, "Pregnancy and Equality: A Precarious Alliance," *Southern California Law Review* 60(1987), p. 1349.

2. Wendy Williams, "The Equality Crisis: Some Reflections on Culture, Courts, and Feminism," *Women's Rights Law Reporter* 7(1982), p. 193.

3. Eva Rubin, *The Supreme Court and the American Family* (Westport: Greenwood Press, 1986), pp. 77–78.

4. Alice H. Cook, *The Working Mother* (New York: Cornell University School of Industrial and Labor Relations, 1978), p. 5.

5. One manifestation of this ambivalence has been the issue of employer limitations on female workers to protect their fetuses or potential fetuses, the so-called fetal protection policies. On March 20, 1991, in *International Union, United Automobile, Aerospace and Agricultural Implement Workers v. Johnson Controls*, 59 U.S.L.W. 4209 (1991), the Supreme Court held that Title VII of the 1964 Civil Rights Act, as amended by the Pregnancy Discrimination Act of 1978, forbids sex-specific fetal protection policies. For a discussion of the history of fetal protection litigation, see Brian Hembacher, "Fetal Protection Policies: Reasonable Protection or Unreasonable Limitation on Female Employees," *Industrial Relations Law Journal* 11(1989); Wendy Williams, "Firing the Woman to Protect the Fetus: The Reconciliation of Fetal Protection with Employment Opportunity under Title VII," *Georgetown Law Journal* 69(1981); Mary Becker, "From *Muller v. Oregon* to Fetal Vulnerability Policies," *University of Chicago Law Review* 53(1986).

6. Elizabeth Duncan Koontz, "Childbirth and Childrearing Leave: Job-Related Benefits," *New York University Law Forum* 17(1971), pp. 481–82 n. 11, quoting from Citizens' Advisory Council on the Status of Women, Job-Related Maternity Benefits (Statement of Principles adopted on October 29, 1970), reprinted in *Citizens' Advisory Council on the Status of Women, Job Related Maternity Benefits* (November 1970), Appendix D at 20.

7. Koontz, "Childbirth and Childrearing Leave," pp. 487–88.

8. General Counsel Opinion Letter, November 10, 1966. Cited in Note, "Current Trends in Pregnancy Benefits—1972 EEOC Guidelines Interpreted," *DePaul Law Review* 24(1974), pp. 129–30 n. 15. Opinion letters are written to specific employers. See Note, "Pregnancy and Sex-Based Discrimination in Employment: A Post-*Aiello* Analysis," *Cincinnati Law Review* 44(1975), pp. 76–77.

9. Wendy Williams, "Equality's Riddle: Pregnancy and the Equal Treatment/Special Treatment Debate," *New York University Review of Law and Social Change* 13(1984–85), pp. 335–36.

10. See Note, "Pregnancy and Sex-Based Discrimination," pp. 61–67. The section dealing with disability insurance and leave, 29 C.F.R. §1604.10(b), states that

disabilities caused or contributed to by pregnancy, miscarriage, abortion, childbirth, and recovery therefrom . . . should be treated as [temporary disabilities] under any health or temporary disability insurance or sick leave plan available in connection with employment. Written and unwritten employment policies and practices . . . shall be applied to disability due to pregnancy or childbirth on the same terms and conditions as they are applied to other temporary disabilities.

11. Note, "Current Trends in Pregnancy Benefits," pp. 133–34.

12. Bureau of National Affairs, *Pregnancy and Employment* (Washington, DC: Bureau of National Affairs, 1987), p. 3.

13. Maternity leave policies in public schools became subject to Title VII in 1972.

14. In his concurring opinion, Powell criticized the majority's reliance on the irrebuttable presumption doctrine. He argued that the cases should have been decided on equal protection grounds and that the board's classifications could have been struck down as irrational under minimal scrutiny analysis. Speaking for himself and Burger, Rehnquist's dissent attacked the Court for interfering in a state's decision to draw lines as part of the legislative process.

15. *Cleveland Board of Education v. LaFleur,* 414 U.S. 632, 644 (1974).

16. *LaFleur,* 414 U.S. at 647.

17. *Turner v. Department of Employment Security,* 423 U.S. 44 (1975).

18. Katharine T. Bartlett, "Pregnancy and the Constitution: The Uniqueness Trap," *California Law Review* 62(1974), p. 1547.

19. Disabilities resulting from court commitment as a dipsomaniac, drug addict, or sexual psychopath were also not covered by the plan. During oral argument, the State admitted that the exclusion was virtually meaningless as the courts almost never commit people for such illnesses. *Geduldig v. Aeillo,* 417 U.S 484, 499 n. 3 (1974) (Brennan, J., dissenting).

20. Ann Scales, "Towards a Feminist Jurisprudence," *Indiana Law Journal* 56(1980–1981), p. 378.

21. *Geduldig,* 417 U.S. at 494. Shortly before the lower court's ruling, in another case brought by a woman disabled by an abnormal pregnancy, the California Court of Appeal held the state plan must provide disability payments to women missing work because of complications from abnormal pregnancies. As a result of the California court decision, the disability program was revised so that the three women with the abnormal pregnancies were given benefits for time lost from work; the fourth woman, disabled by normal pregnancy, was not. The only issue before the Supreme Court was the exclusion of benefits for normal pregnancy.

22. *Geduldig,* 417 U.S. at 493.

23. Under a stricter standard of review, the Court would have demanded more and better evidence from the state that the addition of pregnancy disability insurance would have severely disrupted the disability insurance program. Even if such evidence were available, under a stricter form of scrutiny the Court would have been less willing to accept financial exigency as a basis for discrimination. See Scales, "Towards a Feminist Jurisprudence," pp. 391–93; Harriet Hubacker Coleman, "Barefoot and Pregnant—Still: Equal Protection for Men and Women in Light of *Geduldig v. Aiello,*" *South Texas Law Journal* 16(1975), pp. 227–32.

24. *Geduldig,* 417 U.S. at 496–97.

25. *Geduldig,* 417 U.S. at 496–97 n. 20.

26. *Geduldig,* 417 U.S. at 501 (Brennan, J., dissenting).

27. See Comment, *Geduldig v. Aiello:* Pregnancy Classifications and the Definition of Sex Discrimination," *Columbia Law Review* 75(1975).

28. Comment, "Pregnancy Disability Benefits and Title VII: Pregnancy Does Not Involve Sex," *Baylor Law Review* 29(1977), p. 266.

29. See Scales, "Towards a Feminist Jurisprudence," pp. 380–81.

30. "Comment, *Geduldig v. Aiello,*" pp. 469–71. Eventually, the California legislature revised its disability program and extended benefits to women temporarily disabled by normal pregnancy. Williams, "Equality's Riddle," p. 344 n. 78.

31. Patricia Huckle, "The Womb Factor: Policy on Pregnancy and the Employment of Women," in Ellen Boneparth and Emily Stoper, eds., *Women, Power and Policy,* 2d ed. (New York: Pergamon Press, 1988), p. 135.

32. *Gilbert v. General Electric Company,* 519 F.2d 661, 664 (4th Cir. 1975).

33. Scales, "Towards a Feminist Jurisprudence," p. 399.

34. *General Electric Company v. Gilbert,* 429 U.S. 125, 133–34 (1976). The district court decision in favor of plaintiffs preceded *Geduldig.* The appellate court reached its decision after *Geduldig* but declined to be controlled by it because *Gilbert* was a Title VII case.

35. *Gilbert,* 429 U.S. at 138–39 (emphasis in the original). Rehnquist's analysis was not entirely factual. As in *Geduldig,* the plan allowed the payment of benefits for such male-specific risks as circumcisions, vasectomies, and prostatectomies. There were *some* risks unique to men covered by the plan; Rehnquist never bothered to explain why risks unique to women did not have to be covered as well.

36. *Gilbert,* 429 U.S. at 162 n. 5 (Stevens, J., dissenting).

37. *Nashville Gas Company v. Satty,* 434 U.S. 136, 142 (1977).

38. *Los Angeles Department of Water & Power v. Manhart,* 435 U.S. 702, 715 (1978).

39. Joyce Gelb and Marian Lief Palley, *Women and Public Policies* (Princeton: Princeton University Press, 1987), p. 167.

40. Section 701(k) of the Pregnancy Discrimination Act states that

> the terms 'because of sex' or 'on the basis of sex' include, but are not limited to, because of or on the basis of pregnancy, childbirth, or related medical conditions; and women affected by pregnancy, childbirth, or related medical conditions shall be treated the same for all employment-related purposes, including receipt of benefits under fringe benefit programs, as other persons not so affected but similar in their ability or inability to work.

41. H.Rep. No. 948, 95th Cong., 2d Sess. 2 (1978).

42. H.Rep. No. 948, 95th Cong., 2d Sess. 10–11 (1978).

43. H.Rep. No. 948, 95th Cong., 2d Sess. 5 (1978).

44. 123 *Cong. Rec.* 29,663 (1977).

45. The final bill provided that an employer is not required

> to pay for health insurance benefits for abortion, except where the life of the mother would be endangered if the fetus were carried to term, or except where medical complications have arisen from an abortion: Provided, That nothing herein shall preclude an employer from providing abortion benefits or otherwise affect bargaining agreements in regard to abortion.

46. *Newport News Shipbuilding & Dry Dock Company v. EEOC,* 462 U.S. 669, 684 (1983).

47. Note, "Pregnancy and Equality," pp. 1357–58.

48. *California Federal Savings and Loan v. Guerra,* 758 F.2d 390, 396 (9th Cir. 1985).

49. Martha Minow, "Foreword: Justice Engendered," *Harvard Law Review* 101(1987), p. 19.

50. *California Federal Savings and Loan (Cal Fed) v. Guerra,* 479 U.S. 272, 281 (1987).

51. *Cal Fed,* 479 U.S. at 289, quoting 123 Cong. Rec. 29,658 (1977).

52. *Cal Fed,* 479 U.S. at 289.

53. *Cal Fed,* 479 U.S. at 294 n. 4 (Stevens, J., concurring).

54. *Cal Fed,* 479 U.S. at 297 (White, J., dissenting).

55. *Cal Fed,* 479 U.S. at 300 (White, J., dissenting).

56. *Wimberly v. Labor and Industrial Relations Commission,* 479 U.S. 511, 516 (1987).

57. *Wimberly,* 479 U.S. at 517.

58. Brief for Petitioner at 7, *Wimberly,* cited in Note, "Pregnancy Discrimination in Unemployment Benefits: Section 3304(a) (12) Merely an Antidiscrimination Provision," *Stetson Law Review* 17(1987), p. 234 (emphasis in the original).

59. *Brown v. Porcher,* 660 F.2d 1001, 1004 (4th Cir. 1981).

60. Montana Code Annotated, §§39–7–203(1)–(2). In 1983, §39–7–203 was recodified as §49–2–310. The maternity leave functions of the Commission of Labor and Industry were transferred to the Commission of Human Rights.

61. *Miller-Wohl Company v. Commissioner of Labor and Industry,* 479 U.S. 1050 (1987).

62. This case had a very complex history. The first test of the law arose when Miller-Wohl sought a declaratory judgment in a Montana federal district court asking the court to

declare the MMLA invalid because it violated the equal protection and due process clauses of the Fourteenth Amendment and was preempted by the PDA. In June 1981, the district court upheld the MMLA, denying, among other things, that the Act was preempted by the PDA.

The court held that the MMLA does not conflict with Title VII because the latter would also invalidate a no-leave policy because of its disparate effect on women. Both statutes, said the court, were intended to protect "the right of . . . man and woman alike, to procreate and raise a family without sacrificing the right of the wife to work." Employers, added the court, could comply with both Title VII and the MMLA by allowing reasonable disability leaves to first-year employees of both sexes. *Miller-Wohl Company v. Commissioner of Labor and Industry,* 515 F.Supp. 1264, 1266–67 (D. Mont. 1981).

A year later, in August 1982, the Ninth Circuit Court of Appeals, finding the lower court lacked jurisdiction, vacated its judgment. *Miller-Wohl Company v. Commissioner of Labor and Industry,* 685 F.2d 1088 (9th Cir. 1982).

63. *Miller-Wohl Company v. Commissioner of Labor and Industry,* 692 P.2d 1243, 1252 (Mont. 1984).

64. Frances Olsen, "The Family and the Market: A Study of Ideology and Legal Reform," *Harvard Law Review* 96(1983), p. 1558.

65. This is also known as the "liberal" model of equality. See Williams, "Equality's Riddle"; Williams, "The Equality Crisis." See also Koontz, "Childbirth and Childrearing Leave."

66. Linda J. Krieger and Patricia N. Cooney, "The Miller-Wohl Controversy: Equal Treatment, Positive Action and the Meaning of Women's Equality," *Golden Gate University Law Review* 13(1983), p. 533.

67. *Abraham v. Graphic Arts International Union,* 660 F.2d 811, 819 (D.C. Cir. 1981). Given the Supreme Court's recent ruling in *Wards Cove Packing Company v. Atonio,* 109 S.Ct. 2115 (1989), the disparate impact argument might require revision.

68. Krieger and Cooney, "The Miller-Wohl Controversy," p. 529.

69. Herma Hill Kay, "Equality and Difference: The Case of Pregnancy," *Berkeley Women's Law Journal* 1(1985), p. 26.

70. Kay, "Equality and Difference," p. 22.

71. Kay, "Equality and Difference," p. 27.

72. Scales, "Towards a Feminist Jurisprudence," pp. 438–39.

73. Lucinda Finley, "Transcending Equality Theory: A Way out of the Maternity and the Workplace Debate," *Columbia Law Review* 86(1986), pp. 1155–57.

74. Christine Littleton, "Restructuring Sexual Equality," *California Law Review* 75(1987), p. 1297.

75. Eschel M. Rhoodie, *Discrimination against Women: A Global Survey* (Jefferson, NC: McFarland, 1989), p. 260.

76. *Congressional Quarterly,* June 28, 1986, p. 1485.

77. Sheila B. Kamerman and Alfred J. Kahn, "Family Policy: Has the United States Learned from Europe?," *Policy Studies Review* 8(1989), pp. 585–87.

78. See Patricia Spakes, "A Feminist Case against National Family Policy: View to the Future," *Policy Studies Review* 8(1989), p. 614. Spakes argues that the European model is flawed because it perpetuates the primary role of women as mothers.

79. Note, "Pregnancy and Equality," pp. 1357–58.

80. The states are California, Colorado, Connecticut, Hawaii, Illinois, Iowa, Kansas, Massachusetts, Montana, New Hampshire, Oregon, Tennessee, and Washington. The state laws or regulations provide for childbirth leaves—except for Massachusetts, which guarantees reinstatement to *female employees* for giving birth or adopting a child under three. See Christine Neylon O'Brien and Gerald A. Madek, "Pregnancy Discrimination and Maternity Leave Laws," *Dickinson Law Review* 93(1989), pp. 326–30.

81. The four states are Connecticut, Minnesota, Oregon, and Rhode Island. See O'Brien and Madek, "Pregnancy Discrimination," pp. 331–36.

82. *Congressional Quarterly,* June 28, 1986, p. 1485. As originally proposed and approved by the House Education and Labor Subcommittee in a 9–6 vote, the bill would have reached employers with as few as five workers. See *Congressional Quarterly,* June 14, 1986, p. 1361.

83. *Congressional Quarterly,* May 16, 1987, p. 999; *Congressional Quarterly,* November 21, 1987, p. 2884.

84. Note, "Pregnancy and Employment: Three Approaches to Equal Opportunity," *Boston University Law Review* 68(1988), pp. 1040–45.

85. According to a General Accounting Office study, the fifty-employee cutoff would exempt 95 percent of the nation's employers from the bill. The remaining 5 percent of employers covered by the bill employ 39 percent of the work force, about 42 million people. *Congressional Quarterly,* November 21, 1987, p. 2884.

86. *Congressional Quarterly,* January 6, 1990, p. 17. The Senate Labor and Human Resources Committee approved S. 345 on April 19, 1989. The House Education and Labor Committee approved its bill on March 8, 1990; the House Post Office and Civil Service Committee approved it on April 12, 1990, and the House Administration Committee voted in favor on April 26, 1990.

87. *Congressional Quarterly,* April 22, 1989, p. 892.

88. *New York Times,* May 8, 1990.

89. *Congressional Quarterly,* June 16, 1990, p. 1873; *Congressional Quarterly,* June 30, 1990, p. 2055. The bill would have given federal workers eighteen weeks of parental leave and twenty-six weeks of medical leave. House workers would get the same benefits as private employees; Senate workers were not included in the bill.

90. *Congressional Quarterly,* June 16, 1990, p. 1873.

91. *Congressional Quarterly,* July 7, 1990, p. 2178.

92. *New York Times,* July 26, 1990; *Congressional Quarterly,* July 28, 1990, p. 2405.

7

Equality in Education

In the historic *Brown v. Board of Education* decision in 1954, the Supreme Court announced that "segregation of children in public schools solely on the basis of race, even though the physical facilities and other 'tangible' factors may be equal, deprive[s] the children of the minority group of equal educational opportunities."[1]

The Separate but Equal Doctrine

In *Brown*, the Court held that it was unconstitutional to separate students in public schools on the basis of race. Especially in high schools and elementary schools, the Court proclaimed, separating children "from others of similar age and qualifications solely because of their race generates a feeling of inferiority . . . that may affect their hearts and minds in a way unlikely ever to be undone."[2]

In its only full-scale opinion on sex-segregated education, in 1982, the Court refused to echo *Brown* and rule "that in the field of public education the doctrine of 'separate but equal' has no place [and that with respect to sex] separate educational facilities are inherently unequal."[3] The timidity with which the Court addressed the separate but equal doctrine in single-sex schools stands in stark contrast to the forcefulness with which it has attacked the separate but equal doctrine in racially separate schools.

Lower Court Rulings against Sex Segregation

In the 1970s, there were three lower court decisions that appeared to support the abolition of sex-separated public schools. A closer look reveals that even though the school districts' separate admissions policies were ruled unconstitutional, the separate but equal doctrine survived intact.

The first lower court decision advancing sexual equality in education was a 1970 Virginia district court opinion that approved a resolution adopted by the University of Virginia Board of Visitors. The case arose when four women sued the university because the main campus at Charlottesville, the most prestigious in the state university system, was denied to them. With the court urging settlement of the case, the Board of Visitors agreed to implement a three-year plan during which female students would be phased into the Charlottesville campus. Under this plan, by 1972 men and women would be admitted on an equal basis with no limitations on the number of women allowed into the school.

Concerned that the plan for integration depended on final consent by the Virginia legislature and could be undone by a future Board of Visitors, the plaintiffs wanted a judicial order to solidify the board's intention. Noting that until recently, separate-sex education was widely accepted, the court ruled that the Charlottesville campus could no longer exclude women. Excluding women limited their educational opportunities because it blocked women's access to the greater diversity of courses at Charlottesville and the greater prestige associated with a degree from that campus. And the availability of coeducational and women-only schools in the state system did not adequately compensate for the deprivation.[4]

Even though the young women had also challenged the other sex-separated colleges within the state system, the court restricted its holding to the Charlottesville campus. It declined to order the entire system to integrate, in part because the court was not anxious to order the state to admit women into its men-only military academy.

In 1972, a Massachusetts federal district court upheld a challenge against the Boston School District by ruling that Girls Latin could no longer impose higher admissions standards than Boys Latin. The city argued that its admissions policy was based on the number of seats available in each school. Since the boys' high school had more space available (with three thousand seats to the girls' fifteen hundred seats), its entrance examination requirements were lower than the girls' high school. Boys were admitted with scores of 120, while girls needed at least 133 points to gain admission. The court found that the higher admissions standards for girls denied them equal protection and ordered a uniform cutoff score for boys and girls.[5]

Then, in 1974, another discriminatory admissions policy was success- · fully challenged. The prestigious Lovell High School, a San Francisco public school, was committed to a 50/50 boy to girl ratio. To achieve this, the school accepted boys with a 3.25 grade point average but required girls to have a 3.50 average.

Although the Ninth Circuit Court of Appeals did not believe the school's policies were motivated by invidious discrimination, it rejected the city's argument that a balance of sexes improved the education environment. Nor did the court accept the city's explanation that the policy was legitimate because girls were academically superior in their early years and boys needed time to catch up to them.[6]

While these three cases furthered sexual equality, they did not have much impact on the legal status of sex-separated education. In part, the reach of these cases was limited because two were decided at the district court level and had no precedential value. The Ninth Circuit opinion, while more authoritative, was premised on an unusual factual situation. Moreover, in all three cases, because women were being denied a benefit available to men, the school boards were unable to claim that the education was separate but equal. This allowed the courts to avoid answering the question of whether separate was "inherently unequal."

Support for Separate but Equal in the Lower Courts

When the lower federal courts were later forced to rule on the separate but equal issue, they accepted separation by sex at both the high school and college levels. And although the Supreme Court did not issue opinions in these cases, the high court declined to reverse the lower court rulings. While such summary affirmances carry no precedential value for future cases, the Supreme Court seemingly indicated its satisfaction with, or indifference to, the separate but equal doctrine as applied to sex.

In 1970, in *Williams v. McNair* a three-judge district court in South Carolina allowed the state to maintain separate colleges for men and women: Winthrop College for "girls" and the Citadel for men.[7] The suit was brought by men who sought admission to Winthrop because it was closer to home and therefore less expensive for commuting. South Carolina's undergraduate and graduate educational system consisted of coeducational institutions, with these two exceptions: the Citadel, a military academy, restricted to men, and Winthrop College, established as

> a first-class institution for the thorough education of the white girls of this State, the main object of which shall be (1) to give to young women such education as shall fit them for teaching and (2) to give instruction to young women in stenography, typewriting, telegraphy, bookkeeping, drawing . . . designing, engraving, sewing, dressmaking, millinery, art, needlework, cooking, housekeeping and such other industrial arts as may be suitable to their sex and conducive to their support and usefulness.[8]

While conceding that there was a growing national trend toward coeducational colleges, the district court found the state's restrictive admissions policy constitutional. It reasoned that

> the Constitution does not require that a classification "keep abreast of the latest" in educational opinion, especially when there remains a respectable opinion to the contrary; it only demands that the discrimination not be wholly wanting in reason.[9]

Following the minimal scrutiny analysis used by the Supreme Court in sex-based decision-making, the court held that it was not arbitrary or irrational to have single-sex schools, and the state did not violate the Fourteenth Amendment by restricting Winthrop College to women.[10]

Some years later, in 1974, Susan Lynn Vorchheimer, a Philadelphia teenager who was refused admission to the city's all-male Central High School, also went to federal court. Although she won at the district court level, the Third Circuit Court of Appeals reversed and the Supreme Court upheld the appellate court.

The Philadelphia School District maintained only two "academic" high schools (with exclusively college preparatory classes): Central High for boys and Girls High. Although Vorchheimer preferred to attend a coeducational academic high school, the city offered her no opportunity to do so. She applied to Central High because she was convinced that it was better than Girls High. Although she was well qualified, she was denied admission to Central solely because of her sex.

Both district and appellate courts found that, except for the better science facilities at Central, the two schools were generally "comparable." Relying on the Supreme Court's stricter scrutiny of sex-based classifications, utilized in *Reed v. Reed* and *Frontiero v. Richardson*, the district court concluded it was inappropriate to apply the minimal scrutiny used in *Williams*. Although the Supreme Court had not yet formally adopted a higher level of scrutiny for sex-based classifications, the district court judge felt that a stricter standard was necessary. He found that Vorchheimer was adversely affected by the two–high school policy and that the sex-based classification was unconstitutional because it did not have a "fair and substantial" relationship to the district's educational objectives.

On appeal, in a 2–1 vote the Court of Appeals for the Third Circuit reversed. Pointing out the difference between race and sex classifications, the court explained,

> race is a suspect classification under the Constitution but the Supreme Court has declined to so characterize gender. We are committed to the concept that there is no fundamental differences between races and therefore, in justice, there can be no dissimilar treatment. But there are differences between the sexes which may, in limited circumstances, justify disparity in law.[11]

The appellate court said the facts in *Vorchheimer* were different from those in the sex discrimination cases cited by the district court. In those cases, "there was an actual deprivation or loss of a benefit to a female which could not be obtained elsewhere."[12] In this case, both sexes were equally affected by the sex-segregated school system. And because there was evidence that adolescents benefited from single-sex high schools, both sexes might even be advantaged. The appellate court held that despite the Supreme Court's decision in *Reed v. Reed*, there was no reason to use a stricter scrutiny. Applying minimal scrutiny, the court found a rational basis for the city's educational policy and that Vorchheimer's desire to attend Central High did not warrant changing the policy.[13]

A strong dissent by one of the judges on the three-judge appellate panel drew comparisons between the majority view and the 1896 opinion of *Plessy v. Ferguson*, in which the Supreme Court sanctioned "separate but equal" in racial classifications. He was outraged at the majority's decision because he "was under the distinct impression" that separate but equal was no longer acceptable—especially in the area of public education.[14] Notwithstanding the judge's plea for abandoning the discredited separate but equal doctrine, the Supreme Court affirmed the lower court.[15] The highest court in the land refused to repudiate separate but equal schooling—more than twenty years after *Brown*.[16]

Separate but Equal Survives

The Supreme Court finally addressed the issue of a restrictive admissions policy in a full opinion in 1982 in *Mississippi University for Women v. Hogan*. Because of the circumstances of the case, however, the decision was narrowly focused and left important questions unanswered.

Joe Hogan, a registered nurse, sought admission to the Mississippi University for Women (MUW) to get a bachelor's degree in nursing. While the state offered other opportunities for coeducational nursing, he chose MUW because it was close to home and easier for commuting. Although qualified, Hogan was rejected because of his sex. He filed suit against MUW, the oldest public women's college in America.

Mississippi established a School of Nursing at MUW in 1971; as part of a women's university, only women were admitted into the nursing program. Men were allowed to audit classes. The university's charter defined the purpose of the school, essentially unchanged since its founding in 1884, as providing

the moral and intellectual achievement of the girls of the state by the maintenance of a first-class institution for their education in the arts and sciences, for their training in normal school methods and kindergarten, for their instruction in bookkeeping, photography, stenography, telegraphy, and typewriting, and in designing, drawing, engraving, and painting, and their industrial application, and for their instruction in fancy, general and practical needlework, and in such other industrial branches as experience, from time to time, shall suggest as necessary or proper to fit them for the practical affairs of life.[17]

MUW's founding principles were similar to Winthrop College's. But unlike South Carolina, which maintained separate—and theoretically equal—educational facilities, Mississippi only had a women's school. Because of this, the Supreme Court was able to avoid considering the separate but equal issue and could limit its decision to the narrow question of whether men should be admitted to the nursing program.[18] In contrast to its far-reaching opinion in *Brown v. Board of Education*, the Court explained in a footnote that it was "not faced with the question of whether States can provide 'separate but equal' undergraduate institutions for males and females."[19]

Somewhat inexplicably, using the minimal scrutiny approach abandoned by the Supreme Court for sex-based classifications in 1976 the district court dismissed Hogan's claim. It found that the single-sex school was constitutionally permissible because it was *rationally* related to the state's goal of providing the fullest range of educational opportunities for its female student population. Moreover, said the lower court, the decision to preserve MUW as a single-sex school was not arbitrary because it was consistent with respected educational theory about the benefits of single-sex education. The court of appeals reversed, holding that excluding Hogan because of his sex denied him equal protection of the law.

The state appealed to the Supreme Court, arguing that its restrictive admissions policy was intended to compensate women for past discrimination. Speaking for a 5–4 majority, Justice Sandra Day O'Connor ruled that the nursing program must open its doors to men. O'Connor pointed out there was no evidence that women suffered from discrimination in nursing. She instructed the state that it could

evoke a compensatory purpose to justify an otherwise discriminatory classification only if members of the gender benefited by the classification actually suffer a disadvantage related to the classification.[20]

Actually, O'Connor noted, the state's policy served the opposite goal of maintaining the stereotypical image of nursing as a female occupation.

Mississippi was also unable to show that its policy was substantially related to its compensatory goal. Because men were admitted to the classroom as auditors, with full participation privileges, MUW did not even provide female nursing students with a classroom all to themselves.

As a last resort, the state argued that the Title IX (of the Education Amendments of 1972) exemption for traditionally single-sex public undergraduate schools indicated Congress's intent to screen such institutions from the constitutional requirement of equal protection. O'Connor brushed this aside, saying that it was "far from clear that Congress intended, through §901(a)(5) [Title IX], to exempt MUW from any constitutional obligation. Rather, Congress apparently intended, at most, to exempt MUW from the requirements of Title IX."[21]

The *Hogan* decision raised almost as many questions as it answered and left both sides dissatisfied. Some are critical because O'Connor's opinion failed to address (and overturn) the separate but equal doctrine and left open the possibility that a state can justify a single-sex admission policy that compensates for "a disadvantage" adhering to one sex.[22]

Others are distressed because the Court's equal treatment approach failed to recognize that a single-sex school serves women's needs in a way that a coeducational school does not. Moreover, they argue that a single-sex school empowers women by allowing them to assume nontraditional leadership roles.[23]

Echoing this view in his dissent, Lewis Powell argued that the equal protection clause had never been invoked against an expansion of women's opportunities. In his view, the state should be able to consider women's differing educational needs; identity of treatment, he said, is not a prerequisite of equality. Speaking for himself and William Rehnquist, Powell maintained that MUW's admissions policy was constitutional because Mississippi was simply offering women "an *additional* choice."[24] Acknowledging that coeducational institutions are more common, he insisted that single-sex schools are legitimate and the Court should defer to the views of MUW students and alumni who wished to continue the restricted admissions policy.[25]

Powell concluded by pointing out that Hogan could attend other public nursing schools, although further from his home. He refused to attribute more importance to Hogan's convenience than to the benefits women derive from single-sex education.

Despite the Court's ruling against MUW's nursing school, separate but equal survived. The Court's continued acceptance of the separate but equal doctrine is troubling because "in light of the many vestiges of sexism which remain in American society, it is difficult for a fair-minded observer to conclude that an all-girl school can be separate but equal to an all-boy school."[26] Like racially separate education, separate-sex schools stem from prejudicial and stereotypical notions about women and "whatever their curricula and facilities, [they] are remnants of an earlier era."[27]

Title IX and Gender Equality

In 1972, Congress responded to the issue of sexual inequality in education by passing Title IX of the Education Amendments. The essence of Title IX is found in section 901, which states that no person in the United States shall, on the basis of sex, be excluded from participation in, be denied the benefits of, or be subjected to discrimination under any education program or activity receiving Federal financial assistance.[28]

The act came about largely through the efforts of two Democratic members of Congress: Oregon Representative Edith Green and Indiana Senator Birch Bayh.

As head of the House Special Subcommittee on Education, Green sponsored a bill increasing federal aid to higher education that included provisions barring sex discrimination. Hearings were held in June and July 1970. Although the bill focused attention on the problem of sex inequality in education, it never cleared the subcommittee.

During 1971, similar bills were introduced in the House, and after battles over the question of restrictive admissions, a committee-approved bill was eventually sent to the full House. Although weakened by amendments, the bill was approved by the House late in 1971.

During the summer of 1971, when the Senate was considering a higher education bill that did not include a sex discrimination provision, Bayh introduced an amendment to prohibit sex discrimination in higher education. The Senate rejected his justification of the proposed measure, and the amendment was defeated in a parliamentary maneuver.

The House-approved bill, with the sex discrimination provisions, was then sent to Senate committee, but the version that passed out of committee, similar to the earlier Senate version, still did not contain a sex discrimination provision. In early 1972, during Senate floor debate, Bayh again proposed an amendment banning sex discrimination. This time he was successful. Senate acceptance was prompted, in part, because the new bill exempted admissions policies in private undergraduate colleges.

During conference committee consideration, the conferees were forced to conciliate 250 differences between the two versions of the education bill, only 11 of which concerned sex discrimination. Because conference debate was primarily centered on court-ordered busing for racial integration, little attention was paid to the sex discrimination provisions, and they were approved with little discussion. The conference version passed both houses with little conflict, and the bill was signed by President Richard Nixon on June 23, 1972.

Provisions of Title IX

Title IX bans discrimination in admissions to all vocational, professional, graduate, and most public undergraduate schools. According to Secretary of Health, Education, and Welfare (HEW) Caspar Weinberger, the statute covered sixteen thousand public school systems and nearly twenty-seven hundred post-secondary institutions. However, while it represented an important and far-reaching step toward equal educational opportunity, it fell short of a comprehensive attack on sex discrimination in education. It left major gaps in at least two important areas: admissions and athletics.

Single-sex admissions remained legal in most elementary and secondary schools, private undergraduate schools, and in public undergraduate institutions "that traditionally and continually" from their inception only admitted students of one sex.

The statute excluded two classes of institutions from the reach of Title IX: schools whose "primary purpose" was to train students for the military services or merchant marine and religious schools "to the extent that the provisions of Title IX would be inconsistent with the basic religious tenets of the school."

Two years later, Congress amended Title IX to exempt single-sex groups such as sororities and fraternities, YM and YWCAs, and the Boy Scouts, Girl Scouts, and Campfire Girls. In 1976, further amendments restored father-son and mother-daughter activities as well as scholarships awarded to beauty contest winners.

Legislative Intent of Title IX

Despite their importance, the sex discrimination provisions received little attention during passage of the Education Amendments of 1972. Moreover, because of its scant legislative history, there was no committee report to guide the courts on legislative intent. While intent can only be gathered from the brief debate on the floor of the Senate and the remarks of Senator Bayh, there are some clues to Congress's design. The first section of Title IX is modeled after the identically worded first section of Title VI of the 1964 Civil Rights Act. To the extent that they discussed it, members of Congress indicated their intent to have the two laws similarly interpreted by the judiciary.[29]

Title IX Regulations

Title IX included a provision ordering the secretary of health, education, and welfare to promulgate regulations for its implementation.[30] Because Congress writes in broad strokes, administrative agencies, such as HEW, have responsibility for translating the intent of Congress into specific policy by issuing regulations. Reflecting the agency's interpretation of the statute, regulations have the force of law until challenged in court. While courts often follow the agency's lead in interpreting the statute, they are not bound to do so and can strike regulations on the grounds they do not express legislative intent.

HEW issued its proposed Title IX regulations in June 1974 and set aside a four-month period to receive public comments by interested groups. The publication of the proposed regulations set off a flurry of lobbying activities by anti- and pro-Title IX advocates.[31] The coalition known as the Education Task Force, which included such organizations as the National Student Lobby, Project on Equal Education Rights, and the Project on the Status and Education of Women, led the fight for an expanded interpretation of the statute. Their primary opposition came from the National Collegiate Athletic Association (NCAA) and the American Football Coaches Association.[32] That HEW received nearly ten thousand comments during the public comment period from June to October 1974 indicates the intensity surrounding the debate. Since Congress had authority to disapprove the regulations, some of the lobbying efforts—especially over athletics—were directed at it as well.[33] The final regulations, signed by President Gerald Ford on July 2, 1975, and made effective on July 21, 1975, were weakened during the long lobbying process despite the energy expended by the women's groups.[34]

The Title IX regulations, written by HEW's Office of Civil Rights, encompassed physical education classes; course offerings, such as shop and home economics; extracurricular activities; financial aid; and counseling. Although expressing concern about sex stereotyping in textbooks, because of the possible conflict with First Amendment guarantees of freedom of speech the regulations did not include restrictions on books and other curricular materials.[35] Also, not wanting to encourage the sexual revolution, the rules allowed schools to maintain separate housing facilities for the sexes.

Title IX and Athletics

Although the issue of athletics was not highlighted during its passage, the major battles over Title IX were fought over the anticipated changes in intercollegiate athletics.[36] Congress ordered HEW to propose reasonable regulations for intercollegiate athletic activities "considering the nature of the particular sports." According to Weinberger, athletics received the most attention during the public comment period.

During passage of the Education Amendments of 1974 (before the final regulations were promulgated), Republican Senator John Tower of Texas proposed an amendment that would have exempted revenue-producing intercollegiate sports from inclusion within the ban on discrimination. Although the Senate accepted it in a voice vote, it was deleted in conference. Instead, the Conference Committee adopted the Javits amendment (after Jacob Javits, Republican Senator from New York), which directed that the regulations identifying discrimination in intercollegiate athletics consider "the nature" of the individual sport.

The final Title IX regulations contain many contradictions—undoubtedly resulting from compromises necessitated by the battles over promulgation.[37] While the rules generally bar schools from having separate teams in the same sport on the basis of sex, there are two major exceptions. First, separate teams are permitted in sports where selection is based on competitive skill. Second, single-sex teams are permitted in sports requiring body contact among the players. Such sports include wrestling, boxing, football, basketball, ice hockey, and rugby.

The 1975 regulations required "equal athletic opportunity for members of both sexes." Yet, they allowed differential spending on the basis of sex because "unequal aggregate expenditures" alone did not constitute failure to comply with the regulations. When the regulations were attacked by women's groups, HEW proposed a new policy interpretation requiring equal per capita spending in such areas as scholarships, recruitment, and equipment. HEW also tried to address the effects of past discrimination against women by asking institutions to encourage women to participate in sports, to increase the number of sports offered to women, and to raise the level of awareness of women's sports.

With criticism now leveled at it from the other side, HEW released a much watered-down version calling only for equal per capita funding in scholarships. Equal funding was not required in other areas; equivalency became the new watchword. Also, in the revised version, the requirement for redressing past discrimination became less burdensome for college athletic programs.[38] Debate over sex equality in sports continued after new guidelines were issued in 1979 but, ironically, the major impact on sports programs came from a 1984 Supreme Court ruling that had nothing to do with athletics.

Private Rights of Action under Title IX

For reasons not readily apparent, a number of federal civil rights statutes do not authorize litigation as a remedy for discrimination.[39] This omission frequently leaves courts in a quandary about whether victims of discrimination should be allowed to sue.

The Supreme Court addressed this issue in a lawsuit filed in 1976 by Geraldine Cannon against the University of Chicago's Pritzker School of Medicine. When Cannon, a thirty-nine-year-old surgical nurse, was denied admission to the medical school, her suit charged that her rejection was motivated by discrimination against her on the basis of age and sex.[40] She claimed that the university's policy of discouraging applications from persons over thirty had a discriminatory impact on women. The lower court dismissed her suit, primarily because Title IX did not authorize a suit by a private individual.[41]

The Seventh Circuit upheld the lower court, distinguishing cases in which the Supreme Court had allowed private suits under Title VI of the 1964 Civil Rights Act because those "involved an attempt by a large number of plaintiffs to enforce a national constitutional right."[42] The court added that "from a policy viewpoint we see little to be gained by involving the judiciary in every individual act of discrimination based upon sex."[43]

Reversing the courts below, in *Cannon v. University of Chicago*, 1979, the Supreme Court held that a private suit was permissible under Title IX.[44] The Court primarily based its decision on the identity between Title VI and Title IX. "We have no doubt that Congress intended to create Title IX remedies comparable to those available under Title VI and that it understood Title VI as authorizing an implied private cause of action for victims of the prohibited discrimination."[45]

In deciding whether to allow a private suit, the Court is guided by a four-part test derived from the 1975 case of *Cort v. Ash*. The test is a search for the legislative intent that allows the Court to determine whether a private suit is compatible with the purpose of the statute. It requires consideration of four questions: first, is the person bringing the suit someone for whose "especial benefit" the statute was designed; second, is there evidence of congressional intent, either explicit or implicit, to create or deny a private remedy or suit; third, is a private suit consistent with the legislative purpose of the statute; fourth, is it inappropriate to infer a cause of action in federal law because the suit is in an area that traditionally concerns state law.[46]

Speaking for the 6–3 majority of William Brennan, Potter Stewart, Thurgood Marshall, Rehnquist, and Warren Burger, John Paul Stevens announced the opinion of the Court in *Cannon*.[47] He addressed each of the *Cort* factors and approved a private suit (or private right of action) in Title IX. Stevens devoted most of the opinion to a discussion of the purpose of Title IX and discerned two: first, to prevent institutions from using federal funds to support discriminatory practices; and second, to protect individuals against discrimination. While cutting off federal funds to a guilty institution would prevent the federal government from subsidizing discrimination, it would not help the victim. A private suit would serve the victim better and fulfill the second aim of the statute.

After the Supreme Court ruled on Cannon's Title IX claim, it sent the case back to the district court for trial on the merits of her sex discrimination complaint. Her suit was again dismissed, this time because she could not prove the university intentionally discriminated against her.[48] On appeal, the Seventh Circuit affirmed.

Cannon's lawsuit paved the way for future Title IX plaintiffs, but it did not bring her closer to achieving her goals. So despite her important victory for future civil rights litigation, Geraldine Cannon lost.

Damages under Title IX

A few years after Cannon's lawsuit, Judy Lieberman also sued the University of Chicago Medical School for sex discrimination.[49] Lieberman had been waitlisted by the university but never admitted. Unlike Cannon, however, she had been accepted at a number of prestigious medical schools and was attending Harvard when her case came before the court.

Lieberman's suit was the first to claim money damages under Title IX.[50] She asked for $350,000 as compensation for moving and living expenses, loss of consortium (she was separated from her husband for ten months while she lived and attended school in Massachusetts), pain and suffering for disruption of her life, and punitive damages.[51]

The district court dismissed her claim. In 1981, in *Lieberman v. University of Chicago*, the Seventh Circuit affirmed, declining to expand the scope of Title IX.[52] Ignoring the *Cort v. Ash* legislative intent test, the court instead relied on the Supreme Court's ruling in *Pennhurst State School and Hospital v. Halderman*.[53] In *Pennhurst*, the Court held that states receiving federal aid entered into a contract with the federal government and agreed to accept conditions in return for federal funds. But the contract is only valid if Congress clearly specifies the terms of the agreement in the statute because it would be inconsistent for Congress to insert a financial obligation into an aid statute without adequate warning.

Characterizing Title IX as part of a package of aid to higher education, the circuit court ruled that it was not intended to allow an additional drain on an institution's finances through suits for money damages. *Cannon* only enlarged the class of persons who could sue under the contract, it did not expand the institution's financial liability. The court insisted on evidence showing that the university was aware that receiving federal funds increased its potential liability for financial losses. It concluded by observing that "if a damages remedy is to be created, it should be fashioned by Congress and not by the Courts, thus providing the institutions with ample notice and an opportunity to reconsider their acceptance of financial aid."[54]

How could Congress have specified money damages in a statute that did not expressly state a cause of action in the first place? the dissent asked. Decrying both the reasoning and the result, the dissenting judge warned that the "preclusion of a damage remedy will impair the enforcement of Title IX."[55] Because the more qualified applicants, like Judy Lieberman, will accept positions at other schools, the enforcement of Title IX will be left to lesser qualified persons who have not been accepted at any schools. A university will more likely win these suits because it will be easier to cover up discrimination. "I would allow," he argued, "those who are best able to prove discrimination, i.e., the most highly qualified, to bring actions to enforce Title IX. Provision of a damage remedy will allow these actions to go forward."[56]

Employees Protected under Title IX

Title IX's ban on discrimination against persons in educational institutions clearly included students within its protective reach. Did it also include employees of educational institutions, specifically, teachers? This was the next major issue, addressed by the Supreme Court in 1982.

HEW regulations included far-reaching prohibitions on employment discrimination covering recruitment, hiring, compensation, and fringe benefits, including maternity leave and pregnancy disability. Additionally, the regulations banned employment discrimination on the basis of marital and parental status.

Employment discrimination against women constituted the largest number of complaints to HEW—almost 40 percent—between 1972 and 1976. A June 1979 survey of complaints pending with HEW showed that over 55 percent charged employment discrimination.[57] The legal controversy was triggered when HEW began to investigate these complaints and the schools under investigation went to federal court to declare that Title IX did not govern conditions of employment. Most federal courts agreed with the schools and held that Title IX did not apply to employment discrimination. Only the Second Circuit allowed a Title IX suit for employment discrimination.[58]

North Haven v. Hufstedler (known as *North Haven v. Bell* in the Supreme Court) began with a complaint to HEW against the North Haven Board of Education by Elaine Dove, a tenured teacher who was not rehired after a one-year maternity leave. Initially refusing to comply with HEW's request for information on its employment practices, the board went to district court, asking to have HEW's employment regulations declared invalid. The board won the first round as the district court agreed that Title IX did not cover employees.

On appeal, the Second Circuit Court of Appeals reversed and upheld the HEW regulations encompassing employment practices of schools receiving federal funding. The Supreme Court agreed with the Second Circuit that employment policies were a proper subject of inquiry for HEW. In a 6–3 vote with Harry Blackmun, Brennan, Byron White, Marshall, Stevens, and O'Connor in the majority (and Powell, Rehnquist, and Burger dissenting), the Court adopted most of the circuit court's reasoning.[59]

Speaking for the Court in *North Haven v. Bell*, 1982, Blackmun noted that it was more plausible to interpret section 901's ban on discrimination against any "person" to include rather than exclude employees. In the absence of committee reports to explain legislative intent, he looked to the Senate floor debate and statements by Birch Bayh that clearly revealed *his* intent to include employment practices within Title IX. Introducing the amendment, Bayh explained that it would "cover such crucial aspects as admissions, procedures, scholarships, and faculty employment."[60] Based on its analysis of the legislative history, the Supreme Court agreed with the Second Circuit that the regulations mirrored the legislative intent of Title IX.[61]

Narrowing the Reach of Title IX

North Haven ended with a warning by the Court about Title IX's program-specific language in section 902 that restricts termination of funds for noncompliance to "the particular program, or part thereof, in which such noncompliance has been so found."[62] Although it refused to define the word *program* the Court held that HEW's authority to enforce Title IX regulations was limited to the program receiving federal funds. The case was remanded to the lower court with instructions to the court to find the parameters of the federally funded program in the North Haven school system.

The Supreme Court returned to the question of program-specificity — that is, whether Title IX's ban on discrimination applied to the entire institution or only to the isolated program receiving federal funds — in 1984, in *Grove City College v. Bell*. In *Grove City*, the Court also addressed another important unresolved question: whether indirect aid to students triggered Title IX coverage of the institution.

Indirect Aid

Grove City was a private, coeducational, liberal arts college with approximately 2,200 students in western Pennsylvania. The college received no federal or state financial assistance other than aid to students through the Basic Education Opportunity Grant (BEOG) or Guaranteed Student Loan (GSL) programs; almost one-quarter (about 480) of the students were assisted through these programs. The 1975 Title IX regulations classified schools whose students received BEOG funds as recipients of federal financial assistance.[63]

The case arose when Grove City College and four students sued to prevent the Department of Education (DOE) from terminating the student aid program. DOE decided to cut off funds when the college refused to file an Assurance of Compliance as required by Title IX regulations. Grove City argued that because none of its programs received federal funds, it was not a program or activity within the meaning of section 901.

After surveying the legislative intent and post-enactment history (Congress's reaction to the regulations) of Title IX, the Third Circuit Court of Appeals held that Grove City College received federal funds within the meaning of Title IX. The court supported DOE's interpretation that Title

IX could be applied to institutions that received indirect aid through grants to students.

Pointing to section 902's language limiting termination of funds to particular programs, the college maintained that HEW could only withhold funds from the specific programs guilty of sex discrimination. And in cases where the aid is indirect and not funneled to a particular program, Grove City argued that Title IX applied to no part of the school.

On the contrary, said the circuit court, "where the federal government furnishes indirect or non-earmarked aid to an institution, it is apparent to us that the institution itself must be the 'program.'"[64]

With White delivering the opinion, the Supreme Court agreed with the circuit court and held that indirect aid to students subjected the college to Title IX regulation. White said he found no evidence in the language, legislative intent, or post-enactment history to suggest that Congress intended a distinction between direct and indirect aid.

> With the benefit of clear statutory language, powerful evidence of Congress' intent, and a longstanding and coherent administrative construction of the phrase "receiving Federal financial assistance," we have little trouble concluding that Title IX coverage is not foreclosed because federal funds are granted to Grove City's students rather than directly to one of the College's educational programs.[65]

Program-Specificity

Grove City College also contended that even if Title IX were applicable, its coverage was limited to the program receiving the aid — in this case, the financial aid office. It urged the Supreme Court to reverse the lower court's ruling that federal aid to students through the BEOG program subjected *all* programs within Grove City College to Title IX.

The majority agreed that Congress intended the "program or activity" language of Title IX to be narrowly interpreted. It accepted the college's argument that financial aid to students attending the school did not trigger institutionwide coverage of Title IX. The high court rejected DOE's broad interpretation of Title IX that, by relieving the college of the burden of financial aid, federal funds to students effectively served as a grant to the institution as a whole. The Court "found no persuasive evidence" that Congress meant to have HEW's "regulatory authority follow federally aided students from classroom to classroom, building to building, or activity to activity."[66] HEW could only apply Title IX regulations to the college's financial aid office.

While they concurred in the Court's opinion on the indirect aid issue, Brennan, Marshall, and Stevens objected to the part of the opinion on program-specificity because it narrowed the remedial reach of Title IX. The implications of the decision were soon apparent as collegiate athletic programs began to claim exemption from the ban on sex discrimination within the statute, arguing they were not programs or activities receiving federal funds.

In the end, however, although the lawsuit had a substantial effect on narrowing the scope of Title IX, there was no cause for celebration of the Supreme Court opinion in Grove City because the Court held that the college was required to provide assurance to HEW that its financial aid office was in compliance with Title IX.[67] If Grove City refused, the Court held, DOE could terminate financial assistance to the student aid program.

The Congressional Response to *Grove City*

The *Grove City* decision was greeted with dismay by the civil rights community and their supporters in Congress. In part, they were displeased because the Court's opinion extended beyond the bounds of sex discrimination. The "program" or "activity" language in Title IX was identical to language in Title VI of the 1964 Civil Rights Act banning race discrimination in federally funded programs, to language in section 504 of the Rehabilitation Act of 1973 prohibiting discrimination against the disabled in programs receiving federal financial aid, and to language in the Age Discrimination Act of 1975 banning age discrimination in programs receiving federal aid.

Their concern was well founded, as the decision had a drastic effect on pending civil rights litigation. "According to the Leadership Conference on Civil Rights, the Department of Education had 'closed, limited or suspended hundreds of [discrimination] cases' because of the *Grove City* ruling."[68]

The Supreme Court's insistence on constructing walls around individual programs within institutions threatened to set back the major civil rights advances of the 1960s and 1970s. The fear became reality when, in 1986, the Supreme Court decided that federal aid to airports and the air traffic control system did not bring commercial airlines within the reach of the 1973 Rehabilitation Act prohibiting discrimination against the disabled.[69]

There was sharp displeasure with the Court's opinion in Congress. This was not surprising, because in August 1983 (while the case was pending), fifty members of the House and Senate had urged the Court to adopt an expansive view of Title IX. On November 16, 1983, Democrat Paul Simon of Illinois had proposed House Resolution 190, proclaiming that it is the "sense of the House of Representatives that Title IX . . . should not be amended or altered in any manner which will lessen the comprehensive coverage of such statute in eliminating gender discrimination throughout the American educational system." Speaking in support of the resolution, Simon stressed the importance of interpreting Title IX broadly and accused the Reagan administration of "singl[ing] out Title IX as a regulation to be cut back."[70] He reminded his colleagues that the Justice Department had entered the case pending before the Supreme Court at the time on the side of Grove City. The resolution was adopted by a bipartisan group of 414 members.[71]

Shortly after *Grove City* was handed down, a bill aimed at reversing it was introduced in the House on April 12, 1984. Termed the Civil Rights Act of 1984, the bill proposed three changes in all civil rights legislation affected by the Court's ruling in *Grove City*: (1) to replace the words *program* and *activity* with *recipient;* (2) to define a recipient as an institution receiving assistance "directly or through another"; and (3) to specify that the entire institution or system would lose funding if one of its units violated the ban on discrimination.[72]

After hearings in the Education and Labor and Judiciary Committees, the House easily passed the bill on June 26, 1984, in a 375–32 vote. But opposition from the Reagan administration and the Republican-controlled Senate, despite the support of sixty-three bipartisan cosponsors, stalled the Senate version of the bill in the Ninety-eighth Congress. The measure was tabled by a 53–45 vote on October 2, 1984. Republican Senator Orrin Hatch of Utah was primarily responsible for defeating the Senate bill, arguing that it would expand federal control over society in its zealous attempts to prevent discrimination.

In the Ninety-ninth Congress, two House committees approved versions of a bill that would have reversed the *Grove City* decision, but neither reached the floor for consideration. Congress adjourned with these two bills in limbo as well as two other bills pending in the Senate Labor and Human Resources Committee. A Senate version of the Grove City bill, as it was informally known, was subsequently approved in committee in May 1987, but no further action was taken that year.[73]

The Debate over Abortion Stalls the Grove City Bill

Although neither Title IX nor the proposed bill mentioned abortion, Senate debate, often bitter, primarily revolved around the implications of the bill for abortion rights. After 1985, controversy over the bill's effects on abortion stymied it for three more years.

The U.S. Catholic Conference and the National Right to Life Committee lobbied against it, insisting that the bill would expand abortion rights. Current administrative regulations specified that federal aid recipients were required to treat pregnancy and termination of pregnancy "in the same manner and under the same policies as any other temporary disability." The regulations also barred discrimination against students or employees who had abortions. Opponents of the Grove City bill argued that it would force hospitals with religious ties that received federal aid to perform abortions or be subject to suits for discrimination.[74] Proponents insisted that such hospitals could claim exemption and the bill only addressed coverage of the civil rights laws, not definitions of discrimination.

The Senate finally passed the Grove City bill, S. 557, on January 28, 1988, by a 75–14 vote. The price for its passage was the Danforth amendment. Supported by the Catholic Conference and other antiabortion groups, the amendment contained a so-called right to conscience clause that permitted federally funded hospitals (and their medical personnel) to refuse to perform abortions and allowed educational institutions to exclude abortion from health and disability leave plans. Described by its supporters as abortion-neutral because it also prohibited discrimination against women who had abortions, opponents charged that there was "a certain anti-woman animus in the proponents of this amendment." The Senate approved the Danforth amendment in a 56–39 vote.

In the House, civil rights advocates were torn over whether to support the Senate version of the bill with the Danforth amendment. Women's groups, despite their desire to see the *Grove City* decision overturned, were upset with the abortion language and did not lobby for the bill in the House. The Senate-passed bill was approved in the House on March 2, 1988, in a 315–98 vote.[75]

Entitled the Civil Rights Restoration Act, the bill extended Title IX coverage to all of the operations of state or local government units, including public school systems; to all of the operations of a college, university, or other public school of higher education, as well as vocational schools or any other school system that received federal aid; to all of the operation of corporations, partnerships, or other private organizations if aid is given to the enterprise as a whole, or if the enterprise is "principally engaged" in providing education, housing, health care, parks, or social services.[76]

On March 16, 1988, President Ronald Reagan vetoed S. 557, saying the bill "would vastly and unjustifiably expand the power of the Federal government over the decisions and affairs of private organizations, such as churches and synagogues, farms, businesses, and State and local governments. In the process," he said, "it would place at risk such cherished values as religious liberties." Reagan offered a weaker substitute bill, entitled the Civil Rights Protection Act, that proposed to extend the religious exemption to institutions that are "closely identified" with but not "controlled by" a religious organization. By limiting coverage to the entity receiving federal aid, the bill would substantially undercut the government's ban on discrimination in private businesses, religious school systems, and state and local government units.[77]

Less than a week later, on March 22, 1988, Congress overrode the president's veto. The vote to override in the Senate was 73–24, in the House 292–133.[78] With this action, the Supreme Court's interpretation of federal nondiscrimination legislation was overruled. According to congressional sponsors of the 1988 act, the original intent of Title IX and other civil rights legislation was now restored.

NOTES

1. *Brown v. Board of Education*, 347 U.S. 483, 493 (1954).

2. *Brown*, 347 U.S. at 494.

3. *Brown*, 347 U.S. at 495. In *Mississippi University for Women v. Hogan*, 458 U.S. 718 (1982), the Court ruled that the women-only admissions policy of the nursing program of Mississippi University for Women was unconstitutional. But unlike *Brown*, the Court did not declare that separate but equal education on the basis of sex was unconstitutional.

4. *Kirstein v. Rectors and Visitors of the University of Virginia*, 309 F.Supp. 184 (E.D. Va 1970).

5. *Bray v. Lee*, 337 F.Supp. 934 (D. Mass. 1972).

6. *Berkelman v. San Francisco Unified School District*, 501 F.2d 1264 (9th Cir. 1974).

7. A decade earlier the Texas state courts refused to order the admission of women to Texas A & M University even though courses were offered there that were not offered at other Texas schools. See *Heaton v. Bristol*, 317 S.W.2d 86 (Tex. Civ. App. 1958); *Allred v. Heaton*, 336 S.W.2d 251 (Tex. Civ. App. 1960). The Supreme Court denied certiorari, that is, refused to hear, both cases.

8. Section 408, Title 22, Code of South Carolina (1962); cited in *Williams v. McNair*, 316 F.Supp. 134, 136 n. 3 (D.S.C. 1970).

9. *Williams*, 316 F.Supp. at 137.

10. *Williams* preceded *Reed v. Reed*, 404 U.S. 71 (1971), in which the Supreme Court began to view gender discrimination with heightened scrutiny. See John D. Johnston, Jr., and Charles L. Knapp, "Sex Discrimination by Law: A Study in Judicial Perspective," *New York University Law Review* 46(1971), pp. 723–26 for criticism of *Williams*.

11. *Vorchheimer v. School District of Philadelphia*, 532 F.2d 880, 886 (3d Cir. 1976).

12. *Vorchheimer*, 532 F.2d at 886.

13. *Vorchheimer* was decided by the court of appeals nine months before the Supreme Court adopted heightened scrutiny for sex-based classifications in *Craig v. Boren*, 429 U.S. 190 (1976). The appellate court ruled that the school system would have survived constitutional scrutiny under the stricter district court "substantial relationship" formula as well as the rationality test.

14. *Vorchheimer*, 532 F.2d at 888 (Gibbons, J., dissenting).

15. *Vorchheimer v. School District of Philadelphia*, 430 U.S. 703 (1977). With Justice Rehnquist not participating, the vote to uphold the lower court was tied 4–4. A tie vote in the Supreme Court affirms the lower court opinion.

16. In *Newburg v. Board of Public Education*, 26 Pa. D.& C.3d 682 (1983), the Court of Common Pleas of Philadelphia ordered three female students admitted to Central High School. Applying the more stringent test for sex classifications demanded by the Pennsylvania Equal Rights Amendment, the court ruled that separation of the sexes was not sufficiently related to the asserted educational benefits. Unlike the *Vorchheimer* court, this court actually looked at the quality of education offered in the two schools—on both tangible and intangible grounds—and found that Girls High suffered in comparison to Central. See Rosemary Salomone, *Equal Education under Law* (New York: St. Martin's Press, 1986), pp. 120–21.

17. Mississippi Code Annotated §37–117–3 (1972), cited in *Hogan*, 458 U.S. at 720.

18. Title IX's ban on sex discrimination in admissions did not apply to MUW because the act exempted public undergraduate schools that traditionally maintained a single-sex admissions policy.

19. *Hogan*, 458 U.S. at 720 n. 1.

20. *Hogan*, 458 U.S. at 728.

21. *Hogan*, 458 U.S. at 732.

22. *Hogan*, 458 U.S. at 731. The Court's opinion was limited to the unconstitutionality of MUW's women-only restrictions in its nursing school admissions.

23. See Janella Miller, "The Future of Private Women's Colleges," *Harvard Women's Law Journal* 7(1984) for an argument in favor of separation of men's and women's colleges.

24. *Hogan*, 458 U.S. at 736 (Powell, J., dissenting) (emphasis in the original).

25. This issue surfaced again in 1985 in a New York City school that had been ordered to open its doors to males. Washington Irving High School in Manhattan, an all-girls school for eighty-four years, was directed to begin admitting boys by September 1986. When the Board of Education decided that Title IX required that last single-sex school become coeducational, opposition arose from students, teachers, and administrators within the school. The arguments ranged from financial reasons (the money spent on remodeling to provide for male washrooms and locker rooms), to programmatic concerns (the influx of boys would disrupt the programs for which the school was known—secretarial studies, nursing, and child care), to socialization issues (girls cannot act naturally when boys are around). Regardless of the outcome of this decision, this case is a microcosm of the separate but equal issues raised—whether under Title IX or the equal protection clause. *New York Times*, July 2, 1985.

26. Alfred Blumrosen, "Single-Sex Public Schools: The Last Bastion of 'Separate but Equal'?" *Duke Law Journal* (1977), pp. 276–77.

27. Comment, *"Plessy* Revived: The Separate but Equal Doctrine and Sex-Segregated Education," *Harvard Civil Rights–Civil Liberties Law Review* 12(1977), p. 622. Deborah L. Rhode, "Association and Assimilation," *Northwestern University Law Review* 81(1986), argues that sex-segregated education must be phased out. See also Patricia Werner Lamar, "The Expansion of Constitutional and Statutory Remedies for Sex Segregation in Education: The Fourteenth Amendment and Title IX of the Education Amendments of 1972," *Emory Law Journal* 32(1983).

28. Section 901 of the Education Amendments of 1972. See Andrew Fishel and Janice Pottker, *National Politics and Sex Discrimination in Education* (Lexington, MA: Lexington Books, 1977) for discussion of the events surrounding passage of Title IX.

29. Because Title IX is limited to specified educational institutions, Title VI has a broader reach by barring racial discrimination in federally assisted programs or activities such as public elementary and secondary schools, hospitals, highway departments, and housing authorities.

30. See Joyce Gelb and Marian Lief Palley, *Women and Public Policies*, 2d ed. (Princeton: Princeton University Press, 1987); Salomone, *Equal Education under Law* for discussion of how the Title IX regulations were written.

31. Congressperson Green had asked women's groups not to lobby in favor of Title IX because she felt it would draw attention to the widespread implications for equality in the statute. Gelb and Palley, *Women and Public Policies*, p. 99.

32. Anne Costain, "Eliminating Sex Discrimination in Education: Lobbying for Implementation of Title IX," in Marian Lief Palley and Michael Preston, eds., *Race, Sex, and Policy Problems* (Lexington, MA: Lexington Books, 1979), p. 11.

33. The regulations were subject to a newly enacted provision of the 1974 Education Amendments that allowed Congress to issue a concurrent resolution within forty-five days if it disapproved of any administrative regulations dealing with education because they were inconsistent with legislative intent.

34. Gelb and Palley, *Women and Public Policies*, p. 106.

35. The original Title IX regulations, published by the Department of Health, Education, and Welfare, were codified at 45 C.F.R. Part 86. In 1980, the regulations were recodified essentially unchanged by the Department of Education, which was given responsibility for implementing Title IX, at 34 C.F.R. Part 106. Individual departments with authority to enforce Title IX have issued their own regulations based on the 1975 and 1980 models.

36. Sports were only mentioned twice in the Title IX debates and were never addressed in any congressional reports. Note, "Title IX and Intercollegiate Athletics: HEW Gets Serious about Equality in Sports?" *New England Law Review* 15(1980), p. 577; see also Note, "Sex Discrimination and Intercollegiate Athletics: Putting Some Muscle on Title IX," *Yale Law Journal* 88(1979).

37. Regulations pertaining to sports were divided into two categories, one involving physical education classes and the other school team activities—at all levels of performance. Coeducation was ordered for all physical education classes except those involving ability grouping and contact sports. Elementary schools were given one year to achieve full compliance with the regulations on physical education and athletics; because of the greater complexity of the problems, high schools and colleges were given three years within which to attain sex equality according to the regulations.

38. See Note, "Title IX and Intercollegiate Athletics."

39. Title IX, like its predecessor Title VI—the statute prohibiting discrimination on the basis of race in federally assisted programs—did not contain an explicit cause of action for private individuals. As written, the statute only provided that HEW could cut off funds to an institution found to be guilty of discrimination. Although many statutes, such as Title VII, for example, explicitly authorize suit for violation of the law, others, such as Title IX, merely proscribe a type of conduct and leave enforcement to federal administrative agencies or suit by the U.S. attorney general. In such cases, when an individual wishes to file suit, the courts must first decide whether to "imply a cause of action" from the statute. See Susan Gluck Mezey, "Judicial Interpretation of Legislative Intent: The Role of the Supreme Court in the Implication of Private Rights of Action," *Rutgers Law Review* 36(1983) for analysis of the implication doctrine.

40. Cannon sought reconsideration of her denial and when that proved unsuccessful, she filed a complaint with HEW in April 1975. Three months later, receiving only an acknowledgment of her complaint from the agency, she filed suit.

41. Title IX only authorized victims of discrimination to file complaints with HEW, and if HEW decided there was merit in the complaint, it could order federal funds to be cut off to the offending institution.

42. *Cannon v. University of Chicago*, 559 F.2d 1063, 1072 (7th Cir. 1976).

43. *Cannon*, 559 F.2d at 1074.

44. The Seventh Circuit's refusal to allow a private cause of action was not unique. Other cases also denying private rights of action included *Leffel v. Wisconsin Interscholastic Athletic Ass'n*, 444 F.Supp. 1117 (E.D. Wis. 1978); *Jones v. Oklahoma Secondary School Ass'n*, 453 F.Supp. 150 (W.D. Okla. 1977); *Cape v. Tennessee Secondary School Athletic Ass'n*, 424 F.Supp. 732 (E.D. Tenn. 1977).

45. *Cannon v. University of Chicago*, 441 U.S. 677, 703 (1979).

46. *Cort v. Ash*, 422 U.S. 66, 78 (1975). In *Cort* the Supreme Court refused to allow a private suit against Bethlehem Steel for the actions of its corporate officers in making contributions in the 1972 election campaign in violation of federal statute. The Court reasoned that Congress created the Federal Election Commission to deal with illegal campaign expenditures and that civil suits by citizens or shareholders should not be allowed.

47. The dissenting opinions were based on other grounds. White, speaking for himself and Blackmun, disagreed with the majority over allowing private suits under Title VI.

Cannon also raised questions about the proper role of the courts in the United States political system, and Powell, always concerned about proper boundaries between the courts and legislatures, accused the Court of straying too far into legislative prerogatives by creating a remedy that Congress did not intend to create. "Absent the most compelling evidence" of positive congressional intent, he argued, federal courts should not infer private causes of action. *Cannon*, 441 U.S. at 749 (Powell, J., dissenting).

48. Cannon claimed that the University of Chicago's age limit of thirty *had the effect of* discriminating against women because women are more likely than men to stay home to raise children when they are under thirty. She did not allege that the University *intentionally* discriminated against her. The court held that a Title IX suit requires a showing of intentional discrimination.

The issue of intentional discrimination under Title IX has never been addressed by the Supreme Court, but in *Guardians Ass'n v. Civil Service Commission*, 463 U.S. 582 (1983), the Court held that an administrative agency could design Title VI regulations that prohibited disparate impact. In *Marby v. State Board of Community Colleges*, 813 F.2d 311 (10th Cir. 1987), the Tenth Circuit allowed a Title IX suit for employment discrimination using disparate impact analysis. Then in *Sharif v. New York State Education Department*, 709 F.Supp. 345 (S.D.N.Y. 1989), the trial court extended the disparate impact model in the education context by upholding a disparate impact challenge to the use of the Scholastic

Aptitude Test (SAT) scores to determine merit scholarship awards. See Recent Cases, "Civil Rights—Disparate Impact Doctrine—Court Prohibits Awarding Scholarships on the Basis of Standardized Tests That Discriminatorily Impact Women—*Sharif v. New York Education Department*, 709 F.Supp. 345 (S.D.N.Y. 1989)," *Harvard Law Review* 103(1990).

49. Lieberman based her claim of sex discrimination on the fact that she had been interviewed six times by the university and questioned about her husband, her plans to have children, and other intimate matters. Note, "*Lieberman v. University of Chicago*," *John Marshall Law Review* 16(1982), p. 155 n. 14.

50. The question of damages was obliquely mentioned in a footnote in *Cannon*, 441 U.S. at 689 n. 10.

51. Lieberman sought $100,000 each for pain and suffering, punitive damages, and loss of consortium; she claimed $49,742 for out of pocket expenses. See Note, "*Lieberman v. University of Chicago*: Refusal to Imply a Damages Remedy under Title IX of the Education Amendments of 1972," *Wisconsin Law Review* (1983), p. 183 n. 9.; Comment, "Implied Private Rights of Action for Damages Under Title IX—*Lieberman v. University of Chicago*," *Georgia Law Review* 16(1982), p. 523, n. 83.

52. *Lieberman v. University of Chicago*, 660 F.2d 1185 (7th Cir. 1981). The Supreme Court denied certiorari.

53. *Pennhurst State School and Hospital v. Halderman*, 451 U.S. 1 (1981).

54. *Lieberman*, 660 F.2d at 1188.

55. *Lieberman*, 660 F.2d at 1194 (Swygert, J., dissenting).

56. *Lieberman*, 660 F.2d at 1195.

57. Rosemary Salomone, "Title IX and Employment Discrimination: A Wrong in Search of a Remedy," *Journal of Law and Education* 9(1980), p. 438.

58. *North Haven Board of Education v. Hufstedler*, 629 F.2d 773 (2d Cir. 1980). Five courts of appeal ruled that employment practices were outside the scope of Title IX. See, for example, *Romeo Community Schools v. HEW*, 600 F.2d 581 (6th Cir. 1979); *Islesboro School Committee v. Califano*, 593 F.2d 424 (1st Cir. 1979); *Junior College District of St. Louis v. Califano*, 597 F.2d 119 (8th Cir. 1979). The Supreme Court denied certiorari in these five cases.

59. *North Haven Board of Education v. Bell*, 456 U.S. 512 (1982). See Susan Gluck Mezey, "Gender Equality in Education: A Study of Policymaking by the Burger Court," *Wake Forest Law Review* 20(1984).

60. 118 *Cong. Rec.* 5802–03 (1972), cited in Rosemary Salomone, "*North Haven* and *Dougherty*: Narrowing the Scope of Title IX," *Journal of Law & Education* 10(1981), p. 195.

61. The key to solving this puzzle, said the Supreme Court, lay in the relationship between Title VI and Title IX. Although virtually identical, Title VI contained a provision (§604), absent in Title IX. Section 604 allowed Title VI to be applied to employment practices only "where a primary objective of the Federal financial assistance is to provide employment." The House version of Title IX had contained an equivalent provision—section 1004—which was deleted in conference committee. The question was why Congress omitted §1004 from Title IX. North Haven argued that the omission was merely to correct a drafting error (the unwitting duplication of Title VI in the House version of the bill) and did not signify that Congress intended to include employment discrimination within the reach of Title IX. The court of appeals held that the elimination of §1004 from the final version reflected Congress's intent to make Title IX applicable to employment.

62. Section 902 of the Education Amendments of 1972 states that

> compliance with any requirement adopted pursuant to this section may be effected (1) by the termination of or refusal to grant or to continue assistance under such program or activity to any recipient as to whom there has been an express finding on the record, after opportunity for a hearing, of a failure to comply with such requirements, *but such termination or refusal shall be limited to the particular political entity,* or part thereof, or other recipient as to whom such a finding has been made, *and shall be limited in its effect to the particular program, or part thereof, in which such noncompliance has been so found* (emphasis added).

63. Department of Education regulations describing a "recipient" of federal aid, cited in

the *Grove City* case, are found at 34 C.F.R. §106.2. These regulations were in accordance with HEW regulations enforcing Title VI. See Note, *"Grove City College v. Bell:* Restricting the Remedial Reach of Title IX," *Loyola University Law Journal* 16(1985).

64. *Grove City College v. Bell,* 687 F.2d 684, 700 (3d Cir. 1982).

65. *Grove City College v. Bell,* 465 U.S. 555, 569–70 (1984). All nine justices agreed that indirect aid triggered Title IX coverage.

66. *Grove City,* 465 U.S. at 573–74.

67. Under the Reagan administration, the Department of Education changed its position in favor of a narrow interpretation of Title IX, that is, it now argued that Title IX's ban on sex discrimination only applied to the particular program receiving federal funds—and not to the whole institution.

68. *Congressional Quarterly Almanac,* 1987, p. 281.

69. *Department of Transportation v. Paralyzed Veterans of America,* 477 U.S. 597 (1986).

70. 129 *Cong. Rec.* H10,085–86 (daily ed., November 16, 1983).

71. Norman Amaker, *Civil Rights and the Reagan Administration* (Washington, DC: Urban Institute Press, 1988), pp. 71–72.

72. H.R. 5490, 98th Cong., 2d Sess. (1984); S. 2568, 98th Cong., 2d Sess. (1984). See Note, *"Grove City College v. Bell:* Restricting the Remedial Reach of Title IX," pp. 348–51 for analysis of the attempts to reverse *Grove City* through legislation.

73. S. 557, 100th Cong., 1st. Sess. (1987).

74. *Congressional Quarterly Almanac,* 1985, p. 24.

75. *Congressional Quarterly Almanac,* 1988, pp. 65–66. The Danforth amendment provided that

> nothing in this title shall be construed to require or prohibit any person or public or private entity to provide or pay for any benefit or service, including use of facilities, related to abortion. Nothing in this section shall be construed to permit a penalty to be imposed on any person because such person has received any benefit or service related to legal abortion.

The amendment superseded Title IX regulations that barred educational institutions from treating health insurance, leave policy, and other services related to abortion differently from services provided for pregnancy and childbirth and prohibited discrimination against students who had abortions.

76. *Congressional Quarterly Almanac,* 1988, pp. 63–64.

77. *Congressional Quarterly,* March 19, 1988, pp. 752–53.

78. *Congressional Quarterly,* March 26, 1988, pp. 774–76.

8

Sexual Harassment

Sexual harassment is debilitating to the female worker because it sends a message that she is viewed as an object of sexual gratification rather than as a serious employee.[1] In the 1986 case of *Meritor Savings Bank v. Vinson,* the Supreme Court ruled that sexual harassment was a form of discrimination under Title VII of the 1964 Civil Rights Act. The decision was welcome news to women who had been struggling to get courts to accept their pleas for relief from sexual harassment for over ten years. Although the law was applicable to women harassing men, the overwhelming number of suits had been brought by women complaining of harassment by men.

Prior to 1976, there was little reliable data on harassment of women in the workplace. Then in November 1976, *Redbook* magazine released the results of a survey of nine thousand clerical and professional women. Ninety-two percent of the respondents reported experiences of physical harassment, sexual remarks, and leering. Almost 50 percent claimed that they or someone they knew had been fired or had resigned because of harassment; 75 percent felt that complaining to a supervisor would accomplish nothing.[2] Other studies conducted in the late 1970s substantiated findings such as these.[3] In 1985, the Equal Employment Opportunity Commission (EEOC) received 7,273 sexual harassment complaints.[4]

Despite the widespread occurrences of sexual harassment in the workplace, for a long time it was a problem with no name—each victim struggling with it on an individual basis. Women were reluctant to report episodes of harassment; they felt shamed, embarrassed, and fearful of losing their jobs if they brought attention to it. When women began to take their cases to the federal courts, the majority of courts dismissed their suits without even examining the evidence. Federal court judges ruled that even if plaintiffs were telling the truth about what happened to them at work, their employers' and supervisors' actions did not violate the law.

In her path-breaking work on sexual harassment in the workplace, Catherine MacKinnon distinguishes between two types of behavior: *quid pro quo* harassment and condition of work harassment.[5] The harassment labeled *quid pro quo* occurs when a person in authority, typically a male, requires sexual favors from an employee, typically a female, in return for an employment advantage. Advantages include getting hired, getting promoted, obtaining better working conditions, and not getting fired.

Condition of work harassment, also known as environmental or workplace harassment, is less direct and arises when an employee, again typically a female, is subjected to requests for sexual favors, sexual comments, or sexual insults but no negative employment consequences follow from the employee's refusal to accede to the demands made on her. MacKinnon asserts that

> unwanted sexual advances, made simply because she has a woman's body, can be a daily part of a woman's work life. She may be constantly felt or pinched, visually undressed and stared at, surreptitiously kissed, commented upon, manipulated into being found alone, and generally taken advantage of at work—but never promised or denied anything explicitly connected with her job.[6]

Judicial Reluctance in Sexual Harassment Suits

Although the courts would eventually distinguish between the two types of harassment and require different kinds of proof for each, the early cases made no distinctions between the two and saw no illegality in either situation. In denying legitimacy to complaints of harassment, courts were reflecting the prevalent attitude toward sexual harassment and women in the work force. Additionally, the judiciary's hesitation stemmed from fear that the floodgates of litigation would open and the federal courts would be inundated.

Initially, the courts regarded suits for sexual harassment as forays into forbidden and uncharted territory of (mutual?) sexual attraction. They attributed the harassing behavior to the attractive dress, manner, or physical characteristics of the female employee. Perhaps as well, judges were reluctant to entertain suits for sexual harassment because they believed that the female employee encouraged the advances.

Sexual harassment cases were brought to the federal courts as Title VII suits in which plaintiffs were required to show that the employer imposed a term or condition of employment on them in a sexually discriminatory manner. Although courts eventually accepted sexual harassment as a violation of Title VII, acceptance developed only gradually.

The cases show that courts distinguished sexual harassment from other types of harassment on the job. Judges were more receptive to suits complaining of racial or religious harassment than suits complaining of sexual harassment; they were more willing to acknowledge a Title VII violation in a racially oppressive atmosphere in the workplace than a sexually oppressive atmosphere. Single incidents of racial harassment were more readily labeled as discrimination by the courts, while single incidents of sexual harassment were often dismissed as personal conduct without employment consequences.[7]

The first case allowing a claim for workplace harassment was decided in 1971. Brought by a Hispanic worker, it was followed by others claiming harassment based on religion, national origin, and race.[8] It was not until 1981 that a court finally accepted the concept that sexual harassment creates a hostile working environment. By the early 1970s, the courts had begun to hold employers accountable for the actions of their supervisory personnel in cases of religious or racial harassment.[9] But the courts refused to hold employers liable for the actions of their supervisors in sexual harassment suits.

Proving discrimination by harassment is a difficult process in all circumstances. And while courts often denied relief in cases alleging racial or religious harassment, at least they were not telling the victims that their treatment was "normal," "natural," and a "private affair."[10]

Reasons for Dismissing Sexual Harassment Suits

Courts typically cited any or all of three reasons for dismissing the sexual harassment cases that came before them. The initial hurdle was the court's refusal to acknowledge sexual harassment as a form of sex discrimination. Because either sex *could* be harassed by a member of the opposite sex or the same sex, the courts held that sex was not a determining factor in the harassment. A related problem that made it more difficult for victims of sexual harassment to win their suits was the court's view that their demotion or dismissal was not attributable to sex but rather to their refusal to engage in sexual activity with their supervisors. This "sex-plus" defense had been discredited in the early 1970s when the courts ruled in other Title VII cases that employment barriers applied to one sex only constituted sex discrimination.[11]

Second, courts were unwilling to recognize that harassment had consequences for the employee's work conditions. Courts considered sexual advances made by one employee to another, and even from supervisor to employee, merely personal conduct and not employment related. Flirtatious comments, off-color jokes, invitations to engage in sexual relations were dismissed as individual actions with no relationship to the terms and conditions of employment—even when the consequences of not going along was a demotion, an unfavorable job evaluation, or dismissal.

Finally, and most troublesome for the courts, was the question of where the liability lay. Title VII forbids discrimination by employers. Most of the harassment was committed by supervisors or coworkers in large companies, and courts were reluctant to hold the company legally responsible for these acts by their employees. Their reluctance was heightened when companies had policies forbidding sex discrimination, including harassment, and the plaintiff did not attempt to resolve the problem through internal grievance procedures.

Early Sexual Harassment Litigation

Because of these obstacles, sexual harassment suits met with a chilly reception in the federal courts as victims lost most of the cases. Between 1974 and 1977, five district courts heard sexual harassment cases. Three held that Title VII does not apply to sexual harassment. One held that although Title VII did not apply to the case before the court, it might apply to other cases in the future. Only one court ruled in the woman's favor. Each of these cases illustrates at least one of the barriers sexual harassment plaintiffs faced in court.

In *Barnes v. Train*, 1974, the district court for the District of Columbia dismissed a case brought by Paulette Barnes, an employee of the Environmental Protection Agency (EPA). She claimed that shortly after she began working at the EPA, the director asked her to join him in after-hours social activities. He made sexual remarks to her and promised her extra privileges if she would have an affair with him. She said that she turned him down and that he retaliated by decreasing her job duties and eventually abolishing her job. The court ruled that her supervisor's actions were not motivated by her sex but stemmed from her refusal to engage in sexual relations—not a Title VII problem.[12]

One year later, in *Corne v. Bausch and Lomb*, an Arizona federal district court heard a case filed by Jane Corne and Geneva DeVane against the Bausch and Lomb company. They claimed that their supervisor's verbal and physical harassment created an intolerable working condition and that their employer, Bausch and Lomb, was responsible for allowing them to be supervised by a man who harassed them. The district court dismissed their complaint, saying that the supervisor's behavior was not company-directed policy that negatively affected their employment opportunities. The supervisor's conduct "appeared to be nothing more than a personal proclivity, peculiarity, or mannerism." He was merely "satisfying a personal urge."[13] The court concluded there was no sex discrimination because the supervisor could have harassed male employees as well. The judge also expressed concern that a flood of litigation would follow if their suit were successful.

The plaintiff also lost in *Tomkins v. Public Service Electric and Gas*, 1976, when the district court of New Jersey also refused to apply Title VII to sexual harassment. Despite Tomkins's claim of a physical attack by her supervisor, the court considered sex irrelevant to her claim. Adrienne Tomkins was invited to lunch by her supervisor to discuss his evaluation of her work and the possibility of a future promotion. He propositioned her at lunch and made it clear that her compliance was a job requirement. Not concerned that her supervisor's behavior affected her employment status, the court dismissed her claim, describing the supervisor's acts merely as "abuse of authority . . . for personal purposes."[14]

Then, in *Miller v. Bank of America*, 1976, the district court of the Northern District of California rejected Margaret Miller's Title VII claim for sexual harassment. Miller complained that she was promised a better job if she agreed to engage in sexual activity and was then fired for refusing.

The court dismissed her suit in part because she had not presented evidence of a systematic policy of harassment of women; the court balked at applying Title VII to a case where only one victim was involved. Reluctant to interfere in a personnel decision involving sexual attraction, the judge asked "whether Title VII was intended to hold an employer liable for what is essentially the isolated and unauthorized sex misconduct of one employee to another."[15]

The court noted that the bank had a policy against moral misconduct and that Miller did not avail herself of the complaint procedure. Although not ruling out the possibility that a future Title VII suit *could* be brought against an employer for allowing sex to be a condition of employment, the court felt this was not the time. Warning of the possible abuse of Title VII in these situations, the court stated that "it would not be difficult to foresee a federal challenge based on alleged sex motivated considerations of the complainant's superior in every case of a lost promotion, transfer, demotion or dismissal."[16]

A Sexual Harassment Suit Finally Succeeds

Finally, in *Williams v. Saxbe*, another 1976 decision, the first sexual harassment suit succeeded in federal district court. Diane Williams, an information officer for the Department of Justice, brought suit when she was fired from her job less than two weeks after she refused her supervisor's sexual advances. For the first time, a court recognized a link between a supervisor's conduct and a victim's employment status and agreed that a plaintiff had made a legitimate claim of sex discrimination. Rejecting the argument that sexual demands could be made to both sexes, the district court found that the actions of her supervisors "created an artificial barrier to employment which was placed before one gender and not the other."[17]

Sexual Harassment Is Based on Sex

Following *Williams*, a number of circuit courts began to reverse lower court decisions and permit Title VII suits for sexual harassment. The first major breakthrough came in 1977, in *Barnes v. Costle* (*Barnes v. Train* in the district court), when the District of Columbia Circuit Court ruled that plaintiff's complaint of sexual harassment at the Environmental Protection Agency constituted sex discrimination.[18]

The primary issue in *Barnes* was whether the harassment was "based on sex," as Title VII required. The district court had accepted the EPA's argument that Barnes had not been a victim of sex discrimination, that her position had been eliminated because she refused to give in to her supervisor's sexual demands—not because she was a woman.

The circuit court found that Barnes had been treated differently from other EPA employees because of her sex. Citing examples of her supervisor's attempts to persuade (coerce?) her to engage in sex with him, the court agreed that she had successfully shown that "retention of her job was conditioned upon submission to sexual relations—an exaction which the supervisor would not have sought from any male." The court continued, "[But] for her womanhood . . . her participation in sexual activity would never have been solicited."[19]

The court recognized that her job was eliminated because she refused to cooperate with her supervisor. But the judge explained that Title VII does not require sex to be the sole cause of discriminatory treatment as long as it "contribut[es] to the discrimination in a substantial way."[20] Employers cannot subject men and women to different conditions of employment, fire the women for not complying, and then disclaim any responsibility for sex discrimination.

Employer Liability

Following *Barnes*, the lower court rulings against plaintiffs Miller and Tomkins were reversed by the circuit courts. Both courts agreed that employers could be held liable for the acts of their employees.[21] In *Tomkins*, the Third Circuit found that the sexual demands made on Adrienne Tomkins were based on sex and linked to her employment status. The court held that a Title VII violation occurs when a supervisory employee "makes sexual advances or demands towards a subordinate employee . . . and the employer does not take prompt and appropriate remedial action" after learning of it.[22]

When Margaret Miller appealed the district court ruling against her to the Ninth Circuit, it was no longer possible for the Bank of America to argue that Title VII is indifferent to sexual harassment. Instead, the bank tried to disclaim responsibility because it had a policy against the kind of conduct Miller complained of and because it provided an internal grievance procedure that she did not utilize.

The Ninth Circuit analogized the bank's position to that of a taxi company under the tort doctrine of respondeat superior (in which an employer is held liable for an employee's acts).

> It would be shocking to most of us if a court should hold, for example, that a taxi company is not liable for injuries to a pedestrian caused by the negligence of one of its drivers because the company has a safety training program and strictly forbids negligent driving. Nor would the taxi company be exonerated even if the taxi driver, in the course of his employment, became enraged at a jaywalking pedestrian and intentionally ran him down.[23]

Citing similar rulings in *Barnes* and *Tomkins*, the circuit court determined that Congress did not intend that Title VII exempt employers from the normal rules of employer liability. Although it was an employee (the supervisor) who violated company policy by harassing Miller, the court held the bank responsible for the actions of a superior with authority to "hire, fire, discipline or promote."[24]

The bank also argued that Miller forfeited her right to sue when she bypassed its personnel office. The court disagreed, holding that Congress did not intend to require a Title VII plaintiff to exhaust company grievance procedures before filing suit in federal court.

The EEOC Guidelines

At the same time that the courts became more accepting of sexual harassment suits, the Equal Employment Opportunity Commission issued guidelines reaffirming the linkage between sexual harassment and employment discrimination. Based in large part on prevailing Title VII case law, the guidelines were formally added as an amendment to the EEOC Guidelines on Discrimination Based on Sex.

On April 11, 1980, the EEOC published a set of interim guidelines on sexual harassment and, after a public comment period of sixty days, drafted the final regulations. They were then released on November 10,

1980. Going beyond case law, the guidelines accomplished the two major tasks of providing a comprehensive definition of sexual harassment, including both *quid pro quo* and workplace harassment, and expanding the prevailing view on employer liability.

The 1980 guidelines stated that

> (a) Unwelcome sexual advances, requests for sexual favors, and other verbal or physical conduct of a sexual nature constitute sexual harassment when (1) submission to such conduct is made either explicitly or implicitly a term or condition of an individual's employment (2) submission to or rejection of such conduct by an individual is used as a basis for employment decisions affecting such individual, or (3) such conduct has the purpose or effect of unreasonably interfering with an individual's work performance or creating an intimidating, hostile, or offensive working environment.[25]

The EEOC's position on a company's liability for harassment by supervisory personnel was a broad one. The commission urged that the company be held strictly (that is, always) liable even if the harassment violated company policy and was unknown to company officials. The guidelines made no distinctions between hostile environment harassment and *quid pro quo* harassment when supervisors were involved. When other employees (nonsupervisors) were the harassers, the guidelines placed responsibility on the company if officials knew or should have known about the harassment and failed to take corrective measures.

Hostile Environment Harassment

The judiciary proved to be more sympathetic to *quid pro quo* harassment suits than to hostile environment suits because it was more apparent in *quid pro quo* cases that the harassment affected the employee's terms and conditions of employment. Because the courts were not convinced that workplace harassment violated Title VII, these cases were less successful in court. Then, in 1981, in *Bundy v. Jackson*, the District of Columbia Circuit recognized that a woman could be injured when sexual harassment created a hostile work environment.[26]

The district court had ruled that Title VII did not forbid the harassment experienced by Sandra Bundy, an officer with the Department of Corrections. The judge dismissed her complaint on the grounds that she was not denied employment benefits—that is, she was not fired for refusing her superiors' sexual advances. He found that "the making of improper sexual advances to female employees [was] standard operating procedure, a fact of life, a normal condition of employment in the office."[27]

The court's finding was substantiated by the tales of the sexual propositions directed at Bundy, including the one by a high-level supervisor who, when she complained to him of his subordinates' actions, told her that "any man in his right mind would want to rape you."[28] Despite these incidents, the district court denied Sandra Bundy relief because it found that sexual attention toward female employees was only sport for her supervisors and a "game" played without retaliation for refusing to play.

On appeal, the circuit court recognized that Bundy was a victim of sex discrimination within the bounds of Title VII. The court cited "numerous cases finding Title VII violations where an employer created or condoned a substantially discriminatory work *environment*, regardless of whether the complaining employees lost any tangible job benefits as a result of the discrimination."[29] Ruling otherwise, said the court, would subject a woman to

a "cruel trilemma" [in which] she can endure the harassment. [Or] she can attempt to oppose it, with little hope of success, either legal or practical, but with every prospect of making the job even less tolerable for her. Or she can leave her job, with little hope of legal relief and the likely prospect of another job where she will face harassment anew.[30]

The Origins of the Vinson Case

The sexual harassment case that eventually reached the Supreme Court began a few years after *Bundy* was decided, when Mechelle Vinson filed suit against her supervisor, Sidney Taylor, and her employer, the Capital City Federal Savings and Loan Association.[31] Vinson had been hired initially as a teller-trainee and was subsequently promoted to teller, head teller, and then assistant branch manager. After working at the branch for four years, she took indefinite sick leave and was fired for excessive time on leave.

At a trial that lasted eleven days, Vinson testified that Taylor propositioned her and, after initially refusing him, that she ultimately capitulated because she was afraid of losing her job. She claimed that she was forced to submit to him during the day as well as after work, that he touched her in front of other employees, that he followed her into the women's room where he exposed himself to her, and that he assaulted and even raped her. She testified that she had sexual intercourse with him forty or fifty times during the three-year period that the harassment continued. She did not report him, she said, because she was afraid.

Taylor completely denied her story, and the savings and loan disassociated itself from him, saying that if he committed these acts, he did so without its knowledge or authorization. Following the trial, the district court judge ruled that Vinson had failed to make out a Title VII claim of sex discrimination. Even though this disposed of the case, the lower court did not stop there but went on to assess the savings and loan's liability as well. Because it had a policy against discrimination, and because Vinson had never complained about Taylor, the court concluded that the savings and loan could not be held accountable for Taylor's actions, if indeed, he committed the acts of which he was accused.

The District of Columbia Circuit Court reversed on appeal, ruling that victims of sexual harassment had two legal theories available to them. Citing *Barnes*, the court stated that it was now settled that *quid pro quo* harassment was illegal under Title VII. It added that *Bundy* had created a second option for a sexual harassment suit: in situations where one employee subjects another to pervasive harassment in the workplace and creates a hostile or offensive environment. Referring to the EEOC guidelines, the court held that Title VII applied to both types of harassment. It remanded the case to the district court for a determination on whether Taylor's actions created a hostile environment.

In remanding, the circuit court also instructed the district court on how to decide several points of law. The district court did not determine whether Vinson and Taylor actually had a sexual relationship; it merely ruled that if they did, it was voluntary and irrelevant to her employment status. In reaching its finding of voluntariness, the lower court had allowed Taylor to introduce evidence relating to Vinson's dress and sexual fantasies.

The appellate court rejected the view that Vinson's "voluntary" acquiescence to Taylor's sexual demands, that is, that she was not forced into having sex with him against her will, defeated her claim. Quoting the EEOC definition of sexual harassment as "unwelcome sexual advances . . . [that have] the purpose or effect of unreasonably interfering with an individual's work performance or creating an intimidating, hostile or offensive working environment," the appellate court stressed that her "voluntariness" was immaterial.[32] Because Congress did not intend a victim to forfeit her right to complain when she was forced to capitulate to sexual demands to keep her job, evidence of Vinson's clothing and sexual fantasies were irrelevant.

The district court had not permitted Vinson to present evidence that Taylor had sexually harassed other female employees, and here too, the appellate court disagreed. The circuit court felt it was relevant to her case that Taylor created a sexually harassing environment for female employees.

Finally, and perhaps most important, the appellate court rejected the lower court view of the employer's responsibility. The grievance procedure required an employee to file a complaint with the supervisor; in this case, because Taylor was the supervisor, Vinson could not comply with the rules. She contended that her employer had notice of Taylor's harassment by other means. The lower court disagreed and refused to hold the savings and loan liable, reasoning that even if Taylor were guilty of sexual harassment, the employer was unaware of it. Although the issue of employer liability had not been directly litigated in *Barnes* and *Bundy*, in both cases employers were held liable for discriminatory acts committed by supervisory personnel. In *Vinson*, the district court absolved the employer from responsibility, believing the claim that it was unaware of Taylor's harassment of women employees under his supervision.

The circuit court pointed out that Title VII forbids discrimination by employers *and* by their agents. And the court held that as an "agent" of the savings and loan, Taylor's violation of Title VII was attributable to his employer, regardless of its knowledge of his behavior. Justifying its decision to assess far-reaching employer liability for the acts of its employees (known as vicarious liability), the circuit court pointed to legislative debate on Title VII. Although there was no evidence that Congress intended to impose vicarious liability, the court believed it significant that Congress had at least discussed the issue and had not ruled it out.[33]

Finding the EEOC guidelines "persuasive," the circuit court accepted the broad interpretation of employer liability. Under the guidelines, an employer is accountable for sexual harassment committed by its supervisory personnel "regardless of whether the specific acts complained of were authorized or even forbidden by the employer and regardless of whether the employer knew or should have known of their occurrence." Moreover, added the court, Title VII case law generally considers supervisory personnel as agents of their employers and holds employers accountable for their acts.

The court broadly defined an agent not only as a supervisory employee, but as any employee with authority to hire and fire. An employee who has power over a subordinate can threaten and coerce and, thereby, harass.[34] While Taylor could not hire or fire, he had authority to recommend salary levels and promotions. The court wanted to create a disincentive for the employer to look the other way and escape responsibility simply by disclaiming knowledge of the harassment. "Much of the promise of Title VII will become empty," declared the court, "if victims of unlawful discrimination cannot secure redress from the only source capable of providing it."[35]

The Supreme Court Rules on Sexual Harassment

Vinson's employer, now known as the Meritor Savings Bank, appealed to the Supreme Court. In 1986, a unanimous Court, with Justice William Rehnquist announcing the opinion, affirmed the circuit court's ruling to send the case back to the district court for a trial on Vinson's complaint of hostile environment harassment. The Supreme Court, however, rejected the circuit court's expansive interpretation of vicarious liability as well as its ruling that evidence of the employee's provocation was inadmissible. Despite these reservations, the high court affirmed the circuit court's holding that a hostile work environment created by sexual harassment violates Title VII even in the absence of demands for sexual favors or loss of tangible job benefits.

The bank argued that legislative history and settled case law show that Title VII protection is limited to sexual discrimination that erects "tangible, economic barriers."[36] Not true, said Rehnquist. The injury caused by the discrimination need not be economic. Title VII was intended to reach an entire array of employment disparity between the sexes. Rehnquist also pointed out that the EEOC guidelines clearly state that Title VII extends to complaints of a hostile environment. Cautioning that not all incidents of offensive or annoying behavior in the workplace would amount to harassment, he agreed that the conduct described by Vinson was sufficiently "severe" and "pervasive" to constitute harassment. On these grounds, the Court affirmed the circuit court's decision to remand.

Rehnquist cited a number of errors the appellate court had made in interpreting sexual harassment law. He found that the appellate court had correctly ruled that it was irrelevant whether Vinson was a voluntary participant in the sexual relationship. The key question, Rehnquist said, was not whether she voluntarily engaged in sex with him but whether the sexual advances were "unwelcome." And although the circuit court had flatly stated that Vinson's dress or speech "had no place in this litigation," the Supreme Court disagreed and held these were relevant in determining whether the sexual attention was welcome to her.

The Court straddled the fence on the issue of the employer's vicarious liability for hostile environment harassment. On the one hand, it refused to impose strict liability in workplace harassment cases. On the other hand, it held that a company would not be relieved of responsibility merely by claiming that it lacked notice of the supervisor's actions. Nor would it be absolved by simply pointing to the existence of a nondiscrimination policy or showing that the victim did not use a company grievance procedure.

The Supreme Court was unwilling to commit to a clear statement on employers' liability in part because of the EEOC's apparent shift in direction. Notwithstanding its earlier (1980) guidelines creating strict employer liability whenever supervisory personnel were involved, the EEOC now argued in its brief to the Court, filed by the solicitor general, that while strict company liability for the acts of agents is appropriate in a *quid pro quo* case, it is not suitable for a workplace harassment suit. In a hostile environment case, the EEOC now urged, employer liability should rest on two factors: whether the employer had an express policy against harassment and a grievance procedure to resolve complaints; and whether the employer knew of the harassment and failed to take action to remedy it.

The Supreme Court adopted a middle ground between the circuit court and the EEOC. It refused to impose automatic liability for sexual harassment by supervisors on the employer, agreeing with the revised EEOC position that employers must have notice in order to be held liable in a hostile environment case. But because Congress intended that Title VII be interpreted as holding employers accountable for *some* of the acts of their employees, the Court held that mere "absence of notice to an employer does not necessarily insulate that employer from liability."[37] Advocating a case-by-case approach, the Court ruled that trial courts must examine the facts of each case to determine when employers are to be held responsible for their supervisors' acts.

Finally, the Court criticized the bank's grievance policy because it was a general policy against discrimination that did not specifically forbid harassment. It required the employee to direct complaints to her supervisor, a questionable procedure when, as here, the supervisor is the harasser. Thus, after more than a decade of litigation, the Supreme Court acknowledged that sexual harassment was an unfair condition of work—based on sex—and could be addressed in a Title VII lawsuit. In *Vinson*, the Court went even further to allow suits for harassment that polluted the work environment, even in the absence of material losses in the woman's employment status.

While *Vinson* advanced sexual equality in the workplace, the decision had two major shortcomings. First, the Supreme Court permitted evidence of the employee's dress, manner, and speech to be introduced at trial as a defense to the harassment charge. Evidence such as this allows supervisors to claim that the employees "asked for" the harassment or that they "enjoyed" it. Second, *Vinson* took a step back from the more stringent—original—EEOC position on the issue of employer liability for workplace harassment.

Some justices objected to the Court's retrenchment on employer liability. Thurgood Marshall, speaking for himself and William Brennan, Harry Blackmun, and John Paul Stevens, concurred in the Court's judgment to affirm the appellate court's decision, but wrote separately to express disapproval of the high court's ruling on employer liability for environmental harassment. Marshall pointed out that under Title VII law, expressed in the 1980 EEOC guidelines, the employer is always liable for harassment by supervisory employees—whether *quid pro quo* or workplace harassment. Lack of notice to the employer is not a defense. He saw no "justification for a special rule, to be applied *only* in 'hostile environment' cases, that sexual harassment does not create employer liability until the employee suffering the discrimination notifies other supervisors."[38]

A Final Note on Harassment in the Workplace

Sexual harassment is inextricably intertwined with the status of woman in the workforce. "Whether at the office or the factory, sexual harassment is nothing more than the assertion of power by men over women, perceived to be in a vulnerable position with respect to male authority."[39]

In her study of sexual harassment, MacKinnon argued that sexual harassment stems from an abuse of power rather than sexual desire; she attributed the problem to women's subordinate position in the labor force. Women are victimized by harassment because they "are generally men's subordinates on the job, with men in the position to do the hiring, firing, supervising, and promoting."[40]

The problem of harassment appears particularly acute for women of color. Many of the suits were brought by women of color with jobs that made them subordinate to males — mostly white males. Adrienne Tomkins, Sandra Bundy, Diane Williams, Margaret Miller, Paulette Barnes, and Maxine Munford are African-American secretaries, payroll clerks, assistant managers, and corrections officers. Although the cases did not stress the racial characteristics of the accused and the accusers, it is noteworthy that such women are especially vulnerable to sexual harassment.[41]

Sexual Harassment in Academia

While the battle to gain judicial recognition of sexual harassment in the workplace was being fought, a corresponding battle was being waged at colleges and universities all over the country. As with workplace harassment, the goals of this struggle were twofold: first, to acquaint educational administrators with the problems of sexual harassment on campus; and second, to convince the courts that Title IX offered protection against harassing behavior.

Sexual harassment on the campus violates Title IX law by restricting women's educational opportunities in the classroom and in the academic environment generally. Harassment of students is similar to harassment of employees. Both reflect an unequal distribution of power between victim and harasser. As in the workplace, in academia men typically occupy roles that enable them to exercise power over female students.[42]

The conduct complained of tends to be the same: reports from the academy indicate a wide range of behavior including assault and rape of female students, pressure for sexual activity, suggestive remarks about their clothing, their bodies, and their sexual activity, as well as leering, touching, patting, stroking, and pinching. As with harassment at work, women are more often victims than men.[43]

Also, like workplace harassment, it is difficult to assess the magnitude of the problem on the campus. A book published in 1984, appropriately entitled the *Lecherous Professor*, cites studies showing that 20 to 30 percent of female students indicate they were victimized by male faculty during their years in college.[44] In a 1978 survey of female students at the University of California at Berkeley, 29.7 percent reported at least one experience of sexual harassment during their college years.[45] Looking at the problem more broadly, in 1985 there were over 6 million female students enrolled in colleges and universities in the United States. If only *1* percent were victims of harassment, the number would be a staggering sixty-four thousand.[46]

Academic harassment differs from workplace harassment because students are particularly vulnerable to faculty authority. In *Korf v. Ball State University*, a case involving a tenured professor in the music department at Ball State, the court ruled that the professor had been justly terminated by the university for "unethical behavior by 'exploiting students for his private advantage.'" It did not matter, said the court, that Korf's sexual relationship with his young male student may have been "private and consensual."[47]

Harassment on campus pollutes the academic atmosphere. Female students report that they often feel reduced to sex objects and not taken seriously, are given less respect, and have their self-confidence undermined by male faculty.[48] Learning becomes secondary to extrication from the sexual encounter.

Aside from the power they hold over undergraduate and graduate students, faculty are often seen as role models and mentors. The student-faculty relationship, unlike the employer-employee relationship, is often based on trust and dependency. The education process typically includes close intellectual, and often personal, interactions between students and faculty. When the interactions become romantic or sexual, the intellectual component of the relationship is threatened.

Applying Title IX to Sexual Harassment

Fear of reprisal, fear of embarrassment, and fear of not being believed keep students from reporting sexual harassment to college authorities. It was probably surprising, therefore, when a suit for sexual harassment was filed against Yale University in 1977.[49] *Alexander v. Yale University*, the first reported case against a university or college for sexual harassment under Title IX, is the landmark decision in this area of law. Despite the hope offered by *Alexander*, however, litigation against sexual harassment under Title IX seems permanently stalled. More than a decade later, there has been only one other judicial opinion reported in this area.[50]

Alexander arose when five female students and a male faculty member of the classics department brought charges against Yale. The professor claimed that his teaching efforts were hindered by "an atmosphere of distrust" of male faculty at Yale. Some of the students complained of direct personal experiences with harassment, others cited their distress on hearing of the harassment of others.

The lower court dismissed the faculty member's complaint as well as the complaints of two students (one current, one former), because "such imponderables as atmosphere or vicariously experienced wrong" are not within Title IX protection.[51] The court also dismissed the complaints of one of the former students because she had graduated and another of the current students because she had not complained to authorities at Yale.

Only one plaintiff, Pamela Price, a current student, was allowed to pursue her complaint to trial. Price had charged that she was offered an *A* in a course in her major field if she would agree to her professor's sexual proposition. She had complained to Yale officials, including the dean, but to no avail. She claimed that her final grade in the course, a *C*, was not a fair measure of her work but was a result of her refusal to accede to his wishes. She argued that Yale was denying her equal educational opportunity in violation of Title IX because it did not combat sexual harassment of female undergraduates and had not instituted a grievance procedure to investigate complaints of this sort.

Although the court agreed that sexual harassment in academia is comparable to harassment in the workplace, Price lost her suit. The judge ruled against her, finding that her grade reflected her academic achievement. The court also denied her request to order Yale to establish a grievance procedure for charges of harassment.

When the female students appealed the dismissal of their complaint to the Second Circuit, the circuit court upheld the lower court. The appeals court explained that Title IX protects against loss of "educational benefits," but when the activities are removed from the "ordinary educational process," the injuries must be more specific. These students' injuries, the court held, were too speculative. One of the plaintiffs charged that the coach's harassment made her quit the field hockey team without receiving a varsity letter. Another claimed that because her flute instructor harassed her, she was forced out of the music program and denied a career in music. Not only are the injuries uncertain but, the court wondered, what could be done to redress their grievances? The judge rejected one suggested remedy of awarding the plaintiff a varsity letter in field hockey.

Moreover, the court ruled that because they had graduated, they were no longer suffering any injury. Ordering Yale to establish a grievance procedure would not benefit them in any way. In any event, because Yale had already adopted "a set of procedures" for receiving complaints, "the major relief sought in this suit has already been granted."[52]

The court of appeals also supported the lower court's finding that Price had not proven her claim of harassment. Because she could not show that she had been harmed by harassment, she could not properly complain about Yale's failure to establish a grievance procedure for receiving students' sexual harassment complaints.

While *Alexander* established the principle that sexual harassment of students may violate Title IX, the Second Circuit was unreceptive to the students' complaints. The opinion does not auger well for future Title IX sexual harassment claims. The court's ruling suggests that a successful harassment suit must identify particular episodes of harassing conduct, must show specific harm arising from the harassment, and if the student bringing the claim graduates before the case is heard, the court will treat the issue as settled. *Alexander* also implies that, unlike Title VII actions, students will be limited to *quid pro quo* situations and will be unable to seek relief for environmental harassment.

In *Moire v. Temple University School of Medicine*, the only other reported federal court case of sexual harassment on campus, the district court allowed an environmental harassment claim by medical student Laura Klawitter who failed her psychiatric clerkship and was forced to repeat her third year of medical school. Klawitter brought suit against her clerkship supervisor, Dr. Loren Crabtree, for sexual harassment, and against Temple University for condoning his conduct. The district court acknowledged her right to bring a sexual harassment claim under Title IX and even suggested that the EEOC Guidelines for Sexual Harassment in the workplace are applicable to Title IX actions. Despite her victory on the legal principle, the student lost her suit. Because the trial judge found that her version of events lacked credibility, the court ruled in favor of the university, holding that the plaintiff did not prove that she was sexually harassed by Dr. Crabtree.[53]

In the midst of the apparent prevalence of sexual harassment on campus, sexual harassment litigation remains rare and winning even rarer. In part, this stems from the court's traditional reluctance to interfere with academic judgments in matters relating to faculty standards and classroom autonomy. In *Regents of the University of Michigan v. Ewing*, the Supreme Court highlighted the need for judges to defer to the faculty's professional judgment. In this 1985 case involving the university's decision to dismiss a student from its medical program, the Court instructed lower courts not to "override" faculty decisions unless they represent "such a substantial departure from accepted academic norms as to demonstrate that the person or committee responsible did not exercise professional judgment."[54] *Ewing* signaled that lower courts should refrain from excessive involvement in determining the validity of grades and other academic rewards.

The tradition of judicial deference to faculty decision-making has led to the court's desire to avoid embroilment in academic sexual harassment cases. But even if courts were less reluctant, cases probably will arise infrequently because students are not eager to become plaintiffs. In contrast to employees with long-term commitments to the job, students are relatively short-term residents at colleges and universities. It is easier to transfer out of the class or even to another school than to file a legal challenge. Also, litigation requires financial resources and incentives. And unlike Title VII, which allows a court to award back pay, a Title IX action does not offer the incentive of monetary damages.[55] Finally, because graduation ends a student's legal interest in the suit, even if these obstacles are overcome, most cases are likely to be dismissed by the time they get to court.

The ruling in *Alexander* suggests that universities should establish internal grievance procedures for student complaints if they want the courts' hands-off policy to continue. And while Title VII law on employer responsibility for workplace harassment is still unsettled, it is clear that courts look unfavorably on companies without antiharassment policies and procedures for reporting violations of the policy.

Because of the importance of internal review processes, a number of colleges and universities have adopted policies for reporting and investigating harassment. Academic institutions and faculty associations, such as the American Association of University Professors (AAUP), have also identified sexual harassment as conduct forbidden on the grounds of professional ethics and responsibilities.[56] Indeed, Professor Korf's dismissal at Ball State University was based on the AAUP Statement on Professional Ethics, published in the faculty handbook.

Influenced by the EEOC guidelines on sexual harassment in employment, many institutions around the country—University of Iowa, University of Rhode Island, Temple University, Harvard University—have defined sexual harassment, forbidden it, and provided redress when the rules were broken.[57] While they do not eliminate harassment on the campus, such actions at least heighten awareness of the problem and put both students and faculty on guard that such behavior will not be tolerated.

NOTES

1. See Joan Vermuelen, "Sexual Harassment," in Carol Lefcourt, ed., *Women and the Law* (New York: Clark Boardman, 1987).

2. Project on the Status and Education of Women, *Sexual Harassment: A Hidden Issue* (Washington, DC: Association of American Colleges, 1978), p. 2.

3. See Marvin F. Hill, Jr., and Curtiss K. Behrens, "Love in the Office: A Guide for Dealing with Sexual Harassment under Title VII of the Civil Rights Act of 1964," *DePaul Law Review* 30(1981), pp. 581–82 n. 2.

4. David Machlowitz and Marilyn Machlowitz, "Preventing Sexual Harassment," *ABA Journal* (October 1987), p. 78.

184 Sexual Harassment

5. Catherine MacKinnon, *Sexual Harassment of Working Women* (New Haven: Yale University Press, 1979). MacKinnon uses the phrase *condition of work* to describe non-*quid pro quo* harassment. The Supreme Court and the Equal Employment Opportunity Commission use the phrase *hostile environment harassment* for non-*quid pro quo* harassment. See P. J. Murray, "Employer: Beware of 'Hostile Environment' Sexual Harassment," *Duquesne Law Review* 26(1987).

6. MacKinnon, *Sexual Harassment of Working Women*, p. 40.

7. See MacKinnon, *Sexual Harassment of Working Women*, chapter 2; Vermuelen, "Sexual Harassment."

8. The 1971 case based on race was *Rogers v. EEOC*, 454 F.2d 234 (5th Cir. 1971). Other cases were *Firefighters Institute for Racial Equality v. St. Louis*, 549 F.2d 506 (8th Cir. 1977); *Gray v. Greyhound Lines, East*, 545 F.2d 169 (D.C. Cir. 1976); *Compston v. Borden, Inc.*, 424 F.Supp. 157 (S.D. Ohio 1976); *Cariddi v. Kansas City Chiefs Football Club*, 568 F.2d 87 (8th Cir. 1977). These cases are cited in *Meritor Savings Bank v. Vinson*, 477 U.S. 57 (1986).

9. Examples of cases in which employers were held accountable for racial harassment are: *Calcote v. Texas Educational Foundation*, 578 F.2d 95 (5th Cir. 1978); *Flowers v. Crouch-Walker*, 552 F.2d 1277 (7th Cir. 1977); *Anderson v. Methodist Evangelical Hospital*, 464 F.2d 723 (6th Cir. 1972). A case in which the employer was held responsible for religious harassment is *Young v. Southwestern Savings and Loan*, 509 F.2d 140 (5th Cir. 1975).

10. See MacKinnon, *Sexual Harassment of Working Women*, chapter 4.

11. Kerri Weisel, "Title VII: Legal Protection against Sexual Harassment," *Washington Law Review* 53(1977), pp. 129–32.

12. *Barnes v. Train*, 13 Fair Empl. Prac. Cas. 123 (D.D.C. 1974).

13. *Corne v. Bausch and Lomb*, 390 F.Supp. 161, 163 (D. Ariz. 1975).

14. *Tomkins v. Public Service Electric and Gas*, 422 F.Supp. 553, 556 (D. N.J. 1976).

15. *Miller v. Bank of America*, 418 F.Supp. 233, 234 (N.D. Cal. 1976).

16. *Miller*, 418 F.Supp. at 236.

17. *Williams v. Saxbe*, 413 F.Supp. 654, 657 (D.D.C. 1976). This decision was reversed on other grounds in *Williams v. Bell*, 587 F.2d 1240 (D.C. Cir. 1978). The circuit court ruled that the district court judge should not have decided the case on the basis of the administrative record and remanded the case back to the district court for a new trial. On remand, the court dismissed the supervisor's testimony as incredible and concluded that "submission to the sexual advances of the plaintiff's supervisor was a term and condition of employment in violation of Title VII." *Williams v. Civiletti*, 487 F.Supp. 1387, 1389 (D.D.C. 1980).

18. In *Garber v. Saxon Business Products*, 552 F.2d 1032 (4th Cir. 1977), in a per curiam opinion, the Fourth Circuit found a Title VII violation when female employees were required to submit to the sexual advances of their male superiors.

19. *Barnes v. Costle*, 561 F.2d 983, 989–90 (D.C. Cir. 1977).

20. *Barnes*, 561 F.2d at 990.

21. Lower courts began to assess liability against employers for the acts of their supervisors in 1977. Shortly after *Barnes* was decided, a Michigan district court allowed a Title VII suit for sexual harassment and also decided that the company could, under some circumstances, be held liable for the acts of their supervisory employees. The court held that the employer had an affirmative duty to investigate complaints and take appropriate action against the offender. Failing to investigate gives the appearance of consenting to the harassing behavior. *Munford v. James T. Barnes & Co.*, 441 F.Supp. 459 (E.D. Mich. 1977). Then in *Heelan v. Johns-Manville*, 451 F.Supp. 1382 (D.Colo. 1978), another district court agreed that sexual harassment of women falls within the prohibited behavior of Title VII as long as it was shown that the sexual demands were sufficiently tied to a condition of employment. Because the plaintiff had complained to company management and had her complaints either ignored or summarily dismissed, the court found the company liable for the harassment by the supervisor.

22. *Tomkins v. Public Service Electric and Gas*, 568 F.2d 1044, 1048–49 (3d Cir. 1977).

23. *Miller v. Bank of America*, 600 F.2d 211, 213 (9th Cir. 1979).

24. *Miller*, 600 F.2d at 213. In *Henson v. City of Dundee*, 682 F.2d 897 (11th Cir. 1982) the Eleventh Circuit stated that strict employer liability was appropriate when sexual harassment by a supervisor led to tangible economic loss.

25. 29 C.F.R. §1604.11(a). See Stewart Oneglia and Susan French Cornelius, "Sexual

Harassment in the Workplace: The Equal Employment Opportunity Commission's New Guidelines," *Saint Louis University Law Journal* 26(1981).

26. The Eleventh Circuit allowed a suit for workplace harassment a year later in *Henson*, 682 F.2d at 897, but declined to impose strict liability. The Fourth Circuit also allowed a suit for workplace harassment in *Katz v. Dole*, 709 F.2d 251 (4th Cir. 1983). In *Robinson v. Jacksonville Shipyards*, 1991 U.S. Dist. Lexis 794, the district court of Florida found that employees and supervisors created a "sexually hostile" work environment by displaying pictures of undressed women and making suggestive remarks demeaning to women. This work environment, held the court, violated the women employees' rights by discriminating against them on the basis of sex.

27. *Bundy v. Jackson*, 19 Fair Empl. Prac. Cas. 828, 831 (D.D.C. 1979).

28. *Bundy*, 19 Fair Empl. Prac. Cas. at 831.

29. *Bundy v. Jackson*, 641 F.2d 934, 943–44 (D.C. Cir. 1981) (emphasis in the original).

30. *Bundy*, 641 F.2d at 946.

31. *Vinson v. Taylor*, 23 Fair Empl. Prac. Cas. 37 (D.D.C. 1980).

32. *Vinson v. Taylor*, 753 F.2d 141, 146 (D.C. Cir. 1985).

33. Employer liability can be premised on various theories: agency law, tort law, or Title VII law. Title VII, as expressed in legislative intent, offers the broadest protection to workers. The doctrine of respondeat superior used by the *Miller* court arises from tort law. The problem with using tort law is that courts then limit the reach of Title VII only to areas where employees could sue under tort law. Traditionally, under tort and agency law, employers are exempt from liability when agents act outside the scope of their duty.

By equating employers with their agents for purposes of Title VII, Congress indicated an intent to go beyond tort and agency law in assigning employer liability. In *Vinson*, the Supreme Court seemed to have adopted a position somewhere between agency law and Title VII law. See *Barnes*, 561 F.2d at 995–1001 (MacKinnon, J., concurring); Vermuelen, "Sexual Harassment," pp. 17–18.

34. The court explained that it was deriving these rules from analysis of statutory language and interpretation rather than from common law tort principles of respondeat superior, which exempts employers from liability when the actions of their employers are outside the scope of their employment. *Vinson*, 753 F.2d at 149–52. Judge MacKinnon's concurring opinion in *Barnes* discussed the employer's vicarious liability for the acts of the employee under traditional agency principles, tort law, and statutory law as developed under Title VII and the National Labor Relations Act. *Barnes*, 561 F.2d at 995–1001 (MacKinnon, J., concurring).

35. *Vinson*, 753 F.2d at 151.

36. *Vinson*, 477 U.S. at 64.

37. *Vinson*, 477 U.S. at 72.

38. *Vinson*, 477 U.S. at 77 (Marshall, J., concurring) (emphasis in the original).

39. Vermuelen, "Sexual Harassment," p. 7.

40. MacKinnon, *Sexual Harassment of Working Women*, p. 12. Donna E. Benson and Gregg E. Thomson, "Sexual Harassment on a University Campus: The Confluence of Authority Relations, Sexual Interest and Gender Stratification" *Social Problems* 29(1982) support MacKinnon's view.

41. Writing about the intersection of race, class, and sex, Angela Davis argues that women of color are especially vulnerable to sexual harassment because of their historic economic and sexual victimization by white men. Angela Davis, *Women, Race & Class* (New York: Random House, 1981), chapter 11. See also Paula Giddings, *When and Where I Enter* (New York: William Morrow, 1984).

42. Benson and Thomson, "Sexual Harassment on a University Campus," p. 239.

43. Elaine D. Ingulli, "Sexual Harassment in Education," *Rutgers Law Journal* 18(1987), p. 285.

44. Billie Wright Dziech and Linda Weiner, *The Lecherous Professor: Sexual Harassment on Campus* (Boston: Beacon Press, 1984), p. 15.

45. Benson and Thomson, "Sexual Harassment on a University Campus," p. 241.

46. Charles Cnudde and Betty Nesvold, "Administrative Risk and Sexual Harassment: Legal and Ethical Responsibilities on Campus," *PS* (Fall 1985), p. 781.

47. *Korf v. Ball State University*, 726 F.2d 1222, 1227 (7th Cir. 1984). *Korf* was not a Title IX case; the suit was brought by the professor after he was dismissed by Ball State.

48. Phyllis Franklin, Helene Moglen, Phyllis Zatlin-Boring, and Ruth Angress, *Sexual and Gender Harassment in the Academy* (New York: Modern Languages Association, 1981), pp. 15–19.

49. *Alexander v. Yale University*, 459 F.Supp. 1 (D. Conn. 1977). Plaintiffs won a crucial victory when the court recognized the existence of a private right of action under Title IX.

50. Ronna Greff Schneider, "Sexual Harassment and Higher Education," *Texas Law Review* 65(1987), p. 527 n. 8. The other case is *Moire v. Temple University School of Medicine*, 613 F.Supp. 1360 (E.D. Pa. 1985). The district court ruling was affirmed without opinion by the Third Circuit at 800 F.2d 1136 (3d Cir. 1986).

51. *Alexander*, 459 F.Supp. at 3.

52. *Alexander v. Yale University*, 631 F.2d 178, 184 (2d Cir. 1980).

53. *Moire*, 613 F.Supp. at 1370.

54. *Regents of the University of Michigan v. Ewing*, 474 U.S. 214, 225 (1985). The court's reluctance to get involved in employment discrimination litigation against universities is discussed in Chapter Nine.

55. Schneider, "Sexual Harassment and Higher Education," pp. 527–29.

56. Dziech and Weiner, *The Lecherous Professor*, p. 23.

57. Ingulli, "Sexual Harassment in Education," pp. 316–22.

9

Equality in the Professions

Professional women are frequently subject to sex discrimination. While discrimination against these women often differs from the discrimination against blue-collar or pink-collar women, it is just as invidious. In some ways, it is even more invidious because it is more subtle and hence more difficult to prove and eradicate.

It is therefore not surprising that despite women's growing numbers in the professional and business world, they are unable to secure jobs offering them the "greatest power, prestige, and economic reward."[1] The federal courts have lately become more hospitable to suits brought by business and professional women, but progress has been slow and women still face significant obstacles in proving discrimination against them in high-level jobs.

Evaluating Professionals

The impediments to advancement in professional and business careers stem from a variety of factors, including bias against women in positions of authority or prestige and the traditional reluctance of courts to interfere with and override collegial judgments of professional qualifications.

Evaluations of professional or managerial employees are mostly based on subjective standards such as collegiality, effectiveness of style in lawyering or teaching, quality of scholarship or legal or accounting skills, ability to generate clients, ability to manage others, and degree of professionalism.

Sexual bias often creeps, perhaps unconsciously, into the decision-making process. Consequently, women are often seen as unprofessional or uncollegial if they are ambitious, aggressive, or outspoken, attributes that are positively valued in men.

Because such vague and indeterminate criteria are employed in assessing the work of professionals and because motives are often mixed and difficult to discern, women have a formidable task in proving that unfavorable job actions are caused by discrimination. Part of the difficulty of proving discrimination at this level arises from the judiciary's unwillingness to probe too deeply into complaints against employers of professional or business women.[2] The problem is magnified by the court's reluctance to substitute its judgment for the professional evaluations of corporate executives, law and accounting partners, and university tenure boards. In ruling on discrimination suits, judges generally do not inquire into the standards used to evaluate the work of professional employees; they limit their review to assessing the fairness of the procedure followed.

Finally, even for women willing to challenge their employer's actions, there are high personal costs, as well as enormous financial burdens. Title VII damages are presently limited to judicial decrees ordering hiring, reinstatement, or promotion; back pay and benefits (provided the plaintiff has not found another job); and attorney fees (if the plaintiff wins). Consequently, individual plaintiffs are often reluctant to initiate litigation. Despite the hardships, a number of women have gone to court and some have even won their lawsuits. On closer examination, it is not always clear how much they won.

Women in Academia

The Civil Rights Act of 1964 exempted educational institutions from the nondiscrimination principles of Title VII.[3] The Equal Employment Opportunity Act of 1972 removed the exemption and placed college and university teachers within the statute's protective reach.[4] The House Committee Report accompanying the 1972 act explained that the exemption was insupportable because "discrimination against minorities and women in the field of education is as pervasive as discrimination in any other area of employment." Especially in "the field of higher education," the committee noted,

> women have long been invited to participate as students in the academic process, but without the prospect of gaining employment as serious scholars. [And] when they have been hired into educational institutions of higher education, women have been relegated to positions of lesser standing than their male counterparts.[5]

While conditions have improved since the act was passed in 1972, studies show that women are still "relegated to positions of lesser standing" in colleges and universities. Generally, it is still true that the higher the rank and the more prestigious the school, the fewer the women. Generally, it is still true that women are less likely to become department chairs or academic deans. And generally, it is still true that women are less likely to receive tenure than men.[6]

Tenure ensures that faculty members may only be removed from their teaching positions for "adequate" cause.[7] An award of tenure is a lifetime appointment, providing job security for the rest of one's career; a denial of tenure is a dismissal notice from the university. Female academics are underrepresented in tenured positions: although they held 37 percent of the academic positions by 1985, they only numbered about 10 percent of the tenured positions, less at the most prestigious universities.[8] Not surprisingly, many of the battles over sex discrimination in higher education have been fought over the denial of tenure to women.

Part of the problem of getting tenure stems from the fact that there are diverse standards of judgment among the twenty-five hundred tenure-granting institutions of higher education. As one scholar pointed out, "It is often difficult to even specify exactly what goes into tenure decisions."[9] A system that allocates rewards based on imprecise standards, vaguely articulated, is ripe for the practice of discrimination. Moreover, because courts are still reluctant to override faculty judgments on the merits of their colleagues' teaching or scholarship, impermissible motives can easily enter into the decision-making process.

Proving Discrimination

Academic discrimination litigation began in the 1970s. During this decade, there were 145 federal court decisions. Up to the middle 1980s, there were an average of 34 cases per year.[10]

Most Title VII complaints of sex discrimination in academia are based on the theory of disparate treatment, which requires plaintiffs to establish a prima facie case of discrimination by following the steps outlined in *McDonnell Douglas v. Green*.[11] Under this test, adapted to the academic setting, the plaintiff has to show that she is a member of the class protected by Title VII; that she was qualified for the position or rank sought; that she was denied promotion or tenure; and that others with similar qualifications were promoted at approximately the same time, or in the case of tenure, that the university sought applicants for the position from similarly qualified persons.[12]

It is not difficult for a plaintiff to establish a prima facie case of discrimination. Few reported cases have been dismissed because a plaintiff was unable to do so.[13] In *Lynn v. Regents of the University of California,* 1981, the Ninth Circuit explained that plaintiffs must only show that it was "more likely than not" that there was discrimination. To this end, a plaintiff may also establish a prima facie case by "offering other evidence which creates the inference that the complained of act was unlawful."[14]

In *Lynn,* plaintiff Therese Lynn's other evidence consisted of statistics showing the university's pattern of basing tenure and promotion (or hiring) decisions on sex. Since its founding, the university tenured twenty-six men and only two women; the last woman was granted tenure in 1972. Lynn also offered what the court called "specific statistical data" that demonstrated she had the same qualifications as men who were granted tenure. Finally, she showed that the university's poor evaluation of her work stemmed in part from its perception that women's studies research was not scholarly enough.

Although the district court judge ruled that a low opinion of women's studies was not discriminatory because the university would have the same negative attitude toward a man who researched in that area, the Ninth Circuit disagreed. "A disdain for women's issues, and a diminished opinion of those who concentrate on those issues," the court stated, "is evidence of a discriminatory attitude towards women."[15] Given these factors, the court found that Lynn showed that her tenure denial was more likely than not motivated by sex discrimination.

Once the plaintiff presents evidence of a prima facie case of discrimination, according to the principles of *McDonnell Douglas,* the university is required to articulate "some legitimate nondiscriminatory reason" for its decision but it does not have to prove that it was actually *motivated* by this reason.[16] In other words, the university merely has to produce an acceptable reason for the denial of tenure; it does not have to prove it acted without discriminatory intent.

In defending itself against a charge of discrimination, a university typically presents evidence that the woman is not qualified for tenure or promotion because she is deficient in either scholarship, teaching, or service, or some combination of the three. Universities have also successfully argued that the plaintiff does not fit in — either personally or intellectually — with the rest of the department.

In the last stage of the case, the plaintiff has an opportunity to show that the university's proffered reason was not the actual one but was merely a pretext for discrimination. Plaintiffs are seldom successful in their attempts to convince courts that the university's explanation for their dismissal is untrue, especially if the university is able to point to a negative evaluation of the plaintiff's teaching or scholarly work.[17]

One of the few cases in which a plaintiff was able to prove that the college's reason for dismissing her was a pretext for sex discrimination was *Kunda v. Muhlenberg College,* a 1980 case decided by the Third Circuit. Plaintiff Connie Rae Kunda established a prima facie case of discrimination in her suit against Muhlenberg College for refusing to tenure and promote her to the rank of assistant professor in the physical education department. The college tried to rebut her case by stating that she lacked the necessary master's degree for tenure and promotion. Because she was able to show that three *male* members of the department who also lacked master's degrees were promoted during her time at Muhlenberg, she satisfied the court that the college's stated reason for failing to promote her was merely a pretext for discrimination. *Kunda* was the first case in which a court awarded tenure for a Title VII violation.[18]

Judicial Deference

In the early 1970s, judicial opinions in tenure review cases were characterized by a "hands off" policy. In *Faro v. New York University*, 1974, the Second Circuit wrote that "of all fields, which the federal courts should hesitate to invade and take over, education and faculty appointments at a University level are probably the least suited for federal court supervision."[19] The *Faro* decision was widely cited for the principle that the federal courts should not intervene in academic affairs.[20]

By the late 1970s, courts began to abandon their extreme deference to academic institutions and became more willing to hold universities accountable to Title VII's ban on discrimination. Illustrating the new approach, in *Powell v. Syracuse University*, 1978, the Second Circuit redefined its task as "steer[ing] a careful course between excessive intervention in the affairs of the university and the unwarranted tolerance of unlawful behavior."[21]

Despite the court's recognition in *Powell* that Title VII required greater judicial scrutiny over tenure decisions, academic women still face an uphill battle in litigation. Even after *Powell*, in *Lieberman v. Gant*, 1980, the Third Circuit echoed the warning of *Faro*, saying that courts

> should not substitute their judgment for that of the college with respect to the qualifications of faculty members for promotion and tenure. Determinations about such matters as teaching ability, research scholarship, and professional stature are subjective, and unless they can be shown to have been used as the mechanism to obscure discrimination, they must be left for evaluation by the professionals, particularly since they often involve inquiry into aspects of arcane scholarship beyond the competence of individual judges.[22]

Academic Freedom

Tenure decisions are highly decentralized and involve a review process in which the applicant's file is forwarded by a department to a dean, then to a college and/or university committee, and finally to a vice president, a president, and a board of regents or trustees. The file usually includes evaluations of the candidate's scholarship from recognized scholars in the field as well as recommendations from administrators and faculty members within the university.

A university's decision to deny tenure is based on confidential information contained in the tenure file. It is often difficult for women who suspect discrimination to be able to prove their claim without access to this file.[23] But universities typically refuse to grant access, citing principles of confidentiality and academic freedom. Plaintiffs argue that a closed file deprives them of the normal right of civil litigants to the discovery process (the exchange of relevant information between parties to a lawsuit).

In balancing the university's need for secrecy of its documents against the plaintiff's need to discover evidence relevant to the case, courts disagreed on the extent to which universities were entitled to protect the confidentiality of the tenure file.[24] Resolving the conflict among the lower courts, the Supreme Court ruled in *University of Pennsylvania v. EEOC*, 1990, that universities were subject to the same discovery rules as other litigants and were not entitled to a special privilege to withhold a tenure file.[25]

The case began in 1985 when the University of Pennsylvania denied tenure to Rosalie Tung, an associate professor in the Wharton School of Business. She filed a charge with the Equal Employment Opportunity Commission, claiming discrimination on the basis of sex, race, and national origin. The EEOC began its investigation and determined that her file contained relevant information. It asked the university to produce it along with the files of five male faculty members mentioned in her charge. Refusing to turn over the files, the university asked the EEOC to modify its request and allow it to exclude a number of items including letters from outside reviewers and the internal faculty committee deliberations.

The university contended that the Personnel Committee's summary letter giving the reasons for her tenure denial provided enough information for the investigation. When the EEOC renewed its request and the university refused to comply, the agency sought a court order to compel disclosure of the file. The order was granted by the district court and affirmed by the court of appeals.

Defending its right to withhold the documents, the university cited earlier Supreme Court cases upholding the principle of academic freedom. It highlighted Justice Felix Frankfurter's 1957 statement in which he proclaimed that one of "four essential freedoms" that a university possesses is its right "to determine for itself on academic grounds who may teach."[26] The tenure process, argued the university, is the way in which it fulfills its right to decide who shall teach. The process requires candid evaluations of the applicant's qualifications, which are assured by promising confidentiality to evaluators. Because of its interest in secrecy, the university sought to require the EEOC to obtain a "judicial finding of particularized necessity of access, beyond a showing of mere relevance."[27]

In a unanimous opinion, with Harry Blackmun speaking for the Court, the Supreme Court ruled against the university. Recognizing the importance of academic freedom to an educational institution, Blackmun distinguished the cited cases because they represented "governmental attempts to influence the content of academic speech through the selection of faculty or by other means." Here, there was no attempt to "direct the content of university discourse toward or away from particular subjects or points of view." Reaffirming its commitment to avoid "second-guessing of legitimate academic judgments," he emphasized that "nothing we say today should be understood as a retreat from this principle of respect for *legitimate* academic decisionmaking."[28]

Despite the Court's holding, Rosalie Tung was unable to claim victory over the university. The decision merely made it possible for her to require the university to reveal the documents and perhaps disclose its real reasons for its decision not to grant her tenure. Although not a final victory, it was a significant one because, as Blackmun noted, "[I]f there is a 'smoking gun' to be found that demonstrates discrimination in tenure decisions, it is likely to be tucked away in peer review files."[29]

Women in Law

Women have been engaged in the practice of law for a long time, but it is only recently that they have made any progress in achieving positions of influence within the legal profession.[30] While the courts have played only a limited role in their success, in 1984 the Supreme Court firmly placed the partnership decision — the equivalent of the tenure decision for lawyers — within the realm of Title VII.

The first female lawyer in the United States was Margaret Brent, who arrived in the colonies from England in 1638. A relative of Lord Baltimore's, Brent proceeded to acquire large land tracts and, within a few years, was appointed counsel to the governor of Maryland. Despite her success, there were no other female lawyers until 1869, when the *Chicago Legal News* reported that Mrs. Mary E. Magoon was practicing law in North English, Iowa. As a county lawyer, Magoon did not require admission to the state bar. Although she may not have been the only woman to practice at a local level, there were no women yet admitted to a state bar.

Then in June 1889, Belle Babb Mansfield was admitted to the Iowa bar, officially becoming the first female lawyer in the United States. In allowing Mansfield to take the bar examination, the Iowa Supreme Court bypassed an Iowa statute that limited membership in the bar to white males over twenty-one. Francis Springer, a liberal jurist of the Iowa court, circumvented the restriction on women by relying on another law that permitted legislative references to the masculine sex to be extended to women.

Other women were not as fortunate, as Myra Bradwell of Illinois was to discover. After successfully passing a qualifying examination, Bradwell was denied admission to the Illinois bar on the basis of a law similar to the Iowa statute. She lost her legal challenge in the United States Supreme Court in a 7–1 vote. Ironically, in 1872, the year before the decision, the Illinois legislature had enacted a statute forbidding the exclusion of women from any profession, other than the military, on the basis of sex. Bradwell was eventually granted a license to practice law by the Illinois Supreme Court, acting on its own initiative in 1890.[31]

The rise in the number of female lawyers was very slow. In 1900, there were a little more than 1,000 (1,010 women to 113,450 men). Before 1970, the number of female lawyers was less than 10,000. There was a dramatic increase in the decade from 1970 to 1980, with female lawyers numbering 13,964 in 1970 (to 273,044 men) and 72,312 in 1980 (to 452,494 men).[32] The rate of female lawyers increased by over 300 percent from 1970 to 1980 compared to a 44 percent increase for men. By 1984, the percentage of female lawyers had climbed to almost 13 percent.[33]

One hundred years after Bradwell was finally recognized as a qualified lawyer, women have become a significant, although still underrepresented, force in the legal profession. But while they appear to be moving into entry-level jobs, they still encounter roadblocks at the higher levels of power.

A 1984 survey of women in law showed that they occupied one-fourth to one-third of associate jobs in the one hundred largest law firms. Young lawyers on the partnership track are hired as associates where they serve a probationary period for five to seven years. If they are found satisfactory, the firm invites them to become partners; if they are found unsatisfactory, the firm generally invites them to look for work elsewhere. The same 1984 survey showed that the percentage of female partners was still in single digits. One New York law firm had 2 women out of 115 partners; a Philadelphia firm had 2 female partners out of 148. A number of firms did not have a single female partner until the late 1970s.[34]

Partnership Decisions

Partnership decisions in law firms, like partnership decisions in accounting firms and tenure decisions in universities, are typically collegial decisions in which the candidate is judged on a variety of dimensions.

In 1972, one of Atlanta's most well-known firms, King & Spalding, hired Elizabeth Anderson Hishon as an associate. A graduate of Wellesley

College and Columbia Law School, Hishon was the first woman at the firm to be considered for partner.[35] In 1978, the partners evaluated her for partnership and declined to invite her to become a partner. After another rejection a year later, she was asked to look for work elsewhere. She left the firm in December 1979 and filed suit in federal court against King & Spalding, claiming sex discrimination and seeking back pay rather than promotion and reinstatement.

Hishon contended that consideration for partnership had played an important role in her decision to work for King & Spalding. Her complaint stated that she had been assured that "advancement to partnership after five or six years was 'a matter of course' for associates 'who receive[d] satisfactory evaluations' and that associates were promoted to partnership 'on a fair and equal basis.'"[36] Because she always received favorable evaluations, she assumed she would receive her promotion in due course. When she did not, she sued, claiming that the firm's refusal to make her a partner was motivated by sex.

The lower court dismissed her case on the grounds that a partnership decision is not an "employment" decision within the meaning of Title VII. Immunizing the partnership selection process from Title VII's ban on discrimination, the district court judge characterized a partnership as a marriage. "To use or apply Title VII to coerce a mismatched or unwanted partnership too closely resembles a statute for the enforcement of shotgun weddings."[37] Having a less romantic view of the partnership relationship, the Supreme Court reversed.[38]

Writing for a unanimous Court in *Hishon v. King & Spalding*, 1984, Chief Justice Warren Burger briefly disposed of the question. He explained that Title VII begins to govern an employment relationship once a contract for employment is established; under Title VII the employer cannot discriminate with respect to "terms, conditions, or privileges of employment." The chief justice said the opportunity for an associate at the firm to be considered for partnership could be characterized as either a "term" of the employment contract or a "privilege" of employment. In either case, Title VII prohibits sex from playing a role in the partnership decision.

King & Spalding argued that applying Title VII to partnership decisions would hinder its constitutional right of expression and association.[39] Burger rejected this argument, saying that considering a woman for partnership on her merits does not interfere with the firm's right of expression. He also noted that private discrimination was never accorded affirmative constitutional protection.

The Court's decision meant that Hishon would be permitted to prove in court she had been a victim of discrimination. It probably would not have been too difficult for her to show that an atmosphere of sex discrimination prevailed at the firm. While her case was pending before the Supreme Court, the firm considered holding a "wet T-shirt" contest for its female summer associates at the annual summer outing. Because of in-house objections, the contest was changed to a swimsuit competition. The winner was a third-year Harvard law student who was subsequently offered a job at the firm. "'She has the body we'd like to see more of,' a partner told the *Wall Street Journal*."[40] There was no trial of the case because Hishon and the law firm settled out of court. Neither party has ever publicly discussed the settlement terms, and Hishon never returned to the firm.

In *Hishon*, the Court established that Title VII applies to law firms (with fifteen or more employees) making partnership decisions about associates at the firm.[41] Although a victory for female lawyers, the extent to which it would change the way in which legal firms select their partners is unclear. Despite the Court's affirmation of the applicability of Title VII, plaintiffs will still have to overcome judges' reluctance to interfere in the decision-making process of law firms. Speculating on the effects of the decision, Justice Lewis Powell noted that "with respect to laws that prevent discrimination, much depends upon the standards by which courts examine private decisions that are an exercise of the right of association."[42]

While applauding the decision, some female lawyers remained skeptical: "One Wall Street associate said, 'I suspect we will see a few more women making partner. But I'm afraid the real result of *Hishon* may just be that firms will keep a more careful watch on their women associates — not in an effort to promote them but to better justify their decisions not to make these women partners.'"[43]

Women in Accounting

Women have been members of the accounting profession since the early days of the United States. Like their colleagues in law, the number of women was very low for a long time. In 1870, for example, the census showed only 1,000 female bookkeepers, accountants, and cashiers keeping the books for American businesses. In 1899, Christine Ross became the first woman to pass the state examination to become a certified public accountant (CPA). By 1910, the number of women in the three combined fields had risen to 190,000 but there were only 10 female CPAs. Most of them were licensed in the eastern states (New York, Pennsylvania, New Jersey, and Maryland); one was certified in Illinois and one in Colorado.

During the 1920s, women continued to enter accounting schools but were not often hired as CPAs. The number of female CPAs was just over a hundred in 1933. The passage of federal securities laws in 1933 and 1934 created a tremendous need for public accountants to file the reports required under these acts. Additionally, the government agencies created by these acts hired accountants by the hundred and created a shortage in the nation. This scarcity of accountants, accentuated during the 1940s because of World War II, opened up opportunities for employment as women entered the public accounting profession in greater numbers. But it remained difficult to find jobs in the larger public accounting firms. This pattern was continued during the 1950s and 1960s as most public accounting firms persisted in their refusal to hire women. The firms gave as reasons for not hiring women that they "were unsuited for out-of-town travel, weren't career-minded and had high turnover."[44]

During the 1970s, the field of public accounting was changed as the number of female accountants increased dramatically. By the 1980s women constituted about 50 percent of the new hires and they are soon expected to comprise more than half the profession. But as in law where women are also being hired in greater numbers, the rise to the top is slow. In 1976, only twenty-nine women had achieved the status of partner or principal in the large accounting firms.[45]

Surveys of the eight largest accounting firms conducted in 1983 and 1986 show that there were 69 female partners in these firms in 1983 and 157 in 1986. Despite an increase of more than double the number of women in partnership positions, the percentage of female partners had only risen to 3 percent in 1986, up from 1 percent in 1983.[46]

Against this backdrop of the shortage of women in positions of authority in the public accounting profession, Ann Hopkins was under review as a potential partner in the "Big Eight" accounting firm of Price Waterhouse in 1982. At the time she was being considered for the position, Price Waterhouse had 7 female partners, out of a total of 662.[47]

Hopkins was the only woman among eighty-eight candidates for partnership in that year.[48] Her application was put on hold for a year but before the year was up, two of the partners in her office withdrew their support. When she was told she would not be reconsidered, she resigned and after filing a claim with the EEOC, sued the firm in federal court.

Not surprisingly, women who aspire to law or accounting partnerships have to overcome barriers erected by the male partners' stereotypical images of professional women. At Price Waterhouse, partnership decisions are based on the evaluations of the current partners in the firm. The evaluations are submitted to the Admissions Committee, which makes a recommendation to the Policy Board, which in turn either submits the candidate's name for a vote to the entire partnership, rejects the application, or simply puts it aside.

In Hopkins's case, thirteen partners supported her, eight recommended she be denied partnership, eight said they did not know enough about her, and three voted to put her "on hold." Although she was highly praised for her competence, her interpersonal skills came under attack. Price Waterhouse primarily attributed its decision to put off her partnership bid to her failings in this area.

Hopkins served as the senior manager in Price Waterhouse's Office of Government Services in the District of Columbia for four years. She was highly rated and brought in more business than any other candidate but was rejected because they said she lacked charm and femininity.

Examination of the partnership evaluations revealed that "some of the partners reacted negatively to Hopkins' personality because she was a woman." Both supporters and opponents characterized her in stereotypical terms. She was described as "macho," was advised to take a "course at charm school"; and it was reported that "she overcompensated for being a woman." Her own supporters provided the most striking evidence of the use of sex-based evaluations. One "explained that Hopkins 'ha[d] matured from a tough-talking somewhat masculine hard-nosed mgr [manager] to an authoritative, formidable, but much more appealing lady ptr [partner] candidate.'" Finally, the partner assigned to explain to her why her candidacy was put on hold, also a supporter, advised her that her professional problems would be solved if she were to "walk more femininely, talk more femininely, dress more femininely, wear make-up, have her hair styled, and wear jewelry."[49]

Because of Hishon's victory in 1984, Hopkins was able to sue the firm for sex discrimination under Title VII when she was passed over by the male partners. What made her case different from all other employment discrimination cases was written evidence that the partners allowed sex bias to play a role in their decision.[50] Perhaps it was this kind of direct evidence that inspired the Court to formulate a new rule for the so-called mixed motive case. In the typical Title VII case, the plaintiff has only indirect (or circumstantial) evidence of discrimination, creating an inference that discrimination occurred. In a mixed motive case such as this, the plaintiff has direct evidence of discrimination. And because she has proof that sex played a role in the decision-making process, the Court requires the defendant to *prove* that its decision would have been the same absent the discrimination.

In *Price Waterhouse v. Hopkins*, 1989, the Court's 6–3 opinion also clarified the relationship between sex stereotyping and sex discrimination. The Court ruled that evidence of sex-biased remarks is not sufficient to show that an employment decision was illegally based on sex. A plaintiff must demonstrate that the employer "relied on her sex" in making its decision.

Hopkins satisfied the Court that the sexual stereotypes underlying the partners' evaluations showed that they "acted" on the basis of sex. Price Waterhouse argued that any stereotypical remarks merely constituted "discrimination in the air," but the Court accepted instead Hopkins's contention that the remarks were "'discrimination brought to ground and visited upon' an employee."[51]

Price Waterhouse denied the existence of sexual stereotyping and contended that stereotypical views of women played no role in its decision to defer Hopkins's partnership. It disputed her expert witness, a psychologist, who testified at trial that the partners' remarks reflected sex stereotyping. Upholding the conclusions of the district court judge that the comments reflected stereotyping, the Supreme Court explained that it viewed the psychological evidence as "merely icing on the cake." Somewhat caustically, the Court added,

> it takes no special training to discern sex stereotyping in a description of an aggressive female employee as requiring 'a course in charm school.' Nor . . . does it require expertise in psychology to know that, if an employee's flawed 'interpersonal skills' can be corrected by a soft-hued suit or a new shade of lipstick, perhaps it is the employee's sex and not her interpersonal skills that has drawn the criticism.[52]

Not only was there stereotyping, the Court ruled, but the Policy Board relied on these stereotypical evaluations in determining Hopkins's fate at Price Waterhouse. The record also showed that partners used sex-based comments in the past in evaluating other women in the firm. The Court concluded that Hopkins had successfully shown that the firm violated Title VII by inserting sex as an element in the employment decision. While the partners may be justified in reacting negatively to Hopkins's personality, the Court explained, Title VII bars them from reacting "negatively to her personality because she is a woman."[53]

Ann Hopkins filed her lawsuit in 1984. She won at every level of the judicial process but, like Hishon and Tung, her ultimate fate was not decided by the Supreme Court.[54] Instead, the high court remanded her case to the district court for trial to give Price Waterhouse an opportunity to show that it would have made the same decision about her partnership regardless of her sex.

On May 14, 1990, District Court Judge Gerhard Gesell "found that the firm maintained a partnership evaluation system that 'permitted negative sexually stereotyped comments to influence partnership selection.'" He ordered Price Waterhouse to award Ann Hopkins the partnership it denied her eight years before. Her case was the first in which a court awarded a partnership in a professional firm as a remedy for sex or race discrimination.

Explaining his ruling, Gesell said that "Price Waterhouse plainly does not want her and would not voluntarily admit her. Partnership, not simply a new vote, is the logical remedy, given the finding that Ms. Hopkins was likely to have been made a partner if not for unlawful discrimination." He also awarded her about $400,000 in back pay and ordered Price Waterhouse not to retaliate against her for bringing suit.[55]

Hopkins, a budget manager at the World Bank at the time Gesell made his ruling, said she would go back to Price Waterhouse because she "was sure of her abilities as a management consultant and wanted a chance to use them at a top-notch concern. In any case, she added, many of the people who criticized her are no longer in the Washington office."[56]

On December 4, 1990, a three-judge panel of the Court of Appeals for the District of Columbia affirmed Gesell's ruling, holding that the firm had failed to prove it had nondiscriminatory reasons for rejecting her partnership bid. When the decision was handed down, a Price Waterhouse representative said the accounting firm was undecided whether to appeal the circuit court decision to the Supreme Court.[57]

Exclusion from Private Clubs

In 1984, the New York City Council drew attention to a problem affecting female professionals and business executives: exclusion from men-only clubs. The council explained that,

> although city, state and federal laws have been enacted to eliminate discrimination in employment, women and minority group members have not attained equal opportunity in business and the professions. One barrier to the advancement of women and minorities in the business and professional life of the city is the discriminatory practices of certain membership organizations where business deals are often made and personal contacts valuable for business purposes, employment and professional advancement are formed.[58]

While women have the option of belonging to women-only clubs, these "have neither the prestige nor occupational importance of men's clubs."[59] Although men belonging to restrictive clubs denigrate the importance of their membership to their business lives, surveys of business executives attest to the enhancement of career or business opportunities in the more relaxed club environment. As Deborah Rhode argues, "In a society in which men obtain almost one-third of their jobs through personal contacts, and probably a higher percentage of prestigious positions, the commercial role of social affiliations should not be undervalued."[60]

Always annoying or enraging, at times the discrimination verges on the ridiculous. In 1936, a female lawyer at a prestigious New York law firm described her experiences at the Yale Club, where she went to attend a business meeting.

> Women were allowed in only if they entered through a side door that led to the elevators. It wasn't considered proper for a woman to be in the main area—you could only stand on the edges of the room. Well, I just walked in, and here I was standing in the middle of the floor when a young page came over to me and said, 'Pardon ma'am, but you can't stand here.' I asked him why not, and he said, 'I don't know why, but I was told to tell you ladies aren't

allowed on the carpet.' My answer was to ask him to go back to whoever gave him those instructions and tell him to come here and move me if he'd like.[61]

Freedom of Association

Almost fifty years later, in a series of decisions on clubs with membership restricted to men, the Supreme Court decreased the likelihood that women would be subjected to this kind of embarrassment. The cases arose when state and local laws against sex discrimination in public accommodations threatened the existence of the men's clubs.[62]

The men-only clubs argued that the nondiscrimination laws did not apply to them; as private associations, they had a right to limit membership for any reason they chose. In the first case to test this argument in the Supreme Court, *Roberts v. United States Jaycees*, 1984, the Jaycees brought suit in federal court challenging the application of a Minnesota Human Rights Act to them. The act was a comprehensive one barring discrimination on the basis of sex (and race, creed, color, religion, disability, and national origin) in public accommodations.

The case originated when the Minneapolis and St. Paul chapters of the Jaycees began to admit women as regular members in 1974 and 1975. The Jaycees, founded in 1920 as the Junior Chamber of Commerce, was an educational and charitable organization that provided *young men* with an opportunity for personal development and participation in the affairs of the community, state, and country.[63]

When the national organization threatened to revoke the charters of the Minneapolis and St. Paul chapters, the local chapters filed charges of discrimination with the Minnesota Department of Human Rights. The department ordered a hearing, but before it was held, the national organization sued to prevent enforcement of the Human Rights Act.

The legal debate over men-only clubs involves the larger issue of the constitutional right of freedom of association. In 1958, the Supreme Court formally recognized that the First Amendment, guaranteeing freedom of speech and assembly, also extends to protection of a right to association.[64] Since then the Court has identified two strands of associative freedom. The first, expressive association, arises from the First Amendment. As the Court elaborated in *Roberts*, "[A]n individual's freedom to speak, to worship, and to petition the government for the redress of grievances could not be vigorously protected from interference by the State unless a correlative freedom to engage in group effort toward those ends were not also guaranteed."[65] Large groups or organizations that would otherwise not be considered private associations are protected from governmental intrusion by this principle.

The second freedom, intimate association, stems from a constitutional right to privacy implicit in the Bill of Rights.[66] Again, in *Roberts*, the Court explained that it "has long recognized that because the Bill of Rights is designed to secure individual liberty, it must afford the formation and preservation of certain kinds of highly personal relationships a substantial measure of sanctuary from unjustified interference by the State."[67] In claiming immunity from public accommodation laws on the basis of a right of associational privacy, club members asserted that their relationships to each other were as close as if they were family members or intimate friends.

The question before the Court in *Roberts* was whether the application of the Minnesota statute infringed on the Jaycees' freedom of expressive and intimate association. In answering this question in the negative, the Court fleshed out the contours of these rights.

Speaking for a seven-member Court (Blackmun and Burger did not participate), William Brennan suggested that associations range from intimate family relationships to large business enterprises; the former is entitled to constitutional protection from governmental intrusion, the latter not. Recognizing that the Jaycees fall somewhere in between, he suggested that certain factors were relevant to determining where a particular organization should be placed on the continuum. The factors include "size, purpose, policies, selectivity, [and] congeniality." Applying these standards, he concluded "that the local chapters of the Jaycees are large and basically unselective" and therefore "lack the distinctive characteristics that might afford constitutional protection to the decision of its members to exclude women."[68]

Turning to expressive associational freedom, Brennan recognized that the Jaycees engage in a wide variety of activities protected by the First Amendment. But he found "no basis in the record for concluding that admission of women as full voting members will impede the organization's ability to engage in these protected activities or to disseminate its preferred views."[69]

Applying the *Roberts* Test

Three years later in *Board of Directors of Rotary International v. Rotary Club of Duarte*, the Court upheld California's Unruh Act against a First Amendment challenge. The Unruh Act entitles all persons regardless of sex, race, color, religion, ancestry, or national origin to full access to all business establishments in the state. As in *Roberts*, the local chapter of the Rotary Club admitted women and, after being expelled from the international organization, filed suit in the California state court. The case eventually reached the United States Supreme Court.

Speaking for the seven justices who participated in the case (Sandra

Day O'Connor and Blackmun did not), Powell applied the *Roberts* test and determined "that the relationship among Rotary Club members is not the kind of intimate or private relation that warrants constitutional protection."[70] Similarly, he concluded, admitting women will not hurt the members' ability to engage in protected First Amendment activities.

The right of expressive association is not an unlimited right. It may be curbed by a state, in the least restrictive way, to serve a compelling state interest unrelated to the suppression of ideas. In both *Roberts* and *Rotary Club*, the Court concluded that the compelling interest in eradicating sex discrimination justified any incidental restrictions by the states on the club members' rights of expressive association.

Distinctly Private Clubs

The Supreme Court's most recent opinion on private clubs, *New York State Club Association v. City of New York*, 1988, also revolved around a public accommodations law. New York City's Human Rights Law, passed in 1965, prohibited discrimination in public accommodations. It exempted "any institution, club, or place of accommodation which proves that it is in its nature distinctly private."[71] Then in 1984, in Local Law No. 63, the city defined a public accommodation as any "institution, club or place of accommodation [that] has more than four hundred members, provides regular meal service and regularly receives payment for dues, fees, use of space, facilities, services, meals or beverages directly or indirectly from or on behalf of nonmembers for the furtherance of trade or business."[72]

Following a familiar pattern, the New York State Club Association, a corporation consisting of 125 private clubs and associations, challenged the constitutionality of Local Law No. 63. Losing in the state courts, the association appealed to the United States Supreme Court. At this point, the case diverged from the two before it. The association argued that the law was invalid "on its face," meaning that it can never be constitutionally applied or that it is so broad it inhibits constitutionally protected speech of parties not before the Court.[73] The Court rejected both arguments in a unanimous opinion delivered by Byron White.

According to White, because a number of the clubs in the association share characteristics of the Jaycees and the Rotary Club—such as size, nonselectivity, and engagement in commercial transactions—they cannot claim a right of private association. Neither, said White, does the law impair expressive associational rights of all the clubs in the association. Simply preventing an association from using race or sex as criteria for membership does not affect the ability of individuals within the clubs to advocate views. Therefore, because the law can be constitutionally applied to at least *some* clubs in the association, it cannot be considered invalid on its face.

The Court was also not persuaded that the law was "substantially overbroad." This was largely a failure of evidence because the association did not identify clubs whose expressive and intimate associational freedoms were threatened by the law.

While the case was pending in the courts, New York City initiated administrative proceedings against four all-male clubs: the 10,000-member New York Athletic Club, the 4,000-member University Club, the 1,900-member Century Association, and the 1,600-member Union League Club. The Supreme Court opinion confirmed that these clubs were guilty of sex discrimination. Following the ruling, officials of the 1,300-man Friars Club in New York City proposed an amendment to its charter to allow female members. And city attorneys in Los Angeles and San Francisco indicated that they would reinforce their efforts to enforce local ordinances against sex discrimination.[74]

Retaining the Right to Discriminate

Taken together, the decisions in these three cases suggest that the Court is willing to restrict the ability of large private clubs with business agendas to discriminate. But the Court stopped short of banning men-only clubs.

None of the cases answered the question of when men-only clubs must comply with state nondiscrimination laws. The Court failed to delineate clear guidelines indicating which clubs or organizations are subject to such laws and which are exempt. It also failed to make clear what degree of membership selectivity enables clubs to exclude people on the basis of sex or race.

The Court also did nothing to disturb a private club's right to discriminate if it can prove that sexual or racial restrictions are necessary to maintain First Amendment associational freedoms. Such a ruling invites litigation to claim exemption from a law's ban on discrimination. Finally, although determining that cities or states can constitutionally ban discrimination in certain clubs, the Court did nothing to change the fact that clubs are still free to discriminate in the absence of state or local ordinances prohibiting discrimination in public accommodations.[75]

Women and Family Responsibilities

Admitting women to men-only clubs is not a panacea for sex discrimination against business and professional women; it is a necessary start. Holding accounting and law firms accountable for sex discrimination in their partnership decisions will not ensure women's rise to the top in these professions; it is a necessary start. Forcing universities to divulge the truth about tenure denials is no guarantee that women will receive tenure; but it is a necessary start.

Legal reform is essential to attack inequalities in upper-level jobs, but it does not solve the problem that perhaps most hinders women in achieving success in their business and professional lives: balancing home and family with career. Contrary to the popular image, studies show that most female professionals are married and have children. Whether accountant, lawyer, college professor, or business executive, a woman's home arrangements play a vital role in her career mobility and advancement.[76]

While men are increasingly becoming confronted with these competing demands, there is still a great imbalance in the degree of burden. Women are still primary caretakers of the home and family and spend more time on domestic labor than do the men they are married to. A 1985 study showed that employed wives spend about twice as much time on homemaking responsibilities as their employed husbands; men married to women with full-time employment spend only about 1.4 hours more on domestic chores than men married to nonemployed wives.[77]

The status of women in corporate career paths has not received much attention from the Supreme Court, but their dilemma has been noted elsewhere, specifically in an article in the *Harvard Business Review* by Felice Schwartz. Noting the conflicting demands made on women in the business world, Schwartz demanded that corporations exhibit more social responsibility toward their female employees to allow them to combine home and career. Not limited only to women in business careers, her concerns and suggestions could apply to professionals as well.

The article received a great deal of publicity in the popular press and gave rise to the expression the "Mommy Track." Although Schwartz called for greater attention to the needs of working women, she expressed no concern over the fact that women assume the larger share of the burden for the home. Indeed, she reinforced the present division of labor by assigning women into two categories: "career-primary" and "career and family." She advised businesses to separate the former women, willing to totally commit to their career, from the latter, those wanting to combine the two.

According to Schwartz, the "career-primary" women, following the male model, put their careers first. Their choice, she says, requires them to sacrifice their personal lives, remain single or at least childless, or if they have children, have someone else bring them up. "The secret to dealing with such women is to recognize them early, accept them, and clear artificial barriers from their path to the top."[78]

The majority of women, however, are the "career and family" women. Because they are valuable to the company, they require special treatment. Most of these women, she argues, "are willing to trade some career growth and compensation for freedom from the constant pressure to work long hours and weekends."[79] Such women would be willing to stay at middle-management levels, and companies would be benefited from a more talented crop of middle managers than it currently has on hand. She offers a variety of proposals that companies should adopt to help women adapt to their roles: childcare, flexible hours, job sharing, and maternity leave.

Many women would undoubtedly welcome the news that their employers will accommodate the demands of their home lives. But by focusing entirely on *women's* dual roles, Schwartz simply reinforces the perception that women have sole responsibility for the care of home and children.

As women achieve success in upper-level positions, the conflict between their work and their family responsibilities will stand in the way of continued progress. This dilemma must be resolved before women can assume their rightful places in the professional and corporate work world.

NOTES

1. Deborah L. Rhode, "Perspectives on Professional Women," *Stanford Law Review* 40(1988), p. 1163.
2. Elizabeth Bartholet, "Application of Title VII to Jobs in High Places," *Harvard Law Review* 95(1982), p. 959.
3. Section 702 of the 1964 Civil Rights Act provided an exemption for an "educational institution with respect to the employment of individuals connected with the educational activities of such institution."
4. The Equal Employment Opportunity Act of 1972 expanded Title VII coverage to all public and private elementary, secondary, and college and university teachers. Congress retained (and even broadened) the exemption for religious institutions to restrict employment to individuals of a particular religion.
5. H. Rep. No. 238, 92d Cong., 1st Sess. 19–20 (1971).
6. Bernice Resnick Sandler, *The Campus Climate Revisited* (Washington, DC: Association of American Colleges, 1986), p. 2. See also Angela Simeone, *Academic Women* (South Hadley MA: Bergin & Garvey, 1987), chapter 2.
7. Elizabeth Kluger, "Sex Discrimination in the Tenure System at American Colleges and Universities: The Judicial Response," *Journal of Law and Education* 15(1986), p. 319. Kluger explains the tenure decision-making process as well as the debate over the effect of tenure on equal opportunity within the higher education system. Because men hold the majority of tenured positions, and women are overrepresented among those seeking new positions, the tenure system has the effect of perpetuating male domination of academic jobs.
8. Rhode, "Perspectives on Professional Women," pp. 1179–80.
9. Kluger, "Sex Discrimination in the Tenure System," p. 320.
10. George R. LaNoue and Barbara A. Lee, *Academics in Court: The Consequences of Faculty Discrimination Litigation* (Ann Arbor: University of Michigan Press, 1987), p. 23.
11. *McDonnell Douglas v. Green*, 411 U.S. 792 (1973). In *Kunda v. Muhlenberg College*, 621 F.2d 532 (3d Cir. 1980), the appellate court stated that plaintiffs can also sue under disparate impact theory.
12. *Smith v. University of North Carolina*, 632 F.2d 316, 340 (4th Cir. 1980). In *Lynn v. Regents of the University of California*, 656 F.2d 1337, 1341 (9th Cir. 1981), the court held that this formulation also applied to claims of discrimination in other university actions involving faculty, including initial hiring decisions. In *Lieberman v. Gant*, 630 F.2d 60 (2d Cir. 1980), the appellate court ruled that plaintiffs must make out a stronger prima facie case

for a tenure appointment than for a contract renewal. According to the court in *Kunda*, this was not a universally accepted view.

13. Kluger, "Sex Discrimination in the Tenure System," p. 323.

14. *Lynn*, 656 F.2d at 1341.

15. *Lynn*, 656 F.2d at 1343.

16. In *Board of Trustees of Keene State College v. Sweeney*, 439 U.S. 24, 25 (1978), the Court pointed out "there is a significant distinction between merely articulating" and "proving absence of a discriminatory motive." Two years later in *Texas Department of Community Affairs v. Burdine*, 450 U.S. 248, 254–55 (1981), the Court elaborated on the defendant's burden by explaining "it is sufficient if the defendant's evidence raises a genuine issue of fact as to whether it discriminated against the plaintiff. To accomplish this, the defendant must clearly set forth . . . the reasons for the plaintiff's rejection."

17. LaNoue and Lee, *Academics in Court*, pp. 38–39.

18. Although Muhlenberg College satisfied the court that Kunda's lack of a master's degree was a legitimate reason to refuse to tenure her, she won her suit because she was able to show that she had been treated differently from male faculty members. Although the men in her department were told they needed the master's degree for tenure, she was not. The court allowed her two years to obtain a master's degree and ordered the College to grant her tenure if she did.

19. *Faro v. New York University*, 502 F.2d 1229, 1231–32 (2d Cir. 1974).

20. *Powell v. Syracuse University*, 580 F.2d 1150, 1153 (2d Cir. 1978).

21. *Powell*, 580 F.2d at 1154 (1978).

22. *Kunda*, 621 F.2d at 548.

23. In *Lynn*, the appellate court ruled that Therese Lynn had been denied due process because the district court judge relied on evidence in her tenure file that she had not been allowed to see. The appellate court suggested that the contents of the file might be particularly relevant to proving that the university's articulated reason for dismissing her was a pretext for discrimination.

24. Note, "Title VII in Academia: A Critical Analysis of the Judicial Policy of Deference," *Washington University Law Quarterly* 64(1986), pp. 628–29.

25. *University of Pennsylvania v. EEOC*, 110 S.Ct. 577 (1990).

26. *Sweezy v. New Hampshire*, 354 U.S. 234, 263 (1957) (Frankfurter, J., concurring).

27. *University of Pennsylvania*, 110 S.Ct. at 581. The university also unsuccessfully argued that it had a "qualified common-law privilege against disclosure of confidential peer review materials."

28. *University of Pennsylvania*, 110 S.Ct. at 586–87 (emphasis in the original).

29. *University of Pennsylvania*, 110 S.Ct. at 585.

30. Cynthia Fuchs Epstein, *Women in Law* (New York: Basic Books, 1981), especially chapters 11–14, discusses how women have begun to assume roles of increasing importance in major law firms, on the bench, as law school professors, and in professional associations.

31. See Karen Berger Morello, *The Invisible Bar: The Woman Lawyer in America, 1638 to the Present* (New York: Random House, 1986), chapter 1, for an account of the "first women lawyers."

32. Terence Halliday, "Six Score Years and Ten: Demographic Transitions in the American Legal Profession, 1850–1980," *Law and Society Review* 20(1986), pp. 62–63.

33. Barbara A. Curran, "American Lawyers in the 1980s: A Profession in Transition," *Law and Society Review* 20(1986), pp. 20–25.

34. Morello, *The Invisible Bar*, pp. 195–97.

35. Morello, *The Invisible Bar*, p. 215. A woman was hired in 1944 as a "permanent associate," the firm's only one. In the 1960s, another woman was hired to work on a special project; when it was over, she left the firm.

36. *Hishon v. King & Spalding*, 467 U.S. 69, 71–72 (1984).

37. *Hishon v. King & Spalding*, 24 Fair Empl. Prac. Cas. 1303, 1305 (N.D. Ga. 1980).

38. The Supreme Court accepted the case only to decide whether Title VII's ban on sex discrimination applies to partnership decisions. Hishon's complaint was dismissed on a motion to dismiss at the initial stage of the litigation. The record of her work performance was not before the courts because for purposes of a motion to dismiss, the allegations made by the plaintiff are assumed to be true. The rule is that "a court may dismiss a complaint only if it is

clear that no relief could be granted under any set of facts that could be proved consistent with the allegations." *Hishon*, 467 U.S. at 73.

39. The firm first argued that Title VII excluded partnership decisions from Title VII. It also claimed exemption because a lawyer became an employer on being elevated to partner and hence outside the reach of Title VII.

40. Nina Burleigh and Stephanie B. Goldberg, "Breaking the Silence: Sexual Harassment in Law Firms," *ABA Journal* (August 1989), p. 46.

41. Because the contract for employment had been established when Elizabeth Hishon was hired, the Court's opinion did not seem to rule out sex discrimination in lateral partnership decisions, that is, women who were not already working for the firm.

42. *Hishon*, 467 U.S. at 80–81 n. 4 (Powell, J., concurring). Powell wrote separately to show that the decision did not mean that Title VII applies to the relationship among partners.

43. Morello, *The Invisible Bar*, p. 217.

44. Glenda Reid, Brenda T. Acken, and Elise G. Jancura, "An Historical Perspective on Women in Accounting," *Journal of Accountancy* 163(1987), p. 344.

45. Reid, Acken, and Jancura, "An Historical Perspective on Women in Accounting," p. 350.

46. Karen L. Hooks and Shirley J. Cheramy, "Coping with Women's Expanding Role in Public Accounting," *Journal of Accountancy* 167(1989), p. 67.

47. *Price Waterhouse v. Hopkins*, 109 S.Ct. 1775, 1781 (1989).

48. Of the eighty-eight candidates, forty-seven were promoted to partner, twenty-one were rejected, and twenty, including Hopkins, had their applications put "on hold."

49. *Price Waterhouse*, 109 S.Ct. at 1782. Price Waterhouse argued that because many of these remarks were made by her supporters, they could not have hurt her.

50. William L. Kandel, "Current Developments in Employment Litigation," *Employee Relations Law Journal* 15(1989), p. 103.

51. *Price Waterhouse*, 109 S.Ct. at 1791.

52. *Price Waterhouse*, 109 S.Ct. at 1793.

53. *Price Waterhouse*, 109 S.Ct. at 1795.

54. The district court judge in *Hopkins v. Price Waterhouse*, 618 F.Supp. 1109 (D.D.C. 1985), Gerhard Gesell, found Price Waterhouse guilty of discrimination but refused to order Hopkins promoted to partner. In *Hopkins v. Price Waterhouse*, 825 F.2d 458 (D.C. Cir. 1987), the appellate court affirmed the lower court ruling on liability and held that Price Waterhouse had to prove the absence of discrimination by "clear and convincing evidence." The appellate court also awarded her additional damages and ordered the firm to promote her to partner.

55. *New York Times*, May 16, 1990.

56. *New York Times*, May 19, 1990.

57. *New York Times*, December 6, 1990.

58. *New York State Club Association v. City of New York*, 108 S.Ct. 2225, 2230 (1988).

59. Lois M. McKenna, "Freedom of Association or Gender Discrimination? *New York State Club Association v. City of New York*," *American University Law Review* 38(1989), p. 1086.

60. Deborah L. Rhode, "Association and Assimilation," *Northwestern University Law Review* 81(1986), p. 121.

61. Morello, *The Invisible Bar*, p. 203.

62. A public accommodation is a place of business such as a hotel, restaurant, department store, or theater that sells or otherwise makes available goods or services to the public. Title II of the 1964 Civil Rights Act prohibited discrimination in public accommodations on the basis of race, color, religion, or national origin. Under the 1964 act, a public accommodation was defined as an establishment that is part of interstate commerce. The law exempted private clubs, and many places of public accommodation unsuccessfully tried to portray themselves as private to escape the law.

The Civil Rights Act was enacted under Congress's authority to regulate interstate commerce because the Supreme Court exempted privately owned public accommodations from congressional regulation by a narrow construction of the equal protection clause's state action doctrine. Congress could only reach associations or clubs that performed a public function or were sufficiently entangled with government regulation. See Laurence Tribe, *American Constitutional Law*, 2d ed. (Mineola, NY: Foundation Press, 1988), chapters 5 and

18, for explanations of the state action doctrine and congressional authority to regulate public accommodations through its interstate commerce power.

63. *Roberts v. United States Jaycees*, 468 U.S. 609, 612 (1984).

64. In *NAACP v. Alabama ex rel. Patterson*, 357 U.S. 449 (1958), the Supreme Court unanimously held that the NAACP did not have to reveal its membership lists to the state because its members' right to associate is inseparable from their right to engage in activities protected by the First Amendment, such as speech and assembly.

65. *Roberts*, 468 U.S. at 622.

66. In *Griswold v. Connecticut*, 381 U.S. 479 (1965), the Supreme Court formally acknowledged a constitutional right of privacy. The Court struck a Connecticut law forbidding the distribution of birth-control devices to married couples because it interfered with the right to marital privacy. *Griswold* is discussed in Chapter Ten.

67. *Roberts*, 468 U.S. at 618.

68. *Roberts*, 468 U.S. at 620–21. Each chapter had about four hundred members, and apart from age and sex, all applicants were admitted into membership. Additionally, large numbers of nonmembers, including women, regularly participated in numerous Jaycees activities.

69. *Roberts*, 468 U.S. at 627.

70. *Board of Directors of Rotary International v. Rotary Club of Duarte*, 481 U.S. 537, 546 (1987). Local chapters have from twenty to nine hundred members and are encouraged to cast their membership nets widely.

71. *New York State Club Association*, 108 S.Ct. at 2229.

72. *New York State Club Association*, 108 S.Ct. at 2230.

73. The latter argument may be made in First Amendment cases. It represents an exception to the rule that only parties who are injured by a law can raise a constitutional challenge. Under this construction, a plaintiff can challenge a law on the basis of its injury to third parties, claiming that the statute's very existence will chill or impair protected First Amendment rights.

74. *New York Times*, June 21, 1990.

75. Note, "*New York State Club Association v. City of New York*: Private Club Sex Discrimination," *West Virginia Law Review* 91(1989), pp. 515–16. See also Note, "*New York State Club Association v. City of New York*: As 'Distinctly Private' Is Defined, Women Gain Access," *Denver University Law Review* 66(1988). On July 3, 1990, the New Jersey Supreme Court found that the all-male eating clubs at Princeton University were "places of accommodation" within the meaning of the state antidiscrimination law. Although the clubs argued they were "distinctly private," the court found that their "symbiotic relationship" with the university brought them within the reach of the New Jersey law against discrimination on the basis of sex in public accommodations. The clubs were ordered to "discontinue their practice of excluding women purely on the basis of gender." *Frank v. Ivy Club*, 576 A.2d 241, 261 (N.J. 1990). The Supreme Court unanimously denied certiorari in this case.

76. See Reid, Acken, and Jancura, "An Historical Perspective on Women in Accounting," p. 353; Epstein, *Women in Law*, pp. 330–31; Hooks and Cheramy, "Coping with Women's Expanding Role in Public Accounting," p. 70.

77. Rhode, "Perspectives on Professional Women," p. 1183.

78. Felice Schwartz, "Management Women and the New Facts of Life," *Harvard Business Review* 67(1989), p. 69.

79. Schwartz, "Management Women," p. 70.

10

Abortion: The Right to Choose Develops

Between 1973, when abortion was legalized in *Roe v. Wade*, and 1990, the Supreme Court decided eighteen major abortion cases. Table 10.1 presents the cases, issues decided, and votes. For the most part, until 1989 the Court sustained a woman's right to choose to terminate her pregnancy. Then in 1989, a new majority on the Court asserted itself and abortion rights began to erode.

The 1989 decision galvanized the prochoice forces, largely quiescent since 1973, into action. Their efforts were matched by the invigorated antiabortion groups. The battle over abortion rights moved from the courts to the state legislatures and Congress as each side sought supremacy in the political arena. Encouraged by the 1989 decision, states enacted new restrictive laws. Yet, at the same time, prochoice supporters saw their candidates win major political offices in campaigns focused on abortion rights.

In her book on the politics of abortion, Kristen Luker argues that the conflict over abortion is different from other public policy debates. She asks, "What is it about abortion—of all the myriad issues we face daily—that makes it so troubling, so hard to deal with in reasoned tones?" She believes the abortion debate is infused with passion, largely because "the two sides share no common premises and very little common language."[1]

The clash over abortion policy-making has become a fight to the finish. It is not clear which side will prevail; what is clear is that neither side can claim victory and that the battle will continue. As with other moral

Table 10.1   Major Abortion Cases 1973–Present

Case	Date	Issue(s)	Vote[a]	P/A[b]
Roe	1973	Abortion criminalized	7–2	P
Doe	1973	Hospital/doctor restrictions; residency requirement	7–2	P
Danforth	1976	Saline abortions; parental/spousal consent; recordkeeping/reporting; physician's duty to fetus; definition of viability	5–4	P
Beal	1977	Medicaid funding limits under Social Security Act	6–3	A
Maher	1977	Medicaid funding limits under equal protection clause	6–3	A
Poelker	1977	Public hospital's refusal to perform abortions	6–3	A
Bellotti	1979	Parental consent	8–1	P
Colautti	1979	Physician's duty to fetus	6–3	P
Harris	1980	Constitutionality of Hyde amendment	5–4	A
Matheson	1981	Parental notice	6–3	A
Akron	1983	Second-trimester hospitalization; parental consent; waiting period; risk/fetal development lecture	6–3	P
Ashcroft	1983	Second-trimester hospitalization; pathology report; second physician; parental consent	5–4[c]	A
Simopoulos	1983	Second-trimester abortions in licensed facilities	8–1	A
Thornburgh	1986	Risk/fetal development lecture; recordkeeping/reporting; physician's duty to fetus; second physician; waiting period	5–4	P
Zbaraz	1987	Parental notice; waiting period	4–4[d]	P
Webster	1989	Preamble defining life; public fund restrictions; viability testing	5–4	A
Hodgson	1990	Two-parent notice	5–4[e]	A
Akron Ctr.	1990	Parental notice	6–3	A

[a]Because votes in abortion cases are often split on the specific regulation, the vote shown may not represent the votes on all issues decided.

[b]P = Prochoice. A majority voted to strike all, or most of, the regulation under review.

A = Antiabortion. A majority voted to uphold all, or most of, the regulation under review.

[c]A 6–3 majority struck the hospitalization requirement; a different 5–4 majority voted to uphold the other provisions.

[d]With an equally divided Court, the lower court ruling (striking the waiting period) was affirmed.

[e]A 5–4 majority found the two-parent notice provision unconstitutional; a different 5–4 majority ruled that it was made constitutional by the judicial bypass procedure.

dilemmas in the public policy arena, the Supreme Court will play a major role in determining the outcome of the struggle.

History of Abortion Legislation

Abortion is one of the most controversial legal, political, and social issues of our time. It was not always so. Prior to the 1800s, when the United States legal system followed English common law, abortion was widely practiced and generally unopposed by most people in both countries. It was even considered a relatively safe medical procedure.

During this time, the law was silent about, and essentially condoned, abortion before quickening, the time at which fetal movement is detected by the mother (generally around the fourth or fifth month of pregnancy). Indeed, United States and English law was not greatly concerned about abortion after quickening. Prescriptions for home abortion remedies were widely used and freely advertised. Criminal charges, rare in any event, were never brought against the woman.

Then in 1803, the British Parliament enacted Lord Ellenborough's Act, abandoning the common law approach and criminalizing abortion at all stages of pregnancy. American states followed suit a few decades later. When the new laws were adopted in the United States, generally after 1820, and successively enacted in all states, they also eliminated the legal significance of quickening. Abortion at any time became a criminal act. As a result of these laws, for the first time—in some states—the woman was subject to criminal sanction for having an abortion. By 1880, legal abortions were no longer attainable in the United States.

In his study of the evolution of abortion policy in the United States, historian James Mohr argues that the new laws restricting abortion were instigated by physicians wanting to professionalize medical care and drive untrained practitioners (who competed for their patients) out of the business of practicing medicine.

The physicians were not only motivated by economic reasons; they wanted to raise ethical standards and foster adherence to their Hippocratic Oath, which specifically opposes abortion. They turned to the state legislatures to enact laws defending their vision of the medical profession. And by the middle of the century, the newly formed American Medical Association began its lobbying efforts to ban abortion.

Although the U.S. legislation was prompted by medical and economic considerations, moral and religious forces soon took up the rhetoric against abortion. According to Mohr, the strong opposition to abortion developed largely because abortion had become more widespread, more visible, and increasingly sought by white, middle- and upper-class, married, Protestant women in contrast to lower-class, immigrant, young women "in trouble."

Abortion Reform

Abortion policy remained unchanged for more than a century. Increasing pressure for abortion reform began to develop during the 1950s and 1960s. In 1962, the nation watched the agony of Phoenix celebrity Sherri Finkbine, star of a children's television show. Finkbine had four children, all under seven. She took thalidomide, a tranquilizer drug, to calm her nerves at the beginning of her fifth pregnancy. Thalidomide had not received government approval and was not sold in the United States; her husband brought it home from a recent trip to Europe. At that time, most people thought pregnant women could safely take drugs, including tranquilizers, because the placenta acted as a shield for the baby.

When Finkbine read reports of thalidomide causing serious birth defects in thousands of European babies and realized that she would very likely give birth to a severely deformed child, she sought an abortion. Under Arizona law, she was only entitled to a legal abortion to save her life. When her attempts to get one in Phoenix failed, she traveled to Sweden for the operation.

At the same time, an outbreak of German measles—a disease often leading to blindness, deafness, or mental retardation in babies when contracted by the mother during the early stages of pregnancy—further focused the public's attention on the restrictiveness of abortion laws when women stricken with the disease were denied legal abortions. The epidemic in the early 1960s resulted in the birth of about twenty thousand severely disabled children to these women.[2]

During this time as well, the women's movement played a major role in demanding changes in abortion laws, arguing that abortion rights were necessary for sexual equality. A women's rights activist in California explained,

> when we talk about women's rights, we can get all the rights in the world . . . and none of them means a doggone thing if we don't own the flesh we stand in, if we can't control what happens to us, if the whole course of our lives can be changed by somebody else that can get us pregnant by accident, or by deceit, or by force. So I consider the right to elective abortion, whether you dream of doing it or not, is the cornerstone of the woman's movement. . . . If you can't control your own body you can't control your future, to the degree that any of us can control futures.[3]

Finally, pressure for abortion reform increased because abortion was a reality for millions of American women. A 1936 study estimated that over half a million illegal abortions were performed each year. Although the number of illegal abortions can only be estimated, studies have concluded that in the years before legalization in 1973, there were roughly 1 million illegal abortions a year in the United States.[4] Many in the medical profession, reversing their earlier position, now favored legalization, believing medical judgments should control the decision.

Between 1967 and 1970, abortion reform legislation was enacted in twelve states, including Colorado (the first), New York, California, Hawaii, North Carolina, Alaska, and Georgia. In 1967, the California law, the nation's third, was signed by Governor Ronald Reagan. The laws differed, but most were modeled on the Model State Abortion Law drafted by the American Law Institute (ALI) in 1959. The ALI law permitted abortion under limited circumstances: for victims of rape or incest, cases of severe fetal deformity, or when the woman's life or health was threatened. Going beyond the ALI model, the New York legislature enacted a law in 1970 that allowed abortion for any reason during the first six months of pregnancy.[5]

By 1973, Texas had not reformed its abortion law; Georgia had. The Texas statute banned all abortions except "for the purpose of saving the life of the mother."[6] The Georgia statute permitted an abortion when "a continuation of the pregnancy would endanger the life of the pregnant woman or would seriously and permanently injure her health."[7] When both laws were challenged in the Supreme Court in *Roe v. Wade* and *Doe v. Bolton*, the Court determined that the laws of both states violated the guarantees of the U.S. Constitution by invading a woman's right to privacy.

Right to Privacy Is Established

The foundation for the Supreme Court's decision in *Roe* and *Doe* was laid in two earlier cases: the 1965 *Griswold v. Connecticut* case and the 1972 *Eisenstadt v. Baird* case.

In *Griswold*, in a 7–2 vote the Court invalidated a Connecticut law prohibiting the use of contraceptives by married couples. The case arose when the executive director of the Planned Parenthood League of Connecticut and a licensed physician who prescribed contraceptives were convicted as accessories to the crime of using contraceptives. The Court allowed them to raise the issue of the constitutional rights of their patients with whom they had professional relationships.

Announcing the opinion of the Court, Justice William Douglas was anxious to avoid the charge that the Court was engaging in judicial activism — that is, that the Court was making law rather than merely interpreting it. He denied that the Court was "sit[ting] as a super-legislature to determine the wisdom, need, and propriety of laws that touch economic problems, business affairs or social conditions." But this law was not an ordinary one. It deserved the Court's special attention, he said, because it directly infringed on "the intimate relation of husband and wife."[8]

Douglas cited earlier Supreme Court decisions going back to the 1920s that supported the principle "that specific guarantees in the Bill of Rights have penumbras, formed by emanations from those guarantees that help give them life and substance."[9] The penumbras of the First, Third, Fourth, Fifth, and Ninth Amendments created a "zone of privacy" protected by the Constitution from intrusion by the state. Because the marital relationship lies within that zone, a law forbidding the use of contraceptive devices is an unconstitutional invasion of privacy.

Individual Privacy and Childbearing

A few years later, in *Eisenstadt*, the Court struck a Massachusetts law prohibiting the distribution of contraceptive devices or materials to single persons.[10] Speaking for a 6–1 majority (with William Rehnquist and Lewis Powell not participating), William Brennan set aside the conviction of William Baird, a Massachusetts Planned Parenthood official. Baird intentionally challenged the law by exhibiting contraceptives during a speech on contraception to a group of students at Boston University and giving a young woman a sample package of contraceptive foam at the end of the lecture.

The Court held that a married couple's privacy, established in *Griswold*, belonged to single persons as well. Brennan emphasized that a couple consists "of two individuals each with a separate intellectual and emotional makeup." Perhaps unknowingly laying the foundation for *Roe* less than a year later, he continued, "[I]f the right of privacy means anything, it is the right of the *individual*, married or single, to be free from unwarranted governmental intrusion into matters so fundamentally affecting a person as the decision whether to bear or beget a child."[11]

The Right to Abortion

In *Roe*, the Court held that a woman's fundamental right to privacy, protected by the due process clause of the Fourteenth Amendment, included the right to decide whether to terminate a pregnancy. In striking the Texas statute in which abortion was legal only to save the woman's life, the Court extended the privacy right articulated in *Griswold*.

The case arose when Norma McCorvy, an unmarried, pregnant carnival worker, sought an abortion in her home state of Texas in 1969. Although initially claiming she was raped, she eventually recanted that story.[12] However she became pregnant, she knew she did not want, and would be unable to support, a child. She already had one child she hardly ever saw, a daughter who was living with McCorvy's mother and stepfather in Arkansas.

McCorvy consulted a doctor who informed her that abortion was illegal in Texas and suggested she try another state. With no money to travel to a state where abortion was legal, nor funds to pay for a "safe" illegal abortion in Texas, she looked for an attorney to arrange a private adoption. The lawyer referred her to two Dallas-Fort Worth attorneys, Linda Coffee and Sarah Weddington. It was a fortuitous meeting as Coffee and Weddington had been looking for a plaintiff to challenge the Texas abortion law in federal court. Although Coffee and Weddington offered to help her obtain an abortion, knowing it would weaken—perhaps even destroy—their case, McCorvy refused and decided to have the baby. (She was already four months pregnant and, in 1969, abortions were almost never performed this late.)

When McCorvy, now known as Jane Roe, challenged the Texas law in a three-judge federal court in Dallas, the court ruled in her favor, finding a woman's right to terminate a pregnancy constitutionally protected. But while the court declared the law unconstitutional, it refused to order the state to cease enforcement. Coffee and Weddington were forced to go to the United States Supreme Court for a final victory.

In their appeal to the Court, Roe's attorneys argued that the restriction on the right of abortion was an unconstitutional invasion of a woman's fundamental right to privacy. In a 7–2 vote, the Court agreed and struck the Texas abortion statute.[13] Harry Blackmun's opinion for the Court was joined by Powell, Brennan, Thurgood Marshall, John Paul Stevens, Warren Burger, and Potter Stewart. Rehnquist and Byron White dissented.

Citing past Supreme Court decisions on the right to privacy, Blackmun ruled that it "is broad enough to encompass a woman's decision whether or not to terminate her pregnancy."[14] But although the right is fundamental, it is not absolute, and a woman may not "terminate her pregnancy at whatever time, in whatever way, and for whatever reason she alone chooses."[15] He emphasized that the woman's right must be balanced against a state's interest in regulating abortions.

The State's Compelling Interests

Texas advanced two reasons to justify its abortion law: first, it safeguarded the woman from the medical risks of an abortion; second, it protected prenatal life. Agreeing these were important, the Court emphasized that, in the past, it has held that "where certain 'fundamental' rights are involved . . . [a] regulation limiting these rights may be justified only by a 'compelling state interest' . . . and that legislative enactments must be narrowly drawn to express only the legitimate state interests at stake."[16]

Roe argued that no compelling interest justified the state's virtual ban on abortions. The state countered that protecting prenatal life is always a compelling reason to prohibit abortion in the absence of a threat to the woman's life. The Supreme Court rejected both views.

To support its claim, Texas argued that as a person, the fetus is protected by the Fourteenth Amendment. The Court was not persuaded because there was no evidence that the framers of the Constitution had ever contemplated protection of the unborn. Texas also contended that because life began at conception, its compelling interest in prenatal life arose at that point and continued throughout the pregnancy. Citing the dispute among religious, medical, and philosophical perspectives about when life begins, the Court proclaimed itself unable to define the onset of life. It refused to accept the state's unproven theory of life as justification for prohibiting abortion.

Although rejecting the state's claim that its interests in maternal health and fetal life were compelling throughout the pregnancy, the Court acknowledged that each became compelling at a specific stage of the pregnancy. This led to the adoption of the trimester approach, the principle that abortion regulations must vary with the stage, or trimester, of pregnancy.

Because abortion carries almost no medical risk when performed in the first three months of pregnancy, the state has no compelling reason to regulate the procedure beyond requiring the physician to be licensed by the state. During the first trimester, Blackmun said,

> the attending physician, in consultation with his patient, is free to determine, without regulation by the State, that, in his medical judgment, the patient's pregnancy should be terminated. If that decision is reached, the judgment may be effectuated by an abortion free of interference by the State.[17]

Although the Court would later retreat from this sweeping statement, with about 90 percent of abortions performed during the first trimester, Blackmun's avowal had enormous consequences for a woman's abortion decision.[18]

The state's "important and legitimate interest" in maternal health becomes compelling at "approximately the end of the first trimester." During the second trimester, the state "may regulate the abortion procedure to the extent that the regulation reasonably relates to the preservation and protection of maternal health."[19] A regulation specifying the place where abortions may be performed (that is, hospitals or clinics), and by whom, would be permissible according to this standard.

Lastly, the "State's important and legitimate interest in potential life" becomes compelling at viability, when "the fetus . . . presumably has the capability of meaningful life outside the mother's womb."[20] The Court located viability at about seven months (twenty-eight weeks) but noted that it may occur even earlier, possibly at twenty-four weeks. In protecting the fetus during this last trimester, the state "may go so far as to proscribe abortion . . . except when it is necessary to preserve the life or health of the mother."[21]

After assessing the Texas criminal law in light of this standard, the Court declared it unconstitutional. A law that permits abortion only to save the woman's life, makes no distinctions among the stages of pregnancy, and acknowledges no competing interests with the state's interest in potential life violates the Fourteenth Amendment's due process clause by interfering with the woman's right to privacy.

Hospital and Physician Approval

In *Doe v. Bolton*, the Court determined the constitutionality of Georgia's abortion statute, one of the 1960s reform laws. The Georgia law exempted certain "necessary" abortions from criminal penalties: when the pregnancy would endanger the woman's life or cause serious and permanent injury, when the fetus would very likely be born with a "grave, permanent, and irremediable mental or physical defect," or when the pregnancy resulted from rape. In addition to the woman's physician, two other physicians had to certify in writing, after examining the woman, that the abortion was "necessary." All abortions had to be performed in licensed and accredited hospitals and required advance approval from at least three members of the hospital's abortion committee. The law authorized hospitals to deny admittance to abortion patients and allowed physicians or staff members to refuse to participate in abortions. It also specified that the woman seeking the abortion must be a Georgia resident.[22]

Mary Doe, twenty-two years old, married, and nine weeks pregnant, had three children — two in foster care and one given up for adoption. She had a history of mental illness and had spent time in a state hospital. The abortion committee at Grady Memorial Hospital in Atlanta denied her application for an abortion because she failed to meet the criteria for a necessary abortion. Doe and a number of others (physicians, social workers, nurses, and clergy) challenged the law in federal district court. The court struck portions of the law and upheld others.

Using the standard just developed in *Roe*, with the same 7–2 majority the Supreme Court struck most of the law. Speaking for the Court, Blackmun found that the state could not require all abortions to be performed in hospitals because it had no compelling interest in first-trimester abortions. He also ruled that the hospital-committee approval and two-physician requirement served no legitimate state interest and "unduly" restricted the woman's right to privacy. The residency requirement abridged the constitutional right to travel and appeared irrational as well.[23]

The Dissents in *Roe* and *Doe*

Rehnquist devoted most of his dissent in *Roe* to condemning the Court's judicial activism. He quarreled with the majority's conclusion that abortion is a fundamental right entitled to strict scrutiny—that is, the compelling state interest test. He conceded that the right of privacy is a liberty protected by the Fourteenth Amendment but emphasized that the "liberty is not guaranteed absolutely against deprivation, only against deprivation without due process of law." The traditional test for assessing the constitutional bounds of economic or social legislation, such as an abortion regulation, is whether the law is rationally related to a "valid state objective"— that is, minimal scrutiny.[24] By applying a lower level of scrutiny, he said, the Court would correctly commit decisions on abortion policy-making to state legislators' judgments.

Dissenting for himself and Rehnquist in *Doe*, White accused the majority of allowing a woman to terminate a pregnancy for almost any reason "or for no reason at all," and without having to demonstrate any risk to her own health. Before viability, he said, the Court shows more concern for "the convenience, whim, or caprice of the putative mother . . . than [for] the life or potential life of the fetus."[25]

Like Rehnquist, he charged the Court with exercising judicial activism in the creation of a new constitutional right for pregnant women. He found no constitutional justification for usurping the power of elected state representatives to decide how to protect human life.

The Trimester Approach

Roe and *Doe* established the standard for future analysis of abortion laws. The trimester framework was a compromise arising out of the Court's wish to balance the woman's fundamental right to control her reproduction with the state's desire to limit access to abortions. Under the trimester approach, a state must show that an abortion regulation furthers its compelling state interest in maternal health (during the second trimester) or potential life (during the third trimester). Additionally, a state has to show that the regulation is reasonably related to the applicable interest.

Following *Roe*, the Court was accused of creating "abortion on demand" by enabling a woman to control her pregnancy for three months before allowing the state to impose limits on abortion. But the Court restricted the woman's access to abortion even within the first three months by proclaiming that until viability, "the abortion decision in all its aspects is inherently, and primarily, a medical decision, and basic responsibility for it must rest with the physician."[26] By superimposing a legal grid on the continuum of pregnancy and casting the constitutional right in medical terms of trimesters, the Court located decision-making responsibility in the physician rather than in the woman.

Despite the Court's conservative approach to the fundamental right of abortion, *Roe* engendered state legislation hostile to abortion. And because medical science soon outpaced the Court's mathematical precision into state interests and trimesters, *Roe* planted the seeds for an attack on the trimester approach. Currently, *Roe*'s trimester framework is under siege from prochoice and antiabortion forces, each seeking a reformulation that will benefit its legal position.

Because of the intense moral battles over abortion, it is often forgotten that abortion policy-making is simply a matter of the government making choices among policy alternatives. It is unlikely that any court or legislature would allow the woman the right to abortion *at all times* throughout her pregnancy. It is also unlikely that *all* states will ban abortion entirely. Studies show that the trimester approach comports with the feelings that most Americans have about abortion, with support for abortion declining in each succeeding trimester.[27] Therefore, the trimester framework, with all its flaws and despite changes in technological development, represents the most realistic compromise; it produces a workable policy guide that is generally acceptable to the American public.[28]

Attempts to Curtail *Roe*

Legal scholars such as John Hart Ely denounced the Court for overstepping its bounds in establishing a woman's constitutional right to abortion.[29] Antiabortion statutes and amendments were quickly introduced in Congress. One amendment, sponsored by Republican Senator Orrin Hatch of Utah, came within eighteen votes of the necessary two-thirds in the Senate in 1983. The amendment stated, "A right to abortion is not secured by this Constitution."[30]

Also following *Roe*, almost two hundred abortion bills were introduced in state legislatures. Within two years, thirty-two states enacted a total of sixty-two abortion-related laws. The laws revolved around seven categories: performance regulations (where abortions could be performed and by whom), consent requirements, recordkeeping and reporting requirements, advertising prohibitions, funding restrictions (state and federal), conscience laws (allowing hospitals or physicians to refuse to perform abortions), and fetal protection.[31]

State laws, largely aimed at second-trimester abortions, were soon tested in the federal courts. The litigation centered on efforts by states such as Missouri, Ohio, and Pennsylvania to require hospitalization and regulate methods of abortion, fix the duty of physicians, and provide definitions of viability. In complex multipart rulings, the courts found that most of these laws restricted the woman's right to privacy established in *Roe*. In part, the Court was persuaded that states were setting abortion procedures apart from other medical procedures and imposing unique duties and liabilities on doctors performing abortions. In other health-related areas, beyond setting initial licensing standards the state usually entrusts regulation of procedures and practices to the medical profession itself. For example, states do not usually prescribe how many "doctors and nurses . . . must be present at a tonsillectomy."[32]

Saline Amniocentesis Abortions

In June 1974, the Missouri General Assembly enacted a regulation predominantly aimed at second-trimester abortions. It also imposed a parental- and spousal-consent requirement as well as recordkeeping and reporting rules that were not specific to any trimester. The Court struck the consent provisions and upheld the reporting requirement because the records were kept confidential and used for statistical purposes only.[33]

The law required second-trimester abortions to be performed in hospitals and prohibited physicians from using the saline amniocentesis method of abortion.[34] The statute also charged the attending physician with the duty to preserve a viable fetus's life and health or face manslaughter charges and civil suits for damages. The law defined viability as "that stage of fetal development when the life of the unborn child may be continued indefinitely outside the womb by natural or artificial life-supportive systems."[35]

Three days after the act went into effect, Planned Parenthood and two Missouri physicians challenged it in federal district court on behalf of themselves and their female patients.[36] The lower court struck the physician's liability section but upheld the other provisions.

In a 5–4 opinion, in *Planned Parenthood of Central Missouri v. Danforth*, 1976, with Blackmun, Brennan, Marshall, Stewart, and Powell in the majority, the Court accepted the state's definition of viability but struck most of the other provisions. White, Burger, Rehnquist, and Stevens dissented.

The majority found Missouri's definition of viability consistent with *Roe*'s statement that viability begins at the point at which the fetus is "potentially able to live outside the mother's womb, albeit with artificial aid."[37] Viability, Blackmun noted, was a flexible concept, and the state did not have to peg it to a certain week of pregnancy. In a statement that would become significant over a decade later, the Court held that

it is not the proper function of the legislature or the courts to place viability, which essentially is a medical concept, at a specific point in the gestation period. The time when viability is achieved may vary with each pregnancy, and the determination of whether a particular fetus is viable is, and must be, a matter for the judgment of the responsible attending physician.[38]

The lower court had upheld the state's ban on saline amniocentesis. It found that although the saline method of abortion was safer than continuing a pregnancy to term and was the most commonly used post-first-trimester abortion procedure, safer alternatives existed.

The Supreme Court reversed, in part because the abortion procedures cited by the lower court as alternatives were not generally available. The state could not claim to be furthering maternal health by banning a safe abortion procedure and forcing doctors to rely on more dangerous methods.

The majority also found the provision requiring the physician to preserve the life and health of the fetus unconstitutional. As it "now reads," the Court said, "it impermissibly requires the physician to preserve the life and health of the fetus, whatever the stage of pregnancy."[39]

Criminal Liability for Physicians

Three years after *Danforth*, in a 1979 opinion the Supreme Court struck a portion of the 1974 Pennsylvania Abortion Control Act that imposed criminal penalties on physicians who failed to preserve the life of a fetus that was viable or one they had "sufficient reason to believe" was viable. Following *Roe*, the law defined viability as the potential ability to survive outside the mother's womb. It required physicians to use the abortion technique most likely to save the fetus unless another technique were necessary to preserve the woman's life or health.[40]

In a 6–3 decision, in *Colautti v. Franklin* the Court found the Pennsylvania law unconstitutional. Blackmun announced the opinion of the Court for himself, Brennan, Marshall, Stewart, Powell, and Stevens. He found the law too vague because it did not indicate when the physician's duty to the fetus came into play—at viability or when the fetus "may be viable." The uncertainty of viability and ambiguities in the statute, concluded Blackmun, together with the resulting criminal and civil liability "could have a profound chilling effect on the willingness of physicians to perform abortions near the point of viability in the manner indicated by their best medical judgment."[41]

Blackmun's opinion cited district court testimony on how physicians interpreted the statute. Most said that under ordinary circumstances, they would use saline amniocentesis in the second trimester. But because saline was almost always fatal to the fetus, they said they would have to abandon the saline procedure. When asked how they would comply with the statute, their responses ranged from refusal to perform the abortion to selection of methods more dangerous and/or more costly to the woman.

Blackmun emphasized that the physician's liability provision was unconstitutional because it showed insufficient concern for the woman's health or life. "It is uncertain," he said, "whether the statute permits the physician to consider his duty to the patient to be paramount to his duty to the fetus, or whether it requires the physician to make a 'trade-off' between the woman's health and additional percentage points of fetal survival."[42] The state must clarify these vital points, he insisted, before subjecting a physician to possible criminal penalties.

White's dissenting opinion, joined by Rehnquist and Burger, complained that the Court has "withdraw[n] from the States a substantial measure of the power to protect fetal life that was reserved to them" in *Roe* and *Danforth*.[43]

The Akron Ordinance

In February 1978, the city council of Akron, Ohio, enacted the most restrictive set of abortion regulations yet devised. The ordinance contained seventeen provisions regulating the performance of abortions, including a variety of consent and notice requirements affecting first-trimester abortions. Perhaps the most important section required all post–first-trimester abortions to be performed in hospitals rather than clinics or doctors' offices. Because of the inaccessibility of hospital abortions and the cost involved, this provision significantly reduced access to abortions for Ohio women.

The sections on informed consent and waiting periods required physicians to obtain a woman's written consent, to notify the father of the child and obtain his consent, to secure the consent of a minor woman's parents, and to wait twenty-four hours after obtaining consent before performing the abortion.[44] To ensure that the woman's consent was "informed," the doctor had to describe to her "in detail the anatomical and physiological characteristics of the particular unborn child at the gestational point of development at which time the abortion[is to be performed]," explaining that "the unborn child is a human life from the moment of conception" and can feel pain.

The doctor's lecture had to indicate that "abortion is a major surgical procedure, which can result in serious complications." It also had to inform the woman that the abortion "may worsen any existing psychological problems she may have, and can result in severe emotional disturbances."[45] The law specified the physician must personally present the information.

The ordinance was authored by the counsel for the Ohio Right to Life

Society, who later argued the case for the city before the Supreme Court. It was adopted in a 7 – 6 vote and allowed to become law without the mayor's signature. The ordinance was immediately challenged by the American Civil Liberties Union on behalf of an Akron physician and several abortion clinics.[46] When *City of Akron v. Akron Center for Reproductive Health* reached the Supreme Court, five provisions remained at issue.

When the Court decided *Akron* in 1983, the vote was 6 – 3. The newest justice, Sandra Day O'Connor, a Reagan appointee, joined White and Rehnquist in voting to uphold the ordinance. The majority, consisting of Powell, Blackmun, Marshall, Brennan, Burger, and Stevens, found the challenged sections of the ordinance unconstitutional. The opinion of the Court, announced by Powell, also substantially reaffirmed *Roe* but revealed some cracks in the edifice constructed by *Roe* that had become evident in the ten years that had elapsed.

Perhaps even more heartening to prochoice advocates than the Court's decision was its rejection of Solicitor General Rex Lee's argument that the Court change the legal standard for abortion cases. On behalf of the Reagan administration, Lee urged the Court to adopt a less rigorous scrutiny for abortion regulations.[47] In the opinion, Powell seemed to be responding to Lee when he said that "restrictive state regulation of the right to choose abortion, as with other fundamental rights subject to searching judicial examination, must be supported by a compelling state interest."[48]

Hospitalization for Second-Trimester Abortions

Powell stated that the hospital requirement, like any second-trimester regulation, is constitutional "only if it is reasonably designed" to advance the state's compelling interest in maternal health. A regulation that "depart[s] from accepted medical practice" cannot reasonably advance the state's interest.[49] Under this principle, a regulation encompassing the entire trimester may be unreasonable.

The Court found that Akron's second-trimester hospital requirement created a "significant obstacle" to the woman seeking an abortion: the cost was more than doubled and Akron's hospitals rarely performed second-trimester abortions. While Akron conceded that its regulation erected a barrier for the pregnant woman seeking an abortion, it defended the ordinance as a reasonable health measure. The Court disagreed.

At the time *Roe* was decided, health considerations prompted the American Public Health Association (APHA) and the American College of Obstetricians and Gynecologists (ACOG) to recommend that all second-trimester (and later) abortions be performed in hospitals. Based on these views, in *Roe* the Supreme Court cited a hospitalization requirement as an example of an acceptable second-trimester regulation. Following the high court's lead, the lower courts upheld the Akron hospital regulation.

In the intervening years since *Roe*, the safety of second-trimester abortions (at least up to sixteen weeks) significantly increased because of expanded use of the dilatation and evacuation (D & E) procedure. These medical advances meant that maternal health could now be effectively protected in clinics. Therefore, by 1983 the medical organizations ACOG and APHA had abandoned their recommendation for hospital abortions during the first sixteen weeks of pregnancy.[50] And because the Akron regulation now "departed from accepted medical practice," the Court found it unconstitutional. It was unreasonable for the city to require *all* second-trimester abortions to be performed in hospitals.[51]

While extending the first trimester to sixteen weeks, a medical and mathematical impossibility, the Court nevertheless reaffirmed its commitment to the *Roe* framework. It reiterated that the state's compelling interest in the woman's health *starts at the beginning* of the second trimester. But by striking the Akron ordinance because it did not recognize a distinction within the second trimester, the Court could be accused of itself eroding the trimester approach.[52]

Informed Consent

The twenty-four-hour waiting period and informed-consent requirements of the Akron ordinance regulated first-trimester abortions, as well as those occurring later in the pregnancy. Despite the Court's statement in *Roe* that first-trimester abortions were beyond state regulation, Powell explained in *Akron* that first-trimester abortion regulations may be valid when they "have no significant impact on the woman's exercise of her right . . . [and are] justified by important state health objectives."[53] But in this case, the Court found that the twenty-four-hour waiting period led to scheduling delays that increased the risk to the woman and did not further any legitimate state interest. With appropriate counseling and informed written consent, the Court held, no purpose is served by an arbitrary twenty-four-hour wait.

The city characterized the mandatory lecture to the pregnant woman as an attempt to ensure that her consent was informed. The Court found instead that the information, "a parade of horribles," was really intended to influence her choice against the abortion.[54] By specifying the content of the warning, the city also intruded on the physician's discretion. Finally, the city offered no proof that others could not deliver the lecture as well as the doctor.

O'Connor's Dissent

Many eyes were on Justice O'Connor. When she was nominated for a seat on the high court, antiabortion groups attacked her for her views on abortion. She had undergone extensive questioning on her attitude toward *Roe v. Wade* in her Senate confirmation hearing. *Akron* was her first abortion case, and her opinion demonstrated that the fears of the antiabortionists were unfounded.

In her dissent, O'Connor, joined by White and Rehnquist, attacked *Roe*'s trimester approach as technologically outmoded. She characterized the trimester framework as "unworkable" because medical knowledge was simultaneously advancing the state's interest in potential life by moving the point of viability to an earlier stage in the pregnancy and delaying the state's interest in maternal health by making abortions safer at a later stage in the pregnancy. She even (erroneously) suggested that viability might move up to the first trimester.[55] These technological changes, she contended, meant the *Roe* framework was "on a collision course with itself."[56]

O'Connor argued against the differentiation of state interests by trimester. In her view, a state had a compelling interest in maternal health and fetal life at all stages of pregnancy. "Potential life," she said, "is no less potential in the first weeks of pregnancy than it is at viability or afterwards. At any stage in pregnancy," she continued, "there is the *potential* for human life."[57]

In deciding on the constitutionality of an abortion regulation, she said, the Court should limit itself to one question throughout the entire pregnancy: is it "unduly burdensome" on the pregnant woman's right to abortion? If the regulation does not "unduly" burden the woman's abortion decision, O'Connor would apply minimal scrutiny and require the state to show the law was rationally related to a legitimate purpose. She would only use strict scrutiny in judging the regulation after determining that it imposed an undue burden on the woman's right to abortion. Seeking to restrain the Court's judicial activism, she urged it to pay "careful attention" to a state legislature's judgment on whether the regulation was unduly burdensome.

Under O'Connor's approach, abortion regulations stand a much greater chance of surviving legal challenge. Although she did not provide examples, she indicated that undue burdens are limited to "absolute obstacles or severe limitations," not regulations that merely "inhibit abortions."[58] O'Connor thought none of the provisions of the Akron ordinance unduly burdensome. And after applying minimal scrutiny, she found each rationally related to a legitimate state interest and therefore constitutionally acceptable.

Akron's Companion Cases

The two cases decided with *Akron* in 1983, *Planned Parenthood, Kansas City, Missouri v. Ashcroft* and *Simopoulos v. Virginia*, also focused on second-trimester hospital requirements, this time in Missouri and Virginia.

Based on its ruling in *Akron*, a 6–3 majority struck the hospital requirement in *Ashcroft*. But a different majority in a 5–4 vote upheld provisions requiring a second physician's presence at a post-viability abortion and the filing of a pathology report after the abortion; the Court also approved a parental-consent section. Revealing the divisions on the Court, almost all justices filed separate concurring and dissenting opinions.[59]

In the Virginia case, the Court affirmed the conviction of a physician who performed a second-trimester abortion in an unlicensed clinic. The law required all abortions after the first three months of pregnancy to be performed in hospitals. With a five-justice majority, the Court upheld it because the definition of hospital, as interpreted by the Virginia Supreme Court, included an "outpatient surgical hospital." Second-trimester abortions could be performed in such outpatient surgical hospitals if they qualified for licensing as hospitals.[60]

The Supreme Court upheld the law, finding that it reasonably promoted the state's interest in the woman's health. The Court seemed untroubled by the fact that its opinion had the effect of restricting second-trimester abortions to hospitals. At the time of the decision, there were only four outpatient surgical hospitals in the state, and none performed second-trimester abortions. Clinics licensed for first-trimester abortions were unable to offer second-trimester abortions.[61]

A New Attack on *Roe*

The drama began anew in 1985, when the Supreme Court agreed to review Pennsylvania and Illinois abortion laws. The Illinois case was ultimately dismissed on procedural grounds because the state was no longer a party when the case came before the Court.[62] But despite the procedural irregularities with the Pennsylvania case, the Court chose to rule on it.

Following the Court's decision to hear these cases, the Justice Department announced it would file briefs on behalf of the states. In a rare move, Acting Solicitor General Charles Fried not only urged the Court to uphold the statutes but also to reconsider its decision in *Roe v. Wade*. When the Court ruled in the Pennsylvania case, although the prochoice majority shrunk to five votes, *Roe* withstood the assault.[63]

In 1982, after its previous abortion laws had been ruled unconstitutional, Pennsylvania enacted a new one developed by an antiabortion group.[64] It was remarkably similar to the Akron ordinance. On June 11, 1986, in *Thornburgh v. American College of Obstetricians and Gynecologists*, the Supreme Court struck all provisions of the 1982 Pennsylvania Abortion Control Act under review. Blackmun delivered the majority opinion, joined by Brennan, Marshall, Powell, and Stevens. White, Rehnquist, O'Connor, and Burger dissented. Antiabortion forces took heart from their increased strength caused by Burger's shift to their side.

The law contained numerous restrictions, including a second-trimester hospitalization requirement, a twenty-four-hour waiting period, a ban on public funds for abortions, and a parental-consent provision. Ruling on the informed consent, the physician's duty of care, and the reporting provisions, the Supreme Court found these invalid because they were not justified by a legitimate state interest. In his opinion, Blackmun frequently referred to the antiabortion intent behind the statute.[65]

Informed Consent

The law required seven kinds of information to be given to the woman, five by the physician personally. Along with usual medical information about risks associated with the procedure, the doctor had to tell the woman "that there may be detrimental physical and psychological effects which are not accurately foreseeable." It was also necessary to inform the woman that she might be entitled to financial support from the state and the father of the child.

Additionally, the woman had to read (or be read) a card telling her that adoption agencies were available to help her and that she was "strongly urged" to contact them. The material had to describe the "probable anatomical and physiological characteristics of the unborn child at two-week gestational increments from fertilization to full term, including any relevant information on the possibility of the unborn child's survival."[66] After receiving the information, the woman was required to wait twenty-four hours before she could legally give consent.

The Court found that, like the "parade of horribles" in *Akron*, the informed-consent provision of the Pennsylvania law was intended to deter abortions. It seemed "to be nothing less than an outright attempt to wedge the Commonwealth's message discouraging abortion into the privacy of the informed-consent dialogue between the woman and her physician."[67]

Rather than ensuring informed consent, the information would likely increase the woman's anxiety and tension about the upcoming procedure and harm the doctor-patient relationship. Furthermore, because much of the information was not relevant to consent, it served "no legitimate state interest." The Court concluded that these provisions were designed to prevent the woman from exercising a free choice rather than to aid her in making a choice. And "States are not free under the guise of protecting maternal health or potential life, to intimidate women into continuing pregnancies."[68]

Physician's Duty

The law required physicians, under the threat of losing their licenses, to file detailed reports of the abortion, including the basis for their determination that the fetus was not viable. Although the reports were not supposed to become public records, they were to be made available for public inspection and copying. Though the woman's name was not part of the record, because of the breadth of information called for, identification would be possible.

Blackmun concluded that the information required in the Pennsylvania law exceeded health-related concerns and served no legitimate interest. This reporting regulation was different from the one in *Danforth*, he said, because the Missouri law kept the records confidential except for public health officers and was designed for statistical purposes only.

The law also instructed a physician performing an abortion on a viable fetus to exercise the same degree of care he or she would in the case of a child intended to be born alive and not aborted. The physician was instructed to use a technique that "would provide the best opportunity for the unborn child to be aborted alive unless . . . [it] would present a significantly greater medical risk to the life or health of the pregnant woman."[69] The penalty for violating the law was a possible seven-year prison sentence and $15,000 fine. The Court found this provision unconstitutional because it promoted an impermissible trade-off between the woman's health and fetal life.

Another section required the presence of a second physician at an abortion after viability to preserve the child's life. The Court had upheld a similar provision in the Missouri law in *Ashcroft* because the statute contained an "implicit" exception to prevent an increased risk to the woman's health if the abortion were delayed to await the second physician. Late abortions tend to be emergency situations, and the Pennsylvania law provided no exception for emergencies when the need for the second physician could override the effort to save the woman's life. Instead, the Court found that "all the factors are here for chilling the performance of a late abortion, which, more than one performed at an earlier date, perhaps tend to be under emergency conditions."[70]

Blackmun ended with an impassioned plea for the preservation of the abortion right. He acknowledged that abortion "raises moral and spiritual questions over which honorable persons can disagree sincerely and profoundly." Yet, he insisted that few decisions are more personal and intimate, more properly private, or more basic to individual dignity and autonomy, than a woman's decision — with the guidance of her physician and within the limits specified in *Roe* — whether to end her pregnancy. A woman's right to make that choice freely is fundamental. Any other result, in our view, would protect inadequately a central part of the sphere of liberty that our law guarantees equally to all.[71]

The *Thornburgh* Dissent

In dissent, Burger accused the majority of going far beyond *Roe*. It is not possible, he said, that the Court would forbid the state from giving the woman "accurate medical information" about the procedure she is about to undertake. How can the Court refuse to allow the state to impose conditions for obtaining consent for a medical procedure? he asked rhetorically. Moreover, he stressed, the second-physician requirement is merely a means of realizing the state's compelling interest in fetal life after viability. He sarcastically noted that Pennsylvania had erroneously assumed that the Court meant its statement in *Roe* that the state could take steps to protect a viable fetus.

O'Connor devoted the bulk of her dissent to attacking the procedural irregularities of the decision. But more important, she continued to advocate the unduly burdensome standard which, she said (as she had in *Akron*), the Court relied on in past cases. She accused the Court of going "well beyond distortion" of that standard. "It [now] seems," she said, "that the mere possibility that some women will be less likely to choose to have an abortion by virtue of the presence of a particular state regulation suffices to invalidate it."[72]

Although O'Connor indicated in *Akron* that she would apply a stricter scrutiny to legislation that unduly burdened a woman's decision to abort, neither her dissent in *Akron* nor her dissent in *Thornburgh* hinted as to what kind of regulation would constitute an undue burden. With her acceptance of the numerous regulations at issue in both cases, it appeared that her threshold was a high one.

White's was the major dissent in *Thornburgh*. Joined by Rehnquist, he urged the majority to acknowledge that *Roe v. Wade* was wrongly decided and to overrule it. He insisted that abortion is not a fundamental right. But, he added, even if it were, the Pennsylvania law is within constitutional bounds because it furthers the state's compelling interest in the fetus before and after viability.

The right to personal autonomy recognized in cases such as *Griswold* and *Eisenstadt* does not extend to abortion, he contended. The decision to abort a fetus is distinct, he said, from the decision not to conceive it in the first place. Because a life is involved, a woman's decision to abort is "*sui generis*, different in kind from other decisions the Court has protected under the rubric of personal or family privacy and autonomy."[73] He charged that by identifying abortion as a fundamental right, the majority wrote its own values into the Constitution. Insisting that abortion policy should be left to the states, he urged the Court to defer to the views of state legislators in assessing abortion regulations.

White argued that the informed-consent regulation, unlike the *Akron* "parade of horribles," merely represents the state's attempt to present truthful information to a woman considering an abortion. He defended the reporting requirements because they furthered the state's accumulation of medical knowledge of fetal and maternal health. He also found the state within its authority to require the physician to preserve the life of a viable fetus. If the state can prohibit an abortion entirely during the last trimester except to save the woman's life, surely, he said, it can compel a procedure that gives the fetus the greatest chance of survival.

Despite the loss of Burger's vote, prochoice advocates rejoiced at the *Thornburgh* decision. But the satisfaction derived from *Thornburgh* would not last long. All four dissenting judges called for a reexamination, if not an outright reversal, of *Roe*. And three years later, in *Webster v. Reproductive Health Services*, a new majority on the Court came close to fulfilling their wishes.

NOTES

1. Kristen Luker, *Abortion and the Politics of Motherhood* (Berkeley: University of California Press, 1984), pp. 1–2.

2. Hyman Rodman, Betty Sarvis, and Joy Walker Bonar, *The Abortion Question* (New York: Columbia University Press, 1987), p. 5.

3. Luker, *Abortion and the Politics of Motherhood*, p. 97.

4. Rodman, Sarvis, and Bonar, *The Abortion Question*, p. 23.

5. The most important source of information on early abortion policy in the United States is James C. Mohr, *Abortion in America* (Oxford: Oxford University Press, 1978). See also Marian Faux, *Roe v. Wade* (New York: Mentor Books, 1988); Eva Rubin, *Abortion, Politics, and the Courts* (Westport, CT: Greenwood Press, 1987); Luker, *Abortion and the Politics of Motherhood* for an overview of U.S. abortion policy before 1973.

6. *Roe v. Wade*, 410 U.S. 113, 118 (1973).

7. *Doe v. Bolton*, 410 U.S. 179, 183 (1973).

8. Douglas denied that the Court was engaging in a *Lochner v. New York* type of decision. *Griswold v. Connecticut*, 381 U.S. 479, 482 (1965).

9. *Griswold*, 381 U.S. at 484. According to Webster's dictionary, a penumbra is the partially shadowed region that surrounds the full shadow in an eclipse of the sun.

10. The law made it a felony, punishable by a maximum five-year imprisonment, to distribute "any drug, medicine, instrument, or article whatever for the prevention of contraception." It exempted licensed physicians and pharmacists from penalty. *Eisenstadt v. Baird*, 405 U.S. 438, 440–41 (1972).

11. *Eisenstadt*, 405 U.S. at 453 (emphasis in the original).

12. The fictitious rape was irrelevant because her lawyers did not argue that she should have been allowed an abortion because she had been raped. See Faux, *Roe v. Wade* for the story of how Norma McCorvy became the Jane Roe of *Roe v. Wade*.

13. The Court first resolved the procedural issues in the case, primarily whether the mootness doctrine compelled dismissal. The federal mootness doctrine requires a live controversy when the case is reviewed by a court. Since Roe was no longer pregnant when the Supreme Court heard the case, and possibly not even pregnant when the case was before the district court, the state argued for dismissal. Because the litigation process will almost always outlast a pregnancy, and because pregnancy will "always be with us," the Court concluded that it "provides a classic justification for a conclusion of nonmootness." *Roe*, 410 U.S. at 125.

14. *Roe*, 410 U.S. at 153. The district court grounded its belief in the woman's right to privacy in the Ninth Amendment; the Supreme Court found it "in the Fourteenth Amendment's concept of personal liberty and restrictions upon state action."

15. *Roe*, 410 U.S. at 153.

16. *Roe*, 410 U.S. at 155. As with a suspect category in equal protection analysis, when a fundamental right is involved, the state must offer a compelling reason to restrict it. Fundamental rights arise out of the guarantee of liberty protected by the due process clause of the Fourteenth Amendment. Not all liberty interests are fundamental rights.

17. *Roe*, 410 U.S. at 163. In *Connecticut v. Menillo*, 423 U.S. 9 (1975), in a per curiam opinion, the Supreme Court upheld a Connecticut statute requiring all abortions to be performed by licensed physicians. In *Sendak v. Arnold*, 429 U.S. 968 (1976), the Supreme Court affirmed without opinion an Indiana three-judge district court ruling that struck a statute requiring first-trimester abortions to be performed by physicians in hospitals or other licensed facilities.

18. Paul Reidinger, "Will *Roe v. Wade* Be Overruled?" *ABA Journal* (July 1988), p. 68.

19. *Roe*, 410 U.S. at 163.

20. *Roe*, 410 U.S. at 163.

21. *Roe*, 410 U.S. at 163–64.

22. *Doe*, 410 U.S. at 183–84.

23. *Doe*, 410 U.S. at 194–200.

24. *Roe*, 410 U.S. at 173 (Rehnquist, J., dissenting).

25. *Doe*, 410 U.S. at 221 (White, J., dissenting).

26. *Roe*, 410 U.S. at 166.

27. Nancy K. Rhoden, "Trimesters and Technology: Revamping *Roe v. Wade*," *Yale Law Journal* 95(1986), p. 669.

28. See Rhoden, "Trimesters and Technology," pp. 684–91, who argues that an exception to this formulation might be to allow a third-trimester abortion when a severe fetal deformity has just been diagnosed. In such circumstances, greater flexibility is needed than the current ban on third-trimester abortions except to save the woman's life.

29. See John Hart Ely, "The Wages of Crying Wolf: A Comment on *Roe v. Wade*," *Yale Law Journal* 82(1973).

30. Rubin, *Abortion, Politics, and the Courts*, p. 157. See Note, "*Thornburgh*: The Last American Right-to-Abortion Case?" *Journal of Family Law* 26(1987–1988), pp. 775–76. See also Raymond Tatalovich, "Abortion," in Raymond Tatalovich and Byron W. Daynes, eds., *Social Regulatory Policy* (Boulder: Westview Press, 1988); Rodman, Sarvis, and Bonar, *The Abortion Question*, chapter 7; Frederick S. Jaffe, Barbara L. Lindheim, and Philip R. Lee, *Abortion Politics: Private Morality and Public Policy* (New York: McGraw-Hill, 1981), chapter 9, for discussion of congressional efforts to overturn and restrict *Roe v. Wade* by constitutional amendment and statute.

31. Rubin, *Abortion, Politics, and the Courts*, pp. 127–30.

32. Rhoden, "Trimesters and Technology," p. 645. While abortions are different from tonsillectomies, the question is what are the limits of permissible regulation of abortion for health reasons when the regulation does not appreciably further health, and, at least in some cases, probably poses greater risk to the woman.

33. The parental-consent provision is discussed in Chapter Eleven.

34. At the time *Roe* was decided, saline amniocentesis was the only second-trimester abortion procedure available. The process involved a saline solution being introduced into the amniotic sac, causing premature labor. This procedure could not be performed earlier than sixteen weeks. First-trimester abortions typically involved dilatation and curettage (D & C), a safer technique that led to the Court's conclusion in *Roe* that a first-trimester abortion presented less risk than carrying a child to term. A D & C could be done up to the

twelfth week of pregnancy. Usually during the gap between weeks twelve and sixteen, no abortions were performed. The difference in health risks between the two procedures was the primary reason behind the Court's decision to attach legal distinction to the trimesters. Rhoden, "Trimesters and Technology," p. 644.

35. *Planned Parenthood of Central Missouri v. Danforth*, 428 U.S. 52, 63 (1976).

36. In general, plaintiffs are not permitted to vindicate the rights of third parties. In abortion cases, the Court typically allows physicians to assert the rights of their patients before the court because the relationships are sufficiently intertwined. See *Singleton v. Wulff*, 428 U.S. 106 (1976).

37. *Roe*, 410 U.S. at 160.

38. *Danforth*, 428 U.S. at 64.

39. *Danforth*, 428 U.S. at 83.

40. The law was a comprehensive one dealing with informed consent, spousal and parental consent, records and reporting, approved facilities, and advertising. The Supreme Court only ruled on the physician's liability issue here as most of the provisions of the Pennsylvania law were considered in other cases.

41. *Colautti v. Franklin*, 439 U.S. 379, 396 (1979).

42. *Colautti*, 439 U.S. at 400.

43. *Colautti*, 439 U.S. at 401 (White, J., dissenting).

44. The parental-consent provision is discussed in Chapter Eleven.

45. *City of Akron v. Akron Center for Reproductive Health*, 462 U.S. 416, 423 n. 5. (1983).

46. In 1981, with a population of 237,000 people, Akron had five abortion clinics performing a total of 7,685 abortions. *New York Times*, December 1, 1982.

47. *New York Times*, December 1, 1982.

48. *Akron*, 462 U.S. at 427.

49. *Akron*, 462 U.S. at 434.

50. A D & E could be performed between weeks twelve and sixteen, so it was no longer necessary to wait for sixteen weeks to have a saline abortion. This advance in medical knowledge meant that abortions up to sixteen weeks were now safer than carrying a child to term. Rhoden, "Trimesters and Technology," p. 649.

51. Of the 10 percent of abortions performed during the second and third trimesters, 90 percent take place between weeks thirteen and twenty, through the first half of the second trimester. Reidinger, "Will *Roe v. Wade* Be Overruled?" p. 68.

52. See Rhoden, "Trimesters and Technology," p. 651. She argues that *Roe* had never "guaranteed that trimesters were, in every instance, indivisible or that a regulation would be constitutional if it was valid for any portion of the trimester to which it applied."

53. *Akron*, 462 U.S. at 430.

54. *Akron*, 462 U.S. at 445.

55. O'Connor's assertion was an exaggeration, at best. Medical evidence strongly suggests that fetal viability is unlikely to ever move back earlier than twenty-four weeks because fetal lung development requires at least twenty-four weeks. According to a 1985 study, more than one-quarter of infants born between twenty-four and twenty-six weeks are born with a severe handicap. Only about 40 percent of infants born between the twenty-sixth and twenty-eighth week of pregnancy survive, and many of those suffer numerous handicaps. At twenty-eight weeks, an infant's chances improve remarkably. Another study showed that 83 percent of infants born at twenty-eight weeks survived. Reidinger "Will *Roe v. Wade* Be Overruled?" p. 69. See also studies reported in Rhoden, "Trimesters and Technology," pp. 660–62.

56. *Akron*, 462 U.S. at 458 (O'Connor, J., dissenting).

57. *Akron*, 462 U.S. at 461 (O'Connor, J., dissenting) (emphasis in the original).

58. *Akron*, 462 U.S. 464 (O'Connor, J., dissenting).

59. *Planned Parenthood, Kansas City, Missouri v. Ashcroft*, 462 U.S. 476 (1983). The Court's ruling on parental consent is discussed in Chapter Eleven.

60. *Simopoulos v. Virginia*, 462 U.S. 506, 516 (1983).

61. Note, "The 1983 Abortion Decisions: Clarification of the Permissible Limits of Abortion Regulation," *University of Richmond Law Review* 18(1983), pp. 151–52.

62. In *Diamond v. Charles*, 476 U.S. 54 (1986), the Court unanimously held that the petitioner, an antiabortion pediatrician, did not have standing to bring an appeal to the Supreme Court. Among other provisions, the law had an informed-consent provision requir-

234 Abortion: The Right to Choose Develops

ing physicians to inform their patients that drugs such as DES (the morning-after pill) and intrauterine devices such as the IUD are "abortifacient[s]" that cause fetal death by preventing the fertilized egg from attaching to the uterine wall.

63. Rubin, *Abortion, Politics, and the Courts*, pp. 147–49.

64. Note, "*Thornburgh*: The Last American Right-to-Abortion Case?" p. 780.

65. David Fernandez, "*Thornburgh v. American College of Obstetricians*: Return to *Roe*?" *Harvard Journal of Law and Public Policy* 10(1987), p. 714.

66. *Thornburgh v. American College of Obstetricians and Gynecologists*, 476 U.S. 747, 761 (1986).

67. *Thornburgh*, 476 U.S. at 762.

68. *Thornburgh*, 476 U.S. at 759.

69. *Thornburgh*, 476 U.S. at 768.

70. *Thornburgh*, 476 U.S. at 771.

71. *Thornburgh*, 476 U.S. at 772.

72. *Thornburgh*, 476 U.S. at 829 (O'Connor, J., dissenting).

73. *Thornburgh*, 476 U.S. at 792 (White, J., dissenting).

11

Abortion: The Right to Choose Narrows

To demonstrate the effects of the Supreme Court's abortion decisions: between 1973 and 1989, about 22 million legal abortions were performed in the United States; by 1989, the number of abortions had risen to almost 1.6 million a year.

With the diminishing prochoice majority on the Supreme Court, abortion rights opponents hoped that the elevation of William Rehnquist as Chief Justice to replace the retiring Warren Burger, and the later appointment of two Reagan-nominees, Antonin Scalia and Anthony Kennedy, would precipitate a movement away from the principles established in *Roe v. Wade*. When the two new justices joined the *Thornburgh* dissenters, Sandra Day O'Connor, Rehnquist, and Byron White, an antiabortion majority emerged on the Court. In 1989, when the Court decided *Webster v. Reproductive Health Services*, the hopes of the antiabortionists seemed to come true: *Roe* was in great jeopardy.

Yet, even before 1989 and the installation of the Rehnquist Court in 1986, the Court accepted significant restrictions on abortion rights for some. Janet Benshoof, director of the Reproductive Freedom Project of the American Civil Liberties Union, argues that "minors' rights to choose abortion are one serious retreat from the firm guarantees of *Roe v. Wade*. The second class of persons who are suffering from another retreat are poor women."[1] By limiting the rights of minors seeking abortions and allowing governmental restrictions on abortion funding for indigent women, the Court has accepted the principle of inequality of abortion rights.

Parental Consent

Shortly after *Roe*, states restricted the minor woman's access to abortion, usually by requiring the consent of one or both parents.[2] In a series of cases beginning in 1976, the Court upheld most of these laws because it was persuaded that a state's interest in parental involvement usually outweighed the minor's right to privacy.[3] Studies have shown that the Court's position mirrors public opinion: according to recent polls, 80 percent of the people of the United States approve of involving parents in a teenager's abortion decision.[4]

The Court first addressed the issue of abortion rights for minors in 1976 in *Planned Parenthood of Central Missouri v. Danforth*. The Missouri law required unmarried women under eighteen to obtain the written consent of a parent (or guardian) unless a licensed physician certified that the abortion was a life-saving measure. A married woman needed her husband's consent.

In a 5–4 vote, the Court struck both consent provisions. Recalling that the abortion decision is between the physician and the woman, the Court held that "the State does not have constitutional authority to give a third party an absolute, and possibly arbitrary, veto over the decision of the physician and his patient to terminate the patient's pregnancy, regardless of the reason for withholding the consent."[5]

Conceding that parents have an "independent interest" in the termination of their minor daughter's pregnancy, the Court believed the daughter's right to privacy should prevail. Missouri argued that the statute "safeguard[ed] the family unit" and promoted "parental authority." But Justice Harry Blackmun doubted it accomplished either goal.

Danforth, the first major abortion case after *Roe*, revealed the division among the justices. The five-justice majority consisted of Blackmun, who announced the opinion, Lewis Powell, Thurgood Marshall, William Brennan, and Potter Stewart. White, Rehnquist, Burger, and John Paul Stevens concurred in the Court's judgment on other parts of the law but dissented on the consent requirements.

Stewart and Powell stressed that their objection to the parental-consent provision stemmed from its "absoluteness." The inclusion of a judicial bypass procedure would have made the law acceptable to them.

Dissenting for himself, Rehnquist, and Burger, White candidly admitted that the statute did not only aim at furthering a parent's interest in a child. It was designed, he said, to support the pregnant minor's right "to decide 'whether or *not* to terminate her pregnancy.'" There is nothing novel, or unconstitutional, he insisted, in the state seeking "to protect children from their own immature and improvident decisions."[6]

Stevens dissented from the majority's stand on parental consent. The state's interest in the welfare of its young entitles it to compel a minor to obtain the "advice and moral support of a parent." Unlike the other three dissenters, Stevens did not believe the law was intended to prevent abortions. He assumed that some parents will "advise" abortions that should not be performed, and others will "prevent" those that should be performed. In his view, "the overriding consideration is that the right to make the choice be exercised as wisely as possible."[7]

Judicial Bypass

With the "blanket" veto forbidden, states began to add a judicial bypass procedure to their consent laws. A bypass allowed the minor who was unable to secure her parent's consent (or unwilling to ask) to seek consent from a state court judge. Under most bypass procedures, the teenager had to prove that she was sufficiently mature to make her own decision or that an abortion was in her "best interests." With the judicial bypass procedure in place, the Court approved most consent laws.

In *Bellotti v. Baird* (*Bellotti II*), 1979, the Supreme Court spelled out the requirements of a judicial bypass procedure. The case revolved around a 1974 Massachusetts law requiring parental consent for unmarried minors under eighteen. If one or both parents refused consent, a judge could, after a hearing, supply the necessary consent. If one parent were dead or had deserted the family, the other's consent was sufficient. The law specified criminal penalties for physicians who performed abortions without the requisite consent.

When the law was challenged in federal district court by a Planned Parenthood official, it was found unconstitutional because it was based on an erroneous assumption that all unmarried women under eighteen were incapable of giving consent. The lower court held that the state was more interested in "recognizing independent rights of parents" than the best interests of the minor. On appeal to the high court in 1976, the Supreme Court unanimously vacated the lower court judgment, ruling that the court should have abstained (refused to decide) to allow the state courts to construe the law. The Court returned the case to the Massachusetts Supreme Judicial Court to interpret the law.[8]

The Massachusetts court found that the statute implied a "best interests" standard that subordinated the parent's interest to the minor's. Under this standard, a judge could disregard parental objections if he or she believed the abortion was in the teenager's best interests. But the judge could also overrule the teen's informed and reasonable decision to have an abortion if the judge determined that it was not in her best interests. The state court also ruled that the minor had to attempt to obtain her parent's consent before resorting to the bypass procedure. Finally, the law offered no exceptions for mature minors, even though they were permitted to consent to other kinds of medical treatment without parental approval. The law was successfully challenged again in federal court, and the state appealed the lower court ruling to the United States Supreme Court.

In the Supreme Court, a four-justice plurality of Powell, Burger, Stewart, and Rehnquist voted to strike the law. In a separate opinion, Stevens, Brennan, Marshall, and Blackmun concurred. White was the sole dissenter.

Powell's plurality opinion recognized that the state had an important interest in furthering the "guiding role of parents in the upbringing of their children."[9] But the state also had to accommodate the minors' privacy right by creating an alternate route for obtaining consent. The state must allow the minor to demonstrate she is mature enough to make an abortion decision on her own *or* that the abortion is in her best interests. Against this standard, the Supreme Court held that the Massachusetts law, as construed by the state supreme court, violated the minor's right to privacy.

Powell articulated three criteria that would later become the standard for determining a proper judicial bypass procedure: it must allow the minor to show either that she is mature enough to decide to have an abortion or, if she is not, that an abortion would be in her best interests; it must ensure the teenager's anonymity; and it must allow expedited appeals.[10]

Stevens's concurring opinion simply found the law unconstitutional because, like the Missouri law in *Danforth*, it subjected a minor's abortion decision to an "absolute veto" by a third party. In all cases, he said, regardless of how mature the minor was, either parents or a judge controlled the abortion decision.

In dissent, White objected that the Court was going beyond *Danforth* by prohibiting the state from notifying parents that their daughter was seeking an abortion.

Applying the *Bellotti* Standard

The Akron ordinance, subject of the Court's 1983 ruling in *City of Akron v. Akron Center for Reproductive Health*, required doctors to notify a parent of a minor under eighteen at least twenty-four hours before performing an abortion. The appellate court's ruling upholding the notification requirement was not challenged in the Supreme Court.

The statute also ordered doctors to obtain the consent of at least one parent or a judge for minors under fifteen. The Supreme Court struck this provision, holding that the city could not make a "blanket determination" that all minors under fifteen are too immature to decide to have an abortion or that it may never be in their best interests to do so without a parent's approval. Although the law contained a bypass procedure, the Court considered it insufficient.[11]

In *Planned Parenthood, Kansas City, Missouri v. Ashcroft*, the companion case to *Akron*, the Court upheld a parental-consent provision because it conformed to the *Bellotti* standard. The 5–4 majority found the law constitutional because it exempted mature minors under eighteen from both the consent requirement and the judicial proceeding.

The appellate court construed the law as requiring a judge to make an initial determination on the minor's maturity. If found sufficiently mature to make her own abortion decision, the judge was not permitted to withhold consent. If the judge found the minor too immature to make the decision herself, he or she could only withhold consent if an abortion were not in her best interests. Based on this construction, a majority of five justices on the Supreme Court voted to uphold the consent provision.[12]

Parental Notice for Immature Minors

In many states, the battle over abortions for minors shifted from consent requirements to notice provisions. Under notice laws, physicians and hospitals were required to notify the parents of a pregnant teenager seeking an abortion. Although the Supreme Court stopped short of endorsing all notification laws, it generally found such statutes within constitutional limits.

In 1981, in *H. L. v. Matheson* the Court ruled on a Utah statute requiring a physician to "notify, if possible, the parents or guardian of the woman upon whom the abortion is to be performed, if she is a minor, or the husband of the woman, if she is married."[13] There was no judicial bypass procedure.

The law was challenged in state court by a fifteen-year-old, pregnant, unmarried teenager who lived in her parents' home and wanted to obtain an abortion without notifying them. The Utah high court found the statute valid for all pregnant teenagers. Limiting its ruling to the facts of the case, the Supreme Court held that a state may require a physician to notify the parents of an immature and dependent minor seeking an abortion and is not obligated to provide a bypass procedure for this class of teenager.[14]

In a 6–3 opinion, with Burger, Stewart, White, Powell, Stevens, and Rehnquist in the majority, the Court found the Utah regulation constitutionally acceptable. Delivering the opinion, Burger found that the law did not establish veto power in the parents, nor did it deter minors from seeking abortions. Instead, he held it furthered the state's interest in promoting the family unit and protecting the teenager by allowing her parents to supply a physician with her medical, emotional, and psychological history. The Court concluded that "the Utah statute is reasonably calculated to protect minors in appellant's class by enhancing the potential for parental consultation concerning a decision that has potentially traumatic and permanent consequences."[15]

Powell and Stewart wrote separately to stress that the ruling did not extend to mature minors or minors whose "best interests" mandated that parents not be notified. Stevens, also concurring, believed that it should be extended to *all* minors — mature or not.

Speaking for himself, Brennan, and Blackmun, Marshall dissented, arguing that the notice requirement unduly burdened a minor's right to abortion. He denied that the statute served Utah's asserted purpose of providing relevant medical information to the physician. It only mandated notice to parents; it did not require parents to communicate medical history or other information to the physician. A physician placing a telephone call to the parents a few minutes before the abortion would satisfy the statute.

Marshall also contended that the statute was "plainly overbroad." Parental consultation, he said, is inappropriate when incest or other physical abuse is involved or when the teenager is afraid that the notice would prevent her from obtaining the abortion she seeks. He doubted that parental notification would strengthen the family, and, in any event, he argued, a state's desire to enforce parental authority cannot override the minor's fundamental right to privacy.

State Notice Laws

The Illinois Parental Notice of Abortion Act of 1983 required a minor to notify her parents and wait twenty-four hours before having the abortion. The district court found both provisions unconstitutional, but the Seventh Circuit affirmed only on the waiting period. Relying on the Supreme Court's ruling in *Akron*, the appellate court found that the twenty-four-hour delay imposes "a far greater burden on a minor's rights than a parental notification requirement . . . and . . . does not significantly further the state's interest in promoting parental consultation when combined with a notification requirement, which itself promotes that interest."[16] In a 4-4 vote, the Supreme Court affirmed.

By 1988, twenty-five states had parental-notice or -consent laws involving at least one parent; most included a judicial bypass procedure. Lower court decrees prevented enforcement of most of the laws.[17] Proponents of notice laws say parents have a right to know of their teenager's decision to have an abortion and that parental involvement reduces teenage pregnancies. Opponents say most pregnant teenagers inform their parents anyway and it is unrealistic and harmful to assume parental involvement benefits every teen.[18]

Benshoof argues that notification laws are counterproductive and result in a "survival of the fittest" effect. Mature, well-connected, and more affluent minors will be able to secure abortions. "The minors who do not get the abortions are the younger, more immature teenagers, those least prepared for the emotional and physical rigors of pregnancy and childbirth."[19]

Studies have shown that most teens notify their parents when they are considering an abortion. A 1980 survey by the Alan Guttmacher Institute found that 75 percent of pregnant teenagers fifteen and under inform their parents; overall, slightly more than half (55 percent) of pregnant teens under eighteen tell their parents they are considering an abortion.

Notification laws apparently have little influence on a pregnant teenager's decision to tell her parents. A 1984 survey of 236 teenagers in Minnesota and Wisconsin found that about 60 percent of the teens in each state confided the news of their pregnancy and possibility of abortion to their parents. Minnesota had a notification law, Wisconsin did not.[20]

Two-Parent Notice

On June 26, 1990, the Supreme Court again addressed the issue of parental notice in two cases arising out of Minnesota and Ohio. The Minnesota law was passed in 1981 as an amendment to the Minors' Consent to Health Services Act, which authorized minors to give valid consent to health care services for pregnancy, venereal disease, alcohol or drug abuse. The 1981 amendment was in effect for five years until, in 1986, it was barred from enforcement by a lower court order.

Subdivision Two of the 1981 amendment required a physician to notify both parents of an unemancipated minor before performing an abortion. There was no exemption for minors with divorced or separated parents, or for those whose parent deserted the family. It was sufficient to notify only one parent if the other one was dead or could not be found after "reasonably diligent effort." No notice at all was required in emergencies, or when both parents consented in writing to the abortion, or if the minor had previously been certified to the authorities as a victim of sexual or physical abuse. The physician was required to wait forty-eight hours after notification before performing the abortion.

Subdivision Six of the law specified that a judicial bypass procedure would take effect if Subdivision Two were declared unconstitutional by a court. The bypass allowed the pregnant minor to attempt to convince a judge that she was sufficiently mature to make the abortion decision herself or that an abortion without notice would be in her best interests.[21]

After a five-week trial, in November 1986 the district court struck the entire statute. A year later, a three-judge panel of the Eighth Circuit affirmed. On rehearing the case, the entire appellate court reversed the panel in a 7–3 vote. The majority concluded that "considering the statute as a whole and as applied to all pregnant minors, the two-parent notice requirement does not unconstitutionally burden the minor's abortion right."[22] The court also upheld the forty-eight-hour waiting period.

The circuit court's ruling indicates the importance of presidential appointments to the federal bench. Six of the seven judges in the majority were appointed by Ronald Reagan; Jimmy Carter appointed the seventh. The three minority judges had been appointed by Lyndon Johnson.[23]

On appeal in *Hodgson v. Minnesota,* 1990, five members of the Supreme Court, Stevens, Marshall, Brennan, Blackmun, and O'Connor, found Subdivision Two unconstitutional because it was not reasonably related to a legitimate state interest. A different five-justice majority, of O'Connor, Kennedy, Scalia, Rehnquist, and White, sustained Subdivision Six, thereby affirming the appellate court and upholding the entire law, including the forty-eight-hour waiting period. Four justices, Kennedy, White, Rehnquist, and Scalia, would have found the law constitutional— with or without the bypass.

Speaking for the Court on Subdivision Two, Stevens distinguished between this case and earlier cases addressing the constitutionality of a notice or consent requirement. "None of the opinions in any of those cases," he explained, "focused on the possible significance of making the consent or the notice requirement applicable to both parents instead of just one."[24]

Stevens highlighted the district court's findings that only about half the minors in Minnesota lived with both biological parents and that the effects of notifying the absent parent were potentially harmful to the teenager. Even when both parents are present, Stevens said, criminal reports show there is a realistic danger of violence against the teen. Additionally, he cited the lower court judge's findings that even though most petitions were granted, the bypass procedure was traumatic to the teenager.

Stevens denied that the two-parent notice furthered the state's interests in the teenager, the parent, or the family. The state can fulfill its obligation to the minor by notifying one parent and permitting that parent to decide whether to notify the other or whether notice would be detrimental to the teenager. Stevens responded to the state's contention that the family functions best if both parents are involved in a teenager's abortion decision by saying that the state cannot legitimately seek to mold the family into its idealized image.

In an odd twist of judicial decision-making, Stevens dissented from the Court's ruling on Subdivision Six. He explained that he was dissenting because this judicial bypass procedure differed from those upheld in previous cases. "A judicial bypass that is designed to handle exceptions from a reasonable general rule, and thereby preserve the constitutionality of that rule, is quite different from a requirement that a minor—or a minor and one of her parents—must apply to a court for permission to avoid the application of a rule that is not reasonably related to legitimate state goals."[25]

In her concurring opinion, O'Connor agreed that Subdivision Two was unconstitutional. But she concluded that "Subdivision 6 passes constitutional muster because the interference with the internal operation of the family required by Subdivision 2 simply does not exist where the minor can avoid notifying one or both parents by use of the bypass procedure."[26] Although O'Connor "broke rank" with the other three Reagan appointees (Scalia, Kennedy, and Rehnquist as Chief Justice), she "then demonstrated once again that she is not prepared to climb off the fence she has long straddled on abortion issues."[27]

One-Parent Notice and Judicial Bypass

The same day *Hodgson* was decided, in a 6–3 opinion in *Ohio v. Akron Center for Reproductive Health,* 1990 the Court upheld an Ohio law with a one-parent-notice requirement and a bypass procedure. The law specified that before performing an abortion, the physician was required to give twenty-four-hour notice to a parent. Another relative could be notified if the teenager and the relative filed an affidavit in juvenile court testifying that the minor feared physical or emotional abuse if the parent were told.

The law allowed the teen to file a complaint with the juvenile court indicating that she is "pregnant," "unmarried, under eighteen years of age, and unemancipated," that she wants an abortion "without notifying one of her parents," and that she "has sufficient maturity and information" to make the decision without notifying her parent, or that she has been physically, sexually, or emotionally abused by her parents, or that notice "is not in her best interests."[28]

Both district and appellate courts declared the Ohio law unconstitutional. On appeal, the Supreme Court reversed. Delivering the opinion of the Court for himself, Rehnquist, White, O'Connor, Scalia, and Stevens, Kennedy left open the question of whether all parental-notification laws *must* be accompanied by judicial bypass procedures. He merely held that because the Ohio statute satisfied the criteria listed in *Bellotti* for consent statutes, it must logically be sufficient for a notice statute as well. "It is a corollary to the greater intrusiveness of consent statutes that a bypass procedure that will suffice for a consent statute will suffice also for a notice statute."[29] Kennedy concluded that the Ohio law did not unduly burden the minor's right to abortion.

Kennedy's finding that the Ohio statute was not unduly burdensome seemed to represent a shift from the Court's holding in *Roe* that an abortion restriction must serve a compelling state interest. Had the majority surreptitiously adopted the "unduly burdensome" standard as O'Connor had urged in her concurring opinion in the other Akron case in 1983?

Public Opinion and Parental Notice

Most Americans approve of parental involvement in a minor's abortion decision. A 1989 national survey found that almost 70 percent of voters support a parental-consent requirement for teenagers seeking abortions. Not surprisingly, most candidates for public office favor a parental-involvement law. And while the National Abortion Rights Action League (NARAL) recognizes that parental-involvement laws are "separate parts of the same campaign to ban abortion," it does not view opposition to a mandatory parental notification law as "a litmus-test issue."[30]

In states such as Oregon, Colorado, and Michigan, parental-notification and -consent initiatives appeared on the ballot in the 1990 elections to allow voters to decide limits on a minor's access to abortion.

Public Funding of Abortions

Proclaiming that a woman has a fundamental right to an abortion, the Court has remained silent on the issue of whether the woman was entitled to *have* an abortion or merely allowed to *seek* one. Although women with resources to pay for abortions were not affected by this distinction, poor women who could not afford to pay were vitally affected. The problem stemmed from the fact that *Roe* "recognized the constitutional privacy right in a negative way—limiting state power to forbid abortions—rather than creating a positive state obligation to implement abortion."[31]

Many states reacted to *Roe* by limiting payment for abortion expenses in their state medical assistance (Medicaid) programs. According to Democratic Senator Birch Bayh of Indiana, the funding restrictions meant that society was "saying that those who have the resources to enjoy their constitutional right to decide to have an abortion may do so. Those who do not have the financial resources have the constitutional right, but," he added, "a right without the ability to use it is absolutely worthless."[32]

The dispute over abortion funding generally revolved around opposing views such as Bayh's and those of Senator John Stennis, Democrat of Mississippi, who opposed "spending millions of tax dollars for the unnecessary slaughter of innocent unborn children."[33]

Most lower federal courts found the funding regulations illegal.[34] Then on June 20, 1977, in a trio of cases arising out of Pennsylvania, Connecticut, and Missouri, the Supreme Court rejected the lower courts' reasoning and upheld the funding limits. By the end of 1978, only ten states and the

District of Columbia voluntarily paid the abortion expenses of poor women.[35]

Medicaid is a joint federal-state program administered by the states, subject to the rules of Title XIX of the Social Security Act. It was estimated that in 1977, almost 3 million women poor enough to be eligible for Medicaid assistance were at risk for having an unwanted pregnancy.[36] By 1977, Medicaid was annually financing about 300,000 abortions at a cost of about $50 million.[37]

Title XIX requires states to provide medical assistance to persons with inadequate "income and resources" to pay for their "necessary" medical care. It allows states to establish "reasonable standards" for deciding how much aid to supply to eligible individuals. Distinguishing between medically necessary (therapeutic) and elective (nontherapeutic) abortions, states generally denied funding for the latter.

The Supreme Court and Funding Limits

In the Pennsylvania case, *Beal v. Doe*, the Court held that Title XIX allowed states to fund only "medically necessary" abortions. *Beal* was a 6–3 decision, with Powell, Burger, Stewart, White, Rehnquist, and Stevens in the majority and Marshall, Blackmun, and Brennan dissenting. Speaking for the Court, Powell noted that it was "hardly inconsistent with the objectives of the Act [Title XIX] for a State to refuse to fund *unnecessary* —though perhaps desirable—medical services."[38] Acknowledging that abortions were cheaper and safer, Powell held that the state's "strong and legitimate interest" in childbirth justified its refusal to fund unnecessary abortions.

In his dissent, Brennan predicted that the majority opinion "can only result as a practical matter in forcing penniless pregnant women to have children they would not have borne if the State had not weighted the scales to make their choice to have abortions substantially more onerous."[39]

Marshall accused the state of abusing its funding power. "It is all too obvious," he charged, "that the governmental actions in these cases, ostensibly taken to 'encourage' women to carry pregnancies to term, are in reality intended to impose a moral viewpoint that no State may constitutionally enforce." He contended that antiabortionists were using "every imaginable means to . . . impose their moral choices upon the rest of society." He protested that "the present cases involve the most vicious attacks ever devised. The impact of these regulations here fall tragically upon those among us least able to help or defend themselves." The result will be that nearly all poor women will be denied access to "safe and legal abortions."[40]

Maher v. Roe was the most important of the three cases because it was decided on constitutional grounds. With the same 6–3 majority as in *Beal* (and Marshall, Brennan, and Blackmun dissenting), the Court upheld a Connecticut Welfare Department regulation restricting Medicaid funds to "medically necessary" abortions. The regulation was challenged as violating the Fourteenth Amendment's equal protection clause by distinguishing among women on the basis of wealth.[41]

Distinguishing the Connecticut regulation from laws abridging fundamental rights, Powell explained that unlike those laws,

> the Connecticut regulation places no obstacles—absolute or otherwise—in the pregnant woman's path to an abortion. An indigent woman who desires an abortion suffers no disadvantage as a consequence of Connecticut's decision to fund childbirth; she continues as before to be dependent on private sources for the service she desires. The State may have made childbirth a more attractive alternative, thereby influencing the woman's decision, but it has imposed no restriction on access to abortions that was not already there. The indigency that may make it more difficult—and in some cases, perhaps, impossible—for some women to have abortions is neither created nor in any way affected by the Connecticut regulation.

"Our conclusion," he insisted, "signals no retreat from *Roe* or the cases applying it."[42]

Because there is no burden on a fundamental right, the state need not demonstrate a compelling interest to justify its decision to pay for pregnancy but not abortion. Applying the minimal scrutiny customarily used in economic or social legislation, Powell found the Connecticut law rationally furthered the state's "strong and legitimate interest" in childbirth.

Brennan, joined by Marshall and Blackmun, again accused the majority of "a distressing insensitivity to the plight of impoverished pregnant women." The state's policy, he charged, "clearly operates to coerce indigent pregnant women to bear children they would not otherwise choose to have, and just as clearly, this coercion can only operate upon the poor, who are uniquely the victims of this form of financial pressure."[43]

The last of the trio, *Poelker v. Doe*, involved St. Louis public hospitals that refused to perform elective abortions under orders from St. Louis Mayor John H. Poelker. In a brief per curiam opinion, echoing *Maher*, the same six-justice majority held that public hospitals are not required to provide or even permit elective abortions. The Court stressed that the city policy was "subject to public debate and approval or disapproval at the polls." And "the Constitution does not forbid a State or city, pursuant to democratic processes, from expressing a preference for normal childbirth as St. Louis has done."[44]

In a press conference following the three rulings, President Jimmy Carter defended the Court. He denied that the funding restrictions unfairly deprived poor women of abortion rights.

As you know, [he said,] there are many things in life that are not fair, that wealthy people can afford and poor people can't. But I don't believe that the federal government should take action to try to make those opportunities exactly equal, particularly when there is a moral factor involved.[45]

Implicitly rejecting Carter's position, Michael Perry argues that the Connecticut regulation was not just unfair but that it clearly aimed at discouraging abortions. He points out that in withholding funds for poor women's abortions, the Connecticut law achieved the same result as the Texas law struck down in *Roe*. He found "the majority's effort to avoid *Roe v. Wade* . . . confused and strained, and ultimately a failure."[46] In his view, the Court failed to acknowledge that the June 1977 decisions effectively overruled *Roe* for indigent women.

Congress and Abortion Funding

Congress entered the policy-making arena on Medicaid funding for abortions by enacting the Hyde amendment, named after Representative Henry Hyde, Republican of Illinois. The Hyde amendment's odyssey through Congress presents an insight into abortion politics of the late 1970s and 1980s. It was no secret that the Hyde amendment was aimed at restricting access to abortions. In 1977, Hyde stated, "I certainly would like to prevent, if I could legally, anybody having an abortion, a rich woman, a middle-class woman, or a poor woman. Unfortunately, the only vehicle available is the HEW medicaid bill."[47] A year later, his cosponsor, Representative Robert Bauman, Republican of Maryland, said, "I think without the availability of Federal funds there would definitely be a decrease in abortions. That is what we seek."[48]

The first attempt to limit government funding for abortion was made in June 1974 when Republican Angelo Roncallo of New York offered a floor amendment to a Labor–Health, Education and Welfare (HEW) funding bill. Defeated by a 123–247 House vote, the Roncallo amendment would have barred federal funding for all abortions. Three months later, a Senate version of the funding limit was defeated. A year later, a second attempt in the House also failed.[49]

Then in September 1976, after breaking an eleven-week conference committee deadlock over the Hyde amendment, Congress included a ban on abortion funding "except where the life of the mother would be endangered if the fetus were carried to term" in the fiscal 1977 Labor-HEW appropriations bill. The ban, effective from October 1, 1976, to September 30, 1977, was never enforced because it was successfully challenged in a New York federal district court on October 1, 1976.[50]

On June 17, 1977, the House approved another Hyde-sponsored amendment to the fiscal 1978 Labor-HEW appropriations bill. This version prohibited government funds for abortion in all cases, including those necessary to save the woman's life. On June 29, the Senate voted to prohibit federal funds for abortion unless the woman's life was endangered, the abortion was medically necessary, or the woman was a victim of rape or incest.

The Senate and the House of Representatives remained deadlocked for over five months on the wording of the restrictions. In December 1977, they finally agreed on compromise language that barred federal funds for abortions unless the woman's life was endangered, or two doctors certified that continuing the pregnancy would result in "severe and long-lasting physical health damage," or in cases of rape and incest promptly reported to the proper authorities.[51] Unhappy with the compromise, Hyde voted against the amendment but it passed both houses.

With the House in favor of increased restrictions, and the Senate generally opposing them, the 1977 compromise language remained in place for several years. In 1981 Congress eliminated the rape and incest exception and limited federal funding for all abortions except those necessary to save the woman's life.[52]

Judge Dooling and the Hyde Amendment

The first attack on the Hyde amendment came when New York City's Planned Parenthood filed suit in federal court after Cora McRae was denied a Medicaid abortion. In 1976, in *McRae v. Califano*, Judge John F. Dooling, Jr., of the Eastern District of New York, handed down his decision. Ruling that his decree affected the Hyde amendment nationwide, he ordered all states to pay for "medically necessary" abortions.[53] On appeal to the Supreme Court, his order was vacated, and the case was sent back for rehearing in light of the June 1977 decisions.[54]

On January 15, 1980, in an opinion exceeding one hundred pages, Dooling held the Hyde amendment violated the First and Fifth Amendments.

The Supreme Court and the Hyde Amendment

Dooling's decision again went to the Supreme Court, and the victory went to Henry Hyde when the Court ruled in a 5–4 decision in *Harris v. McRae* that the amendment reflected a "legitimate congressional interest in protecting potential life."[55]

Stewart's opinion for the Court was joined by Burger, White, Powell, and Rehnquist. Comparing the Hyde amendment to the Connecticut law upheld in *Maher*, he stressed that neither interfered with a woman's constitutionally protected right to an abortion. The Constitution guarantees the right to terminate a pregnancy, but it does not entitle a woman to the funds to do so. Echoing *Maher*, he explained that

> although government may not place obstacles in the path of a woman's exercise of her freedom of choice, it need not remove those not of its own creation. Indigency falls into the latter category. The financial constraints that restrict an indigent woman's ability to enjoy the full range of constitutionally protected freedom of choice are the product not of governmental restrictions on access to abortions, but rather of her indigency.[56]

In a footnote, he added that it would be different if Congress attempted to withhold all medical care because a woman had chosen to exercise her right to abortion. Here, the government action "represents simply a refusal to subsidize certain protected conduct."[57]

Stewart denied that the Hyde amendment violated the First Amendment's establishment clause merely because it "coincide[d]" with the principles of the Roman Catholic Church. The Court did not even address the merits of the "free exercise" argument because none of the plaintiffs could prove they sought an abortion to further a religious belief.

Finally, the Court rejected an equal protection challenge to the Hyde amendment. As in *Maher*, the Court used minimal scrutiny analysis and found a rational relationship between the statute and the government's interest in protecting the potential life of the fetus. Stewart concluded that Congress does not discriminate against poor women by refusing to pay for their abortion expenses.

The *Harris* Dissent

In an indication that the justices were not uniformly supportive of the Hyde amendment, he cautioned that "it is not the mission of this Court or any other to decide whether the balance of competing interests reflected in the Hyde amendment is wise social policy. If that were our mission," he added, "not every Justice who has subscribed to the judgment of the Court today could have done so."[58]

Harris left it up to the states to decide whether to fund abortions out of their own coffers. On the same day *Harris* was handed down, in *Williams v. Zbaraz* the Supreme Court reversed an Illinois lower federal court judge who ordered the state to pay for all medically necessary Medicaid abortions. The high court ruled that Congress did not intend states to fund Medicaid abortions on their own.[59]

The four dissenters, Brennan, Marshall, Blackmun, and Stevens, argued that the Hyde amendment infringed on a woman's constitutional right to privacy by making abortion inaccessible.

Brennan reminded the majority that *Roe* required the government to "refrain from wielding its enormous power and influence in a manner that might burden the pregnant woman's freedom to choose whether to have an abortion." He repeated his earlier charge that withholding funds "serves to coerce indigent pregnant women to bear children that they would otherwise elect not to have." And he accused the Hyde amendment sponsors of trying to impose their moral preferences on women through "coercive financial incentives."[60]

Brennan also attacked the majority's premise that the government placed no obstacle in the way of a poor woman's right to abortion. Denying government funding to women in poverty denies them access to abortion as effectively as criminal sanctions did in the days before *Roe*. While they may choose to have an abortion, "the reality of the situation is that the Hyde amendment has effectively removed this choice from . . . [their] hands."[61] The Hyde amendment, he insisted, forces women to relinquish constitutional rights gained in *Roe*.

Also dissenting, Marshall assailed the decision's effect on poor women. He predicted that women requiring medically necessary — but not life-threatening — abortions would "resort to back-alley butchers, attempt to induce an abortion themselves by crude and dangerous methods, or suffer the serious medical consequences of attempting to carry the fetus to term." He denounced the majority opinion as a "retreat" from *Roe* and a "cruel blow to the most powerless members of our society."[62]

Stevens's dissent centered on the conflict between fetal life and the woman's health. *Roe* placed the pregnant woman's health above all other interests, including potential life, and does not allow a state to protect fetal life at her expense. Yet, by withholding abortion funding, he charged, the government is denying the indigent pregnant woman a benefit to which she is otherwise entitled when she exercises her right to value her life by having an abortion.

Medicaid Funding Restrictions Continue

Congress continued to add a version of the Hyde amendment to each year's appropriations bills. And then, in 1989, prochoice advocates were pleased when Congress liberalized federal financial assistance for abortion — but their victory was short-lived because the legislation was vetoed by President George Bush.

Congress's first step toward a new abortion policy began on September 21, 1989. In a voice vote, the Senate approved a measure to allow federal funding of abortions for victims of rape and incest "promptly reported."[63] Earlier in the summer, the House had voted to retain the old version of the Hyde amendment restricting federal funding to abortions that were necessary to save the woman's life.

The issue went to conference committee and was sent back unresolved. Most expected the House to prevail as it had in the past. But in a close vote on a motion by Representative Barbara Boxer, a California Democrat, the House agreed to accept the Senate version.

The House debate over the bill was highly emotional. "We're talking about 13-year olds, we're talking about little kids who are victims of rape and incest," said Nancy Johnson, Republican of Connecticut. "You compound the horror by killing a second victim. Even the babies of poor women deserve a chance at life," proclaimed Henry Hyde.[64]

The White House sent a message to Congress that the president would veto any bills expanding federal funding of abortions. Because of the close vote in the House, it was unlikely that prochoice supporters could garner the votes to override a veto. Anxious to avoid a confrontation, however, the White House later proposed a compromise in which federal funding would be allowed for rape and incest victims if the crime were reported within twenty-four hours.

President Bush was in a difficult position. Public opinion appeared to be moving in a prochoice direction and a veto might jeopardize Republican chances in the next election, not to mention his own electoral hopes in 1992. But he also had to conciliate his support among antiabortion forces, who mistrusted him because he had favored federal financing for abortions before he became the vice-presidential candidate in 1980.

The White House tried to explain why the president accepted a rape and incest exception for privately financed abortions but not for federally funded abortions. "The President's moral position is that he is opposed to abortion, except when the life of the mother is threatened or in cases of rape or incest period," his press secretary said. But, with federal funding, he added, "you're talking about the management and implementation of Federal taxpayer dollars and whether or not you can control them."[65]

In the end, the president decided to veto. In a letter to Senate Appropriations Committee Chair Robert Byrd, Democrat of West Virginia, Bush said the question was

> whether the federal government and American taxpayers should be forced to pay for the termination of an unborn child's life in the case of rape or incest. That such a child may have been conceived through an unconscionable act of violence makes this question difficult and, indeed, agonizing; it does not, however, alter the basic fact that federal funding is being sought that would compound a violent act with the taking of an unborn life. And in the absence of perfect legislation that would reconcile these difficult issues, if I have to err, I prefer to err on the side of human life.[66]

His veto message on October 21, 1989, simply stated "I have informed the Congress on numerous occasions that I would veto legislation if it permitted the use of appropriated funds to pay for abortions other than those in which the life of the mother would be endangered if the fetus were carried to term."[67]

The House failed to override the veto on October 25, 1989, in a 231–191 vote, fifty-one votes shy of the necessary two-thirds. Again, emotions were high. "This debate is not about forcing people to have children, but it is forcing taxpayers to pay for the extermination of unborn children," Hyde proclaimed. "There is something that is simply obscene in the people of this upper-middle-class body denying to poor young girls a privilege that we would give to our own daughters, sisters or nieces in a heartbeat," declared Charles Wilson, Democrat of Texas.[68]

A spending bill containing the original life-threatening exception only was eventually enacted by the Congress before it recessed in November. At the last minute, prochoice members of Congress refused to accept a seventy-two-hour reporting requirement as the price for a rape or incest exception.

In the midst of the furor over the appropriations bill, Congress authorized a fiscal 1990 District of Columbia spending bill that allowed the District to use its own locally raised tax funds for abortions. This was a change from current District policy that prohibited federal *or* local funds for abortions unless the mother's life was endangered or in cases of rape or incest.

On October 27, 1989, almost a week after he vetoed the appropriations bill, President Bush also vetoed the D.C. funding bill. A second veto followed on November 20, 1989, after Congress approved a ban on the use of federal funds for abortion in the District—except to save the woman's life. This bill was silent on local funding. A third bill containing the language Bush favored, prohibiting the expenditure of federal or local funds for abortion absent a threat to the life of the woman, was finally passed about a week later.[69]

A year later, on October 25, 1990, the House reversed itself when it voted 211–195 against a bill that would have allowed the District of Columbia to use locally raised revenues to pay for abortions for poor women. The abortion language, part of the fiscal 1991 D.C. spending bill, would have permitted the District to use federal funds for abortions for indigent women in cases of rape or incest or to save the woman's life and locally raised funds in any manner.[70]

About a month before the appropriations vote, the House also voted against an amendment to a defense authorization bill that would have allowed a woman to obtain an abortion in a military health facility outside the United States if she paid for it herself.[71]

Another defeat for abortion rights advocates in the 101st Congress came when a Senate-House conference agreed to drop an amendment to a fiscal 1991 spending bill for the Departments of Labor, Health and Human Services, and Education. The amendment would have allowed federal funding of abortions in cases of rape or incest. Although the measure would have been vetoed by the president, it never cleared the conference committee because the amendment also contained language requiring health facilities to notify the parent of a minor seeking an abortion at least forty-eight hours before the abortion can be performed. Because of procedural complexities, the two measures could not be disentangled, and supporters of the rape and incest exception decided to withdraw their support for it rather than to accept the parental-notice provision.[72]

Continually on the losing side, congressional abortion rights supporters have introduced a one-page bill, entitled the Freedom of Choice Act, that forbids states from "restrict[ing] the right of a woman to choose to terminate a pregnancy before fetal viability, or at any time, if such termination is necessary to protect the life or health of the woman." Introduced in the 101st Congress, no action was taken by the time of adjournment. Described as a codification of *Roe v. Wade*, opponents charge that it goes beyond *Roe* by outlawing parental-consent or -notification provisions as well as hospitalization requirements.[73]

The Supreme Court Retreats from *Roe*

On July 4, 1989, the *New York Times* banner headline read:

SUPREME COURT, 5–4, NARROWING ROE V. WADE, UPHOLDS SHARP STATE LIMITS ON ABORTIONS

The day before, in a sharply divided—and often bitterly worded—opinion, the Supreme Court sparked renewed interest in the abortion debate by raising serious doubts about the future of *Roe v. Wade*. The decision, *Webster v. Reproductive Health Services*, was preceded by a massive prochoice demonstration in Washington a few months before. On the day the opinion was announced, demonstrators from both sides of the abortion controversy gathered outside the courthouse to await the decision.

The case revolved around a 1986 Missouri abortion law challenged by doctors, nurses, abortion clinics, and Planned Parenthood. Following a three-day trial, the district court declared seven provisions of the act unconstitutional. The Eighth Circuit affirmed the lower court on all but one issue.[74] On appeal, the Supreme Court reversed.

Oral Arguments

The Supreme Court heard oral arguments on *Webster* on April 26, 1989. Although it is not customary to attempt to persuade the Supreme Court through public opinion, two weeks earlier at least 300,000 prochoice advocates marched in Washington. They carried signs proclaiming "My body, my baby, my business" and "Keep your laws off my body."

The rally drew counterdemonstrators to the scene, shouting "What about the babies?" and "Life, Life, Life." The prochoice demonstration had originally been planned to send a message to President Bush, but the leaders hoped the Supreme Court would be listening as well. The Court also received 200,000 pieces of mail before the April 26 argument day.[75]

On the day of the arguments, demonstrators from both sides gathered outside the Supreme Court with signs and loud voices. It is not known whether the justices heard them. Inside, the Court listened to arguments by William L. Webster, attorney general of Missouri; Frank Susman of the American Civil Liberties Union, representing Missouri abortion clinics; and Charles Fried, former U.S. solicitor general acting as special assistant to the attorney general, representing the Bush administration.

Fried urged the Court to "reconsider and overrule its decision in *Roe v. Wade*." Anxious to demonstrate that he was not advocating the abolition of the privacy doctrine, he stressed that he was "not asking the Court to unravel the fabric of unenumerated and privacy rights." Rather, he said, he was merely "asking the Court to pull this one thread."

In his turn, Susman argued that the right to abortion was an integral part of the right to privacy and procreation. He said Fried was being "disingenuous" by insisting he was "not seek[ing] to unravel the whole cloth of procreational rights, but merely to pull a thread." Susman retorted, "[I]t has always been my personal experience, that when I pull a thread, my sleeve falls off. There is no stopping."[76]

The Preamble

The Supreme Court considered the constitutionality of four sections of the Missouri law: a preamble declaring life begins at conception; a required test to determine fetal viability; a ban on the use of public funds to encourage or counsel women to have abortions not necessary to save their lives; and a prohibition on the use of public facilities and public employees to perform abortions not necessary to save the woman's life.[77]

The preamble to the Missouri law stated that human life "begins at conception" and that "unborn children have protectable interests in life, health, and well-being." The district court held this provision unconstitutional because it conflicted with the Supreme Court's assertion in *Roe* that "a State may not adopt one theory of when life begins to justify its regulation of abortions."[78]

Missouri characterized the preamble as abortion-neutral, saying it merely extended the protections of tort, property, and criminal law to the unborn. Moreover, it argued, the law had no effect on abortion policy because it explicitly stated that it must be interpreted in a manner consistent with Supreme Court decisions.

The appellate court ruled that the beginning-of-life declaration was not abortion-neutral because the preamble was part of a bill almost exclusively concerned with abortion. "The only plausible inference," held the court, "is that the state intended its abortion regulations to be understood against the backdrop of its theory of life."[79]

The circuit court agreed with the lower court that the state relied on its theory of life to justify restrictive abortion regulations. The bill is not saved either by the proviso that it must be compatible with the Constitution. An otherwise unconstitutional law is not made constitutional, the court stated, simply by pointing out that it is bound by the dictates of the Constitution.

Speaking for the Court, Rehnquist, joined by Kennedy, White, O'Connor, and Scalia, held that the Court need not decide on the constitutionality of the preamble. The opinion focused on the question of whether the preamble formed an integral part of the act or was merely an abstract statement. Noting that the preamble itself did not regulate abortion, Rehnquist found it simply a legitimate expression of a value judgment favoring childbirth over abortion. Until it impinged on an abortion right in "some concrete way," the preamble was too abstract to require the Supreme Court to rule on its constitutionality.[80]

Public Facilities

The appellate court also found unconstitutional the prohibition on the use of public employees or facilities in performing abortions not necessary to save the woman's life. It reasoned that this provision could preclude a woman from obtaining an abortion entirely, if, for example, her doctor did not have hospital privileges elsewhere or no private hospital were available.

In 1985, Truman Medical Center in Kansas City, Missouri, performed 97 percent of all Missouri hospital abortions at sixteen weeks or later. Truman is a private hospital, primarily staffed by private physicians, and no public funds were spent on the abortions performed there. But because the hospital was built on land leased from the state, it was considered a "public facility" according to the law.[81]

Comparing this provision to ones found acceptable in *Maher, Poelker*, and *Harris*, Rehnquist found no constitutional problem in banning abortions at Truman. He explained that the state had not created a barrier to abortion by withholding its facilities and personnel. It merely left women in the same position as if it had chosen not to operate a public hospital in the first place. Any restriction caused by a woman's physician being affiliated with Truman or another public hospital was "easily remedied."

If a state may prefer childbirth over abortion by withholding funds,

Rehnquist said, "surely it may do so through the allocation of other public resources, such as hospitals and medical staff."[82] It was irrelevant that the woman was willing and financially able to pay for the abortion. St. Louis's ban on abortions in public hospitals, upheld in *Poelker*, applied to paying patients as well as public-aid recipients.

Public Funds

As with the preamble, the Supreme Court found it unnecessary to rule on the provision of the law forbidding the use of public funds, employees, and facilities to encourage or counsel abortions. The appellate court found the entire provision unconstitutional, but the state only appealed a portion of the lower court ruling to the Supreme Court. The issue before the high court was whether the ban on using public funds to encourage women to seek abortions was constitutional.

Missouri argued that the ban was not aimed at persons engaged in abortion counseling; it was intended to prevent hospital administrators from allocating funds for use in abortion counseling. Given the state's narrow interpretation of the law, the plaintiffs had to withdraw their challenge, being forced to admit they were not "adversely affected" by it. The Court therefore never had an opportunity to determine whether the law restricted freedom of speech by barring physicians from discussing abortion with their patients.[83]

Viability Testing

The most significant part of the law, the viability testing section, provided that

> before a physician performs an abortion on a woman he has reason to believe is carrying an unborn child of twenty or more weeks gestational age, the physician shall first determine if the unborn child is viable by using and exercising that degree of care, skill, and proficiency commonly exercised by the ordinarily skillful, careful, and prudent physician. . . . In making this determination of viability, the physician shall perform . . . such medical examinations and tests as are necessary to make a finding of the gestational age, weight, and lung maturity of the unborn child.[84]

The appellate court interpreted the statute as requiring doctors to perform age, weight, and lung tests in determining fetal viability in all women they believed twenty weeks pregnant. Because the tests are costly and potentially dangerous to the woman and the fetus, the court found the provision unconstitutional.

Speaking for a plurality of three (himself, Kennedy, and White), Rehnquist reversed the circuit court. He construed the law as requiring doctors to test for lung maturity, age, and weight only when, in their professional judgment, they felt such tests were useful in determining viability. He denied the law required these three tests to be used whenever the physician believed the woman was at least twenty weeks pregnant.

Rehnquist acknowledged that the Missouri law clashed with *Roe* by allowing viability tests during the second trimester. But instead of forthrightly overruling *Roe*, the Rehnquist plurality utilized a "backdoor approach [that] allowed it to eviscerate *Roe* without explicitly overruling" it.[85] Rather than attacking *Roe* head-on, Rehnquist proposed to resolve the conflict between *Roe* and the Missouri law by abandoning "the rigid trimester" approach that he said has made "constitutional law in this area a virtual Procrustean bed."[86]

Declining to limit the state's compelling interest in potential human life to the third trimester, Rehnquist approved the fetal test provision because it "permissibly further[ed] the State's interest in protecting potential human life."[87] Conceding that this will allow government regulation of abortion that would have been forbidden under *Roe*, Rehnquist seemed to invite legislatures to challenge *Roe*. Repeating his oft-stated assertion that abortion is not a fundamental right but only a more narrowly defined "liberty interest," Rehnquist implied that the Court will not require the state to show a compelling interest in the future. Indeed, the plurality already appeared to have adopted a new standard by sustaining an abortion regulation as long as it "permissibly" furthered the state's interest.

Rehnquist denied that the Court was overruling *Roe*. He insisted that the facts in the two cases were distinct and that *Webster* offered the Court "no occasion to revisit the holding of *Roe*." But, he added, "to the extent indicated in our opinion, we would modify and narrow *Roe* and succeeding cases."[88]

The Concurring Opinions

O'Connor found the plurality's interpretation of the fetal viability section persuasive and agreed that the viability tests do not impose an undue burden on a woman's abortion right. Her concurring opinion disputed Rehnquist's contention that the viability testing section was inconsistent with *Roe*. In her view, *Roe* was not implicated and the plurality did not have to address it. "When the constitutional invalidity of a State's abortion statute actually turns on the constitutional validity of *Roe v. Wade*, there will be time enough to reexamine *Roe*. And to do so carefully."[89]

Scalia, also concurring, expressed disappointment in the plurality's failure explicitly to overrule *Roe v. Wade*. In a rare attack on a judicial colleague, he criticized O'Connor by saying her refusal to reconsider *Roe* "cannot be taken seriously."[90] He charged that the plurality vitiated *Roe* yet was fearful of saying so openly. Characterizing the Court's decision as "stingy" because it failed to forthrightly address the constitutionality of abortion, Scalia argued that by refusing to dismantle *Roe*, the Court had chosen the "least responsible" path. "It thus appears," he complained, "that the mansion of constitutionalized abortion-law, constructed overnight in *Roe v. Wade*, must be disassembled door-jamb by door-jamb, and never entirely brought down, no matter how wrong it may be."[91]

The *Webster* Dissent

In a passionate dissent, Blackmun, joined by Brennan and Marshall, charged that the plurality and Scalia "would return to the States virtually unfettered authority to control the quintessentially intimate, personal, and life-directing decision whether to carry a fetus to term." He accused the plurality of

> implicitly invit[ing] every state legislature to enact more and more restrictive abortion regulations in order to provoke more and more test cases, in the hope that sometime down the line the Court will return the law of procreative freedom to the severe limitations that generally prevailed in this country before January 22, 1973.[92]

In language seldom seen in judicial opinions, Blackmun described one of the plurality's statements as "totally meaningless"; he charged the other justices with "obscuring" the analysis of the case, and breeding "disregard for the law."

Blackmun focused his attack on the plurality's treatment of the fetal testing provision, denying that it implicated *Roe* at all. Contrary to the plurality's assertion, the plain language of the statute directs the doctor to determine the age, weight, and lung maturity of every twenty-week fetus. Had the Court interpreted the statute as written, it would have been required to strike it even under minimal scrutiny review. In requiring doctors to impose risks on the woman and the fetus, the law was not rationally related to the state's interest in protecting fetal life or maternal health.

Blackmun accused the plurality of manufacturing a conflict with *Roe* and exploiting it to attack the trimester framework. Defending the trimester approach he created almost twenty years before, he described it simply as a tool for evaluating and balancing a woman's constitutional right to procreational privacy against the state's competing interests. *Roe*'s trimester approach and the dividing line of viability, he claimed, still represent the most effective and sensible way to balance a state's interest in regulation and a woman's interest in privacy.

Predicting dire consequences for the future, Blackmun evoked images that

> hundreds of thousands of women, in desperation, would defy the law, and place their health and safety in the unclean and unsympathetic hands of back-alley abortionists, or they would attempt to perform abortions on themselves with disastrous results. Every year, many women, especially poor and minority women, would die or suffer debilitating physical trauma, all in the name of enforced morality or religious dictates or lack of compassion, as it may be.

The plurality's "silence" in the face of these events, he charged, was "callous."[93]

He concluded somberly, "[F]or today, at least, the law of abortion remains undisturbed. For today, the women of this Nation still retain the liberty to control their destinies. But the signs are evident and very ominous, and a chill wind blows."[94]

In his dissent, Stevens took special aim at the state's equation of conception with fertilization, contrary to the medical view that conception begins when the fertilized egg is implanted in the uterus, about six days after fertilization. To the extent that the statute interferes with contraceptive choice, he believed it unconstitutional under the privacy doctrine.

The Impact of *Webster*

Interpretations of *Webster* vary. One view is that *Webster* may pave the way for the state to subordinate the woman's fundamental right of procreational privacy to its compelling interest in the fetus. Logically and legally under this interpretation, a state can criminalize abortion to protect prenatal life—even when the woman's life is at stake. Although a state is unlikely to require a woman to sacrifice her life, *Webster* allows states to exert greater control over the woman's body during the nine months of pregnancy in the name of fetal protection.

Another view of *Webster* is that it would outlaw contraceptive devices that "kill" fertilized eggs by preventing implantation after conception. Under this theory, the privacy "thread" would indeed become unraveled and a woman's right to privacy would be severely jeopardized. Extending this reasoning, it is even possible that a state's interest in the "potentiality" of life could justify an outright ban on all contraceptives. While this seems alarmist at this time, *Webster* does not indicate where the Court would draw the line at interfering with a woman's right to privacy.[95]

The debate over abortion may become mooted by the eventual importation of RU 486, a French drug that interrupts a pregnancy at its earliest stage. So far, antiabortion groups have been able to prevent the import and American manufacture of the drug. Even more important, under the broad interpretation of *Webster*, a state's compelling interest in potential life could allow it to criminalize the prescribing and taking of this drug.

Abortion Clinics

Webster did not lead to outright reversal of *Roe*—as opponents of abortion rights hoped and proponents feared. *Turnock v. Ragsdale*, an Illinois case, seemed a likely vehicle for a formal reexamination—and possible reversal—of *Roe*. Speaking for the Bush administration, U.S. Solicitor General Kenneth Starr urged the Court to uphold the Illinois law and evaluate abortion regulations under minimal scrutiny review rather than the current strict scrutiny standard. At issue in the case was an Illinois law with extensive licensing regulations for clinics.

For a variety of reasons, most hospitals and physicians in the United States refuse to perform abortions. Consequently, specialized abortion clinics have been left the task of performing most U.S. abortions. In 1977, only 31 percent of the 1,661 U.S, non-Catholic short-term (public and private) general hospitals reported performing at least one abortion during the year; 59 percent of the 1,661 reported performing, on average, less than two abortions a week. This means that more than two-thirds of available hospitals in the United States did not perform abortions.

Availability of abortions varies widely across the country. Metropolitan-area hospitals were more likely to offer abortion services, yet, in sixty-one metropolitan areas with over 2 million women living in them, no public or private hospitals performed abortions. One study found that a hospital's refusal to provide abortion services is largely determined by the attitudes of the staff doctors.

Clinics have assumed an increasingly important role in the delivery of abortion services. Most (about two-thirds) of the abortions during 1977 took place in clinics, and each year the proportion of clinic abortions has continued to grow. Clinics are preferred abortion providers for several reasons. They are almost always cheaper, perhaps even safer because the personnel have more experience, and they are generally more supportive of, and accommodating to, the women undergoing abortions.

Clinics, however, are primarily located in metropolitan areas and often duplicate the efforts of hospital abortion providers, leaving women in rural areas and smaller cities without access to abortion. A survey of abortion services in 1988 showed that over 80 percent of the counties in the

United States have no doctors who acknowledge they perform abortions. Some women had to travel hundreds of miles to find an available doctor: in South Dakota, for example, only 1 of 66 counties delivered abortion services; in Kentucky, only 2 out of 120 counties; and in Oklahoma, only 4 of 77 counties.[96]

State laws requiring all second-trimester abortions be performed in hospitals virtually rule out second-trimester abortions of women who live in areas where hospitals refuse to provide abortion services. Similarly, when states impose licensing standards on clinics that threaten their continued existence, abortions will become totally unavailable in areas where only clinics serve the public. This was the issue in *Ragsdale*. Largely because of internal Illinois politics involving the 1990 governor's race, the case was settled and removed from the Supreme Court's docket a few days before it was scheduled for oral arguments.[97]

Public Opinion on Abortion

The majority of the people in the United States are committed to abortion rights, yet their approval usually stops short of the freedom allowed women in *Roe v. Wade*. As a public policy issue, questions on the right to abortion frequently appear on public opinion polls.

Despite shifts that occur because of the wording of the questions, approval of abortion if the "woman's health is seriously endangered by the pregnancy" has been stable for a long time. Since at least 1972, polls conducted by the National Opinion Research Center have shown that between 85 to 90 percent of people surveyed support a woman's right to an abortion for this reason. In a 1989 *New York Times*/CBS News Poll, the figure was at 87 percent.

There has also been strong, although lower, approval for the other so-called "hard" reasons for an abortion: when rape is involved or when the fetus is likely to be seriously deformed. Support usually drops about twenty to thirty percentage points for the so-called "soft" reasons for obtaining an abortion: poverty, being unmarried, or the desire not to have more children.

Other surveys show the ambiguity with which most Americans view the abortion issue. In the 1989 *New York Times*/CBS Poll, 49 percent of the respondents favored keeping abortion legal as it is now. Yet, in the same poll, 48 percent agreed that "abortion is the same thing as murdering a child." But about one-third who felt abortion was murder also agreed that it is "sometimes the best course in a bad situation."

The number of people believing abortion should be illegal in all circumstances has also been consistent over time, varying from about 7 to 10 percent of the population over the last twenty years.

The 1989 *New York Times*/CBS poll also demonstrated that age, education, and marital status divide people's views on abortion: unmarried, younger, and more educated people are more supportive of abortion rights. Religion itself is not as important in affecting attitudes toward abortion as the strength of the religious belief and the frequency of church attendance. Differences in sex and race are not great but men are generally more supportive of abortion rights than women and whites more than blacks.[98]

Post-*Webster* Politics

Reaction to *Webster* was immediate and intense. Polls taken within a few days after the opinion was announced showed that most people disapproved of the decision. The polls also showed that most Americans were in the dark about what it meant; according to a Gallup Poll conducted between July 6 and July 9, 1989, only 59 percent could accurately answer a question on the ruling. But the same poll found that, despite their lack of knowledge, seven out of ten people had strong feelings for or against the opinion. Six out of ten people said they would now be more likely to consider a candidate's position on abortion when voting.[99]

Rehnquist's plurality opinion in *Webster* was perceived as an invitation to state legislatures to enact new laws restricting access to abortion. Moreover, by characterizing the right to abortion as a lesser liberty interest, rather than a fundamental right (and thereby triggering a lower level of scrutiny), the *Webster* plurality appeared to signal that the Court would approve limitations on abortions. Without reversing *Roe*, *Webster* diminished constitutional protection of abortion rights and paved the way for a return to the pre-*Roe* status of individual state abortion laws.

The political battles following *Webster* reflected the importance of the state as an arena for the abortion debate. Abortion played an important role in the victories of prochoice gubernatorial candidates in Virginia and New Jersey. In Virginia, Democrat L. Douglas Wilder defeated Republican J. Marshall Coleman. In New Jersey, Democrat Jim Florio beat Republican Jim Courter. And in the New York mayoral election, prochoice David N. Dinkins was successful against Republican Rudolph W. Giuliani. In each case, the candidate perceived as more prochoice won.

Abortion was also an important issue in the 1990 congressional elections. In most races, the Democratic candidate was more prochoice than the Republican, but in numerous contests, both supported abortion rights or both were opposed.[100] Whatever the candidate's position on abortion, virtually every political campaign was affected.

State Abortion Laws

Within months after *Webster*, a number of state legislatures approved restrictive abortion laws, often with provisions that had been declared unconstitutional by the Supreme Court in earlier cases. Sponsors of the legislation intended to force the Court to reexamine *Roe v. Wade*, and they hoped, to overrule it.

Republican Governor Bob Martinez made the first move by calling the Florida legislature into special session in October 1989 to consider new abortion regulations. His bills would have required viability testing of the fetus at twenty weeks, a one-week waiting period between the woman's consent and the abortion, extensive licensing regulations, and a ban on abortion in public facilities. The legislature rejected all his proposals.[101]

In November 1989, Pennsylvania Governor Robert P. Casey, a Democrat, signed the first state law restricting abortion after *Webster*. The Pennsylvania Abortion Control Act of 1989 banned most abortions in public hospitals; required that a woman notify her husband of a planned abortion, or if she is a minor, required a parent's consent; imposed a twenty-four-hour wait after consent was obtained, and ordered counseling by the doctor to include giving the woman a pamphlet on fetal development.

When the law was challenged in federal court, District Court Judge Daniel H. Huyett III ruled against the state. In a 191-page opinion, issued on August 24, 1990, he found most provisions violated the constitutionally protected right to abortion established in *Roe v. Wade*. The state appealed his ruling to the Third Circuit Court of Appeals and the case was argued in February 1991. By presenting the Supreme Court with abortion regulations that have already been declared unconstitutional, the case will likely force the high court to decide whether *Roe* will remain the law of the land.

In March 1990, Governor Joseph F. Ada, Republican governor of the U.S. Territory of Guam, signed a bill reinstating a criminal abortion law that predated *Roe*. The bill made it a felony to perform or aid in the performance of an abortion; having an abortion was a misdemeanor. An abortion was legal only if two independent physicians agreed that the pregnancy threatened the woman's life or seriously endangered her health.

The territorial statute, quickly challenged in federal court, was ruled unconstitutional by District Court Judge Alex Munson on August 23, 1990. Munson held the constitutional protection of *Roe* applied to Guam, as well as to states. The lower court ruling was appealed to the Ninth Circuit and may reach the Supreme Court as well.[102]

Also in March 1990, in a move that pleased prochoice advocates, Cecil D. Andrus, Democratic governor of Idaho, vetoed a bill that forbade abortion except in cases of rape reported within seven days, or incest when the victim was under eighteen and the crime was reported to authorities, or when the fetus was severely deformed. The law would have imposed a $10,000 fine on a doctor performing an illegal abortion.[103]

Finally, in July 1990, Governor Buddy Roemer, Democrat of Louisiana, vetoed an antiabortion bill for the second time. If passed, it would have been the most prohibitive law in all the states. The first version of the bill allowed legal abortions only to save the woman's life. The second added an exception for cases of rape reported within seven days. Under both versions, performing an abortion was a felony that subjected the doctor to a prison sentence at hard labor.[104]

Back to the Supreme Court

In October 1990, David Souter became an associate justice of the Supreme Court, replacing Justice William Brennan. In his confirmation hearings, Souter suggested support for a right to privacy, yet refused to answer questions about his views on abortion and *Roe v. Wade*. In the meantime, more states continue to enact abortion control measures and both sides anxiously await the next abortion cases to see how the Supreme Court, and especially the newest justice, will vote.

One of the cases the Supreme court will be deliberating on within the next few years will be the most recent and most restrictive abortion law in the nation, enacted by the Utah legislature in January 1991. Intended to test the Supreme Court's commitment to *Roe*, the law was acknowledged to be unconstitutional under current Supreme Court rulings by Utah's attorney general. Passed in the Utah House by a 53–20 vote and in the Senate by a margin of 19–10, the bill was quickly signed into law by Republican Governor Norm Bangerter. The provisions of the Abortion Limitation Bill originally proposed made abortion illegal in all cases except rape, incest, danger to the woman's life, or terminal birth defects. The bill that was signed by the governor softened the language to allow abortion when there is serious danger to the woman's life, in cases of rape or incest promptly reported and the abortion performed within the first twenty weeks of pregnancy, to prevent severe damage to the woman's health, or if the child would be born with serious defects. Persons performing illegal abortions would be subject to a term of up to five years in prison and a $5,000 fine. The American Civil Liberties Union vowed to challenge the law in federal court.[105]

NOTES

1. Janet Benshoof, "The Legacy of *Roe v. Wade*," in Jay L. Garfield and Patricia Hennessey, eds. *Abortion* (Amherst: University of Massachusetts Press, 1984), p. 42.

2. National averages for 1987 reported by the Alan Guttmacher Institute show that about

one-quarter (25.5 percent) of the abortions were performed on women nineteen and under; slightly over one-half (55.4 percent) of the abortions were performed on women between twenty and twenty-nine years old. Most women who had abortions during this year (52.4 percent) had no children; almost one-quarter (22.1 percent) had one child. Over half (57.1 percent) the women had never had an abortion before; almost one-third (28.9 percent) had had one. Just over half (51.3 percent) of the women who had abortions were using contraception at the time they became pregnant. *New York Times*, May 8, 1989; *Chicago Tribune*, July 4, 1989; *Chicago Tribune*, April 26, 1989.

3. Although the Court had generally been moving toward a convergence of rights enjoyed by adults and children, there were still some important areas of difference remaining. In *Tinker v. Des Moines*, 393 U.S. 503 (1969), the Court proclaimed that students do not shed their constitutional rights at the schoolhouse door and overturned the suspension of three Des Moines students who wore black armbands to school to protest the Vietnam War. But in *Bethel School District No. 403 v. Fraser*, 478 U.S. 675 (1986), the Court upheld a restriction on a student's nonobscene speech that would not have been upheld for an adult. Then in *Hazelwood School District v. Kuhlmeier*, 484 U.S. 260 (1988), the Court curtailed freedom of the press in public schools by upholding a principal's regulation of the student newspaper. And in *New Jersey v. TLO*, 469 U.S. 325 (1985) the Court allowed a school search on grounds that would not have satisfied Fourth Amendment standards for a search of adults. In each of these cases, the Court balanced the minor's constitutional right against the state's need to educate the child and maintain discipline in the school.

4. *Washington Post*, June 26, 1990.

5. *Planned Parenthood of Central Missouri v. Danforth*, 428 U.S. 52, 74 (1976).

6. *Danforth* 428 U.S. at 94–95 (White, J., concurring in part and dissenting in part) (emphasis in the original).

7. *Danforth*, 428 U.S. at 104 (Stevens, J., concurring in part and dissenting in part).

8. *Bellotti v. Baird*, 428 U.S. 132 (1976) (*Bellotti I*). The Supreme Court directed the Massachusetts court to determine whether the law imposed an undue burden on a minor's right to abortion. In using the "undue burden" standard, the Supreme Court seemed to be creating a new standard for assessing minors' privacy rights. See Gene Lindsey, "The Viability of Parental Abortion Notification and Consent Statutes: Assessing Fact and Fiction," *American University Law Review* 38(1989).

9. *Bellotti v. Baird* 443 U.S. 622, 637 (1979) (*Bellotti II*).

10. *Bellotti II*, 433 U.S. at 644–45.

11. *City of Akron v. Akron Center for Reproductive Health*, 462 U.S. 416 (1983).

12. *Planned Parenthood, Kansas City, Missouri v. Ashcroft* 462 U.S. 476 (1983). The majority of Powell, Burger, O'Connor, White, and Rehnquist differed from the majority of five that voted to strike the hospitalization requirement that was discussed in Chapter Ten.

13. *H. L. v. Matheson*, 450 U.S. 398, 400 (1981).

14. The Court only addressed the constitutionality of the Utah statute as it applied to teenagers in the plaintiff's class.

15. *Matheson*, 450 U.S. at 412.

16. *Zbaraz v. Hartigan*, 763 F.2d 1532, 1538 (7th Cir. 1985). The appeals court opinion was affirmed by the Supreme Court in a tie vote, *Hartigan v. Zbaraz*, 484 U.S. 171 (1987). Shortly after the Supreme Court's decision in the 1990 Minnesota and Ohio cases (discussed later in this chapter), the attorney general of Illinois, Neil Hartigan, announced that he would ask a federal court to reinstate the Illinois parental-notification law struck by the appellate court in *Zbaraz*. *Chicago Tribune*, July 5, 1990. See Case Notes, "Abortion," *Journal of Family Law* 24(1985–86).

17. *New York Times*, August 9, 1988.

18. *Congressional Quarterly*, May 19, 1990, p. 1575.

19. Benshoof, "The Legacy of *Roe v. Wade*," p. 42.

20. *Chicago Tribune*, July 5, 1990.

21. The statute provided that the bypass procedure be confidential, that it be expedited, that the minor be given court-appointed counsel if desired, and permitted twenty-four-hour-a-day, seven-day-a-week access to the court. Appeal is permitted for a court order denying an abortion, but is not allowed for an order authorizing an abortion without notice. *Hodgson v. Minnesota*, 110 S.Ct. 2926, 2928 (1990).

22. *Hodgson v. Minnesota*, 853 F.2d 1452, 1465 (8th Cir. 1988).

23. *New York Times*, August 9, 1988.

24. *Hodgson*, 110 S.Ct. at 2938.

25. *Hodgson*, 110 S.Ct. at 2948–49.

26. *Hodgson*, 110 S.Ct. at 2951 (O'Connor, J., concurring).

27. *Washington Post*, June 26, 1990.

28. *Ohio v. Akron Center for Reproductive Health*, 110 S.Ct. 2972, 2977 (1990). The statute required the juvenile court to hold a hearing as early as possible but no later than the fifth business day after the complaint is filed. The court had to appoint a guardian ad litem and an attorney to represent the teenager and was required to protect her anonymity. A decision had to be made immediately after the hearing. There was also a right of appeal and a condition that if the juvenile court or the appeals court did not meet the prescribed time limits, the abortion could proceed.

29. *Akron Center*, 110 S.Ct. at 2979.

30. *Congressional Quarterly*, May 19, 1990, pp. 1573–75.

31. Note, "Limiting Public Funds for Abortions: State Response to Congressional Action," *Suffolk University Law Review* 13(1979), p. 926.

32. Alan Guttmacher Institute, *Abortions and the Poor: Private Morality, Public Responsibility* (New York: Alan Guttmacher Institute, 1979), p. 9.

33. Guttmacher Institute, *Abortions and the Poor*, p. 34.

34. Note, "Abortion, Medicaid, and the Constitution," *New York University Law Review* 54(1979), p. 124.

35. The ten states included New York, Colorado, Idaho, Michigan, and Maryland. Of the thirty-nine other states participating in the Medicaid program (Arizona did not), eighteen adopted the precise language of the Hyde amendment, sixteen limited Medicaid funding to women in life-endangering situations, and five paid for abortions in life-threatening situations or cases of reported rape or incest. Seven of the thirty-nine states, including California and Massachusetts, were prevented from enforcing their funding restrictions by court order. See Guttmacher Institute, *Abortions and the Poor*, pp. 22–23.

36. Guttmacher Institute, *Abortions and the Poor*, p. 8. Women at risk are sexually active, fertile, and neither pregnant nor wanting to become pregnant.

37. *New York Times*, June 21, 1977; *Congressional Quarterly*, June 25, 1977, p. 1285.

38. *Beal v. Doe*, 432 U.S. 438, 444–45 (1977) (emphasis in the original).

39. *Beal*, 432 U.S. at 454 (Brennan, J., dissenting).

40. *Beal*, 432 U.S. at 454–55 (Marshall, J., dissenting).

41. The Court cited *Dandridge v. Williams*, 397 U.S. 471 (1970), and *San Antonio School District v. Rodriguez*, 411 U.S. 1 (1973), in which the Court held that wealth is not a suspect category for equal protection analysis. In these cases, the Court refused to apply strict scrutiny to wealth classifications, using a rationality test to scrutinize a state welfare policy and a school financing plan.

42. *Maher v. Roe*, 432 U.S. 464, 474–75 (1977).

43. *Maher*, 432 U.S. at 483 (Brennan, J., dissenting).

44. *Poelker v. Doe*, 432 U.S. 519, 521 (1977). The city's policy also stemmed from the hospital's practice of staffing its obstetrics-gynecology department from a Jesuit-run medical school opposed to abortion.

45. Frederick S. Jaffe, Barbara L. Lindheim, and Philip R. Lee, *Abortion Politics: Private Morality and Public Policy* (New York: McGraw-Hill, 1981), p. 132.

46. Michael Perry, "The Abortion Funding Cases: A Comment on the Supreme Court's Role in American Government," *Georgetown Law Journal* 66(1978), p. 1201.

47. 123 *Cong. Rec.* 19,700 (1977).

48. 124 *Cong. Rec.* 17,260 (1978).

49. Roger Davidson, "Procedures and Politics in Congress," in Gilbert Y. Steiner, ed., *The Abortion Dispute and the American System* (Washington, DC: Brookings Institution, 1983), pp. 38–9.

50. The federal government's fiscal year begins on October 1 and ends on September 30. On June 24, 1976, the House voted to approve Hyde's amendment to forbid the use of federal funds "to pay for abortions or to promote or encourage abortions." Because the Senate struck the Hyde amendment from the appropriations bill, the bill was sent to conference committee. Although named after Henry Hyde, the language of the first Hyde amendment was authored by Representative Silvio Conte, Republican of Massachusetts. Conte offered the compromise

that the conference finally accepted in September 1976 after the long deadlock. *Congressional Quarterly*, November 11, 1989, pp. 3063–66.

51. Federal regulations interpreted "prompt" as within sixty days. See Susan Tolchin, "The Impact of the Hyde Amendment on Congress: Effects of Single Issue Politics on Legislative Dysfunction June 1977–June 1978," *Women and Politics* 5(1985) for language of successive Hyde amendments.

52. The "severe and long-lasting health damage" was dropped in October 1979. *Congressional Quarterly*, November 11, 1989, pp. 3063–66. The House attached restrictions to the fiscal 1979 appropriations bill for the Department of Defense to limit funding for abortions for military personnel and their dependents. It also barred the use of Peace Corps funds to pay for abortions of Peace Corps volunteers. The restrictions on funding for the military matched the compromise language adopted in the Labor-HEW bill in December 1977. *Congressional Quarterly*, October 21, 1978, pp. 3011–12.

53. In *McRae v. Califano*, 491 F.Supp. 630 (E.D. N.Y. 1980), Dooling broadly defined "medically necessary" to include abortions based on physical, psychological, emotional, and familial considerations.

54. Without explanation, in November 1976 the Supreme Court had refused to block enforcement of Dooling's order. *New York Times*, November 9, 1976. See also Albie Sachs and Joan Hoff Wilson, *Sexism and the Law* (New York: Free Press, 1978), chapter 4.

55. *Harris v. McRae*, 448 U.S. 297, 325 (1980). The Court's ruling was based on the current version of the Hyde amendment, applicable for fiscal year 1980. It banned funding for abortions unless the mother's life was endangered or in cases of rape or incest. The Court noted that this version was more inclusive than the fiscal year 1977 approach that did not include the rape or incest exception. It was narrower than the one used in most of fiscal year 1978 and all of fiscal year 1979 that allowed federal funding for abortions in which physical and long-lasting health damage would result if the pregnancy was continued. In sum, the operative version of the Hyde amendment prohibited funding unless the woman's *life* was threatened by the pregnancy. Medically necessary abortions were not funded by Medicaid because they did not rise to the requisite degree of danger to the woman.

56. *Harris*, 448 U.S. at 316.

57. *Harris*, 448 U.S. at 317 n. 19.

58. *Harris*, 448 U.S. at 326.

59. In *Harris*, the Court ruled on two equal protection issues: first, Congress may encourage childbirth through the Hyde amendment to further its interest in protecting potential life; second, because abortion is an "inherently different" medical service, Congress may allow federal reimbursement to states for most medically necessary procedures while refusing to reimburse for certain medically necessary abortions.

In *Williams v. Zbaraz*, 448 U.S. 358 (1980), the Supreme Court held that because the lower court did not have jurisdiction to consider the constitutionality of the Hyde amendment, that part of the lower court's ruling should be vacated. Thus, the Supreme Court's ruling was based on the statutory question of whether Title XIX required states to pay for abortions in the absence of federal reimbursement and on the equal protection question of whether it was constitutional for the Illinois statute to withhold public funds for certain medically necessary abortions while funding other medically necessary medical procedures. Based on its rulings on these questions in *Harris*, the Court upheld the Illinois statute against both challenges.

60. *Harris*, 448 U.S. at 330 (Brennan, J., dissenting).

61. *Harris*, 448 U.S. at 333 (Brennan, J., dissenting).

62. *Harris*, 448 U.S. at 338 (Marshall, J., dissenting).

63. Creating a rape and incest exception for federally financed abortions was mostly symbolic. A 1987 survey by the Alan Guttmacher Institute showed that only 1 percent of the nineteen hundred women who were asked why they were having an abortion named rape or incest as a reason. *New York Times*, October 13, 1989.

64. *New York Times*, October 12, 1989.

65. *New York Times*, October 17, 1989.

66. *Congressional Quarterly*, October 21, 1989, p. 2790.

67. *Congressional Quarterly*, October 28, 1989, p. 2870.

68. *Congressional Quarterly*, October 28, 1989, p. 2869.

69. *Congressional Quarterly*, November 25, 1989, pp. 3235–36.

70. *Congressional Quarterly*, October 27, 1990, p. 3600.

71. *Congressional Quarterly*, November 3, 1990, p. 3702.

72. *Congressional Quarterly*, October 20, 1990, p. 3513. Abortion opponents are increasingly relying on the tactic known as the "poison pill" approach, in which they tack an antiabortion amendment onto a prochoice provision of a bill. This forces prochoice supporters to choose between accepting the antiabortion language or voting against the entire amendment.

73. *Congressional Quarterly*, August 25, 1990, pp. 2713–19.

74. *Reproductive Health Services v. Webster*, 851 F.2d 1071, 1073 n. 2 (8th Cir. 1988). The state appealed all but two aspects of the lower court ruling to the appellate court: the provisions requiring that the physician alone advise the pregnant woman of certain information and tell her whether or not she is pregnant. Thus, the lower court's finding of unconstitutionality remained undisturbed.

75. *New York Times*, April 10, 1989; *Congressional Quarterly*, April 29, 1989, pp. 973–75.

76. *New York Times*, April 27, 1989.

77. *Webster v. Reproductive Health Services*, 109 S.Ct. 3040, 3047 (1989). The lower court struck the provision of the state law requiring all abortions at sixteen weeks of gestational age to be performed in hospitals. The appellate court affirmed and the state did not appeal the lower court's ruling on this issue to the Supreme Court.

78. *Webster*, 851 F.2d at 1075.

79. *Webster*, 851 F.2d at 1076.

80. In her concurrence, O'Connor rejected the argument that the preamble made post-fertilization contraceptive choices and in-vitro fertilization (where fertilized ova may be destroyed) illegal. Recognizing that earlier cases protected such choices, she said there was nothing in the record to indicate that the preamble would have such an effect.

81. *Webster*, 109 S.Ct. at 3068 n. 1 (Blackmun, J., dissenting).

82. *Webster*, 109 S.Ct. at 3052.

83. For a discussion of the first amendment implications of the Missouri law challenged in *Webster*, see Rachel Pine, "Abortion Counseling and the First Amendment: Open Questions after *Webster*," *American Journal of Law and Medicine* 15(1989).

In *Rust v. Sullivan*, cert. granted, 110 S.Ct. 2559 (1990), argued on October 30, 1990, and scheduled for decision in the 1990–91 term, the Supreme Court is expected to take up the question of the Reagan administration policy that bars the nearly five thousand family-planning clinics receiving federal funds from providing information and advice on abortion. At issue are 1988 regulations of the Public Health Services Act that prohibit employees in federally supported family-planning clinics from counseling women about "abortion as a method of family planning," referring women to abortion providers, or answering questions about abortion. The act, passed in 1970, provides support for clinics serving low-income women. As originally enacted, the law prevented federal funds from being used in "programs where abortion is a method of family planning." The 1988 regulations extend the prohibition on abortion funding to pro-abortion speech. See *New York Times*, October 1, 1990; *ABA Journal* (November, 1990), p. 54.

84. *Webster*, 109 S.Ct. at 3054.

85. Walter Dellinger and Gene B. Sperling, "Abortion and the Supreme Court: The Retreat from *Roe v. Wade*," *University of Pennsylvania Law Review* 138(1989), p. 83.

86. *Webster*, 109 S.Ct. at 3056.

87. *Webster*, 109 S.Ct. at 3057.

88. *Webster*, 109 S.Ct. at 3058.

89. *Webster*, 109 S.Ct. at 3061 (O'Connor, J., concurring).

90. *Webster*, 109 S.Ct. at 3064 (Scalia, J., concurring).

91. *Webster*, 109 S.Ct. at 3067 (Scalia, J., concurring).

92. *Webster*, 109 S.Ct. at 3067 (Blackmun, J., dissenting).

93. *Webster*, 109 S.Ct. at 3077–78 (Blackmun, J., dissenting).

94. *Webster*, 109 S.Ct. at 3079 (Blackmun, J., dissenting).

95. See Dawn Johnsen and Marcy J. Wilder, "*Webster* and Women's Equality," *American Journal of Law and Medicine* 15(1989).

96. Jaffe, Lindheim, and Lee, *Abortion Politics*, chapter 3; *Washington Post National Weekly Edition*, October 15–21, 1990.

97. Attorney General Neil Hartigan, the Democratic candidate for governor of Illinois, was running against a prochoice Republican and wanted to portray himself as prochoice. Despite the opposition of antiabortion activists, the case was settled out of court. In *Ragsdale v. Turnock*, 841 F.2d 1358 (7th Cir. 1988), the appellate court found the regulations invalid.

98. See Lucky M. Tedrow and E. R. Mahoney, "Trends in Attitudes toward Abortion, 1972–1976," *Public Opinion Quarterly* 43(1979); Jaffe, Lindheim, and Lee, *Abortion Politics*, chapter 8; Hyman Rodman, Betty Sarvis, and Joy Walker Bonar, *The Abortion Question* (New York: Columbia University Press, 1987), chapter 8; *New York Times*, April 26, 1989.

99. *Washington Post National Weekly Edition*, July 24–30, 1989.

100. *Congressional Quarterly*, March 10, 1990, pp. 765–75.

101. *New York Times*, October 12, 1989.

102. See *ABA Journal* (November 1990), pp. 20–21. The Pennsylvania case is *Planned Parenthood of Southeastern Pennsylvania v. Casey*, 1990 U.S. Dist. Lexis 15775; the Guam case is *Guam Society of Obstetricians and Gynecologists v. Ada*, 1990 U.S. Dist. Lexis 11910.

103. *Washington Post National Weekly Edition*, July 9–15, 1990.

104. *New York Times*, July 28, 1990.

105. *Deseret News*, January 25, 1991.

Bibliography

Aaron, Henry, and Lougy, Cameran, M. *The Comparable Worth Controversy.* Washington, DC: Brookings Institution, 1986.

Allessandra, Anita. "When Doctrines Collide: Disparate Treatment, Disparate Impact, and *Watson v. Fort Worth Bank and Trust.*" *University of Pennsylvania Law Review* 137(1989): 1755–90.

Amaker, Norman. *Civil Rights and the Reagan Administration.* Washington, DC: Urban Institute Press, 1988.

Baer, Judith. *Equality under the Constitution.* Ithaca, NY: Cornell University Press, 1983.

———. *The Chains of Protection.* Westport, CT: Greenwood Press, 1978.

Baron, Ava. "Feminist Legal Strategies: The Powers of Difference." In Hess, Beth B., and Ferree, Myra Marx, eds. *Analyzing Gender.* Beverly Hills: Sage Publications, 1987.

Bartholet, Elizabeth. "Application of Title VII to Jobs in High Places." *Harvard Law Review* 95(1982): 945–1027.

Bartlett, Katherine T. "Pregnancy and the Constitution: The Uniqueness Trap." *California Law Review* 62(1974): 1532–66.

Bayes, Jane. "Women, Labor Markets, and Comparable Worth." *Policy Studies Review* 5(1986): 776–99.

Becker, Mary. "From *Muller v. Oregon* to Fetal Vulnerability Policies." *University of Chicago Law Review* 53(1986): 1219–68.

Benshoof, Janet. "The Legacy of Roe v. Wade." In Garfield, Jay L., and Hennessey, Patricia, eds. *Abortion.* Amherst: University of Massachusetts Press, 1984.

Benson, Donna E., and Thomson, Gregg E. "Sexual Harassment on a University Campus: The Confluence of Authority Relations, Sexual Interest and Gender Stratification." *Social Problems* 29(1982): 236–51.

Bergmann, Barbara. *The Economic Emergence of Women.* New York: Basic Books, 1986.

Berry, Mary Frances. *Why ERA Failed.* Bloomington: Indiana University Press, 1986.

Bird, Carolyn. *Born Female.* New York: Pocket Books, 1970.

Blau, Francine D., and Ferber, Marianne A. "Occupations and Earnings of Women Workers." In Koziara, Karen Shallcross; Moskow, Michael H.; and Tanner, Lucretia Dewey, eds. *Working Women: Past, Present, Future.* Washington, DC: Bureau of National Affairs, 1987.

Blumrosen, Alfred. "The Legacy of *Griggs*: Social Progress and Subjective Judgments." *Chicago-Kent Law Review* 63(1987): 1–41.

———. "Single-Sex Public Schools: The Last Bastion of 'Separate but Equal'?" *Duke Law Journal* (1977): 259–76.

———. "Strangers in Paradise: *Griggs v. Duke Power Co.* and the Concept of Employment Discrimination." *Michigan Law Review* 71(1972): 59–110.

Blumrosen, Ruth. "Wage Discrimination, Job Segregation, and Title VII of the Civil Rights Act of 1964." *University of Michigan Journal of Law Reform* 12(Spring 1979): 399–502.

Boles, Janet. *The Politics of the Equal Rights Amendment.* New York: Longman, 1979.

Brown, Barbara; Emerson, Thomas; Falk, Gail; and Freedman, Ann E. "The Equal Rights Amendment: A Constitutional Basis for Equal Rights for Women," *Yale Law Journal* 80(1971): 871–985.

Brown, Barbara; Freedman, Ann; Katz, Harriet; and Price, Alice. *Women's Rights and the Law.* New York: Praeger Publishers, 1977.

Brown, Judith; Baumann, Phyllis Tropper; and Melnick, Elaine Millar. "Equal Pay for Jobs of Comparable Worth: An Analysis of the Rhetoric." *Harvard Civil Rights–Civil Liberties Law Review* 21(1986): 127–70.

Bryner, Gary. "Congress, Courts, and Agencies: Equal Employment and the Limits of Policy Implementation." *Political Science Quarterly* 96(1981): 411–30.

Bureau of National Affairs. *Pregnancy and Employment.* Washington, DC: Bureau of National Affairs, 1987.

Burleigh, Nina, and Goldberg, Stephanie B. "Breaking the Silence: Sexual Harassment in Law Firms." *ABA Journal* (August 1989): 46–52.

Cary, Eve, and Peratis, Kathleen Willert, eds. *Woman and the Law.* Skokie: National Textbook Company, 1977.

Case Note. "Abortion." *Journal of Family Law* 24(1985–86): 699–706.

Chi, Keon. "Comparable Worth in State Government: Trends and Issues." *Policy Studies Review* 5(1986): 800–14.

Cnudde, Charles, and Nesvold, Betty. "Administrative Risk and Sexual Harassment: Legal and Ethical Responsibilities on Campus." *PS* (Fall 1985): 780–89.

Coleman, Harriet Hubacker. "Barefoot and Pregnant—Still: Equal Protection for Men and Women in Light of *Geduldig v. Aiello.*" *South Texas Law Journal* 16(1975): 211–40.

Comment. "*Geduldig v. Aiello*: Pregnancy Classifications and the Definition of Sex Discrimination." *Columbia Law Review* 75(1975): 441–82.

Comment. "Implied Private Rights of Action for Damages under Title IX—*Lieberman v. University of Chicago.*" *Georgia Law Review* 16(1982): 511–32.

Comment. *"Plessy* Revived: The Separate but Equal Doctrine and Sex-Segregated Education." *Harvard Civil Rights–Civil Liberties Law Review* 12(1977): 585–648.

Comment. "Pregnancy Disability Benefits and Title VII: Pregnancy Does Not Involve Sex." *Baylor Law Review* 29(1977): 257–81.

Cook, Alice H. *The Working Mother.* New York: Cornell University School of Industrial and Labor Relations, 1978.

Corcoran, Mary, and Duncan, Greg. "Work History, Labor Force Attachment, and Earnings Differences between the Races and Sexes." *Journal of Human Resources* 14(1979): 3–20.

Cortner, Richard C. "Strategies and Tactics of Litigants in Constitutional Cases." *Journal of Public Law* 17(1968): 287–307.

Costain, Anne. "Eliminating Sex Discrimination in Education: Lobbying for Implementation of Title IX." In Palley, Marian Lief, and Preston, Michael, eds. *Race, Sex, and Policy Problems.* Lexington, MA: Lexington Books, 1979.

Cowan, Ruth. "Women's Rights through Litigation: An Examination of the American Civil Liberties Union Women's Rights Project, 1971–1976." *Columbia Human Rights Law Review* 8(1976): 373–412.

Curran, Barbara A. "American Lawyers in the 1980s: A Profession in Transition." *Law and Society Review* 20(1986): 19–52.

Davidson, Roger. "Procedures and Politics in Congress." In Steiner, Gilbert Y., ed. *The Abortion Dispute and the American System.* Washington, DC: Brookings Institution, 1983.

Davis, Angela. *Women, Race & Class.* New York: Random House, 1981.

Days, Drew S., III. "The Courts' Response to the Reagan Civil Rights Agenda." *Vanderbilt Law Review* 42(1989): 1003–16.

Dean, Virginia. "Pay Equity/Comparable Worth." In Lefcourt, Carol, ed. *Women and the Law.* New York: Clark Boardman, 1987.

Deckard, Barbara Sinclair. *The Women's Movement.* New York: Harper & Row, 1975.

Dellinger, Walter, and Sperling, Gene B. "Abortion and the Supreme Court: The Retreat from *Roe v. Wade.*" *University of Pennsylvania Law Review* 138 (1989): 683–118.

Dubois, Ellen. "The Radicalism of the Woman Suffrage Movement: Notes toward the Reconstruction of Nineteenth-Century Feminism." *Feminist Studies* 3(1975): 63–71. Reprinted in Hall, Kermit L., ed. *Women, the Law, and the Constitution.* New York: Garland Publishing, 1987.

Dziech, Billie Wright, and Weiner, Linda. *The Lecherous Professor: Sexual Harassment on Campus.* Boston: Beacon Press, 1984.

Ely, John Hart. "The Wages of Crying Wolf: A Comment on *Roe v. Wade.*" *Yale Law Journal* 82(1973): 920–49.

Enloe, Cynthia. *Does Khaki Become You?* Boston: South End Press, 1983.

Epstein, Cynthia Fuchs. *Women in Law.* New York: Basic Books, 1981.

Evans, Sara, and Nelson, Barbara. "Comparable Worth: The Paradox of Technocratic Reform." *Feminist Studies* 15(1989): 171–90.

Faux, Marian. *Roe v. Wade.* New York: Mentor Books, 1988.

Feagin, Joe E., and Feagin, Clairece Booher. "Theories of Discrimination." In

Rothenberg, Paula, ed. *Racism and Sexism: An Integrated Study*. New York: St. Martin's Press, 1988.

Feldberg, Roslyn. "Comparable Worth: Toward Theory and Practice in the United States." *Signs* 10(1984): 311–28.

Feldstein, Merrill D. "*Watson v. Fort Worth Bank and Trust*: Reallocating the Burdens of Proof in Employment Discrimination Litigation." *American University Law Review* 38(1989): 919–51.

Fernandez, David. "*Thornburgh v. American College of Obstetricians*: Return to *Roe*?" *Harvard Journal of Law and Public Policy* 10(1986): 711–27.

Finley, Lucinda M. "Transcending Equality Theory: A Way out of the Maternity and the Workplace Debate." *Columbia Law Review* 86(1986): 1118–82.

Fishel, Andrew, and Pottker, Janice. *National Politics and Sex Discrimination in Education*. Lexington, MA: Lexington Books, 1977.

Fiss, Owen. "Groups and the Equal Protection Clause." *Philosophy and Public Affairs* 5(1976): 107–77.

Flexner, Eleanor. *Century of Struggle*. New York: Atheneum, 1974.

Franklin, Phyllis; Moglen, Helene; Zatlin-Boring, Phyllis; and Angress, Ruth. *Sexual and Gender Harassment in the Academy*. New York: Modern Languages Association, 1981.

Freedman, Ann E. "Sex Equality, Sex Differences, and the Supreme Court." *Yale Law Journal* 92(1983): 913–68.

Freeman, Jo. *The Politics of Women's Liberation*. New York: David McKay, 1975.

Friedan, Betty. *The Feminine Mystique*. New York: Dell Publishing, 1963.

Friedman, Joel, and Strickler, George Jr., eds. *The Law of Employment Discrimination*. Mineola, NY: Foundation Press, 1987.

Gelb, Joyce. *Feminism and Politics*. Berkeley: University of California Press, 1989.

Gelb, Joyce, and Palley, Marian Lief. *Women and Public Policies*. 2d ed. Princeton: Princeton University Press, 1987.

Giampetro, Andrea, and Kubasek, Nancy. "Individualism in America and Its Implications for Affirmative Action." *Journal of Contemporary Law* 14(1988): 165–94.

Giddings, Paula. *When and Where I Enter*. New York: William Morrow, 1984.

Ginsburg, Ruth Bader. "Some Thoughts on Benign Classification in the Context of Sex." *Connecticut Law Review* 10(1978): 813–27.

Goldstein, Leslie Friedman. "The ERA and the U.S. Supreme Court." *Law and Policy Studies* 1(1987): 145–61.

Gunther, Gerald. "Foreward: In Search of Evolving Doctrine on a Changing Court: A Model for a Newer Equal Protection." *Harvard Law Review* 86(1972): 1–48.

Alan Guttmacher Institute. *Abortions and the Poor: Private Morality, Public Responsibility*. New York: Alan Guttmacher Institute, 1979.

Halliday, Terence. "Six Score Years and Ten: Demographic Transitions in the American Legal Profession, 1850–1980." *Law and Society Review* 20(1986): 53–78.

Hamilton, Charles, and Carmichael, Stokeley. *Black Power*. New York: Random House, 1967.

Harrison, Cynthia. *On Account of Sex: The Politics of Women's Issues, 1945–1968*. Berkeley: University of California Press, 1988.

Hembacher, Brian. "Fetal Protection Policies: Reasonable Protection or Unreasonable Limitation on Female Employees." *Industrial Relations Law Journal* 11(1989): 32–44.

Hill, Marvin F., Jr., and Behrens, Curtiss K. "Love in the Office: A Guide for Dealing with Sexual Harassment under Title VII of the Civil Rights Act of 1964." *DePaul Law Review* 30(1981): 581–622.

Hochschild, Jennifer L. "Race, Class, Power, and Equal Opportunity." In Bowie, Norman E., ed. *Equal Opportunity.* Boulder: Westview Press, 1988.

Hodes, W. William. "Women and the Constitution: Some Legal History and a New Approach to the Nineteenth Amendment." *Rutgers Law Review* 25(1970): 26–53. Reprinted in Hall, Kermit L., ed. *Women, the Law, and the Constitution.* New York: Garland Publishing, 1987.

Hooks, Karen L., and Cheramy, Shirley J. "Coping with Women's Expanding Role in Public Accounting." *Journal of Accountancy* 167(1989): 66–70.

Huckle, Patricia. "The Womb Factor: Policy on Pregnancy and the Employment of Women." In Boneparth, Ellen, and Stoper, Emily, eds. *Women, Power and Policy.* 2d ed. New York: Pergamon Press, 1988.

Ingulli, Elaine D. "Sexual Harassment in Education." *Rutgers Law Journal* 18(1987): 281–342.

Jaffe, Frederick S.; Lindheim, Barbara L.; and Lee, Philip R. *Abortion Politics: Private Morality and Public Policy.* New York: McGraw-Hill, 1981.

Johnsen, Dawn, and Wilder, Marcy J. "*Webster* and Women's Equality." *American Journal of Law and Medicine* 15(1989): 178–84.

Johnston, John D., Jr., and Knapp, Charles L. "Sex Discrimination by Law: A Study in Judicial Perspective." *New York University Law Review* 46(1971): 675–747.

Jones, James E., Jr. "The Origins of Affirmative Action." *University of California, Davis Law Review* 21(1988): 383–419.

Kamerman, Sheila B., and Kahn, Alfred J. "Family Policy: Has the United States Learned from Europe?" *Policy Studies Review* 8(1989): 581–98.

Kandel, William L. "Current Developments in Employment Litigation." *Employee Relations Law Journal* 15(1989): 101–13.

Kanowitz, Leo. "'Benign' Sex Discrimination: Its Troubles and Their Cure," *Hastings Law Journal* 31(1980): 1379–1431.

Kay, Herma Hill. "Equality and Difference: The Case of Pregnancy." *Berkeley Women's Law Journal* 1(1985): 1–38.

———. "Models of Equality." *University of Illinois Law Review* (1985): 39–88.

Kirby, Emily. *Yes You Can.* Englewood Cliffs: Prentice-Hall, 1984.

Kluger, Elizabeth. "Sex Discrimination in the Tenure System at American Colleges and Universities: The Judicial Response." *Journal of Law and Education* 15(1986): 319–39.

Kluger, Richard. *Simple Justice.* New York: Alfred A. Knopf, 1976.

Knowles, Louis L., and Prewitt, Kenneth, eds. *Institutional Racism in America.* Englewood Cliffs: Prentice-Hall, 1969.

Koontz, Elizabeth Duncan. "Childbirth and Childrearing Leave: Job-Related Benefits." *New York University Law Forum* 17(1971): 480–502.

Kosaki, Liane, and Mezey, Susan Gluck. "Judicial Intervention in the Family: Interspousal Immunity and Civil Litigation." *Women & Politics* 8(1988): 69–85.

Kraditor, Aileen S. *The Ideas of the Woman Suffrage Movement 1890–1920.* Garden City, NY: Anchor, 1971.

Krieger, Linda J., and Cooney, Patricia N. "The Miller-Wohl Controversy: Equal Treatment, Positive Action and the Meaning of Women's Equality." *Golden Gate University Law Review* 13(1983): 513–72.

Lally-Green, Maureen E. "Affirmative Action: Are the Equal Protection and Title VII Tests Synonymous?" *Duquesne Law Review* 26(1987): 295–378.

Lamar, Patricia Werner. "The Expansion of Constitutional and Statutory Remedies for Sex Segregation in Education: The Fourteenth Amendment and Title IX of the Education Amendments of 1972." *Emory Law Journal* 32(Fall 1983): 1111–65.

LaNoue, George R., and Lee, Barbara A. *Academics in Court: The Consequences of Faculty Discrimination Litigation.* Ann Arbor: University of Michigan Press, 1987.

Law, Sylvia. "Rethinking Sex and the Constitution." *University of Pennsylvania Law Review* 132(1984): 955–1040.

Lehr, Richard. "EEOC Case-Handling Procedures: Problems and Solutions." *Alabama Law Review* 34(1983): 241–62.

Lindsey, Gene. "The Viability of Parental Abortion Notification and Consent Statutes: Assessing Fact and Fiction." *American University Law Review* 38(1989): 881–918.

Littleton, Christine. "Restructuring Sexual Equality." *California Law Review* 75(1987): 1279–1337.

Loudon, Joseph P., and Loudon, Timothy D. "Applying Disparate Impact to Title VII Comparable Worth Claims: An Incomparable Task." *Indiana Law Journal* 61(1986): 165–87.

Luker, Kristen. *Abortion and the Politics of Motherhood.* Berkeley: University of California Press, 1984.

McCann, Michael W. "Equal Protection for Social Inequality: Race and Class in Constitutional Ideology." In McCann, Michael W., and Houseman, Gerald L., eds. *Judging the Constitution: Critical Essays on Judicial Lawmaking.* Glenview, IL: Scott, Foresman, 1989.

Machlowitz, David, and Machlowitz, Marilyn. "Preventing Sexual Harassment." *ABA Journal* (October 1987): 78–80.

McKenna, Lois M. "Freedom of Association or Gender Discrimination? *New York State Club Association v. City of New York.*" *American University Law Review* 38(1989): 1061–92.

MacKinnon, Catherine. *Feminism Unmodified.* Cambridge, MA: Harvard University Press, 1987.

———. *Sexual Harassment of Working Women.* New Haven: Yale University Press, 1979.

Malveaux, Julianne, and Wallace, Phyllis. "Minority Women in the Workplace." In Koziara, Karen Shallcross; Moskow, Michael H.; and Tanner, Lucretia Dewey, eds. *Working Women: Past, Present, Future.* Washington, DC: Bureau of National Affairs, 1987.

Mansbridge, Jane. *Why We Lost the ERA.* Chicago: University of Chicago Press, 1986.

Marshall, Ray, and Paulin, Beth. "Employment and Earnings of Women: Historical Perspective." In Koziara, Karen Shallcross; Moskow, Michael H.; and

Tanner, Lucretia Dewey, eds. *Working Women: Past, Present, Future.* Washington, DC: Bureau of National Affairs, 1987.

Maschke, Karen. *Litigation, Courts, and Women Workers.* New York: Praeger Publishers, 1989.

Mezey, Susan Gluck. "Gender Equality in Education: A Study of Policymaking by the Burger Court." *Wake Forest Law Review* 20(1984): 793–817.

———. "Judicial Interpretation of Legislative Intent: The Role of the Supreme Court in the Implication of Private Rights of Action." *Rutgers Law Review* 36(1983): 53–89.

Miller, Janella. "The Future of Private Women's Colleges." *Harvard Women's Law Journal* 7(1984): 153–87.

Minow, Martha. "Foreword: Justice Engendered." *Harvard Law Review* 101(1987): 10–95.

Mohr, James C. *Abortion in America.* Oxford: Oxford University Press, 1978.

Morello, Karen Berger. *The Invisible Bar: The Woman Lawyer in America, 1638 to the Present.* New York: Random House, 1986.

Murray, P. J. "Employer: Beware of 'Hostile Environment' Sexual Harassment." *Duquesne Law Review* 26(1987): 461–84.

National Committee on Pay Equity. *Pay Equity: An Issue of Race, Ethnicity and Sex.* Washington, DC: National Committee on Pay Equity, 1987.

Norton, Eleanor Holmes. "Equal Employment Law: Crisis in Interpretation— Survival against the Odds." *Tulane Law Review* 62(1988): 681–715.

Note. "Abortion, Medicaid, and the Constitution." *New York University Law Review* 54(1979): 120–60.

Note. "Clearing the Mixed-Motive Smokescreen: An Approach to Disparate Treatment under Title VII." *Michigan Law Review* 87(1989): 863–94.

Note. "Current Trends in Pregnancy Benefits—1972 EEOC Guidelines Interpreted." *DePaul Law Review* 24(1974): 127–42.

Note. "Factually or Statistically Based Commissioner's Charge: A New Approach to EEOC Enforcement of Title VII." *Boston University Law Review* 63(1983): 645–71.

Note. "Finding a 'Manifest Imbalance': The Case for a Unified Statistical Test for Voluntary Affirmative Action under Title VII." *Michigan Law Review* 87(1989): 1986–2025.

Note. "*Grove City College v. Bell*: Restricting the Remedial Reach of Title IX." *Loyola University Law Journal* 16(1985): 319–58.

Note. "*Lieberman v. University of Chicago.*" *John Marshall Law Review* 16(1982): 153–63.

Note. "*Lieberman v. University of Chicago*: Refusal to Imply a Damages Remedy under Title IX of the Education Amendments of 1972." *Wisconsin Law Review* (1983): 181–210.

Note. "Limiting Public Funds for Abortions: State Response to Congressional Action." *Suffolk University Law Review* 13(1979): 923–59.

Note. "*New York State Club Association v. City of New York*: As 'Distinctly Private' Is Defined, Women Gain Access." *Denver University Law Review* 66(1988): 109–21.

Note. *New York State Club Association v. City of New York*: Private Club Sex Discrimination." *West Virginia Law Review* 91(1989): 503–18.

Note. "Not Just Any 'Factor Other Than Sex': An Analysis of the Fourth Affirmative Defense of the Equal Pay Act." *George Washington Law Review* 52(1984): 318–36.

Note. "Pregnancy and Employment: Three Approaches to Equal Opportunity." *Boston University Law Review* 68(1988): 1019–45.

Note. "Pregnancy and Equality: A Precarious Alliance." *Southern California Law Review* 60(1987): 1345–74.

Note. "Pregnancy and Sex-Based Discrimination in Employment: A Post-*Aiello* Analysis." *Cincinnati Law Review* 44(1975): 57–80.

Note. "Pregnancy Discrimination in Unemployment Benefits: Section 3304(a)(12) Merely an Antidiscrimination Provision." *Stetson Law Review* 17(1987): 219–47.

Note. "Sex Discrimination and Intercollegiate Athletics: Putting Some Muscle on Title IX." *Yale Law Journal* 88(1979): 1254–79.

Note. "The 1983 Abortion Decisions: Clarification of the Permissible Limits of Abortion Regulation." *University of Richmond Law Review* 18(1983): 137–59.

Note. "*Thornburgh*: The Last American Right-to-Abortion Case?" *Journal of Family Law* 26(1987–1988): 771–92.

Note. "Title VII in Academia: A Critical Analysis of the Judicial Policy of Deference." *Washington University Law Quarterly* 64(1986): 619–34.

Note. "Title IX and Intercollegiate Athletics: HEW Gets Serious about Equality in Sports." *New England Law Review* 15(1980): 573–96.

Note. "*Watson v. Fort Worth Bank and Trust*: A Plurality's Proposal to Alter the Evidentiary Burdens in Title VII Disparate Impact Cases." *North Carolina Law Review* 67(1989): 725–40.

O'Brien, Christine Neylon, and Madek, Gerald A. "Pregnancy Discrimination and Maternity Leave Laws." *Dickinson Law Review* 93(1989): 311–37.

O'Connor, Karen. *Women's Organizations' Use of the Courts.* Lexington, MA: Lexington Books, 1980.

Olsen, Frances. "The Family and the Market: A Study of Ideology and Legal Reform." *Harvard Law Review* 96(1983): 1497–1578.

Olson, Susan. *Clients and Lawyers.* Westport, CT: Greenwood Press, 1984.

Oneglia, Stewart, and Cornelius, Susan French. "Sexual Harassment in the Workplace: The Equal Employment Opportunity Commission's New Guidelines." *Saint Louis University Law Journal* 26(1981): 39–61.

Perry, Michael. "The Abortion Funding Cases: A Comment on the Supreme Court's Role in American Government." *Georgetown Law Journal* 66(1978): 1191–1245.

Pine, Rachel. "Abortion Counseling and the First Amendment: Open Questions after *Webster*." *American Journal of Law and Medicine* 15(1989): 189–97.

Project on the Status and Education of Women. *Sexual Harassment: A Hidden Issue.* Washington, DC: Association of American Colleges, 1978.

Randall, Vicky. *Women and Politics.* 2d ed. Chicago: University of Chicago Press, 1987.

Recent Cases. "Civil Rights—Disparate Impact Doctrine—Court Prohibits Awarding Scholarships on the Basis of Standardized Tests That Discriminatorily Impact Women. — *Sharif v. New York Education Department*, 709 F.Supp. 345 (S.D. N.Y. 1989)." *Harvard Law Review* 103(1990): 806–11.

Recent Developments. "Beyond Cal Fed: Parenting Leave Possibilities." *Harvard Women's Law Journal* 10(1987): 294–308.

Reid, Glenda E.; Acken, Brenda T.; and Jancura, Elise G. "An Historical Perspective on Women in Accounting." *Journal of Accountancy* 163(1987): 338–55.

Reidinger, Paul. "Will *Roe v. Wade* Be Overruled?" *ABA Journal* (July 1988): 66–70.

Reynolds, William Bradford. "The Reagan Administration's Civil Rights Policy: The Challenge for the Future." *Vanderbilt Law Review* 42(1989): 993–1001.

———. "Comparable Worth: Bad Policy and Bad Law." *Harvard Journal of Law & Public Policy* 9(1986): 89–94.

Rhode, Deborah L. "Equal Protection: Gender and Justice." In McCann, Michael W., and Houseman, Gerald L. eds. *Judging the Constitution: Critical Essays on Judicial Lawmaking.* Glenview, IL: Scott, Foresman, 1989.

———. *Justice and Gender.* Cambridge, MA: Harvard University Press, 1989.

———. "Perspectives on Professional Women." *Stanford Law Review* 40(1988): 1163–1207.

———. "Association and Assimilation." *Northwestern University Law Review* 81(1986): 106–45.

Rhoden, Nancy K. "Trimesters and Technology: Revamping *Roe v. Wade.*" *Yale Law Journal* 95(1986): 639–97.

Rhoodie, Eschel M. *Discrimination against Women: A Global Survey.* Jefferson, NC: McFarland, 1989.

Robinson, Donald. "Two Movements in Pursuit of Equal Employment Opportunity." *Signs* 4(1979): 413–33.

Rodman, Hyman; Sarvis, Betty; and Bonar, Joy Walker. *The Abortion Question.* New York: Columbia University Press, 1987.

Rose, David. "Twenty-Five Years Later: Where Do We Stand on Equal Employment Opportunity Law Enforcement?" *Vanderbilt Law Review* 42(1989): 1121–82.

Rubin, Eva. *Abortion, Politics, and the Courts.* Westport, CT: Greenwood Press, 1987.

———. *The Supreme Court and the American Family.* Westport, CT: Greenwood Press, 1986.

Rutherglen, George. "Disparate Impact under Title VII: An Objective Theory of Discrimination." *Virginia Law Review* 73(1987): 1297–1345.

Rutherglen, George, and Ortiz, Daniel R. "Affirmative Action under the Constitution and Title VII: From Confusion to Convergence." *UCLA Law Review* 35(1988): 467–518.

Sachs, Albie, and Wilson, Joan Hoff. *Sexism and the Law.* New York: Free Press, 1978.

Salomone, Rosemary. *Equal Education under Law.* New York: St. Martin's Press, 1986.

———. "*North Haven* and *Dougherty:* Narrowing the Scope of Title IX." *Journal of Law & Education* 10(1981): 191–206.

———. "Title IX and Employment Discrimination: A Wrong in Search of a Remedy." *Journal of Law and Education* 9(1980): 433–47.

Sandler, Bernice Resnick. *The Campus Climate Revisited*. Washington, DC: Association of American Colleges, 1986.

Scales, Ann. "Towards a Feminist Jurisprudence." *Indiana Law Journal* 56(1980–1981): 375–444.

Schneider, Ronna Greff. "Sexual Harassment and Higher Education." *Texas Law Review* 65(1987): 525–83.

Schultz, Vicki. "Telling Stories about Women and Work." *Harvard Law Review* 103(1990): 1749–1843.

Schwartz, Felice. "Management Women and the New Facts of Life." *Harvard Business Review* 67(1989): 65–76.

Simeone, Angela. *Academic Women*. South Hadley, MA: Bergin & Garvey, 1987.

Sochen, June. *Herstory: A Women's View of American History*. New York: Alfred A. Knopf, 1974.

Spakes, Patricia. "A Feminist Case against National Family Policy: View to the Future." *Policy Studies Review* 8(1989): 610–21.

Speiser, Tina L. "The Future of Comparable Worth: Looking in New Directions." *Syracuse Law Review* 37(1987): 1189–1218.

Stone, Diana. *Pay Equity Sourcebook*. San Francisco: Equal Rights Advocates and Washington, DC: National Committee on Pay Equity, 1987.

Sullivan, Charles S. "The Equal Pay Act of 1963: Making and Breaking a Prima Facie Case." *Arkansas Law Review* 31(1978): 545–606.

Tatalovich, Raymond. "Abortion." In Tatalovich, Raymond, and Daynes, Byron W. eds. *Social Regulatory Policy*. Boulder: Westview Press, 1988.

Taub, Nadine, and Schneider, Elizabeth M. "Perspectives on Women's Subordination and the Role of Law." In Kairys, David, ed. *The Politics of Law: A Progressive Critique*. New York: Pantheon, 1982.

Tedrow, Lucky M., and Mahoney, E. R. "Trends in Attitudes Toward Abortion, 1972–1976." *Public Opinion Quarterly* 43(1979): 181–89.

Thomas, Clarence. "The Equal Employment Opportunity Commission: Reflections on a New Philosophy." *Stetson Law Review* 15(1985): 29–36.

Tolchin, Susan. "The Impact of the Hyde Amendment on Congress: Effects of Single Issue Politics on Legislative Dysfunction June 1977–June 1978." *Women and Politics* 5(1985): 91–106.

Tong, Rosemarie. *Feminist Thought: A Comprehensive Introduction*. Boulder: Westview Press, 1989.

Treiman, Donald, and Hartmann, Heidi, eds. *Women, Work, and Wages: Equal Pay for Jobs of Equal Value*. Washington, DC: National Academy Press, 1981.

Tribe, Laurence. *American Constitutional Law*. 2d ed. Mineola, NY: Foundation Press, 1988.

Tussman, Joseph, and tenBroek, Jacobus. "The Equal Protection of the Laws." *California Law Review* 37(1949): 341–81.

Vaas, Francis J. "Title VII: Legislative History." *Boston College Industrial and Commercial Law Review* 7(1966): 431–58.

Vermuelen, Joan. "Sexual Harassment." In Lefcourt, Carol, ed. *Women and the Law*. New York: Clark Boardman, 1987.

Vose, Clement. "Litigation as a Form of Pressure Group Activity." *The Annals of the American Academy of Political and Social Sciences* 319(1958): 20–31.

Weisel, Kerri. "Title VII: Legal Protection against Sexual Harassment." *Washington Law Review* 53(1977): 123–44.

Whalen, Charles, and Whalen, Barbara. *The Longest Debate: A Legislative History of the 1964 Civil Rights Act.* New York: Mentor Books, 1985.

Williams, Wendy. "Equality's Riddle: Pregnancy and the Equal Treatment/Special Treatment Debate." *New York University Review of Law and Social Change* 13(1984–1985): 325–80.

———. "The Equality Crisis: Some Reflections on Culture, Courts, and Feminism." *Women's Rights Law Reporter* 7(1982): 175–200.

———. "Firing the Woman to Protect the Fetus: The Reconciliation of Fetal Protection with Employment Opportunity under Title VII." *Georgetown Law Journal* 69(1981): 641–704.

Wilson, Joan Hoff. "The Legal Status of Women in the Late Nineteenth and Early Twentieth Centuries." *Human Rights* 6(1977): 125–34. Reprinted in Hall, Kermit L., ed. *Women, the Law, and the Constitution.* New York: Garland Publishing, 1987.

Wood, B. Dan. "Does Politics Make a Difference at the EEOC?" *American Journal of Political Science* 34(1990): 503–30.

Index

Table of Cases